Luis Buñuel: A Critical Biography

Military service (1919)

LUIS BUÑUEL: A CRITICAL BIOGRAPHY

by
Francisco Aranda

Translated and Edited
by David Robinson

A DA CAPO PAPERBACK

Library of Congress Cataloging in Publication Data
Aranda, J   Francisco, 1926-
  Luis Buñuel: a critical biography.

  Filmography: p.
  Bibliography: p.
  Includes index.
  1. Buñuel, Luis, 1900-
PN1998.A3B7513 1976   791.43'0233'0924 [B]   75-31793
ISBN 0-306-70754-3
ISBN 0-306-80028-4 (pbk.)

ISBN 0-306-80028-4
First Paperback Printing 1976

Luis Buñuel: biografía crítica by J. Francisco Aranda first published
in 1969 by Editorial Lumen, Barcelona. The English-language edition, *Luis Buñuel: A Critical Biography,* translated by David Robinson
first published in Great Britain in 1975 by Martin Secker & Warburg
Limited.

First American Edition, 1976, by Da Capo Press, Inc.

Published by Da Capo Press, Inc.
A Subsidiary of Plenum Publishing Corporation
227 West 17th Street
New York, N.Y. 10011

Contents

Contents

1. Out of Innocence

Calanda is a village of 3,000 inhabitants, 115 kilometres from Zaragoza, on the foothills of the Teruel range. It would be a nondescript place but for two phenomena which give it a claim to fame. First, it is the birthplace of one of the most delightful of Spanish dances, the Calanda *jota* – a slow bolero, of aristocratic solemnity and great choreographic invention. It is arguable that ballet owed its birth to the boleros of Calanda and Alcañiz, a few kilometres away. In the sixteenth century, when the bolero reached its apogee, the kingdom of Aragón extended to include among its other Mediterranean territories, Naples; and it may be that Aragonese dances, brought there by the Spanish governors, imported steps which, having been systematized in Italy, provided the origins of the first known academic ballet. (It might also be mentioned that Gaspar Saenz, one of the best contrapuntalists of Spanish Renascence music, was born in Calanda.)

The other reason for the village's celebrity is the Miracle of Calanda. A man very devoted to the Virgin of the Pilar, having had a leg amputated, dreamed that Our Lady disinterred the member and stuck it back on his stump. The flesh, even though it was already putrefying and worm-eaten, resumed its vital functions. No other miracle can compare with this. To revive a dead man or return sight to one who is blind, can be faked; to see a

Procession of Calandan drummers

man who has been without a leg walking with it once more is a proof too absolute to allow a possibility of doubt.

This country – once ruler of European destinies, now eking a living out of arid lands – oscillates between these two poles. The landscape itself affords contrasts: on three sides are the dry, ploughed fields; on the fourth the Sierra, with rocks and richly coloured flora, with trees and little streams of transparent water. Unlike Alcañiz the village presents no remnants of former glories. The people go about in their dark working clothes, with felt hats over their eyes. They are savage, and were until recently mostly illiterate. Yet sometimes, talking to them, there is still a sense of ancient tradition and underlying elegance. Their pleasures are violent and aristocratic. On feast days they organize hunts with packs of dogs, and bring back quantities of game. Afterwards they gorge themselves with an enormous banquet of meat, liberally washed down with the sharp, sweet wine of Cariñena, and accompanied by jotas sung in voices that resemble the rasp of files. Best of all is Semana Santa (Holy Week). Then four hundred men go into the streets with great drums. From the evening of Good Friday, the day of Our Lord's Crucifixion, until the morning of His Resurrection, two days later, the percussion echoes for many kilometres around. The strongest keep up the drumming with all their might, and stop only for swigs from their leather wine bottles. Others take the place of those who succumb to exhaustion.

In the middle of the village is the church – an ugly one – which forms the end of a triangular plaza. In the centre of this is a crude monument. This was first dedicated to the victors of the Civil War, and 'Die for God and the Fatherland'. Later, as the slogan became less fashionable, a bust of Goya, who was born in a village not far away, was substituted. Perhaps one day a monument to Luis Buñuel will replace Goya on the same pedestal.

The Buñuel family comes from Calanda. Its genealogy can be traced back to Spain's glorius sixteenth century. Some Buñuels emigrated to Aragón; a less distinguished branch established itself in the North, and it is supposed that they were the founders of Buñuel, a Navarrese village fronting the south of Huesca. Luis Buñuel's grandfather was born at the beginning of the nineteenth century and died at the end of it. He had two sons, Joaquín, who died of cholera at the end of the century, and Leonardo, the father of Luis. Leonardo was a restless boy. At fourteen he left home to join the army as a bugler. He took part in the Cuban War against the United States and rose to the rank of Captain. After the war he stayed in Cuba and opened a fancy-goods store in partnership with two associates, Vizoso and Lasteleiro, who subsequently between them made one of the largest fortunes in Spanish America. Leonardo had no such ambitions. In 1899 he visited his birthplace and announced that he would choose the healthiest and prettiest woman in the

Leonardo Buñuel during the Cuban War

Maria Buñuel with Luis on the right

village. This he did.* Leonardo fell in love, and married, at forty-three years of age, a girl more than twenty years younger than himself, María Portolés. She was the daughter of the landlord of the *posada* (inn) facing the church. Although educated as a *señorita*, she was accustomed to lend a hand at the bar. Once married, he settled in Calanda for good, buying an estate there.

Don Leonardo had fine features and large clear eyes. Although he had no formal education, he acquired a culture. Friends who still remember him talk of his lively intelligence and the wide range of his knowledge. When he moved to Zaragoza he mixed with the intelligentsia of the Aragonese capital, where rich landowners made up a considerable part of the bourgeoisie. He died in 1923.

Luis's mother was born in 1883 and died on 29 June 1969. She was a model wife, and made the marriage very happy. A woman of remarkable beauty, she was tall, broad-boned, with such an aristocratic bearing that even when she was past sixty, heads still turned when she went to Mass along the Paseo de la Independencia. She brought up her children in the most devout and strict conventions of those days. There were seven of them: Luis, the first-born and strongest, born in 1900; María (1901), Alicia (1902), Conchita

* Even today, when a girl of the village repeatedly refuses offers of marriage, risking remaining an old maid, the villagers say: 'She'll marry when Buñuel comes back from Cuba.'

Buñuel family: (l. to r.) María – Conchita – Leonardo – Alicia – Luis

(1904), Leonardo (1910), who became a radiologist, Margarita (1912) and Alfonso (1915–61), an architect and adherent of the Spanish Surrealist group. To know the Buñuel family is a considerable help in understanding the work of Luis, which can be so disconcerting at times. Their character is a mixture of energy and honesty. They are violent and gentle at the same time. Their taste for paradox and bizarre expressions is inborn; the constant slips on the treacherous ground of blasphemy, inevitable. Anecdotes on this subject are numerous and delightful. When Señora Buñuel's daughters were imprisoned, she protested to the police, asking 'How dare you imprison people who are all descendants of canons?' For her, Luis was a saint. To prove it she showed me his portraits on an improvised altar in a wardrobe where they were surrounded by photographs of the late Popes. Knowing the Buñuels, it was impossible to question her sincerity. Looking into her great limpid eyes, one felt submerged in a deep, translucent lake. Surrealism is not the creation of Luis, or of his family: the world is surreal. But above all, Spain.

At the end of the last century the Buñuels had a fine house in Calanda. Just before Luis was born they pulled down their cottage on the outskirts of the town in order to build a new one, where they intended to live. They rented a stately mansion from a noble Lower Aragonese family, the Ram de Viu, who had palaces in Alcañiz and Cataluña. There Luis was born. In his autobiography, written for the Museum of Modern Art in 1938,* and never till now published, he recalled:

* It was written in English and is printed here without editorial revision or correction.

'I was born February 22, 1900, in Calanda, a town in the province of Teruel, Spain.

'My father had spent almost all his life in America, where, as a wholesale merchant, he succeeded in amassing something of a fortune. When well in his forties he decided to return to his native town, Calanda, where he married my mother who was then barely seventeen. I was the first of the seven children of this marriage who are now living in Spain.

'My infancy slipped by in an almost mediaeval atmosphere (like that of nearly all the Spanish provinces) between my native town and Zaragoza. I feel it necessary to say here (since it explains in part the trend of the modest work which I later accomplished) that the two basic sentiments of my childhood, which stayed with me well into adolescence, are those of a profound eroticism, at first sublimated in a great religious faith, and a permanent consciousness of death. It would take too long here to analyse the reasons. It suffices that I was not an exception among my compatriots, since this is a very Spanish characteristic, and our art, exponent of the Spanish spirit, was impregnated with these two sentiments. The last civil war, peculiar and ferocious as no other, exposed them clearly.'

Luis was baptized in Calanda. Then his parents moved to Zaragoza, the

Birthplace of Buñuel in Calanda

Luis as a child

capital of Aragón, to live in a flat at number 29, Paseo de la Independencia. From then on Luis spent four months every summer, as well as Holy Week and other holidays, at Calanda. From 1915 to 1931 he spent his holidays at San Sebastian, but always returned home for Easter, to take part in the Procession of the Drums, in which he was one of the most dogged performers. In the country the Buñuels lived in the rebuilt house, surrounded by a beautiful garden full of cypresses and running down to the edge of the river. He played with his brothers and sisters and the village children, and was a quiet little boy. Like all the sons of good provincial families, he learned to serve at mass, and sang in the choir with a very good voice. Sometimes he played games with the girls, pretending to be the priest saying mass – a very common first sexual manifestation among Spanish children. All the Buñuel children liked dressing up. Sometimes they organized theatrical entertainments with texts of their own invention. Conchita recalls one in which they all wore kerchiefs on their heads (like the bandits in *L'Age d'or* and characters from so many Buñuel films) and Luis recited:

With this pair of scissors
And will to fight, it's plain
We'll have a revolution
And capture all of Spain.

At other times they had shadow shows. Luis was kind to his sisters, but also very attracted to the other girls, whom he sometimes gave dolls which he had taken from the house. There were elements of sadism, natural enough in little boys, in his games. One of them, typically Calandan, consisted of poking a match inch by inch towards the eyes of a little girl, very slowly, to see how long she could resist closing them. When she gave up, she had to shout 'Coñe!' ('Cunt!') and run away. 'We tried doing the same thing to bats,' Buñuel recalls. 'They never said "Coñe!" of course, though we always hoped they would.' Other times they dared one another to swallow cigarette butts picked up in the street and washed down with water, or to eat sandwiches spread with ants * – an activity which has given rise to tortuous interpretations of Buñuel's gastronomic habits. In fact, his only peculiarities were to be a vegetarian between the ages of eighteen and twenty, and always to eat day-old bread.

'At six he was sent to the College of the Brothers of the Sacred Heart, an order which, having been expelled from France, had finally settled in Zaragoza. There he encountered the idiom which was later to become an important part of his culture. At seven he moved to the Jesuit College, where he worked for his *baccalaureat* until he was sixteen. He always had top marks, receiving the "Laurel Crown" and the titles of "Emperor", "Carthaginian Consul" and so on, which embarrassed him immoderately and more than once led him to misbehave deliberately so that they would not award him such honours.'

This extract from a letter from Alfonso Buñuel (26 January 1955) brought a protest from Luis, who wrote in another letter:

'My marks at the Jesuit College were sometimes good and other times bad; and I *never* was Emperor or Prince, although I had one or two minor prizes.' The records of the college itself show that Buñuel is, as usual, exact. His worst marks were generally for mathematics. There is a record of a second prize for good conduct, honourable mention in French and Latin, and good marks for piety, politeness and neatness, and other Jesuitical virtues. The exquisite photograph reproduced here, showing the infant Buñuel invested with the Image of the Immaculate Conception at the Congregación Mariana comes from the college, through the kindness of the present Rector. This priest also reveals that he was a school-friend of Buñuel in the last baccalaureat year. It is strange, he told me, that he should have left the college in this

---

* Buñuel denies this.

Buñuel 'invested with the Image of the Immaculate Conception'

last and most difficult year; 'but it could not have been a case of being expelled, because that would have been established in the school records'. The Rector remembers him as a serious boy, bigger, better dressed and much more responsible than the majority of the others in his class. 'We very much envied him, because he was like a man, which is what we all wanted to be.'

Such details are not irrelevant. Everyone's childhood is decisive in his subsequent development. For the artist, the atmosphere and the landscape in which his early years are passed form the character of his work. Buñuel is one of the most outstanding illustrations. It is impossible to understand his cinema without taking into account his character as a Spaniard and an Aragonese, and all that goes with these things. Most of the errors and the elaborate and difficult interpretations put upon Buñuel's work come from this ignorance: indeed, for many years most critics thought that they were dealing with a Frenchman. If he had been French, the anti-clerical content and the insistence on religious problems would have had a different character. It might have been an intellectual and rational game, perhaps with a degree of wishing to *épater le bourgeois*. As it is, there is no question but that Buñuel's is far from an *Encyclopédiste* mentality; and that, as his autobiography suggests, religion was an anxious preoccupation from which he liberated himself by reacting violently against it. The same may be said of his social vision. Buñuel is the product of a bourgeoisie which entered the new century with the 'Generación del '98',* defeated, disillusioned, with few supports to prop their pride of caste. His family shared in an urban culture, liberal and semi-intellectual, at the same time as they were landowners. They remained in contact with the land. Above all they were the children of that generation which achieved its revolution. During the first quarter of the century they were deeply conscious of national and personal crisis. And there were many among them who reacted as he did.

Throughout his work, Buñuel attacks – sometimes bitterly and angrily – those things which constituted his own youthful patrimony. In *L'Age d'or* and *El* there are gardens recalling the family garden in Calanda, complete with the horrid, scaled-down reproductions of classical statuary, the creation of the society which built its neo-Gothic or *art nouveau* villas. The brilliantly conceived, idiotic decorations of the house in *El* are, according to Buñuel's sister Conchita, like those of their home in Calanda. The house in *Viridiana* must be a recollection of the home of his respected canon uncle. Buñuel's work is a pitiless analysis of the atmosphere which surrounded him. It is full of aesthetic reminiscences (literary, musical and plastic) of the nineteenth century, as, it may be mentioned in passing, is all Surrealist art. Some enemy of the Surrealists has said that 'to be a Surrealist you have only to come from a "good" family'.

Living in the country acquainted him with agricultural life: in his films he often alludes to the way men treat beasts of burden. In almost all of them, too, he returns to the landscape of Calanda. Buñuel uses a large proportion of exteriors, stressing landscapes of dust and soil. At most he frames only a narrow strip of sky. But this sky tells you nothing. In the midst of the land, among the dry tree-trunks, the rocks and the stones – there he places the centre of his interest, the human being, geometrically composed and dwarfed in a very particular kind of long shot. A frame from Buñuel is unmistakable, distinguishable among thousands, linked with the great tradition of Griffith, Ince, Pudovkin, Dovzhenko, Ivens, but carried to an extreme of exasperation. In all his work there emerges a plastic style which has its own grandeur. We are far from the narcissism of Welles: yet despite himself Buñuel has an aesthetic personality, a way of going directly to what he has seen and felt, without aiming to beautify it. And the content, the absolute presence of the matter and its space, illuminates the unique message of his 'being'. The

* 1898 was the year in which Spain lost her last colonies.

17

physical type of the Aragonese peasant appears in very many of his films: short-legged, bearded, wearing the old, dirty clothes of a labourer, with skins and a crumpled hat. (Cf. *L'Age d'or*, *Nazarín*, etc.) The Jesuits taught him to be conscious of his duties and obligations, even the disagreeable ones, and this has enabled him to express all he wants to express in the cinema, with regal discretion. All his life Buñuel has borne this formation with an elegance that Voltaire, James Joyce and Jean-Paul Sartre – good students who emerged from just such a school as his, as equally vehement anti-Catholics – might themselves have envied.

Other constant themes in his cinema also appear to be tastes from his youth: Alfonso Buñuel recalled in a letter:

'Entomology and the study of animals in general attracted him. He always had some live animal in his room: snakes, rats, giant lizards, owls and so on. He was a favourite pupil of the entomologist Cándido Bolívar, whom he helped in classifying insects in the Museum of Natural History in Madrid, near to the Student Residence in which he lived.

'Extremely fond of music, he played the piano and violin from childhood; and I remember him playing the ocarina in the morning, before he had breakfast. His favourite composer was Richard Wagner, whom he greatly venerated, especially *Tristan and Isolde*' (the music of *Un Chien andalou*, *L'Age d'or* and *Cumbres borrascosas*).

Conchita writes:

'When he was about thirteen he started to study the violin, at his own very strong desire; and he seemed to show an aptitude for it. He used to wait till we had gone to bed, then, with his violin all ready, would come to the room where we, his three sisters, slept. He would begin by telling us the "plot", which as I recall it was a very Wagnerian tale, although he was not aware of it at the time. I don't think his music was so Wagnerian, but it was a gift which enriched the adventures of my childish imagination.

'In those days we spent the summers at our house in Calanda. There he managed to form an orchestra, and at the great religious ceremonies, from the choir of the church, he would launch the strains of Perosi's *Mass* and Schubert's *Ave Maria* over the admiring populace. My parents often went to Paris, showering us with new toys on their return. From one of these trips came a theatre which, looking back, I reckon must have been about one metre square. It had a back-cloth and scenery. I remember two sets: a throne-room and a wood. The cardboard characters represented a King, a Queen, a Jester, Courtiers. They were only ten centimetres high, and always faced the front, even when they were moving sideways, pushed by a wire. To augment the cast my brother brought in a ferocious lion, which normally stood on an alabaster base and served as a paperweight. Also he used a gilt Eiffel Tower which until then had passed its time between the kitchen, the drawing room and the barn. I can't remember whether the Eiffel Tower represented a fortress, or some sinister personage in the play, but I do recall that I saw it enter the throne-room, leaping and bounding, harnessed to the tail of the lion. A week before the shows, Luis started preparations. He rehearsed with his chosen ones who, as in the Bible, were few; though many were called. He arranged chairs in one of the barns. Invitations were prepared and distributed among those boys and girls of the village who had achieved the age of twelve. At the last moment he prepared a small collation of sweets made of egg-white and, as a drink, water flavoured with vinegar and sugar. As we were persuaded that this drink came from an exotic land, we drank it with pleasure and devotion. To make him admit us, his sisters, my father had to threaten him with prohibition of the event.

'He ate like a squirrel, and even when the temperature was below zero and there was snow on the ground, he wore as little clothing as possible, and monkish sandals on his feet. My father was opposed to all this, but under-neath, very proud of having a son capable of these things. He hid his pride, and was particularly angry with Luis when he saw him lift up his feet one after the other and wash them in the wash basin – in cold water – every time he washed his hands. At that time, or perhaps a little earlier (I find dates very confusing) we had in the house a rat as big as a hare, which was perfectly repulsive with its vixen tail, but which we treated as one of the family. Whenever we went anywhere we took it in a parrot's cage, and for quite a time it made our lives very complicated. The poor creature died like a saint, and with definite symptoms of poisoning. As we had five servants, it was not easy to discover the murderer. At all events we had forgotten it even before its smell had completely vanished from the house. We always kept some animal. Monkeys, parrots, falcons, toads and frogs, some sort of snake, a large African lizard which the cook, in a moment of fright, killed outright with the kitchen poker and an iron. I still remember the ram, Gregorio, who prac-tically crushed my femur and pelvis when I was ten years old. I believe that they had brought him from Italy when he was little. He was always untrust-worthy, and only liked Nene the horse. We were already older when we had a big hatful of grey mice. They belonged to Luis, but he allowed us to look at them once a day. He had selected several couples which, well fed and housed, procreated without cease. Before leaving home, he took them to the barn and let them go, so that they might increase and multiply.

'We all loved and respected everything that lived, even vegetable life. I believe that they also respect and love us. We could walk through a forest of wild animals, like those Salgari describes, without fear of molestation. There is one exception. THE SPIDERS. Horrid and fearful monsters which at any

19

moment can deprive us of all the joy of living. Thanks to a strange, "Buñuelesque" morbidity, they are a principal theme of our family conversation. Our discussions on spiders are legendary. One story alleges that my brother Luis, seeing a monster with eight eyes and a twisted mouth emerge when he was eating in an inn in Toledo, fell into a swoon and did not recover until he arrived back in Madrid.

'Nearly all the animals which we bought belonged to my brother Luis and I never saw beings better cared for, each one according to its biological needs. Even today he still loves animals and I think that he even tries not to hate spiders. In *Viridiana* we are shown a long, long cart-track, and a poor dog tied beneath a cart. Looking for locations for the film, he had been very upset to see this actual scene, but played for real. He tried to put a stop to it once or twice, but the habit is rooted among Spanish peasants, and it was like fighting windmills. While they were shooting these scenes, he ordered a kilo of meat to be bought every day for the dogs, and for any others that might come into the neighbourhood.

'We had many delightful adventures. In one of those summers that we spent at Calanda, we experienced the greatest adventure of our childhood. At that time Luis was thirteen or fourteen. We decided to go to a nearby village without the permission of our parents. We were joined by some cousins of our own age, and left the house, I don't know why, all dressed up as if for a holiday. The town, five kilometres away, was called Foz. We had estates and smallholdings there. We visited everyone, and everyone gave us sweet wine and little cakes. The wine produced such euphoria and Dutch courage in us that we did not hesitate to go to the cemetery. For the first time I walked there without fear. I recall Luis stretching out on a grave as if on the autopsy table and asking to be cut open. I also remember our efforts to help one of our sisters to release her head from a hole which the weather had worn in a tomb. She was so firmly stuck that Luis had to tear away the plaster with his nails in order to free her. After the war I went back to the cemetery to remember. It seemed much smaller, and older. Thrown into a corner was a crumbling little white coffin, with the mummified remains of a child, which made a strong impression on me. A big cluster of red poppies was growing where its stomach once was.

'After our heedless and sacrilegious visit to the cemetery, we undertook to walk across the bare and burning hills in search of the – to us – fabled "Brown Cave". The sweet wine continued to sustain us and enabled us to do what older people had not dared to do: to jump into a deep, narrow hole, to drag ourselves along a horizontal fissure, and arrive at the first cavern. Our only speleological equipment consisted of a stub of wax candle, left over from some burial, which we had picked up in the cemetery. We walked as long as its light held out. Suddenly everything went – lights, courage, joy. Luis insisted that the fluttering bats were prehistoric beings; but that he would protect us. Later, when someone said that he was hungry, Luis chivalrously offered himself to be eaten. Because my brother was my idol, I whimpered that *I* wanted to be the one to be eaten, since I was the littlest and silliest of the senior group of Buñuel children. I have forgotten the anguish of all those hours, just as one forgets physical pain. I remember however the joy of being found, and the fear of punishment. There was no punishment, on account of our pathetic state. We made the return journey to home, sweet home in a cart drawn by Nene. My sister was unconscious, though I am uncertain whether from drunkenness, weakness or discretion. Our parents only addressed us in the most formal terms for the next few days. When he thought we were not listening, my father recounted the adventure to visitors, exaggerating the dangers, and praising Luis's offer to be eaten. Nobody mentioned my offer, though it was just as heroic.'

Luis's autobiography takes up the story:

'My eight years as a student with the Jesuit fathers only increased these sentiments instead of diminishing them. Until my baccalaureat at sixteen years of age one can say that I had not been a part of modern society. I went to Madrid to study. The change from the province to the capital was as amazing to me as it would have been to a crusader who had suddenly found himself on Fifth Avenue, New York City.

'When I graduated with my bachelor degree my father asked me what I wanted to study. I had two chief interests: one, music (I had taken several violin courses) and the other, natural sciences. I asked my father to allow me to go to Paris and enrol in the Schola Cantorum and continue the study of composition. He refused, arguing that with the career of an artist one was more apt to die of hunger than to prosper. This was the attitude of any Spanish father (and perhaps of a father of any nationality). Flattering my other interest, he urged me to go to Madrid to study for the career of Agricultural Engineer.

'In 1917 I therefore found myself settled in Madrid in the Students' Residence, which in Spain is the only really modern institution of pedagogy, inspired and created in imitation of the English universities, by the Institución Libre de Enseñanza.

'A curious thing is that in Spain the career of engineer is the most difficult and honorable which a young man can pursue. The aristocratic thing to do in Spain is to study to be an engineer or a diplomat. The only young men who had access to these careers were those who, besides having the necessary intelligence and application, had sufficient funds, as the cost was excessive for the modest Spanish way of living.

'In agricultural engineering there was the absurd situation in which, although it was essentially a career of natural sciences, it was necessary for one to study mathematics for several years. And, if my inclinations led me to the study of nature, I in no way felt inclined to solve equations with the grade of "n". Nevertheless I studied mathematics for three years. With this they succeeded in making me hate my studies.

'Determined to try on my own and without my father's permission, I enrolled in 1920 as a pupil of the learned Spanish entomologist, Dr Bolívar, director of the Museum of Natural History of Madrid. This and the following year I dedicated to the study of insects which, as far as my material future was concerned, was less lucrative than if I had studied music at the Schola Cantorum.

'I worked with interest for over a year, although I soon arrived at the conclusion that I was more interested in the life or literature of insects than in his [sic] anatomy, physiology and classification.

'During that time I formed a close friendship, in Students' Residence, with a group of young artists who were to influence me strongly in finding my bent. Some of them have become famous, such as the poet, Federico García Lorca, the painter, Salvador Dalí, Moreno Villa, poet and critic, etc. I began to collaborate in the vanguard of literary publications, publishing some poems and preferring to chat with my friends in the café rather than to sit at the table with the microscope at the Museum of Natural History.

'My new literary leanings made me realize that my goal was art and letters rather than natural sciences. Thus I changed my career and began the study of Philosophy and Letters in the University of Madrid, and graduated with a degree in 1924.

'I cannot say that I was a good student. I alternated between interminable gatherings of our group of friends and the writing of poems, and sports. In 1921 I became amateur boxing champion of Spain, because, as the saying goes, "In the land of the blind, the one-eyed man is king." '

Alfonso Buñuel, in the letter already quoted, relates this episode:

'In his adolescence, apart from natural sciences and intellectual pursuits, he was a great athlete: very muscular in build, unbeatable at elbow-wrestling. As an amateur boxer he made public appearances in Madrid, losing the amateur heavyweight championship on points at nineteen.

'His father having finally forbidden him boxing, especially in public, he went to the ring rather nervously. In the previous bout, it happened that one of the boxers was killed. With great trepidation Luis was on the defensive in every round. The judges, seeing his superiority over his opponent, asked him to adjourn the fight. The opponent accepted another round, and Luis said: "Twenty more or none at all"; so his opponent was declared winner on points.'

Of Luis's friendships, Alfonso adds:

'In the Residencia he formed warm friendships with various other inmates: Federico García Lorca, Pepín Bello, Salvador Dalí,* José María Hinojosa, José Moreno Villa. His group was in general that whole generation of writers and their circle: Alberti, Guillén, Dámaso Alonso, Ramón Gómez de la Serna, Altolaguirre, Pedro Garfias, Barradas, Palencia, Vázquez Díaz, José

---

* Dalí was never a formal member of the Residencia, though he was a constant visitor there.

Boxer Buñuel and punchbag marked 'RESI 1919'

Ortega y Gasset, Adolfo Salazar, etc.' He might also have included two very great friends, Vicens and Sanchez Ventura.

Buñuel's period in the Residencia de Estudiantes is important. The Residencia was a formative place, an exceptional catalyst of talents in the story of modern Spanish art. Its history has still to be written, and will be a significant one. To understand it, it is necessary to link it with two sister institutions: the Institución Libre de Enseñanza and the Instituto Escuela. Since 1920 almost all Spain's outstanding names in the sciences, arts and sociology – internationally celebrated figures – have come from these three centres.

The contact between young intellectuals, their shared existence, the interminable talks in the common rooms, dormitories and cafés to which Buñuel refers, describing them as idling away the time (and the description is correct if we apply the Aristotelian definition of idling as the germinating period of creation), resulted in the work of the Generation of '27. Buñuel, Val y Gay and García Lorca would organize lectures, shows and excursions. Federico was later to found, with Eduardo Ugarte as secretary, 'La Baracca' ('The Barn'), a touring theatrical company; with this company Buñuel was to visit Las Hurdes where he would subsequently make the film of the same title; and he was to develop the literary and cinematographic activity described in Chapter 3.

In the Residencia there were concerts, poetry recitals, entertainments, literary discussions, scientific lectures, a Sociedad de Cursos y Conferencias. The cinema had begun to interest intellectuals in France after 1918, and

Buñuel with Federico García Lorca (1923?)

consequently in the Spanish centre – always in the forefront – there was a favourable atmosphere for what they were beginning to call 'The Seventh Art'.

Buñuel interested himself in the theatre, especially the puppet theatre, thanks to his friends Juan Chabas and Federico García Lorca, who wrote some excellent farces for puppets. The three of them met a little man called Mayeu who was presenting children's shows in the Retiro Park, passing the hat around to make a little money. Chabas and Buñuel organized shows of a superior kind, helping Mayeu to prepare the plays and performances. They ended up taking the show to the Residencia where they presented performances with this delightful theatre which Lorca had already conscientiously rehearsed with Manuel de Falla, during his adolescence in Granada.

Buñuel was also an amateur actor. His troupe were much admired for their interpretation of Zorrilla's *Don Juan Tenorio* which they played every 1 November. The performance was faithful, but the students let themselves and their fantasy loose on the production and the decors. Each year the director and designer changed. Sometimes it was Lorca, sometimes Buñuel. As actor, Buñuel always played Don Juan: exuberant, exaggerated, nervously moving from one side to the other, and carrying a portable typewriter for writing love-letters. The students of the Residencia saw in the ultra-romanticism of *Don Juan Tenorio* a fount of Freudian significances and other precursors of Surrealism, which practically all the members of the group were to assimilate. (Buñuel notes: 'My first contact with Freud was reading in 1921 *Psychoanalysis of Daily Life*, translated and with an introduction by Ortega y

24

Gasset. This introduction earned the Spanish philosopher a letter of harsh censure from Freud.') The custom of presenting this annual performance still continues as a sort of ritual among the survivors who remain in Madrid. Something resembling the Residencia production was seen in 1951 when Salvador Dali mounted *Don Juan Tenorio* for the National Theatre, with settings which he had designed and used in America. Buñuel's stage experience in the Residencia was later to prove useful when he began his professional career with the direction of *El Retablo de Maese Pedro*, and afterwards came to direct film actors.

Generally the activities of this period influenced the whole artistic formation of Buñuel. His passion for insects is reflected in all his films. Insects played a great part in Spanish literature at that period, in the work of Lorca, Dámaso Alonso and others, providing our writers with an authentic poetic image – of anxiety, fear, desire, terror. Buñuel's use of big close-ups of insects interpolated in the action of his films, has been attacked as affected and pretentious; but those who make this criticism fail to recognize the expressive origins of such images. Although they come from entirely personal sources, their use is never simply gratuitous: they always have an additional purpose, as shock images, as methods of transition between sequences, as a reminder to the spectator of the other dramas that are played out on the sidelines of the main theme. As well as symbols of unbalanced states of mind, too, there is an element of objective vision, a gesture of curiosity and affection towards these other living creatures.

His Surrealist formation can also be traced to his years in the Residencia. Although his orthodox initiation into the movement dates from his stay in Paris, his first literary works, published in Madrid, already clearly show his inclinations. The beginnings of Surrealism in Spain were contemporary with the French movement.* We can trace the germs from 1916 and the appearance in Barcelona of Francis Picabia's † Dada magazine *391*. In 1919 a Dada group formed in Barcelona around a fashionable milliner, Joan Prats, and some of his dilettante friends. Almost at the same time Dada made its appearance in Madrid. If the rapid assimilation of Surrealism in Barcelona was due to the city's thirst for cosmopolitanism, in Madrid it had an indigenous origin which made it quite different from French Surrealism. Although integrated in the international Paris group, Buñuel's Surrealism always retained its essentially Spanish character.

Madrid in 1920 was a hubbub of 'isms', which were later noted and

---

* Buñuel in fact corrects this statement. He says that it was only four months after the première of *Un Chien andalou* that he introduced Dali to the Surrealist group in Paris.

† Picabia, whose baptismal name was Francisco Martinez de Picabia, was of Spanish–Cuban origin.

Pepín Bello, Moreno Villa, María Luisa González, Luis Buñuel, Salvador Dalí and José María Hinojosa

classified by Ramón Gómez de la Serna, who was very roughly Spain's equivalent to Apollinaire. Encouraging all his contemporaries, inciting them to discover new forms, accustoming them to his extravagant literary techniques, he was the catalyst if not the master of the new styles. The Spanish Surrealist group was undoubtedly on the march before 1925. There is a study of this movement,* which represented an important, though not exclusive activity of the Generation of '27; and the present writer has made a *Chronology of Spanish Surrealism*. The Surrealist influence and the style of the new 'belief' were marked in Buñuel's Spanish friends – Dalí, Hinojosa, Prados, Lorca, Alberti, Bello, Duran, Garfias, Gerardo Diego and later Ceruda Alexandre and many others. It is important to recognize that these owed not everything to French Surrealism; only Juan Larrea was indebted to Paris. Spanish Surrealism did not drink at the same fountains as the French – Swift, De Sade, De Quincey, Hegel, Lautréamont, Jarry – but from *La Celestina* and the Spanish picaresque novel, and the nineteenth century indigenous theatre.

For Buñuel, as a good Aragonese, fantasy is impossible: paradoxical though it may seem, his Surrealism is without fantasy, a purified form of

* H. B. Morris, 'Surrealism and Spain', Cambridge University Press, 1972.

Surrealism. Surrealism was a movement of revolt against the last century's strict and stultifying naturalism. Buñuel is a materialist, but no longer admits *only* what he can see and touch. He accepts as real, things which we do not *know* but which can be sensed, although they may continue to remain undemonstrable by experiment. (It is strange, however, to observe that since Surrealism many of these things have become capable of scientific demonstration.) Generally, even despite Maurice Nadeau's classic *Histoire du Surréalisme* (1945), there is still misconception about what the movement really was. For many it was simply an aesthetic movement. And in effect it was so from the time of the defection to an artistic formalism of some of its members, who were for other reasons expelled from 'the party'. Fundamentally, however, it was a philosophical and active position applied to the contemporary world as an embattled intellectual movement, and deeply involved in the social and political currents of the time. To an extent elevating reality through a process of poeticizing it, its practitioners fought against and despised the idea of 'art for art's sake' and the idealist aesthetic still dominant in many areas of the old European capitalist culture. If Surrealism in Spain never had a defined programme as it had in France, it nevertheless possessed the advantage of alliance with the temperament and art of a people traditionally devoted less to logic, and more to reality than the French. With the Spanish, Surrealism does not imply an intellectual distortion of reality, but a rupture: 'The ship on the sea and the horse on the mountain,' pleaded Lorca. To put the boat on the mountain and the horse on the water would be worse, for the Spanish Surrealists, than simply a fantastic paradox: it would be an injustice and an offence against nature and the natural order. Hence the Spanish are able to understand Buñuel, and not find in his work any of the betrayal and renunciation of which some French critics accuse him.

It is quite true that Buñuel's work can be divided into distinctive periods according to its language: the first and the latest by orthodox Surrealist vocabulary; and the middle period by images and situations apparently belonging to the commercial cinema, although in reality we can discover within them the same processes as in the other films. It is also true that Buñuel has changed in the course of thirty years, as all men must; and as he has himself said: 'At seventy you see things with a different passion and from a different viewpoint. In thirty years the world has changed, and you have to attack with different weapons.' Yet his feelings and convictions have continued unchanged. Buñuel's processes of intellectual connection do not observe traditional logic. He affirms the absurd, but only in that part of cinematic structure which is not concrete: in the development of the sequence and its articulation with the rest. But his material is, in a wholly Spanish style, always objective, undistorted. I cannot bring to mind a single shot or a single frame in Buñuel which does not contain some real, familiar, everyday object, directly shown. Here lies the difference between him and Jean Vigo, the son of a Catalan, and the cinema's other great Surrealist. Vigo also employs objective reality, but records it with the illuminations, the unexpected angles of an eccentric vision which gives new significances to the object, through aesthetic addition. For Buñuel the element of surprise and contradiction in things resides in those things just as they are. He shows pig-killing quite faithfully in *Cumbres borrascosas*, just as it might be seen in any village; but when he presents it to us it seems incredible, inadmissible. When he presents the actual world as harsh and cruel, it is no sadistic deformation. On the contrary, Buñuel shows violence with discretion, in brief shots, which never linger over details, but bring us a genuine sense of shame. Vigo, as artist and poet, was the prophet of a new social class. Buñuel is the chronicler of a dying class; and without wanting to make anything more beautiful or optimistic than it is, simply and laconically offers us his document.

This Spanish essence of Buñuel clearly links him quite as much with his contemporaries of the Generation of '27 as with the artists with whom he was associated in his French period. His intellectual origins in the Residencia de Estudiantes are fundamental to a knowledge of him. His contact with it continued after his years as a student of philosophy and literature. After going to Paris in 1925, Buñuel continued regularly to visit the Residencia, and kept up his contact with his friends – even after his marriage, when he was living in an apartment in Calle Menendez y Palayo, between 1934 and his departure for France in 1937.

Returning to 1924:

'Upon completing my career, I found myself at loose ends. My only out was to try for a professorship in an institute or university, a profession for which I felt I had no calling. As I was twenty-four years old I realized that I must think seriously about getting established, but nevertheless I felt more undecided and perplexed than ever. This is a fault prevailing among the Spanish. Instead of a youth's developing according to his likes and aptitudes, he must follow the course marked out by his parents. The student, upon leaving the bosom of his family and feeling himself independent, is more drawn to life itself than to study. The Spanish University did very little, one must realize, to attract the students or inspire their affection.

'My nervousness and uncertainty was dissipated immediately when my mother gave me permission to go to Paris. My father had died the year before.'

This was the time of Primo de Rivera's dictatorship. Buñuel lived in a time in which politico-social problems were becoming progressively graver. The bourgeoisie tried to ignore them. The Residencia with its educated bourgeois élite and its English-style education of exclusive minorities had felt an ill-defined anxiety, which manifested itself in the pre-Surrealist rebellion. The liberal and progressive tone of the Residencia would not succeed in shaking the young artists out of their heritage and their 'symbolist' education.

Buñuel, like Larrea and Hinojosa, will breathe the cosmopolitan air of Paris. He will perhaps be the first of the Institute's ex-students to react, the first of the Generation of '25 (or the Generation of the Dictatorship, or the Generation of '27, to use alternative titles for it) to adopt a radically new position. It is a fact of considerable importance, which can explain the late acceptance and understanding of his work as much as his present-day recognition, now that a new generation has taken a fresh step forward, and the Buñuel period can be regarded as 'classic'. Despite this Buñuel remains firmly linked to his Generation of the Residencia. He overcomes a crisis, but it will be expressed in terms of conflict. It is the path which leads from 'Modernism' to realism, from idealism to Marxism. His whole work reflects the path of a nation from the 'Golden 1900s' through the Dictatorship and the Civil War up to our own times.

2. Initiation

'In 1925 I arrived in Paris without having any idea of what was to become of me. I wanted to do something – work, earn my living – but I didn't know how. I continued writing poems, but this seemed to me more like the luxury of a "senorito". Then, as even now, I was opposed to luxury and to the "senoritos", although, because of my birth, I was one of them.

'Among the Spaniard's defects is that of improvisation, which arises from the belief that he knows everything. I must confess that this fault was a virtue for me, since, thanks to it, I found my walk in life, and in a profession which appears to be conclusive for me. Because I could improvise I was able to make my debut as "metteur en scène" in Amsterdam, direction [*sic*] the scenic part of:

"EL RETABLO DE MAESE PEDRO"

'I had gone to Paris with a letter of introduction to the illustrious pianist, Ricardo Viñas. One day, when I was calling on him, Viñas told me that the director of the Dutch orchestra, Maestro Mengelberg, had told him to gather all kinds of artistic elements in Paris, in order to present in Amsterdam "El Retablo de Maese Pedro", a musical composition, for orchestra, voice and stage, by Manuel de Falla.

'The aforementioned work, perhaps the most exquisite of the Spanish master, had up to then been given only once, in the palace of the Princesse de Polignac in Paris. The Princess had expressly commissioned Falla to do it.

'*El Retablo de Maese Pedro* is an episode taken from *Don Quijote de la Mancha*.

El Retablo de Maese Pedro: original programme cover

In the play are Don Quijote, Sancho and other Cervantes characters who are present during the performance of a puppet show put on by Maese Pedro. At the performance in the home of Princesse de Polignac, both the Cervantes characters, as well as the puppets, had been dolls.

'It occurred to me to "improvise"; I suggested to Viñas that the human characters be actors, so that in this way there might be a more pronounced difference between them and the puppets, which could only be dolls. It seemed a good idea to him, and I offered to execute it. I still can't understand why he accepted. I was named "Regisseur", and consequently charged with the scenic part.

'I looked among my friends for the eight flesh and blood characters which we needed. Or, to be more accurate, I added their inexperience to mine, inasmuch as one was a painter, another a medical student, still another a newspaperman and none actors.

'The decoration, costumes, masks and dolls were commissioned from good artists in Paris. The singers were from the Opera Comica [*sic*], among others Vera Yanocopulos, and they were to sing from the orchestra. The characters in the play had to follow the action of the song with pantomime.

'I still tremble when I think of my audacity and that of my friends, who accepted in order to be able to visit Amsterdam gratis. Collaborating with Falla, one of the greatest contemporary musicians; with Mengelberg, famous orchestra conductor; with singers of the Opera Comica. Orchestra seats for the premiere at 200 frs. This spectacle formed the most discordant and heterogeneous conglomeration which music and the theatre have ever seen together.

'I must say that we didn't do so badly and that both my friends and I gave all our efforts to succeed in such a disproportionate enterprise. None of the public suspected that the plastic part of the spectacle was an experiment, for once not catastrophic, of Spanish improvisation. I should add that we had been having rehearsals for a month.

'Drunk with my success, which it was for me by virtue of not being a failure, I felt that a great love of the "mise en scène" had awakened within me. Shortly afterwards, in Paris, I saw a film by Fritz Lang, *Les Trois Lumières,** which greatly impressed me. For the first time, I felt that the movies could be a vehicle of expression and not merely a pastime, which up to then I had thought them. I succeeded in getting Jean Epstein, who was then the most famous director in France, to take me as assistant. I worked with him for two years, and with him learned the technical side of moving pictures.'

The team of Spanish collaborators on *El Retablo*, as it appears on the original programme was as follows:

EL RETABLO DE MAESE PEDRO

Produced: Amsterdam, Holland, 26 and 27 April 1926 (World première)

Book and music: Chamber opera by Manuel de Falla (1919)

Decor: Hernando Viñes, executed by Marcel Guérin (Proscenium and portable stage: Manuel Angeles Ortiz; puppets: Manuel Angeles Ortiz and Adolfo Armengot; scenic devices: José Viñes).

Costumes: Manuel Angeles Ortiz.

Musical direction: Willem Mengelberg (Concertgebouw Orchestra)

Scenic director: Luis Buñuel

Operators: Rafael Sauras, Francisco Cossío, Paquín Peinado, Juan Esplandíu, José Viñes, Hernando Viñes, Juan Aramburu, Roger Whettnalh

Players: Hector Dufrance, Thomas Salignac, Vera Janocópulos.

Despite Buñuel's modesty about it, the success of the production was deserved. The young people involved were exceptional. The director's decision to replace puppets by real people was generally praised by the critics; among others Adolfo Salazar wrote very favourably in a series of articles later collected in the books *Música y músicos de hoy* (Madrid, 1928) and *La música contemporánea en España* (Madrid, 1930). The Dadaist solution to the difficult problem of the period *mise en scène* was very characteristic of Buñuel. At one stroke he simplified seemingly insoluble problems arising from the simultaneous action of the glove-puppets, the

---

* English title: *Destiny.*

marionette theatre representing the live audience, and the orchestra and singers who were present throughout. At the same time, the desire to humanize remains very characteristic of Buñuel's work. The opera in its initial conception tended to be an intellectual, *avant-garde* game, favouring the abstraction which Falla favoured at the time. Buñuel converted the people to flesh and blood and the story to legend.

In Paris Buñuel got off on the right foot. He arrived with a recommendation from Don Pedro Azcárate, later Ambassador to London, and with the promise of a job in the future International Institute of Intellectual Cooperation. Azcárate had guessed the potential of this young man whose only activity until then had been the publication of some minor literary pieces. Buñuel went to Paris as his protégé on a kind of cultural mission, which meant that he had a grant. He was introduced into the best intellectual circles of the city, and seems to have made an immediate impression. Sport was fashionable in Paris; and his having been a boxer gave him a certain allure. Well-dressed and in his own fashion elegant, Buñuel was by no means flamboyant. A friend of his Paris period told me that basically Buñuel was a rather timid and nervous man; and when he walked in the streets at night would always choose the well-lit centre as if superstitiously avoiding the darkness of the footpaths. Buñuel is one of the privileged few who know how to listen, and it is safe to suppose that at that time he was all ears. He was introduced to Jean Epstein by Guillermo de Torre, to whose *avant-garde* magazines *Ultra* and *Tablero* both Epstein and Philippe Soupault had contributed. Epstein was responsive to interesting personalities and must have been impressed by Buñuel. The film director had formed a sizeable group of cinema apprentices around him, and initiated them with stimulating lectures. For each of his films he would select assistant directors from among his pupils, not only using their services but also advising and guiding them. Of Polish extraction, Epstein was the only director of that bleak era of the French cinema to merit the title of an intellectual film-maker. He, Camille Bardoux and Alex Alain, who ran it with him, called their private film school the Académie de Cinéma. Most of the students were white Russians. Buñuel was enrolled as student no. 19, presenting himself along with the painter Uzelay and the son of the painter Regoyos, to study acting.

Buñuel went to work. An assistant director must be above all a good messenger; the job consists in getting on and preparing things. Claudio de la Torre gives a good idea of this activity in a short account he gave the readers of *La Gaceta literaria* of the work of his fellow editor:

'TRAMCAR IN SLOW MOTION – THE ROAD FOR LUIS BUÑUEL

'. . . But for the moment *Maison Usher* has not opened to the public. When we visited it, it was still under construction. We saw a room or two, a lot of scaffolding, the complete electrical installation. We also discovered a lake, a lot of owls, two or three skeletons. Their owners, slow and pale, gesticulated solemnly before the camera. Epstein's shouts served to indicate our friend to us:

' "Buñuel! Lights!"

'Luis Buñuel – whoever would recognize Madrilene inertia in him now – rapidly consults his papers.

' "Buñuel! Number!"

'Again he consults his fan of papers as if it were the wheel of fortune.

' "32!"

' "Buñuel!"

' ". . . !" '

In this way he learned his job, without receiving any payment. Marie Epstein has told me that he used to go to the house of the director, in Neuilly, where Epstein had a sort of laboratory; and there he learned editing from the master. Buñuel has told me that this was not so, and that he was used just as a simple worker:

'The fact is that I learned very little from Epstein. When I began *Un Chien andalou* I knew very little about the cinema. You can only learn with practice. The work that can help you most is that of script-girl: that way you learn all the secrets of filming, and you see the creation of the work. What happens with the cinema is that people have written and said a great deal about its technique. There's a lot of hot air in all that: cinema is easy to do, and has no secrets . . . The specialists solve the technical problems. To be a good director in the cinema is the same as being a good writer – to have clear ideas, to know what you want to say and to say it as directly as possible. If I had known the technique of editing properly, I would not have had to spend so many nights in New York over the work on my *Triumph of the Will* with an assistant, because among other things we did not know where to fit the sound, which as you know comes a few frames later on the film, so that it would coincide with the image.'

Such a view of the craft is understandable in a film-maker like Buñuel, for whom technique has never been an end in itself or a pretext for artistic flourishes. He learned something, no doubt, but nothing important. On the other hand, none of Epstein's ideas could have much interested the very different temperament of a man who, though still young, was completely formed. There were few things about Epstein of which Buñuel could wholeheartedly approve. In the conversation already quoted he explained to me:

'When I watched Epstein direct he frequently made me think – with the

Checking a set for *Mauprat*

temerity of every newcomer — that this was not the way to do it, that the placing of the camera, lights or cast ought to be in such or such another way. Epstein was patient with me. Above all I learned by mentally elaborating the picture being made, seeing it in a different fashion.'

Epstein represented the culmination, and already the decadence of the French cinema's second *avant-garde*. His exquisite taste for metaphor, literary symbolism, gaunt images — or rather *flou* — and ultra-romantic themes carried him into a baroque style that was sometimes very poetic, but also sometimes soft and confusing. In one respect he might have had something to impart to the young assistant. According to Henri Langlois, the supreme virtue of Epstein was his ability to 'rendre insolite les objets les plus quotidiens'. Is not this one of Buñuel's prime virtues also? Is not one of the essential postulates of the Surrealists, to 'rehabilitate everyday reality', giving it a weight of importance, almost a magical quality? Of course the two cinéastes used this ability in very different ways. Epstein tried to create an atmosphere of beauty, an aesthetic impression of romantic mystery. He would photograph a candelabra, an armchair, a curtain; and the object would acquire an unusual weight of lyrical resonances. When Buñuel does the same,

35

Buñuel as an extra on *Mauprat*

the process is precisely inverse. Instead of photographing the object wrapped up in a diffused, mystical halo, and from some unexpected angle, Buñuel presents it in such a way that its material essence seems never to have appeared so directly, with a reality so physical and strong. The two Epstein films on which he worked, though their treatment is radically opposed to all Buñuel has done, have certain elements about them not completely alien to him. Of *Mauprat* Buñuel has said, 'It could only be of any interest to the warped minds of film archivists.' And though he has not been so specific about *La Chute de la Maison Usher*, his opinion cannot be much different. Langlois, with his usual critical acumen, has characterized *Mauprat* as the perfect instance of French neo-Classic cinema. The cold quest for correct lines and balance in this film recalls *pompier* architecture and painting. The plot in itself could have produced a very romantic film. There is something pre-romantic about it, along with something of the Sadic novel, with its looming castles in the darkness of leafy woods, its murderous family feuds, its acts of violence and, vanquishing all, love – *l'amour fou* of the Surrealists.

Between the two Epstein films, Buñuel was found a job by the cameraman

La Sirène des Tropiques: Pierre Batcheff, Josephine Baker

Duverger, who was later to shoot *L'Age d'or*. *La Sirène des Tropiques* was a *film d'art*, a commercial vehicle for the beauty of Josephine Baker – then at its peak – and for the sort of Modernist decors and furniture, walls of polished and diffused glass, which were currently the rage in Paris. There were two changes of director. The plot involved the attempt to adapt the naked and gleaming Venus to the social life of Paris, and provided opportunities to alternate the ultra-modern atmosphere of high society with the no less sophisticated scenes of African jungles from which the 'Bronze Venus' was supposed to have emerged. A series of extravagant situations succeeded in exciting a certain *succès de scandale*. Opposite the star they had prudently cast Pierre Batcheff, one of the most fashionable actors in the European cinema. Batcheff was a kind of James Dean of his day, admired both for his beauty and for certain intellectual attributes which made him the idol of the intelligentsia. Like the American, he indulged eccentric habits, and also died young, though by suicide. He was a relatively good actor, pale and elegant, and a useful contrast to the exuberance of Josephine Baker.

Buñuel's work was mechanical and unrewarding. Still photographs showing guns hanging from the wall or the actress emerging from a wardrobe recall scenes from his own subsequent pictures; but Buñuel has assured us that he had nothing to do with it, in regard to the decoration or anything else. The experience served as practice in shooting in exteriors; and he also discovered Batcheff, who would later give a much superior performance in Buñuel's first film, *Un Chien andalou*, than in any of the roles in which he had made his name.

Buñuel was contemplating making his first film. Letters to friends indicate his impatience:

Paris, 22 July 1927

I am still an assistant on *La Sirène des Tropiques*. I am working ten hours a day. I am neglecting my book – *Polisinos* – for want of time. I have thought up two stupendous scenarios, but I haven't time to write them. In the Spring I shall make a film in Greece. For this Winter in Spain: project with Ramón (Gómez de la Serna). Project with Sánchez Mejías (Ignacio)

La Glacière, 5 September 1927

... I have finished the interiors already. Tomorrow we leave for Dieppe and then to Fontainebleau. All if the *metteur en scène* (Etiévant) does not change, which I would like. I will send you a photograph of Baker, the crew and myself...

Paris, 8 November 1927

... I start with Epstein again soon, hoping that Ramón will send me his work. The ****** promised me I would have it here by the 15th of last month; but so far there is no news of it. I pin all my hopes on making my debut. I have an excellent project. The film will be Franco-Spanish, but without the scenario I can do nothing. As soon as I have it I will have to work on it for a month, with another two to sort out the company and to make a start on it. Because of this, if all goes well I won't start my first film at least until March. I will bring German, French and Spanish actors, a friend or two – you, if you like – and even Cruz.

Paris, 14 February 1928

... I have now been in Paris ten days looking after my affairs. They are going quite well. Within a week I shall be signing a contract which will oblige me to make a film this Summer, and the other party in his turn will commit himself to contributing 50,000 pesetas. I cannot tell you the name of that 'party'...

Paris, 21 March 1928

... I've been a month and a half employed as assistant assistant-director with Jean Epstein, making a Poe film. A few days ago I had a fight with *my boss* (*Cahiers d'art*) over a rave I had written about the American cinema:

the following day I handed in my resignation which was joyously accepted. So much the better. My affairs are going very badly. I did not believe it was going to be so difficult to start. The film in Greece will not now be made, in spite of the fact that it was certain. Ramón has still not sent me his scenario! You will recall that both of us were working in Madrid and thought it was finished. So I find myself not knowing what to do. Of course I won't let myself get disheartened, and I'm keeping on. The experience which I'm getting in my not-yet-begun career makes me see life in quite a different light from when we used to drink rum in my room. The business which I was so mysterious about was a work of Claudio de la Torre and the son of Sota de Bilbao. The other day I had dinner with them, taking advantage of Sota's being in Paris.

In brief, here I sit in my room with not an idea what to do.

Saint Michel en Grêve, 1 August 1928

In October I shall go to the Cinema Congress in Spain.

It's quite probable that I shall sign a contract with the Julio César company, whose president thinks well of me. Julio César accepted my Goya treatment, and will pay me 4,500 pesetas for it.

I am making the *découpage* for my next film, *Caprichos*, based on a scenario by Ramón. The film consists of six stories. Shooting starts in September or October, with a Paris company.

I have 25,000 in my current account, destined for the film *Caprichos*.

Buñuel had rejoined Epstein for the shooting of *La Chute de la Maison Usher*, of which Carlos Fernández Cuenca gives the following account:

'During the months of February and March 1928 Jean Epstein shot the bulk of *La Chute de la Maison Usher* in the Epinay Studios near Paris. The exteriors were also shot near the capital, taking advantage of the wintry desolation, and especially the misty days. The subject was a favourite of Epstein's, to the extent that after the introduction of sound, he dreamed of re-making it, improving it with modern technical means. When he conceived the idea of filming Poe's terrifying story, he had not foreseen the inclusion of other literary elements from the same source; but while he was preparing the script, he decided to introduce the poetic finale of *The Oval Portrait*, another of Poe's great stories, in which an artist, in putting the image of his loved one on to canvas, tears out of her, stroke by stroke, her physical existence. From the fusion of this with the hallucinating story of the last Lord of Usher, whose tainted line ends beneath the ruins of the crumbling castle, there resulted one of the finest examples of the final period of the so-called French *avant-garde* cinema.'

Buñuel insists that as assistant he had no part in the direction of the film.

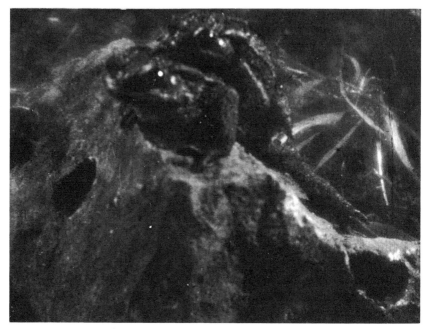

La Chute de la Maison Usher: the mating toads

Even so the two best sequences have shots which it is tempting to attribute to him. One is the magnificent scene of the last moments of Lady Madeline: at ₂very brush-stroke on the canvas of her husband's portrait of her, she fades away until finally she dies. The death-pangs are expressed with Epstein's own peculiar sensitivity, through a complex montage of close-ups of the brush giving nervous strokes upon the canvas, the enquiring glances of Roderick Usher, the eye-lids of his wife flickering into unconsciousness. Epstein adds poetic symbols: the flickering candle-flame agitated by an eerie wind; the pendulum of the clock moving ever more slowly; the fallen leaves dragged in whirlpools on the floor. At the moment of death, the pendulum stops, the candles die. Beside these images of hallucinatory visual and auditory force, which are all suggested by Poe, there is one that is more impressive than all: a guitar on a table whose strings are seen to tighten. At the moment of death the strings snap. There is no precedent for this anywhere in Poe; and on the other hand the image appears in Lorca as a symbol of the death crisis. Hence I deduce the possibility that Buñuel could have suggested this shot to the director.

The other sequence is the burial. Epstein again makes use of the slow-motion, *flous* and superimpositions which he so strenuously commended in his theoretical and practical work, as well as a subjective camera, which moves at the same pace as the hesitant steps of the coffin bearers. Once the corpse has been deposited in its niche in the abandoned vault, the unreal takes over. Through the cracks begins to ooze the bridal veil which shrouded Lady Madeline; and finally Lady Madeline herself lifts the flag-stone and goes out into the misty park. Prior to this there are six rapidly alternating shots, of no narrative value, but simply poetic in intention: an owl cries from a branch, with a moon in the background. Two toads mate in the warm undergrowth. Apparently two further symbols from Poe's sinister imagery. What is admirable though is that these animals are presented in an activity which affirms life, as a counterpoint to the dead world which surrounds them and to the meaning which literary symbolism normally attributes to them. This sounds distinctly like a cry from Buñuel; and it is the kind of *trouvaille* that abounds in his later work.

After *La Chute de la Maison Usher* Epstein proposed that Buñuel might work as assistant director on Gance's *Napoléon*. Buñuel replied in terms so insulting to Gance (compare also his criticism of the finished film, page 271) as to end his friendship with Epstein. While working for the last time as assistant director, he was continuing the hard struggle of every beginner in a creative career. All the plans referred to in the letters quoted above were frustrated; and another project with Ramón Gómez de la Serna also proved impossible. His insistence on wanting to make his first film with Ramón as scriptwriter again indicates how bound up he was with the Spanish group. There was another reason also: Gómez de la Serna was at that time the only Spaniard who belonged to the Académie Française, and therefore enjoyed a certain celebrity in the neighbouring country. Working with him, Buñuel could kill two birds with one stone, appealing to both countries, with a collaborator to whom he was himself personally attached. The découpage was ultimately finished; but not the film. *El Mundo por diez céntimos* was to have been a reportage on the bric-à-brac contents of a typical magazine, including critical, social and political material.

Many other projects were in his mind; for instance the one which he discussed with a friend, and which is already close to *L'Age d'or*:

The title, *La Sancta Misa Vaticanae* is in macaroni Latin. It would be a short film in which would be shown a competition of masses in St Peter's Square in Rome. The church, 'always attentive to the progress of civilization and of sport', wishes to set the mass to the living rhythms of our own times. For this purpose, functional altars have been placed between each pair of gigantic columns in Bernini's square; and on each of them a priest officiates. On the word 'Go!' the priests start to recite the mass as fast as they are able. They reach incredible speeds as they turn to the faithful to say the Dominus Vobiscum, to cross themselves and so on, while the servers pass constantly backwards and forwards with the missal and other ritual objects. Some of them collapse exhausted like knocked-out boxers. Finally there remains only the champion, Mosén Rendueles from Huesca, having set up a record for saying the entire mass in one and three quarter minutes. As a prize he receives a monstrance.

Such projects might appear simply as games for his own amusement, with no intention of realization, if it were not that two years later Buñuel created a work in which derision of ritual, lust for sacrilege and other characteristics which will be described later on, were fully and openly exploited in order to shock the world at large.

One of the projects of this period was brought to fruition in 1928. For want of a producer, *Un Chien andalou* was produced independently.

3. The Critical Man

This is perhaps the moment to consider Buñuel's literary career, which constituted his first activity after he had decided definitively not to follow a technical profession. This period of his life was too short to be really consolidated, and his writing lacks polish. At the same time, from the very beginning his creative personality, clearly defined, asserts itself. It is fascinating to see his future fundamental preoccupations as film-maker already evident in his work as a writer. Not only the ideas but many of the images of his films already appear in work written between the ages of twenty-two and twenty-eight.

Buñuel first contributed to the magazine *Horizonte*, a well-produced Madrilene publication dedicated to minor literature and *avant-garde* ambitions. Among his first works we find a series of paradoxes, *Los Instrumentos de la Orquesta*. Some of these betray the influence of Ramón Gómez de la Serna, which was practically obligatory among the young of 1920. Already that interest in the anthropology of musical instruments, later seen in *L'Age d'or* and – in the destruction of instruments – in *El ángel exterminador* is evident. We know half a dozen poems, completely in the mode of the period, which are rich in ideas and metaphors that are practically Surrealist, and abound above all in images of tactile qualities. Some short prose poems which appeared between 1927 and 1929 (published in *Hélix* and

The literary years ... 1924

La Gaceta literaria) are also surrealist and clearly predict his first cinematographic phase. *Palacio de Hielo* (*Palace of Ice*) (page 255) is a poem from the book *El perro andaluz*, which also includes a very long poem on Cortes, the conqueror of Mexico, and a series of titles devoted to Hosts: *Combat between Consecrated Hosts and Ants*; *Consecrated Hosts Emerging from the Arsehole of a Nightingale and Taking a Bow*. Buñuel also wrote lots of short stories, the majority of them unprintable. One of these is included in the Appendix (page 257): it dates from 1927 and relates to the 'carnuzo', the concept of a lump of meat, rotting yet still alive (cf. the miracle of Calanda), which has also the same roots as the film *Un Chien andalou*.

A few poems were published in the *avant-garde* magazine *Ultra*, 1922, edited by de la Torre; and two stories appeared in the *Revista oficial de ciegos* (*Official Review for the Blind*) the same year. These stories are more traditional, with clear influences from the picaresque and from authors of the *fin de siècle* and the first quarter of this century. One of them indicates that the Mexican period of Buñuel's films marked no radical change from his previous attitudes: *El ciego de las tortugas* describes a character who in

L U I S

... and 1927

compensation for being deprived of sight possesses a sixth sense and a cunning that permit him to go about with insolent ease, an early precursor of the depraved blind men of *Los Olvidados* and *Viridiana*. His attack on charity does not preclude a humanitarian feeling towards the blind – any more than his mocking use in his films of romantic music, symbolic for him of the ideals of bourgeois decadence, prevents him from loving music. In this as in everything else, Buñuel reveals his instinctive reaction. The man who in *L'Age d'or* showed his protagonist kicking a blind man who blocks his way in the street is the same man who, seven years earlier, collaborated on a magazine for the blind by writing short stories to help in their psychological rehabilitation.

His most important work as a writer is to be found in his scripts. The director has always been story-writer and co-scenarist of his films. These stories have a functional value in the creation of a picture, always containing situations and ideas of great polemic strength and human interest. They are also of substantial literary quality. When these scripts are adapted from existing literary works, Buñuel approaches his originals with intense intelligence and complete freedom, once and for all settling the old question of

45

whether the adaptor should remain faithful to the spirit or the letter. His treatment of *Robinson Crusoe* and *Wuthering Heights* alone would confirm Buñuel as one of the best adaptors for the cinema. He has a unique gift for discovering the essence of a work and the intention of an author, and transposing these into cinematographic forms.

Buñuel is a cultured rather than an erudite man. In any event he has followed literary trends much more closely than might appear at first sight. Although he often expresses scorn of 'the reader', he has in fact read a great deal, especially in his formative years in Madrid and in the Parisian Surrealist circles. His letters reveal his passion for literature. The opinions are those of a young man in the full Surrealist euphoria, with a destructive urge which lasts until *L'Age d'or*. They reflect a dominant and persisting attitude, for although his methods of expression may have changed, his thought and his being have never deviated. The following paragraphs are from personal letters. In published criticism their writer might have expressed himself with less violence. These intimate commentaries contain necessary passion against people to whom he was in fact closely attached. Buñuel felt the need to combat a kind of poetry which was still marked by bourgeois ideals and Modernist forms.*

I saw Federico in Madrid (14 September 1928) and we made friends again, so if I say that his book of ballads, *El Romancero Gitano*, to me and to everyone who has spent any time outside Seville is very bad, my judgment will appear the more sincere to you. It is a poetry which has the delicacy and *approximate* modernity which any poetry today must have if it is to appeal to the Andrenios, the Baezas and the Cernudas of Seville.†

---

* On reading this section of the text, Buñuel asked that it should be pointed out that the reader must recognize the particular circumstances of the time, which are perhaps hard to appreciate today. 'Our Surrealism was fighting against "Culture"; that meant that we were theoretically enemies, but friends in fact.'

† Here may be the significance of the title *Un Chien andalou* which has created so much debate among cinema critics and historians. Buñuel has often said that it is a meaningless title, chosen at random. From this paragraph and other correspondence of Buñuel, however, we know that he, Dalí, Bello and other friends from the North, applied the name 'perros andaluces' in the Residencia to Andalusian Modernist poets who were insensible to the revolutionary poetry of social content praised by Buñuel long before anyone else in Spain, although years later Alberti and others were to follow him. In effect we can see that the film *Un Chien andalou* describes many members of the group in its subconscious and proto-paranoiac aspect, its complexes of infantilism, castration, sexual and personality ambivalences and so on, and its inner struggle for liberation from the bourgeois burden and for affirmation of maturity. As it happens Batcheff even physically seems to represent this type of poet; and it is not surprising that Dalí (in *The Secret Life of Salvador Dalí*, 1943) congratulates himself on having discovered in the actor the right physique for the character.

The 'Generation of 27'

There is dramatization for those who like that kind of flamenco dramatization; there is a soul of classical romance for those who like to perpetuate classical romance for century after century. There are even fine and very new images; but they are very few and far between, and mixed up with a plot which I find insupportable. Of course I prefer it to Alberti, who has reached the very limits of lyrical absurdity. Our exquisite poets belong to an anti-cant élite: Larrea above all, Garfias (pity he has so little imagination: with half the fantasy of Federico his work would be divine), Huidobro, sometimes the fool of Gerardo Diego; and, in fact, apart from them there is nobody who *excites* me as much as the Southern Group.

Letter to Juan Ramón Jiménez (1928):

Our distinguished friend:

We believe it is our duty to inform you – disinterestedly – that your work is deeply repugnant to us because of its immorality, its hysteria, its arbitrary quality.

Especially: MERDE! for your *Platero y yo*, for your facile and ill-intentioned *Platero y yo*, the least donkeyish and the most odious donkey that we have ever encountered.

Sincerely, Luis Buñuel, Salvador Dalí.

As it happened, Jiménez, who was spiritual father of the Andalusian group of poets of the Generation of '27, received the Nobel Prize for Literature in 1956 – largely on account of *Platero y yo.*

For his friends of Paris days:

Paris, 1 October 1928

Péret is something very big in Surrealism. If we were together we could enjoy the beauty of his things. I've only been able to show you the leftovers. Take into account the difference between Surrealism and sheer idiocy, which nevertheless share something of the same quality. Surrealism only animates current reality with every kind of occult symbol, with strange life, lying in the depths of our subconscious, and which intelligence, good taste, traditional poetical shit, had managed completely to suppress. This is why it is so vital, so close to the primal founts of the savage and the child. It is authentic reality without any *a posteriori* corruption. When we say that Menjou's moustache does such and such a thing, we speak more truth than when we discuss the speed developed by the latest type of torpedo. To discuss this last matter demands a whole culture and a finished experience; the moustache of Menjou displaces more space than a 50 h.p. vehicle. We have to fight with all the scorn and anger we possess, against all traditional poetry, from Homer and Goethe, including Góngora – the foulest monster born of a mother – right up to the ruinous debris of today's poetasters . . .

You will understand the distance which separates you, Dalí and me from all our poetic friends. They are antagonistic worlds, the earth's pole and the south of Mars; and they all belong in the crater of vilest putrefaction. Federico wants to do Surrealist things, but they are false, done with *intelligence*, which can never discover the things which instinct discovers. His last piece published in the *Gaceta* is an instance of his trouble. It is as artistic as his *Ode to the Blessed Sacrament* and will raise an erection in the feeble member of Falla and other Andalusian artists. In spite of everything, within the traditional context, Federico is one of the best.

Buñuel writes of another poet that 'he manages to make me feel sicker than the idea of a God, than the faecal matter that gurgles in the bellies of pretty women, than the Society of Lectures and Conferences, than the Aragonese *jota*, than concerts of the Sinfonica'.

Buñuel began diligently as critic for *La Gaceta literaria hispanoamericana*, an important *avant-garde* literary magazine which ran from 1928 to 1932; and he earned deserved admiration and influence in the Spanish literary world. His work on this publication is important because he was not only critic, but editor of the cinema section. The creation of a complete cinema page in *La Gaceta* was something unprecedented, revolutionary and very fruitful. From that moment no cultural magazine could ignore the cinema; and whether they liked it or not, the intellectuals had to come to terms with it. Buñuel's page reflected his personal preoccupations and the friendships and acquaintances he had established in Paris. The reportage was extensive and intelligent, with illustrations, drawings and literary material on the same level as the rest of the magazine, and with famous names from Paris appearing alongside those of young Spanish intellectuals. Buñuel actually ran it from Paris, where he was living, sending back material written either by himself or by French writers, and at the same time soliciting contributions from his friends by letter. When his work in the cinema finally prevented him from continuing his work for the magazine, he passed the job on to his friend Juan Piqueras – founder of the first film society in Spain, 1925, shot in 1936 – who was later to create *Nuestro Cinema*, the only important cultural magazine in the Republican period. Piqueras gave the page a less literary quality than Buñuel and was more concerned with sociological and specialized cinematic aspects. In its four years of life, *La Gaceta* published contributions – practically none of which have been reprinted – by Luis Buñuel, Jean Epstein, Eduardo G. Maroto, Marcel L'Herbier, Sebastián Gasch, Salvador Dalí, Robert Florey, Miguel Pérez Ferrero, Vinicio Paladini, Francisco Ayala, César M. Arconada, Rafael Laffon, R. Blanco Fombona, Léon Moussinac, Ernesto Giménez Caballero, Vicente Huidobro, Carlos Fernández Cuenca, Jaime Miratvilles, Guillermo de Torre, Francisco G. Cossío, M. García Blanco, Alberto Corrochano, André Beuclair, Pierre McOrlan, Enrique Lafuente Ferrari, Concha Méndez-Cuesta, Ramiro Ledesma Ramos, Carlos Ruiz Funes Amorós, Juan del Brezo, E. Salazar Chapela, Francisco Ginestal, Ramón Martínez de la Riva, Ramón Gómez de la Serna, Jean Cassou, Rosa Chacel, Juan Piqueras, Julio Alvarez del Vayo, Humberto Rivas, Luis Gómez Mesa, Claudio de la Torre, Eloy Yanguas, Marqués de Guad-al-Jelú, Augustín Aragón de Leyva, Antonio G. Solalinde, Rafael Resa, L. Martínez Ferry, Pío Baroja, Eugène Deslaw, Eugenio Montes and Rafael Alberti.

The editor of the magazine, Giménez Caballero, introduced Buñuel to the readers in the following note:

'THE CINÉASTE BUÑUEL

'As editor of *La Gaceta literaria* – as a friend and an admirer – I have pleasure in offering a close-up of Luis Buñuel, cinéaste.

'(Luis Buñuel – chief of this cinema page which we shall periodically present to our readers.)

'Who is Luis Buñuel?

'Luis Buñuel is a new name which is written into your young calendar with two marks – one of exclamation (admiration), the other of interrogation. So: Buñuel!?

'Admiration – because he has accomplished what none of our cinéastes has managed: to lodge himself in High Studies of Cinema. To set himself in the best seats of the Seventh Art and to succeed – before the screen – with the humility of a conscientious student.

'While the cinema-crazy rush to Hollywood to make themselves stars in the siren-luring beams of light – moths against the headlights of a car – this solid and perceptive spirit has confronted the cinema like a laboratory.

'Luis Buñuel is one of those young men whom I have called – in a currently fashionable phrase – "normaliens", coming from that great home of culture, the Residencia de Estudiantes in Madrid.

'With his previous studies, this young man of great new sensitivity set out for Paris in search of the cinema, in the same spirit as an Ortega once went to Marburg in quest of philosophy. And there he now is. Preparing . . . Preparing what? This is the interrogation mark.

'We know that he is going to make his debut with his own film, to be made with Gómez de la Serna, who essays literature . . . We have great hopes in Buñuel.

'His first work as a technician, seen this spring in the Sociedad de Cursos y Conferencias, in the context of films of the *avant-garde* (as we noted at the time) has already confirmed our faith. Luis Buñuel, an Aragonese. A Cyclops. Clearly outlined. Like a Heraclitan silhouette. And a xylographic face.

'Luis Buñuel honours us in taking the helm of this cinema page. For if it is not rich in material things, it will be in personal things, in quality.'

La Gaceta was to continue to follow Buñuel's career with much affection, reporting the success of *Un Chien andalou* and publishing a critique of *L'Age d'or* (by Agustín Aragón de Leyva, in No. 112, 15 August 1931) – a film which was ignored by other Spanish magazines, except the Surrealist.

Buñuel's personal contribution to *La Gaceta* consisted of the eight articles which are reprinted in the Appendix. They reflect above all the contemporary Parisian climate, with which Buñuel was closely involved. It is interesting that in these critical articles, Buñuel goes beyond the context to introduce his own personality. His essays on *découpage* and the photogenic reflect theories – of Epstein and to a certain extent of Dulac – which also have influenced his practice. Epstein's near obsession with slow motion found an echo in the work of Buñuel the director, who uses the effect functionally (for dream and hallucination sequences), never for the purely aesthetic ends of Epstein. There is slow motion in *Un Chien andalou*, in the dream sequences of *Los*

Olvidados, Subida al cielo and *Robinson Crusoe*, to cite only the most typical. There is use of the freeze frame (a device introduced by Buñuel in *Los Olvidados*, though later borrowed by Truffaut and an endless number of subsequent directors); of superimpositions, dissolves and other devices.

Other articles – 'Hollywood News' and 'The Moustache of Adolphe Menjou' – manifest the Surrealist influence; and the criticisms of *Camille* and *La Passion de Jeanne d'Arc* contain extremely personal reflections. The most revealing article however is the one on Von Stroheim. Today it is clearer that Buñuel's position is that of a realist; and anyone who still finds such an assertion surprising has only to read this enthusiastic essay on the great master of cinema naturalism, written in 1928. Has Buñuel been directly influenced in his work by Stroheim, or is there merely a coincidence of temperament? It is irrelevant: what is certain is that anyone who knows the work of both directors will find points of coincidence: much in *The Wedding March*; the brutal butcher in *El Bruto* who eats lumps of raw meat with the same effect of mixed revulsion and fascination which Buñuel repeatedly exerts on his audience; the pathological jealousies, the tyranny over women; the sort of primary and brutal instincts that are to be found in *Greed*. His tastes and interests reveal that the Buñuel of 1928 was already essentially the same Buñuel that we only began to perceive clearly after 1950.

Another important activity of Buñuel at this time was his organization and programming of cinema clubs. Again he was organizing events in Madrid from his vantage point in Paris, arranging cinema sessions at the Residencia. Alfonso Buñuel claimed that he had already programmed such sessions in 1920, and this has been confirmed in a recent book by Alberti – which represent an unusually early instance of visual education and cinema culture in university activities. He also organized cinema activities in other centres; and this curious programme, devised for the Sociedad de Cursos y Conferencias in Madrid in early 1927, is additional evidence of Buñuel's curiosity about slow motion techniques:

'Cinema Session of the Sociedad de Cursos y Conferencias
'1. – "Cinema of the invisible" of Lucien Bull (of the Marey Laboratories) and Studies in slow motion.
'2. – Dream sequence from *La fille de l'eau*, by Jean Renoir (shot in slow motion)
'*Entr'acte*, by René Clair (with several scenes in slow and accelerated motion).'

Such tentative beginnings resulted in the creation of the Cineclub Español in the Autumn of 1928. Its organizers were mainly the friends of *La Gaceta literaria*, who made it complementary to the magazine. The official founder and director was Ernesto Giménez Caballero, but the true originator was Buñuel, who had numerous French models for the idea. From Paris he sent by post programmes of cinema material which he knew was available in Madrid, and films which he himself managed to send from France. Sometimes he would select lecturers from Madrid; two or three others came from Paris. Here is an example of one of his programmes:

Meeting of the Cineclub Español.
Saturday 4 May 1930, at 4 p.m. in the Goya Cinema.

COMIC CINEMA

First anthology of comedians – 13 personalities – presented in a European cineclub.

Some declarations by Buñuel:

'This session will be something definitive; and, strangely, it has not been done in any cineclub or in any other cinema in the world. People are so stupid, with so many prejudices, that they think that *Faust* and *Potemkin* are superior to these lunacies which are not lunacy at all but what I would call the new poetry. The Surrealist equivalent in the cinema is to be found *only in these films*. Much more genuine surrealism than in the films of Man Ray.'

PART ONE

1. Robinet (primitive comic)
   100 metres of *Robinet Nihiliste*
2. Tancredo (primitive comic)
   100 metres of *Tancred the Sheriff*
3. Clyde Cook (Lucas)
   600 metres of *The Bullfighter*
4. Ben Turpin
   600 metres of *Ben Turpin's News*
5. Harold Lloyd, Snub Pollard and Bebe Daniels
   300 metres of *Harold the Politician*

Ten-minute interval

Reading of *Poems to the cinema comedians*, by Rafael Alberti

PART TWO

6. Chaplin
   700 metres of *Sunnyside*
7. Buster Keaton
   300 metres from *The Navigator*
8. Glenn Tryon
   600 metres from *A Father's Afflictions*

9. Harry Langdon
   600 metres from *Long Pants*
   Special music for this programme: gramophone records (arranged by Luis
   Buñuel).

Another example:

> MEETING OF FILMÓFONO CINECLUB
> Only projection in Spain of Luis
> Buñuel's *L'Age d'or*.

People who gave lectures at the Cineclub Español included Giménez
Caballero, Ramón Gómez de la Serna, Pío Baroja, Federico García Lorca,
Rafael Alberti, Luis Buñuel, Ricardo Urgoiti and Germaine Dulac. Some of
these intellectuals subsequently became film-makers. The Cineclub Español
was the second in Spain, and a model for many more created in succeeding
years. By 1932 there were already forty of them throughout the country,
organizing meetings and congresses, devising methods of popular education
through the cinema. The Cineclub Español, with programmes of French and
German *avant-garde* films and the first showings in Spain of the great Soviet
classics along with documentaries, mostly German, and such items of exotica
as Chinese films, can be reckoned an influence on the little-known Spanish
avant-garde of the early thirties, and on the documentary movement which
achieved its greatest importance around 1936. The society was one of the
organizers of the international congress of *avant-garde* film-makers held at La
Sarraz, in Switzerland, in 1929. Giménez Caballero was an actor in the film
Storm Over La Sarraz which Eisenstein began there with a team of congress-
ists. (If the film was ever finished, all trace of it now seems lost.)

Buñuel's activity as critic extended elsewhere. *L'Amic dels arts*, a cultural
review in the Catalan language, in which Dalí was an important figure, asked
him for an interview on the subject of Chaplin. It was a combined interview
with Dalí and Buñuel, who took the opportunity to heap insults on Chaplin,
his Judo-Christian morality and all his artistic work with the exception of *The
Gold Rush*. A Surrealist scandal? Recently the author has discussed Chaplin
with Buñuel; and his view has not been altered at all by the years between:
'Chaplin deserves all his fame and universal acclaim; but only for two films:
The Gold Rush and *Monsieur Verdoux*.' His views on films, as on everything
else, are mordant and precise.

He was also publishing criticism in France; on 8 November 1927 he wrote
to José Bello:

> I am very busy. I have been made editor of the cinema page which *La
> Gaceta literaria* is going to run. I have to devise the page, find contributors,

decide on rejections, give news and interviews, etc. .... Nearly every day brings letters from Giménez Caballero, who is very nice and gives me practically complete freedom. At the same time, and this is marvellous news, I was appointed critic for the *Cahiers d'art* just the day before yesterday. There too I am in charge of the movie page, and responsible for accepting and rejecting articles. This opens every door in Paris to me. I begin with the next issue. Maybe you already know that it is the best modern art magazine in Paris. I am very grateful to the director, M. Zervos, for the honour. Yet in spite of my successes as a critic – what horror! – I am no critic. I want other people to criticize my work. Anyhow, it all serves as a start to my career.

The collaboration on the French magazine lasted only a short time, since Buñuel very soon achieved his objective. In the succeeding years he has not lost the attitudes of a critic, even if he has not always kept up with the latest novelties in cinema. His position is revealed in his 1954 interview with *Cahiers du Cinéma*:

ANDRÉ BAZIN – How many times a year do you go to the cinema?

LUIS BUÑUEL – Very rarely. I won't exaggerate: maybe four times. It could be six, or two. But the average is four.

ANDRÉ BAZIN – On those occasions it must be something fairly profound in order to keep you in the cinema in spite of your lethargy, the difficulty you have in making films and the little pleasure it gives you. Why do you make films rather than writing novels or painting or using some other means of expression?

LUIS BUÑUEL – I don't like going to the cinema, but I like the cinema as a medium for expressing myself. I find it the best medium to show a reality which we cannot actually touch with our hands in everyday life. With books, with newspapers, with our own experience, we acquaint ourselves with an exterior, objective reality: the cinema, with its mechanism, opens up for us a little window on the extension of this reality. My hope as a member of the audience is always that the film will *reveal* some slight thing to me, but this happens to me very rarely. The rest does not amuse me; I am already too old. I'm very glad to have had the chance to see so many things in this Festival.* I have seen great films, but it does not mean very much to me. The cinema very rarely reveals to me what I am looking for, and for this reason I hardly ever go. Naturally I have friends who tell me about the pictures that have pleased them, and they sometimes force me to go and see them. That is why I saw *Les Jeux interdits*, which has opened up a little window for me; it is an admirable film. I also saw *Portrait of Jennie*,

* The interview was recorded during the time of the Cannes Film Festival.

which I liked a lot and which opened up a big window for me. From the professional point of view I am unforgiveable. I ought to know more films. I ought to go to the cinema every day . . . I am the first to accuse myself. In Mexico, when they want me to select my cast, I can never give an answer because I don't know the actors. This is very bad, I know, but I prefer to stay peacefully at home with friends and a bottle of whisky, rather than go to the pictures.

ANDRÉ BAZIN – You told me one day that thanks to Denise Tual you were able to see Robert Bresson's *Les Anges du péché* and that your principal memory of the film was the image of a nun whose feet were being kissed.

LUIS BUÑUEL – Ah, yes. A very beautiful scene and a very beautiful film.

ANDRÉ BAZIN – I was a bit surprised, because this image does not seem in any way the most characteristic of *Les Anges du péché*.

LUIS BUÑUEL – I know what you mean. In practice I am neither a sadist nor a masochist. I am only these things in theory, and I don't accept these elements as anything more than elements of struggle and violence. Throughout Bresson's whole film I had a feeling of something about to happen, which attracted me a lot, and in the final scene, sure enough, it came disturbingly into the open. For this reason I only remember the kissing of the dead nun's feet. But having said this, I don't *myself* feel like kissing the feet of dead nuns, of green cows, or any other sort of feet. But at that point there was the flowering of certain occult sentiments that had been present throughout the film.

Though he no longer expresses himself as reporter or critic, as in the twenties, Buñuel's interviews are always revealing in that he talks of his own problem in relation to the cinema, and seriously attempts to define his theory.

4. Un Chien andalou

'In 1929 I entered the Surrealist group of Paris. Its moral and artistic intransigence, its new social political field, fit in perfectly with my temperament. As I was the only moving picture person in the group I decided to take the aesthetics of Surrealism to the screen.

'That same year I asked my mother for $2,500 to make my first cinematographic experiment. Only she would have financed an idea that seemed ridiculous to everyone else. My mother gave me the money more out of love than understanding of my venture, which I was careful not to explain to her.

'Thus I produced my first film, which was at the same time the first Surrealist film, entitled:

"UN CHIEN ANDALOU"

'It is a two-reel short in which there are neither dogs nor Andalusians. The title had the virtue of becoming an obsession with some people, among others the American writer Harry V. Miller, who, without knowing me, wrote an extraordinary letter which I still have about his obsession.

'In the film are amalgamated the aesthetics of Surrealism with Freudian discoveries. It answered the general principle of that school, which defines Surrealism as "an unconscious, psychic automatism, able to return to the mind its real function, outside of all control exercised by reason, morality or aesthetics".

'Although I availed myself of oniric elements, the film is not the description of a

Salvador Dalí photographed by Buñuel

dream. On the contrary, the environment and characters are of a realistic type. Its fundamental difference from other films consists in the fact that the characters function, animated by impulses, the primal sources of which are confused with those of irrationalism, which, in turn, are those of poetry. At times these characters react enigmatically, in as far as a pathological psychic complex can be enigmatic.

'This film is directed at the unconscious feelings of man, and therefore is of universal value, although it may seem disagreeable to certain groups of society which are sustained by puritanical moral principles.

'When I made the film, I was absolutely sure that it was going to be a failure; but I didn't care because I had the conviction that it expressed something, until then never said in pictures. Above all it was sincere.

'The film was christened in June, 1929, in the theater "Ursulines" in Paris, before a select public. I was stupified [sic], confused, by the avalanche of enthusiasm which its showing awakened. I actually believed it was a joke. It was not, since it ran for nine consecutive months in the moving picture theater, "Studio 28", for the general public. Hundreds of articles were written and controversies were started. Other films were made along the same lines, such as *La Perle* by George Hugnet and *Bateaux Parisiens* by Gorel, and other attempts which were not very successful.'

A letter from Buñuel to José Bello, written from Paris in January 1929, describes the genesis of the film:

Tomorrow or the day after I am going to spend a fortnight with Dalí to collaborate on some mutual and very cinematographic ideas. Even if the world crumbles about us, this film will begin shooting at the beginning of April with the money which I still have left; and when we start I shall go on adjusting it so that we can keep within the budget and I do not need to ask anyone for economic assistance.

A letter of 10 February 1929, also to Bello, says:

You are right: we should have written from Figueras, but I had so many things to tell you that I preferred not to do so. We didn't even send anyone a postcard. Dalí and I are more united than ever, and we have worked together to make a stupendous scenario, quite without precedent in the history of the cinema. It is something very big. You will love it. I'll begin filming in March. At the moment I am preparing everything. We were going to call it *El marista de la ballesta* but for the moment it is provisionally entitled *Dangéreux de se pencher en dedans*.

Simultaneously Buñuel was planning a book of poems with the title subsequently given to the film:

My book is at the printers ... There are plenty of things which you know, and even if slightly *démodés* they are not bad.

This is just to open fire. Then I am going to publish great things. Dalí and I will collaborate on a book this summer in Cadaqués. And I will do another, with you, as soon as the occasion presents itself. The title of my present book is *The Andalusian Dog*, which made Dalí and me piss with laughter when we thought of it. I should point out that there is no dog anywhere in the book. But it is very good and very docile. Besides being funny it is idiotic. As soon as it comes out – in about a month – I'll send you a copy. Read one of the poems from it:

How many *Maristas* can you pack on a rope-bridge? Four or five . . .*

Not only the title, but some images from the book reappear in the film; more are to be found in *L'Age d'or* where, for instance, we effectively verify that one tiny garden bridge *can* hold only four or five *Maristas*: the image appears briefly during the persecution of the lovers hidden in the garden.

Buñuel added the following comment in the filmography published by the Mexican review *Nuevo Cine*:

I was able to make *Un Chien andalou* thanks to the 25,000 pesetas which my mother gave me to make it. In fact the film was made with half this sum; the rest I spent in Paris. I was to have made it with Ramón Gómez de la Serna who would have been the writer. I am aware what Dalí has said about me.† Really the idea of the newspaper film which he criticizes so much, is a good one: the stories would include not only the dramatized news items, but would also treat in documentary form the processes of producing a newspaper. The plot of *Un Chien andalou* is a joint work. On some things we worked very closely together. In fact Dalí and I were extremely close during that period. Then he met Gala and married her, and she completely changed him. But the film is mine. I lived for a time in Figueras while I was preparing the plot; and Dalí's contribution to the film consists only in the scene of the priests who are dragged in on ropes. Although it was a joint decision to exclude all narrative sense, all logical association . . . The title was a problem. We thought of many. *Défense de se pencher à l'extérieur.* Then we thought of the opposite: *Défense de se pencher en dedans.* But we couldn't agree. Then Dalí discovered the title of a forgotten book of my poems, *Un Chien andalou.* 'That's the title!', he exclaimed; and so it was.

Un Chien andalou was made very quickly, as the short space of time between Buñuel's letters to Bello and the première in April reveals. (Note that Buñuel in the unpublished autobiography recalls the Ursulines première as being in June 1929.) Although, says Buñuel, 'Dalí was present only on the

---

* See Appendix.
† In *The Secret Life of Salvador Dalí.*

last day of shooting', he played, alongside the Catalan anarchist Jaime Miratvilles, one of the two priests dragged along the ground. Other people, besides the painter himself, have sought to attribute the film to Dalí; but the perspective of 44 years enables us to see the facts more clearly. When *Un Chien andalou* is compared with the later and separate works of Buñuel and Dalí, we see that not only the cinematographic quality, but also all the positive values of the film are those of Buñuel. Mary Meerson, of the Cinémathèque Française, who was in Paris in the thirties, has said that anything not good in *Un Chien andalou* must be attributed to the influence of Dalí: some recherché images, the symbolist tendencies, an element of *snobisme*, the danger of *avant-garde* preciosity. Buñuel himself says: 'The film was 50% of each of us. For instance I did the cutting of the eye and the ants in the hand; Dalí did the garden scene and the cocktail shaker bell. We simply acquired the psychoanalytical practice of remembering our dreams. We had no script, but every morning would tell each other our dreams and select a few images of each to put into the film.'

The scenario – evidence of the cinema's first use of the 'automatic' language of Surrealism – was first published in the official Surrealist review in 1929. Since then both the scenario and the shooting script of the finished film have been frequently reprinted,* and it is necessary here only to give a synopsis of the action. The first scenario and the finished film differ in such slight details that it is clear that the plan of the film was little altered in the shooting.

UN CHIEN ANDALOU (synopsis)

Once Upon a Time

A man (Buñuel) stands by a window, sharpening a razor and looking up at the moon.

As a light cloud crosses the face of the moon, a razor slices the eye of a young woman.

Eight Years Later

A man in a dark grey suit, wearing white frills at cuffs and waist and a white hat, and with a black and white striped box on a strap round his neck, cycles along an empty street.

A woman, reading in a third-floor room, starts, listens and goes to the window in time to see the cyclist come to a halt and fall off his machine. She goes to the door, and rushes down to the street where she kisses him as he lies motionless and expressionless.

* In *Luis Buñuel*, by Ado Kyrou (Paris, 1962; scenario only); *l'Avant-Scène du Cinéma* (Paris, 1963); in English, by Lorrimer Publishing Ltd, as *L'Age d'or* and *Un Chien andalou* (London, 1968).

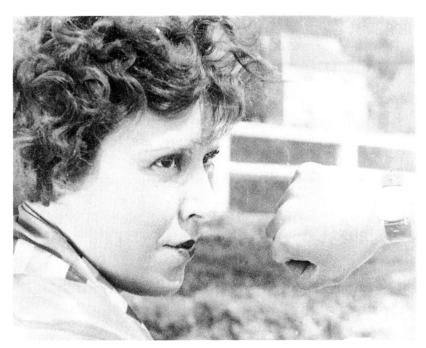

Un Chien andalou

In close-up, a hand opens the striped box and takes out a striped tie wrapped in striped paper.

The frills and the collar and tie worn by the cyclist are laid out on a bed in the form of a figure. The girl replaces the dark tie with the striped one she has taken from the box. She turns to find the young man standing beside her, gazing with alarm at the palm of his hand. In close-up, the palm is revealed as having a large hole in the centre, from which crawl ants.

Close-ups of the armpit hair of a woman; a sea-urchin; the top of a head. The camera irises out from this image; the head belongs to an androgynous woman who is standing in the centre of an agitated crowd of people, poking with a stick at a severed hand which lies on the floor. A policeman pushes through the crowd and places the hand in the striped box, which he politely hands to the girl. She appears to be transported, oblivious of the traffic rushing past her.

Above, a couple watch from a window. They see the girl knocked down by a car. The man approaches the girl with him in the room, and mauls her lustfully (she appears momentarily naked; her breasts become thighs under his hands). The girl retreats. The man picks up two ropes, and approaches

Un Chien andalou

her, dragging behind him with these ropes a heavy burden of cork mats, melons, two Marist priests, two pianos, each bearing the carcase of a donkey and oozing from the lid entrails and excrement.

The girl rushes from the room; as the man hurls himself after her she slams the door to trap his hand – a hand which in close-up has a hole in its palm, crawling with ants. The room she has entered is identical to the one she has left. On the bed lies the same man, once again clothed in his frills.

About 3 in the Morning

Outside the door a stranger rings the bell (but instead of a bell we see two hands protruding through holes in the door and shaking a cocktail shaker). The girl admits the stranger, who forces the man on the bed to get up, then tears off his frills and flings them out of the window into the street, along with the striped box. He then obliges him to stand against the wall of the room, like a naughty schoolboy. Till this point the audience has not seen the stranger's face. He turns; and it is again the same as the cyclist in frills.

Sixteen Years Before

The stranger picks up from a school desk, two ink-stained books which he hands to the man against the wall. In his hands they become revolvers and he shoots the stranger.

As the wounded man falls, he is no longer in the room but in a park, beside a nearly naked woman. The woman disappears; the man's body is carried off by passers-by.

Back in the room, the girl is alone. She looks at the wall where the cyclist was previously standing, and sees only a black spot which enlarges to become a death's-head moth. The death's-head pattern itself enlarges till it fills the screen.

The young man is again in the room with her. He claps his hand to his mouth in alarm, then takes it away to reveal that his mouth has vanished, to be replaced with the girl's under-arm hair. She is in turn startled, annoyed, disdainful and walks out of the room . . .

. . . on to a vast empty beach, where a man is waiting for her. Lovingly they walk together along the water's edge. The waves wash up the frills, hat, cuffs and finally the box of the cyclist. The man kicks the broken box; the girl picks up a couple of items but throws them carelessly away.

In the Spring

A desert. The man from the beach and the girl are buried alive up to their chests, ragged and blinded, 'being eaten alive by the sun and by swarms of insects'.

END

The Parisian public had been bombarded with so-called Surrealist films which had proved to be no more than feeble *avant-garde* intellectual essays. One such was Germaine Dulac's *La Coquille et le Clergyman*: leaving the screening of the film, the uninitiated asked André Breton if it was truly Surrealist. The reply was unhesitating: 'No; it is only an aesthetic essay.' But Breton left *Un Chien andalou* declaring: 'Yes, this is a Surrealist film.'

From the start the film was the subject of intellectual debates and impassioned polemic – at first in the cinematic, artistic, philosophic and cultural press of France and Belgium; later throughout the world. Few noncommercial films have had such a triumphal career or attracted such intelligent and such unjust criticism. The original controversy and the rivers of ink spilled over it have led film historians to class *Un Chien andalou* as an *avant-garde* film. Buñuel has had to insist that it is not such. In *La Révolution Surréaliste*, No. 12, he declares that it is not an aesthetic essay but 'a desperate appeal to murder'. His aim was not to please but to provoke.

When he presented the film in the Cineclub de Madrid, with Ortega, Juan Ramón Jiménez and others present, he announced:

'I don't want the film to please you but to offend you. I would be sorry if you enjoyed it.'

Many years later, Buñuel again explains his intention:

'Historically the film represents a violent reaction against what in those days was called "avant-garde", which was aimed exclusively at artistic sensibility and the audience's reason ... In *Un Chien andalou* the film-maker for the first time takes up a position on a poetic-moral plane ... His object is to provoke instinctive reactions of revulsion and attraction in the spectator. Nothing in the film symbolises anything.'

(*Art in Cinema*, San Francisco Museum of Modern Art, 1947)

This declaration may be unexpected; but Buñuel was sincere, and did not have as his intention to *épater la bourgeoisie*. Of course it is possible to deduce very many symbols in so far as the film is the objectivization of desires irrationally presented, whose images, as Freud clearly showed, are always transpositions of other images left by the subconscious. But this cannot properly be called symbol or metaphor as the terms are understood in art. In the same way we cannot speak of symbols in the imagined images of Surrealist 'automatic writing' some examples of which from Buñuel appear in the Appendix. Much later Dalí also explained the intention of the film: 'To disrupt the mental anxiety of the spectator, and to reveal the principal conviction which animates all Surrealist thought: the overwhelming importance of desire.' According to Dalí, this reconstructed dream arises from 'the critical paranoia (which) ... is based in the critical and systematic objectivization of mad associations and interpretations'. Breton for his part had defined this as 'The ultra-confusional activity whose sources lie in an obsessive idea.'

Reading the script gives no idea of the dizziness which overtakes the spectator in the succession of shots deprived of any traditional logic, of the sense of being absorbed into a universe in which the cartesian coordinates of space and time, on which our whole thinking and culture are based, have disappeared. He feels that he is not watching a chance game, but a succession of events which possess some internal logic, which we can identify with certain memories of our subconscious. The spectator is made anxious; his innermost psyche has been violated. It is easy then to understand how it can be possible to react against the picture; even so, few would dare accuse it of being an exhibition of gratuitous eroticism or an elaborate hoax.

Un Chien andalou retains its importance while the works of the *avant-garde* have retreated into oblivion, or historical curiosity, or ridicule. The reason is that for the first time, as Buñuel says in his autobiography, the subjective world of the subconscious was freed as a language of communication with laws more authentic than the traditional laws of the language employed for expressing conscious thought. Buñuel did not make the discovery, but he was the first to apply it to the cinema. He did so at the same moment that others were applying it to other areas of art, philosophy, medicine and even the exact sciences (consider Picasso; or the fetishist-inspired sculpture of such modern artists as Lipchitz, Alberto, Archipenko, Gonzalez; or Young, Einstein, Sartre, etc.). Buñuel's genius lies in its application not to art but to pure rebellion against that reason which has governed the ideals of a disintegrating society. His work of destruction, of withdrawal of faith, is finally constructive, since it helps us to seek the profound reality of phenomena. Through his story, showing desire as a prisoner of all the 'respectable' values and describing the liberation which his personages seek, Buñuel created a work of great aesthetic and revolutionary sensibility, and of lasting value.

Even so the film would not have kept its immediate freshness but for its surprising artistic merit. The use of angles, focus, opticals, transitions; the alternation of long-shots and close-ups, interiors and exteriors, reveal a very rich and individual cinematographic language. Nor (with rare exceptions which are confidently attributable to Dalí) are these effects gratuitously used. They are justified and demanded by the narrative – a typical virtue in Buñuel. For instance the high-angle shot in which we see the young androgyne in the street, prodding the severed hand with a stick and surrounded by a circle of onlookers, might recall the *recherché* plastic effects of German Expressionism and is certainly a Surrealist image of anal fixation; yet it is shot in this way because it is justified and called for by the preceding shot in which the antagonists look down out of the window, seeing the scene from exactly the camera's point of view.

The structure of the film has, moreover, an interior cohesion not easy to account for immediately. It is true that the narrative is not continuous, that events happen helter-skelter, that there are non-real jumps in time and space, that the characters doubt, retract, repeat themselves, very much as in dreams. Yet at no point does the spectator feel lost, or worry that the succession of events is arbitrary. Everything appears linked by a fatality. I do not know whether this comes from the scientific exactness with which subconscious conduct has been studied, from sheer chance or from artistic intuition. There is, of course, conscious structure in the division of prologue, establishment, development and epilogue; for Buñuel is much more a classicist than might at first be evident.

At first sight all his films seem different in form, sharing only a certain casualness in conception. Closer examination shows that all of them are submitted to an almost conservative rhythmical ordering: the prologue in which the author proposes the *règle du jeu*; the establishment, at times very rapid, at others very slow, especially in the psychological pieces; the development, with a couple of violent climaxes to startle the spectator in the fifth and ninth reels, each followed by some minutes of lighter content (a documentary sequence, an anodyne episode, a comic scene) whose object is to relax the spectator again. And always the very precipitate finale, bringing us to a pitch of anxiety and stupefaction a few seconds before the film is finished and the lights go up in the cinema. Buñuel does not like people to talk of his aesthetics, but there is no doubt that they exist.

The problem of form in Buñuel deserves particular study. Why, for instance, are some of his shots so unfinished technically, some transitions so awful, the sound defective, performances weak. Are we simply Buñuel fanatics, those of us who insist that the bad lighting and sound in *L'Age d'or* only make his film doubly beautiful? When we find it enchanting that Buñuel suddenly and shamelessly introduces an obvious model among the exteriors of *Subida al cielo*, to save money on costly locations? Does Buñuel do these things out of incompetence, carelessness, laziness – or out of some genius?

I am convinced myself that it is through laziness. I also know that Buñuel is only lazy when he can afford to allow himself to be so. When he neglects some element of polish such as we have mentioned, he does so in the knowledge that it will affect neither the story nor the content, but only the technical correctness of the film. Technical correctness in inessential aspects leaves Buñuel quite indifferent. He has a feeling for mischief too and knows that these things disconcert the critics and the decent bourgeois who likes to see everything done nicely. The model in *Subida al cielo* was used for reasons of economy; at the same time there is no doubt that the very evident trompe-l'oeil, so much to the Surrealist taste, indicates the distinction between the realistic sequences and the shots which have a symbolic value: the scenes of the ascent and the descent of the mountain in the bus might be taken to allude to the incidences of the biological curve of the human life.

One further element to be considered in *Un Chien andalou* is its Spanishness. The confusion of space and time constitutes an important tradition of Spanish theatre and Spanish story-telling. The extremely nervous rhythm is characteristically Latin. The brutality is characteristic of our art.

The tactile quality of many shots is very important as being one of the basic discoveries of Surrealism. The Surrealist painters invented a kind of painting in which the effects of traditional spatula technique and use of thick pigments were exaggerated to an excess; even to the extent of introducing sand and cement under the paint. They added to this *collages* of objects, pictures made not just with bits of newspaper and engravings as the Cubists had already done, but with glass eyes, false teeth, crushed glass, stones or twigs. Sculpture too wanted to appeal to the sense of touch at the same time as that of sight – to appeal, finally, to our nerves. Man Ray's flat-iron with nails beneath it is famous.

Buñuel was deeply aware of these new directions in art; but his own aggressiveness was so rooted to his temperament that the familiarity was not a prerequisite. In his case distinction between form and content is absurd, for the expression is a unity in which both are fused. Violence and sadism as a means of communication appear not only in his plots, ideas and situations but – as he affirmed in drawing my attention to *Un Chien andalou* – in the way of presenting particular scenes, in the violent impact which they aim to produce in the spectator by means of a deliberate technique and shock rhythm, by elimination of any aesthetic beauty which could produce a sensation of pleasure, finally by the unnerving, tactile quality of many images. This plastic quality is found, long before the birth of Surrealism, in traditional Spanish art: wrought iron, tinplate jewellery and sculpture itself appear to seek to appeal to the finger-tips. It is enough to recall the Christ of Palencia, vividly described in a poem by Unamuno, made out of hair, blood and real nails, and which produces in the spectator a distinct physical discomfort, 'because this Christ of my earth *is* earth'. Many shots in *Un Chien andalou* are already significant: the hand trapped in the door, with the ants crawling out of the black hole in its palm, is more than a symbol; it is the visualization of the pain which the crushing has produced. Many spectators report that they sense their arm asleep or feel the sensation of itching (in Spanish the words for ant, *hormiga*, and for itching, *hormigueo*, are closely associated). The most brutal and the most celebrated shot in the film is the cutting of the eye. No one fails to experience a shudder at the physical sensation; even after seeing the film many times it is hard to resist covering one's eyes.

The malicious have said that all Buñuel's success stems from this repulsive image which began his career. 'They are right,' says Buñuel. He would not have become so famous so quickly without it. But to question its artistic justification is to ignore Surrealist theory, the Spanish Surrealists' obsession with lacerated eyes, and the whole Spanish tradition of tactile impact.* More important still is Buñuel's own explanation: 'To produce in the spectator a state which could permit the free association of ideas, it was necessary to produce a near traumatic shock at the very beginning of the film; hence we began it with a shot of an eye being very efficiently cut open. The spectator entered into the cathartic state necessary to accept the subsequent events of the film.'

* See Appendix, and also H. B. Morris. In fact the image of the cut eye dates back as far as a poem of 1919 by Larrea.

5. L'Age d'or

The success of *Un Chien andalou* gave Buñuel the chance to make a film for the intelligentsia of Paris. He had now to surpass himself in order to come up to the expectation he had aroused. He began work at once:

'I am immediately starting the film which is going to please you more than anything. All our things on the screen. It will be finished at the beginning of May. Dalí will come to Paris in a few days for a long stay. Dalí and I are going to do a revue' (letter to José Bello, 25 March 1929).

But time passed before it was possible to realize the project:

'I don't know if you've heard that Noailles has given me a million francs to make a talking picture, with complete spiritual freedom, which I hope, in consequence, will make all who see it blush with shame. It is a feature film and more than an hour long. I'm thinking of calling it *La Bestia Andaluza* though I would prefer *Abajo la Constitución*. Naturally neither the National Assembly nor any other legislative body actually go down. The story, like *Un Chien andalou*, I have done in collaboration with Dalí. I would love you to come for the opening, which will be in the middle of June. Afterwards we can go to Toledo for a week. Even if you don't come, tell me if you want us to organize the trip. Write directly to Hinojosa. Dalí will come as well.

'You cannot imagine how I've changed, and the progress I think I've made, especially in the field of morality and intransigence. But it will be best to wait till we see each other and can talk a lot so that I can tell you everything properly' (letter to José Bello, from Paris, 11 May 1930).

The film was finished after a month of intensive work at the Billancourt Studios in Paris, where the big interior of the house in which the party is held was shot. Apart from the technicians and leading actors, the people who took part in the production were all friends. This did not mean that the work was without discipline. Buñuel, though not very sure either of his technique or his French vocabulary, rehearsed a great deal, and made many retakes, according to Simone Cottence, sister of the intelligent young documentary film-maker Jacques B. Brunius who was the director's assistant and also acted in the film. But the atmosphere was extremely happy. The material was completed with exteriors shot on location in the suburbs of Paris, with bits of newsreel, and the exteriors for the Majorcan prologue, for which the unit went to Cadaqués, the home of Salvador Dalí. Letters reveal that Buñuel had spent part of the previous summer there, preceded by García Lorca. Dalí was not present during the Paris shooting. Moreover before starting to film, Buñuel completely changed the story; and there was a total break between the two old friends. Thus the film was Buñuel's alone:

'I made it with the million francs which the Vicomte de Noailles made available to me, out of which I was able to hand back two hundred and sixty thousand. Dalí had nothing to do with the filming; and I put his name alongside mine on the titles out of friendship. Dalí and I were separated through the fault of his wife. Thanks to him I had to give up, many years later, my job at the Museum of Modern Art in New York.'

Dalí's autobiography confirms this, by attacking Buñuel and alleging that 'he made a caricature and betrayal of the idea'. He had some reason for his charges ... Buñuel even thought of changing the title of the film to *In the Icy Waters of Egoist Calculation*, a phrase from Karl Marx.

In his autobiography Buñuel writes of the film:

'Shortly after the opening of *Un Chien andalou*, Georges Henri Rivière, assistant director of the Museum "Trocadéro" and an intimate friend of Vicomte de Noailles, patrons and exquisite generous people, called me. Rivière took me to their home and introduced me. My present friends, Charles and Marie Laure de Noailles, wanted to give me the means to make another film, in which they gave me complete liberty in the choice of subject. They only asked that the score of the film be written by Stravinsky. I had to refuse the latter, since my Surrealist discipline and the artistic tendencies of our group were incompatible with those of Stravinsky, above all from a moral standpoint. The patrons agreed to do without the musician and the score was taken from fragments of classical music. So my second film was called
L'AGE D'OR

'It consists of six reels. It was one of the first talkies made in France and cost about $25,000, a small amount if one considers the ambitiousness of the film.

'The story is also a sequence of moral and Surrealist aesthetic. Around the principal characters, a man and woman, is disclosed the existing conflict in all human society between the sentiment of love, and any other sentiment of a religious, patriotic, humanitarian order; here, too, the setting and characters are realistic, but the hero is animated by egoism, which imagines all attitudes to be amorous, to the exclusion of control or of other sentiments. The sexual instinct and the sense of death form the substance of the film. It is a romantic film performed in full Surrealistic frenzy. In it were certain experiments in the use of sound and speech which were later used in commercial films. For example, in *A Nous la Liberté*, by René Clair, a love scene in a garden. Jean Cocteau produced, a year later, *La Vie d'un Poète* (sic), also subsidized by the Noailles, in which film the great influence of *L'Age d'or* can be noticed.

'When this film was first shown the whole Surrealistic group launched a manifesto on the purpose of *L'Age d'or* which was answered by Léon Daudet, from L'Action Française, an extreme rightist paper, so inciting their readers that they attacked the theatre. The attack was brought to an end six days after the first showing of the film by reactionary young Frenchmen, causing damages in the theatre and vestibule to the amount of 120,000 frs. The projection continued two days more in the devastated theatre but as the partisans of the film wanted to exercise reprisals, the chief of police in Paris, Chiappe, suspended the showing. Deputy Gaston Borgery appealed to the Congress on behalf of the film, although to no avail.

'Hundreds of articles were written about the film; some for, others against, and, whenever it was shown, either in France or outside, it was at private societies or theatres. The producers, the Vicomte and Vicomtesse de Noailles, withdrew it from circulation in 1934 to keep it in their archives, since it was almost impossible actually to show it.'*

Following the scandal, the Surrealist group distributed the following questionnaire: †

1. What is your view of the prohibition by the police of the film *L'Age d'or* following the demonstration by the League of Patriots and the Anti-Jewish League on 3 December 1930 at Studio 28?

2. Since when has there been no freedom in France to question seriously religion, its roots, the habits of its representatives, etc?

Since when have the police been dedicated to antisemitism?

Is the police action, in sanctioning the programme of the League of Patriots, an official encouragement to the setting up of fascist methods in France?

---

* Buñuel recalls that the de Noailles liked the film very much and went to the première in happy expectation of congratulation. It was only after seeing the shocked reaction of the audience that they themselves began to have any doubts about it. Buñuel also corrects the cost of the film to 650,000 francs.

† It was later reprinted in *Le Surréalisme au Service de la Révolution*.

Is this police action to be understood as an authorization, granted analogously to those who find religious propaganda intolerable, to interrupt by any means its manifestations (films of Roman propaganda, pilgrimages to Lourdes and Lisieux, centres of obscurantism such as Bonne Press, Congregation of the Index, churches, etc. . . . perversion of youth in church schools and military training, radio sermons, crucifixion revues, virgins, crowns of thorns)?

3. Does the fact of the prohibition of *L'Age d'or* constitute a simple new abuse of power by the police, or rather does it prove the incompatibility of Surrealism with bourgeois society?

Must it be considered as the recognition of this incompatibility that after bourgeois youngsters have destroyed Surrealist paintings and stolen Surrealist books, after the bourgeois newspapers have published a letter of provocation signed by the Provost of Daunay and instigated the suppression of the review *Surrealism in the Service of Revolution* and raids on the offices of this magazine, their police should prohibit a Surrealist film, as Soviet films have been prohibited and as Hitler's police have prohibited *All Quiet on the Western Front* in Germany?

4. Is not the use of provocation to justify the subsequent intervention of the police the sign of a movement towards fascism?

Can it for one moment be pretended that this intervention, under pretext of protecting children, youth, the family, the fatherland and religion, this clear conversion to fascism, has not the object of destroying everything that might oppose the approaching war?

And particularly the war against the U.S.S.R.?

The leaflet containing this questionnaire was signed by Maxime Alexandre, Aragon, André Breton, Luis Buñuel, René Char, René Crevel, Salvador Dalí, Paul Eluard, Max Ernst, Georges Malkine, Benjamin Péret, Man Ray, Georges Sadoul, Yves Tanguy, André Thirion, Tristan Tzara, Pierre Unik and Albert Valentin.

The impassioned atmosphere which resulted from the incidents surrounding the première of the film had repercussions in French criticism, in which there was already a very chauvinist and political tendency. Notices swung between eulogy and wild condemnation, with few half-tones:

'*L'Age d'or* contains an obsessive vision of sexual love, which grips the flesh of the spectator and will not release him. There has never been anything like this before in the cinema' (Paul Rejac, *Cinémonde*, 11 December 1930).

'A film entitled *L'Age d'or*, whose minimal artistic merit is an offence to any recognized technical standard, puts together, as a public spectacle, the most obscene, repellent and paltry episodes. Country, family and religion are dragged through the mud . . .' (Richard Pierre Bodin, *Figaro*, 7 December 1930).

'Let us say at once that this "production" is of evident tedium. It is inspired by the cockadoodling Surrealists who astonished the bourgeoisie in 1920. This pretentious and trivial rubbish has nothing to do with the art of the *avant-garde* nor with any other art. The technical execution is so bad that it would be booed off the screen of the most wretched provincial flea-pit . . . With the aim of relieving the frightful tedium of every centimetre of this film, the director has intertwined scenes of the lowest and most dismal pornography' (G. M., *Echo de Paris*, 10 December 1930).

'The public – which is not yet so corrupted as to accept without protest the lucubrations of false thinkers, hiding their foreign origins under recently acquired French nationality and creating works rejected by the entire world – has put itself in the place of a negligent authority.

'It is right, in so far as the censorship will not fulfil its duty, that spectators should protect themselves, on the strength of traditions of honesty and decency which are the basis of French culture' (*Ami du Peuple*, 7 December 1930).

'The role of the sound and speech in this film reveals Buñuel's astonishing sense of the new possibilities of the cinema' (Henri Tracol, *Vu*, 3 December 1930).

'Never before in the cinema, or with such vigour, such scorn of the "conventions" and of bourgeois society and its appurtenances – the police, religion, the army, morality, the family, the State itself – has one been so assailed by blows from head to foot.

'Whatever one's intellectual position or literary experience, one feels readily the direct violence of these images . . . Clearly in making *L'Age d'or*, the authors wanted to make sure that the snobs and smart audiences who had gratuitously admired *Un Chien andalou*, thereby insulting them, should make no mistake this time about their meaning and should feel the disgust in which they, the authors, hold them' (Léon Moussinac, *L'Humanité*, 7 December 1930).

The passion surrounding *L'Age d'or* has never really cooled, though nowadays eulogy has become almost general. Bit by bit the film has become a classic and few critics would dare attack it. On the contrary, we now have the quite different phenomenon of critics who dislike Buñuel and who for purely ideological motives will make a show of objectivity by praising the early films at the cost of the later ones which they violently attack.

The Surrealists themselves accepted the film from the first as one of their most authentic expressions. André Breton wrote: 'This film remains a unique exaltation of total love, as I see it; and the violent reactions which greeted its first appearance in Paris have only strengthened my sense of its incomparable worth. Within this love there exists a potential, true Golden Age, totally apart from the Golden Age which Europe formerly experienced; and an infinite wealth of future possibilities' (in *L'Amour Fou*).

Critical exaltation reaches its peak, however, with Ado Kyrou, for whom 'There is *L'Age d'or*; and after it come all other films. *L'Age d'or* is the most beautiful film in the world' ('Le Surréalisme au Cinéma, et *L'Age d'or*, centre et tremplin du cinéma surréaliste', in *L'Age du Cinéma*, 1951). In *Amour, érotisme et cinéma*, Kyrou writes: 'Buñuel is the most honest and sincere man that I know. Impermeable to the filth of the cinema business, he has expressed himself, expresses himself and will continue to express himself simply, freely and valiantly. He has spoken and will always speak of love and the enemies which love must fight.'

The definitive contribution to the conversion of Buñuel into myth, however, was that of Henry Miller, then established in Paris. In 1931 he wrote about *L'Age d'or* in the May issue of *La Nouvelle Revue de Paris*, offering his interpretation of the film as 'an exposition of the collision between the sexual instinct innate in man, and his intellect, as the glorification of death and of the lost rhythm of life'. In 1937 he published the book *Cosmological Eye*, which included a chapter devoted to *L'Age d'or*. It was an opportune reminder of the forgotten film-maker at a time when his former friend and collaborator, Dali, had made himself a millionaire by supplying art to the bourgeoisie of the United States. Buñuel at that period was recalled as the ghost author of old forbidden films. Many reckoned these as the works of a prophet, a messiah who had actually been sacrificed for his cause. Miller began the total canonization:

'Those who are disappointed because they cannot find order or reason (in *L'Age d'or*) will never find order anywhere ... Perhaps it is the baroque element in human life, or rather in the life of civilized man, that gives to the work of Buñuel its dimension of cruelty and sadism; cruelty and sadism isolated, because the great virtue of Buñuel is in refusing to be entrapped in the glittering cobweb of logic and idealism which tries to mask the truthful naturalness of man. Perhaps, like Lawrence, Buñuel is only an inverted idealist. Perhaps his great sensibility and the enormous purity and poetry of his vision oblige him to expose the abomination, the malice, the ugliness and the false hypocrisies of man. Like his precursor he feels an enormous hatred towards the untruth.

'The normal, instinctive, decent, lively being, without pretensions, is met with only in the topsy-turvy currents of social forces. The completely normal and honourable being is considered as something strange. Like Lawrence he divides the world into two completely opposed camps – those who are with him and those who are against him. In this dilemma there is no possibility of indecision. Either you are made like the rest of civilized humanity, or you are proud and whole like Buñuel. And if you are whole and proud, then you are an anarchist, and throw bombs.

'I could no more prevent myself from holding this opinion of Buñuel than tomorrow morning I will be able to keep myself from washing my face. My past vital experience leads me to this moment and despotically controls me. In affirming the value of Buñuel, I am affirming my own values, my own faith in life. In singling out this unique man, I am doing only what I am constantly doing in every part of existence: selecting and evaluating.'

The full scenario of *L'Age d'or* has been frequently reproduced (it is available in English in the Lorrimer Classic Film Script Series); and a synopsis of the action will be adequate here.

The film opens with a shot of two scorpions on a doorpost; and the sequence moves into what appears to be a documentary study of the habits of scorpions, with long explanatory titles:

> The scorpion belongs to a class of arachnids frequently found in the hot regions of the Ancient world ...

> The tail is formed by a series of five prismatic joints ...

> The claws resemble the larger claws of the crayfish; they áre organs of aggression and information ...

> The tail ends in a sixth, bladder-like joint, which contains poison. A curved and pointed sting injects poisonous fluid into a ....

> A lover of darkness, it burrows beneath stones to escape the glare of the sun ...

> Not at all sociable, it ejects the intruder who comes to disturb its solitude ...

> What lightning speed and what virtuosity in its attack!
> Despite its fury, even the rat falls to its blows ...

A scorpion is shown killing a rat.

A title 'SOME HOURS AFTERWARDS' introduces a bleak and rocky shore landscape, where an armed and ragged bandit keeps lookout. Organ music swells up as the audience sees, from the bandit's viewpoint, four Archbishops in full robes performing mysterious rites and singing the *Dies Irae*. So feeble that he keeps tumbling on the rough ground, the bandit makes his way to a wretched hut where a group of his fellow-bandits, as starved and ragged as himself, sit languidly around. The youngest, Péman, lies dying on a pallet. When the lookout bursts in and announces 'The Majorcans are here!' they all

L'Age d'or: the bandits

struggle out, except Péman, who makes his excuses: 'But you have accordions, hippopotami, keys, climbers and paintbrushes.' As the debilitated bandits clamber across the steep ground, they fall one by one until only the leader remains. A fade into the spot where the bishops were previously seen reveals that they are still there in their robes, but transformed into skeletons.

A group of ten little boats is rowed into a rocky inlet, and a caravan of distinguished persons – soldiers, priests, monks, nuns, policemen and silk-hatted civilians – disembark to file in procession to the place where the bishops stand, now very tattered. The crowd forms up in front of the skeletons, and the Governor prepares to deliver an oration, when cries are heard from behind the crowd. The people turn to see a man and woman rolling in the mud, in lascivious embrace. The woman's face expresses indulgent adoration, the man's crazed lust. The crowd tear them apart and the woman is dragged away, looking back longingly at the man. He half-closes his eyes in ecstasy as a shot of the young woman apparently sitting on a lavatory is introduced. There is a sound of a flushing cistern, and a shot of lava flowing at the base of a volcano. The man is dragged away by the police, but breaks away to kick a yapping dog held by one of the crowd, and again to crush a beetle with his foot. As he and his escort disappear into the distance, the Governor lays a foundation stone:

> In the Year of Our Lord, 1930,
> on the site of the last resting-place
> of the four Majorcans, this stone was
> laid as the foundation for the city of . . .

Title: IMPERIAL ROME. Shots of the Vatican are followed by scenes of city streets. A title, SOMETIMES ON SUNDAY, introduces a shot of houses being blown up. Title: VARIOUS PICTURESQUE VIEWS OF THE METROPOLIS: alongside dull street scenes are bizarre incidents – a well-dressed man kicks a violin along the street; an old gentleman walks through a park with a stone balanced on his head in emulation of a nearby statue.

The handcuffed man is dragged along the streets by the police. He gazes at a poster advertising hand-cream; and a real hand makes onanistic gestures in a bunch of hair. Again, he gazes at a pair of women's legs on a passing sandwich-board, and a photograph of a young woman in a hairdresser's window.

The face mixes to the face of the man's mistress, who is lying on a sofa in an elegant room. Her mother sits reading, and comments on her daughter's finger being bandaged. A cutaway shows the girl's aristocratic father, the Marquis, with the same finger stuck in the neck of a bottle which he is vigorously agitating. The girl discusses the rather bizarre arrangements for a party; but her mother interrupts her: 'Hurry, the Majorcans will come at nine o'clock.'

The girl goes into her bedroom and shoos a cow which is lying on the bed. The noise of its bell continues throughout the succeeding scene. She sits before her dressing-table mirror, absently polishing her nails: this scene intercuts with shots of the man being escorted by the two policemen. Both man and girl seem to share the same sadness. Instead of her own reflection she sees drifting clouds in the mirror of her dressing table, and her hair is blown by a wind.

In the street the man insults a well-dressed passer-by; then produces documents which seem to establish his identity as a man of rank, and alarm the police, who release him. Leaping into a taxi he pauses only to knock down a passing blind man.

A title announces: IN THEIR MAGNIFICENT VILLA NEAR ROME THE MARQUIS OF X AND HIS WIFE PREPARE TO WELCOME THEIR GUESTS. Elegant guests are ushered from cars and into a ballroom where they are graciously received by the Marquis who endeavours vainly to brush away the flies which crawl on his face. Among the arrivals at the party is a reliquary which is heaved out of a limousine.

Inside the ballroom the guests politely ignore the irruption of a farm-cart which trundles through their midst bearing drunken labourers; and take no more notice when a screaming maid rushes out of the kitchen from which belch fire and smoke. Through a window the gamekeeper is seen to shoot his little boy for some trivial provocation. The guests show mild interest as the man indignantly justifies his action to valets who question him.

The young woman is clearly bored and anxious until the arrival of the man, now elegantly dressed, who enters trailing a dress identical with the one she is wearing. The two lovers are totally indifferent to what goes on around them, even when the man causes a scandal by slapping the Marquise for spilling a drop of wine on him. The Marquise swoons and the man is ordered out of the house. He reappears behind a curtain to signal the girl to go into the garden; and she leaves by the French windows. Meanwhile the man reappears and haughtily crosses the room and follows her out into the garden.

In the garden, by night, the girl waits for the man by an urn raised on a pedestal. As they make off down a gravel walk between high hedges, the other guests begin to fill the seats arranged in front of an orchestra, conducted by an aged bearded man, and with a priest as first violinist. The film cuts between the orchestra's preparations and tuning-up and the young couple's violent and ungainly efforts to make love while sitting on two garden chairs. As they fumble and tumble, they are startled as the orchestra suddenly strikes up with the Liebestod from *Tristan and Isolde*.

L'Age d'or: the erotic sequence in the garden – Gaston Modot, Lya Lys

L'Age d'or: the Minister's corpse on the ceiling

The man's attention is suddenly captured by the phallic form of the toe of a statue in the garden. At that moment four startled priests (including the first violinist) scurry across a little bridge. Now the lovers' struggles become more desperate and they fall together on the gravel. Suddenly a servant arrives and calmly announces that the Minister of the Interior wishes to speak to the man on the telephone. Resentfully he goes off, leaving the girl to suck the phallic toe of the statue, passionately.

Inside the house the man has a furious conversation on the telephone with the Minister, who is seen in his office. As the Minister upbraids him, there are cut-in shots from newsreels of demonstrating crowds and police. The Minister accuses the man of being the cause of hundreds of deaths – 'children . . . honourable old men . . . and women'; the man, furious to be disturbed for this, puts down the phone. The Minister's telephone is seen dangling on its wire, with, near by, a revolver, a pair of shoes and a pool of blood. The Minister's corpse lies on the ceiling.

When the man returns to the garden and the girl, their relationship is changed. Instead of the frenzied passion they are gently affectionate. For a moment the girl's face changes into an old woman's. When she again appears as she was before, the conversation heard on the sound-track is the soft talk of a couple in bed.

As the music reaches a crescendo the woman again becomes passionate and cries out, 'I've waited for you so long. What joy, what joy! To have murdered our children.' The man's face is covered in blood as he murmurs ecstatically 'Mon amour! Mon amour! Mon amour! Mon amour!'

L'Age d'or: Gaston Modot

Suddenly the conductor of the orchestra hurls away his baton, clutches his head in his hands and walks off the platform. The music stops and the audience watches in surprise as the conductor staggers noisily over the gravel and away to where the lovers are. The girl starts up and rushes to embrace him. He kisses her loudly through his beard. The hero starts up in anger but bumps his head on a branch. Seizing his head in the same attitude as the conductor had done, he staggers back the way the other man had come. As he approaches the camera we see that one of his fly-buttons is undone. His retreat is accompanied by loud drums which continue till the end of the sequence. He enters the young woman's bedroom, still evidently in great pain. He throws himself on the bed, and begins to tear at the pillows, throwing the feathers about the room. He gets up and picks up and throws down in turn a marble bust of a Roman senator and a wooden plough. He goes over to the window.

Cut to exterior of the window. From it there emerges a flaming Christmas tree. The man throws out an archbishop, who is followed by a plough, a bishop's crook, a stuffed giraffe and feathers.

The feathers cut to snow; and the scene to a mediaeval castle on a precipitous mountain.

Title: AT THE EXACT MOMENT WHEN THESE FEATHERS, TORN OUT BY HIS
FURIOUS HANDS, COVERED THE GROUND BENEATH THE WINDOW: AT
THAT MOMENT, AS WE SAID, BUT VERY FAR AWAY, THE SURVIVORS OF
THE CHATEAU DE SELLINY WERE COMING OUT, TO RETURN TO PARIS

There is a cut to a big close-up of their features, then a further

Title: FOUR WELL-KNOWN AND UTTER SCOUNDRELS HAD LOCKED THEM-
SELVES UP IN AN IMPREGNABLE CASTLE FOR ONE HUNDRED AND
TWENTY DAYS TO CELEBRATE THE MOST BRUTAL OF ORGIES. THESE
FIENDS HAD NO LAW BUT THEIR DEPRAVITY. THEY WERE LIBERTINES
WHO HAD NO GOD, NO PRINCIPLES AND NO RELIGION. THE LEAST
CRIMINAL AMONG THEM WAS DEFILED BY MORE EVIL THAN YOU CAN
NAME. IN HIS EYES, THE LIFE OF A WOMAN — WHAT DO I SAY, OF ONE
WOMAN, OF ALL THE WOMEN IN THE WORLD — COUNTED FOR AS
LITTLE AS A FLY'S. THEY TOOK WITH THEM TO THE CHATEAU, SOLELY
FOR THEIR DISGUSTING DESIGN, EIGHT MARVELLOUS GIRLS, EIGHT
SPLENDID ADOLESCENTS, AND SO THAT THEIR IMAGINATION
(ALREADY TOO JADED) SHOULD BE CONTINUALLY STIMULATED, THEY
ALSO TOOK WITH THEM FOUR DEPRAVED WOMEN WHO CONSTANTLY
FIRED THE EVIL LUST OF THE FOUR MONSTERS BY THEIR TALES.

A long shot of the castle is followed by a third

Title: HERE, NOW LEAVING THE CHATEAU DE SELLINY, ARE THE SURVIVORS
OF THESE CRIMINAL ORGIES, THE LEADER AND CHIEF INSTIGATOR OF
THE FOUR: THE DUC DE BLANGIS.

The castle gates open, and four decrepit and worn-out orgiasts emerge to
cross the drawbridge. The first of them is the Duc de Blangis, a Christ-like
figure, long-haired, bearded and in Hebrew robes. A little girl, blood-stained
and terrified, runs out after them. The Duc tenderly picks her up from where
she has fallen, exhausted, and helps her back into the castle. There is a pause
as the camera lingers on the open door. Then a terrible shriek from inside the
castle. The first three orgiasts walk off into the snowy mountain, while the
Duc, with an expression of infinite pity once more emerges, and advances
towards the camera. There is a dissolve to a snow-covered cross hung with
the scalps of women, agitated by the wind; and the fade-out is accompanied by
a gay little phrase of music.

L'Age d'or was innovatory, astonishing and scandalizing to a far greater
degree than *Un Chien andalou*. This was the first feature-length Surrealist
film. It was one of the first European sound films to use sound consciously.
For the first time in history, love appeared on the screen in its total dimension,

L'Age d'or: the epilogue

analysed philosophically, sociologically and morally. Completely and deliberately, *L'Age d'or* ignored every traditional aesthetic value.

Although *Un Chien andalou* had been a Surrealist film – in a way that the *avant-garde* aesthetic essays which claimed to be Surrealist were not – it was a short, almost experimental effort. It affirmed the language and the visualization of the subconscious and of dreams, laying them out almost didactically. It could almost be regarded as a catalogue of Surrealist images, a manual of Surrealist aesthetic; and its critics have seen it as such. *L'Age d'or* left no doubt of its status as a Surrealist expression.

Although full of shock images, it was on a more realistic and everyday plane than *Un Chien andalou*; and the exclusion of Salvador Dalí probably had more than a little to do with this. The Surrealist images arose from more developed situations – which might be styled 'story' or 'narrative' or 'dramatic' – than were present in the short. Certainly the narrative is a great virtue of *L'Age d'or*: through apparently disconnected facts there runs an internal logic. 'It is a story film,' Jacques B. Brunius wrote.

This story extracts the essence of the Surrealist postulates. Its content was more evidently political than the previous film, or than most of the plastic works of Surrealism, with the exception of those of certain artists like Max

Ernst, André Masson and the collage artists. Also central to Surrealist orthodoxy was the principle of not wanting 'to make art'. From this point of view no film was ever purer than *L'Age d'or*; nor in this sense would Buñuel himself ever achieve anything else like it.

The theme and the impudence of its treatment preclude the possibility either of enjoying or being repelled by the technique. The deliberately intellectual intention of 'not making art' exculpates or justifies the technical deficiencies.

An excellent cameraman, Duverger, allows his camerawork to be without polish. Strong overhead lighting falls mercilessly on the actors' faces. It was the habit in that period of cinema to use big spotlights on built sets, without ceilings. In *L'Age d'or* the lighting was even less varied than normally, which might in anyone else be attributed to technical negligence. Yet today we realize that this is intentional. Buñuel has obliged directors of photography as distinguished as Gabriel Figueroa to produce work of a simplicity approaching crudity. Here the camera scarcely moves, long shots predominate, and within the shots the movement of the actors creates an interior montage – of a kind which is today in fashion, but was then regarded as lack of initiative in the direction of the camera. Editing, scarcely existent within sequences, is limited to linking the shots indicated by the script.

The poor quality of the direct sound can certainly not be reckoned as an intentional deficiency, but must be attributed to the imperfect techniques of early European sound films. The technical defects of the recording do not prevent the sound track of *L'Age d'or* from being the most important in this first stage of sound films. Not until Pudovkin's *Deserter* was the richness of the sound language in Buñuel's film surpassed – not even in Fritz Lang's brilliant use of sound in *M*, where he translated into the cinema discoveries in the dramatic use of sound made in theatre and literature. In *L'Age d'or* it is a different matter. Buñuel is really putting into practice the image-sound counterpoint theoretically discussed by Eisenstein, Pudovkin and Alexandrov in their famous *Manifesto on Cinema Sound* of 1928. It is not known if Buñuel was acquainted with the manifesto, but it is possible that he applied the theory intuitively, with the help of the Surrealist experience of collage. For the first time the music of gramophone records was used with the images not as a rhythmical accompaniment, but as an intellectual discovery. Buñuel and his imitators have used the effect many times since. Fragments of romantic symphonies, ideals of bourgeois society, collide with the crudity and brutality of the visuals. It is a matter of a scandalizing counterpoint, which instead of making the visuals sweeter, makes them still more insolent. The same idea impels the off-screen commentaries accompanying the documentary fragments. What the commentator tells us does not illustrate the picture but gives a sense of outrage thanks to a veiled allusion or some discord with the images. The same effect is produced by the subtitles, introduced as in a silent film or in *Un Chien andalou*; for instance the title 'Sometimes on Sundays', which is followed by a collapse of houses in a working-class district. Buñuel was to use the ironic counterpoint of commentary and image with outstanding brilliance in his next film, the short documentary *Land Without Bread*.

The dialogue is often at odds with the action. One of the best episodes of this sort is the scene in the garden where the lovers' voices are heard off-screen murmuring a bedroom conversation while they sit chastely looking into one another's eyes. Natural sounds take on poetic qualities. The heroine, Lya Lys, gazing at herself in a looking-glass, sees her reflection agitated by a sea wind, which we also hear as the echo of her passion; then her mother interrupts, and the sound-track starts in with the ting-ting of the cowbell which might represent, in Freudian terms, the mother. By means of the new language it discovered, *L'Age d'or* could express its complex content with a minimum of cinematic rhetoric.

The cinema ages rapidly, but not its outstanding works. *L'Age d'or* has suffered not at all from the passage of time. Because it has absolutely no period style, it has not dated. Above all its meaning remains contemporary. A political film, it presents a society on the edge of a cataclysm. At the time it appeared exaggerated but exact. A few years later came the World War; and the sequels of the content seemed to be resolved with the rhythm of that cataclysm. It was a film not about the past or the future, but a vigorously actual present: in order to make its criticism not of individual facts but of a whole civilization and social structure, it embraced a wide space and time.

Politics and poetry were for many years considered contradictory elements: there is no longer such an equivocation. *L'Age d'or* is a film of aggressive political intent, though it attacks principles of moral and social organization that are atavistic and deep-rooted. These principles are today still vigorously defended by the bourgeoisie and in this sense the work still has a concrete purpose. What *L'Age d'or* affirms above all else is the pre-eminence of love. When it says 'above all else' it truly means everything. 'Love or destruction' or 'love and death' are eternal themes in Spanish poetry, and, essentially, Buñuel has said nothing new. André Gide said: 'We have been shouting it for two thousand years, but since no one has listened yet, we shall say it again.'

6. Las Hurdes – Tierra sin pan

Buñuel told Bazin and Truffaut in the interview already quoted, 'In 1930, after *L'Age d'or* I was in Hollywood . . . Metro had seen the film in Paris and as a result signed up the feminine lead of the film, Lya Lys. Then they proposed that I should go to Hollywood with a contract. But I refused. Basically I was not interested to make films in those conditions. In Paris I was free to make the films I wanted, with friends who gave me the money. Then I was signed up as an observer, to go for six months to observe how they made films there, from script to editing.'

Buñuel embarked for America with Julio Peña and about ten other Spaniards hired by Hollywood for Castillian versions. These involved shooting every scene with Spanish actors, since the system of dubbing was not yet developed. An incident that happened during the Atlantic crossing is worth recalling as an illustration of the destructive and antisocial exaltation of an orthodox Surrealist cinéaste, as well as of the frequent fits of intransigence which have earned him the joking nickname of 'Mussolini' in his family.

The Captain of the American liner invited all the passengers to a party, at the end of which the orchestra played the United States national anthem. The guests all stood, as usual, but Buñuel remained seated with his feet on the table, whistling 'La Marseillaise'. When an explanation was demanded he

Buñuel and Eisenstein in Hollywood, 1930

replied violently 'Merde!', 'Je m'en fiche' and so on. Things became serious when the captain challenged Buñuel to a duel (recall the irony with which Buñuel treats the subject of duellists in *La Voie Lactée* and *Tristana*). All was finally settled after the intervention of friends and Buñuel proffered gentlemanly excuses to the good captain. 'National anthems and flags are symbols which fascinate me and seem to me to be imbued with marvellous power,' Buñuel once said, 'seeing that millions of men have gone gaily to death for them.'

Another instance of the fury of Surrealist iconoclasm is the story of Chaplin's Christmas Eve party. Chaplin had invited some of the then numerous Spanish colony in Hollywood: Edgar Neville, Miguel Mihura, López Rubic and Buñuel among them. The host had erected a huge Christmas tree in the hall of his house, with a present for every guest. The Spaniards, egged on by Buñuel, burst into the house armed with huge pruning shears, and at the cry of 'Down with symbols!' fell upon the tree, leaving it reduced to the vertical essence of its trunk. Chaplin was amused. Buñuel has a photograph of himself with Chaplin and Eisenstein, of which he is very fond, although his opinion of Chaplin is immutable: 'Chaplin,' he has told me, 'is a man of marvellous courtesy and very nice – but anodyne.' Buñuel's opinion of the Soviet director appears elsewhere in this book. He had known Eisenstein in Paris: 'Eisenstein's friends have tried to blame Alexandrov for the debâcle of the dreadful and shoddy production of *Romance sentimentale*. But I saw Eisenstein making it with my own eyes, since he was shooting it on the stage next to me when I was making *L'Age d'or*.'

No doubt Buñuel sought out Eisenstein on his arrival in Hollywood. The Eisenstein Museum in Moscow has a note: 'Cher Eisenstein: Je viens vous voir et vous êtes parti. Je serai très content de vous rencontrer. Voulez vous me téléphoner un matin avant dix heures CR 6668? A bientôt: Luis Buñuel.'

The first meeting of Buñuel and Chaplin is recorded in the Hollywood diary kept by Ivor Montagu:

'Once Charlie was caught in a situation despite Kono's* best precautions. A young man-about-Hollywood of perfect exterior and elegant manners – here designated Count B. – one day brought to Charlie's two visiting Spaniards, men of infinite dignity and intelligence but who could not at that time muster one word of English between them. Only Sergei Mikhailovich † was fluent in their language. The name of the older was Ugarte – a noble writer, I learned to know him in the Spanish war. ‡ That of the younger and darker with a flashing eye was Luis Buñuel. Charlie's two children by his second marriage were visiting us, Charles and Sidney (what an excellent actor the latter is now), two dark curly-haired small boys with an accordion. Ugarte entertained them by making little horns with his forefingers and prancing light-footed before them as a bull while Buñuel helped to teach them passes with their handkerchiefs. That afternoon was a triumph, but less so two days later when Count B. arrived once more with his protégés, deposited them on the lawn, and dashed off to keep an appointment with a girl. Sergei Mikhailovich happened not to be there that day, and we had a complicated four hours trying to converse with Charlie's few words and otherwise by signs, for although Buñuel spoke French excellently it never occurred to the rest of us to try him out.' §

Buñuel's interview with *Cahiers du Cinéma* takes up the story of his work in Hollywood:

'The first day the supervisor looked at my contract and said, "It's a funny contract, but still . . . Where do you want to start, with the studio, the script department or the editing?" I chose the studio. So he said, "On stage 24,

---

* Chaplin's loyal and protective Japanese valet.

† Eisenstein, who was then, with his team, in Chaplin's house.

‡ Montagu made a very important documentary in Spain, *The Siege of Madrid* (1938). It is not generally known that his crew included a seventeen-year-old boy later to become a classic figure in cinema history: Norman McLaren.

§ Ivor Montagu: *With Eisenstein in Hollywood*, Berlin, 1969.

Greta Garbo is working. Do you want to go there for a month as an observer?" I went, and when I entered saw Greta Garbo who was being made up. She looked at me out of the corner of her eye, asking herself who this stranger was, so I said something in an incomprehensible idiom – it was supposed to be English but at that time I could only say "Good morning" – and she made a gesture and someone threw me out. After that I collected my pay each Saturday at noon, and nobody bothered any more with me. After three months of this, I went back to see the supervisor who, in spite of everything, asked me to look at a piece of film with Lili Damita – do you remember Lili Damita? – He said to me: "Are you Spanish?" I said: "Yes, but I'm here as a Frenchman, since they engaged me in Paris." "Never mind," the supervisor replied; "Mr Thalberg wants you to look at a Spanish film of Lili Damita's." I replied, "Tell Mr Thalberg" (and he was the boss at Metro) . . . can I say the word I said?'

JACQUES DONIOL-VALCROZE – 'Of course.'

LUIS BUÑUEL – 'I said that I hadn't time to spare listening to a p . . . Then it was all over. A month later they cancelled my contract. There were two months outstanding. I went back to France. They paid my return trip, and one month instead of the two. That's all I did in Hollywood.'

ANDRÉ BAZIN – 'So you were in France at the beginning of 1931?'

LUIS BUÑUEL – 'Yes. In April 1931 to be precise. At the moment of the founding of the Spanish Republic. I stayed in Paris two days. Then I borrowed money to go by taxi from Paris to Madrid. I took one taxi in Paris and another in Irun for Madrid . . . Then I came back to Paris.'
(*Cahiers du Cinéma*, 36).

'After making *L'Age d'or* I received some offers to make films of a commercial type which I had to refuse, not because they were commercial but because I disagreed with the theme.

'In 1932 I separated from the Surrealist group although I remained on good terms with my ex-companions. I was beginning not to agree with that kind of intellectual aristocracy, with its artistic and moral extremes, which isolated us from the world and limited us to our own company. Surrealists considered the majority of mankind contemptible or stupid, and thus withdrew from all social participation and responsibility and shunned the work of the others.

'To earn a living I began to collaborate anonymously in my profession, entering as a writer in Paramount Studios in Paris, adapting pictures from English to Spanish. I was then supervisor for "dubbing" at Warner Bros in Madrid. I have a pleasant memory of my association with that company and of its chief in Spain, Mr Huet . . .

'Between 1932 and 1936 I made only one picture under my own name. It was shown in Paris in 1937, although its completion dated from 1933. This picture was called *Land Without Bread*.

'There exists in Spain a section almost unknown by the Spanish, until King

Alfonso made a trip to it in 1923. It still remained on the outskirts of Spanish life and civilization, its obstinacy a social problem and enigma.

'This section, called "Las Hurdes", is one of the most miserable on the face of the globe, isolated from the outside world by mountains difficult to pass and with a population of 6,000 inhabitants distributed in 52 hamlets.

'It originated at the beginning of the 16th century, when some of the survivors of the Jewish expulsion and persecution, ordered by the Catholic Kings, went to inhabit it. Its population was increased later by outlaws who were seeking refuge in its mountains, fleeing the rigors of justice.

'Only sixty miles from Salamanca, one of the centres of European culture, and two miles from Las Batuecas, one of the most interesting centres of paleolithic culture, Las Hurdes, nevertheless, has remained unbelievably backward.

'Bread is almost unknown in Las Hurdes Altas. The inhabitants have to work, with great effort, their fields which barely yield enough to sustain them for nine months. They almost completely lack utensils or work implements. There are no domestic animals. There is no folklore. During the two months I stayed there, I didn't hear one song, nor see a single picture in their little shacks and hovels. Impoverishment, hunger, incest, a product of the horrible misery, have made many inhabitants cretinous. Nevertheless, the majority possess normal mental faculties, being rather quick in intelligence.

'The pathetic thing about this country, and for this reason its psychological and human interest is very superior to that of barbaric tribes, is that, though its material civilization is rudimentary and almost prehistoric, its religious and moral culture and ideas are like those of any civilized country.

'There are Hurdanos who speak French because they have emigrated. Why don't these people entirely abandon their country? Geographers are agreed that it is uninhabitable. Neither books nor the film have been able to explain the reasons for their continuance there.

'Through the king's visits and the magnificent book by the French Professor Legendre on this country which he studied deeply for twenty years, I became acquainted with its existence, and my desire was to make an objective document, a sort of human geographical study about it. However, no one wanted to give me the little money I asked in order to produce it. Some it repelled, others were afraid of losing their money, the rest said that it wasn't fair to show Spain in that light. As if hiding the truth would remedy the evil.

'A school master from Huesca, Ramón Acín, to whom I had spoken of this project in friendly conversation, became very interested by my idea and offered me part of his savings for the undertaking. He could only give me $2,000. Considering the smallness of the budget, I looked in Paris for disinterested collaborators whom I could interest in Las Hurdes. The poet, Pierre Unik, the cameraman, Eli Lotar, Professor Sanchez Ventura and the teacher, Ramón Acín, helped me in my enterprise. We passed two unforgettable months in that remote civilization.'

In the interview with *Cahiers du Cinéma* Buñuel gave more details:

LUIS BUÑUEL – 'I had read something by Maurice Legendre, who was director of the Institut Français in Madrid, about the life of certain backward human groups. It was a doctorate thesis of 1,200 pages, a very complete and minute study of this kind of life. This book excited me, and I thought about a film. I had a Spanish friend, called Acin, who had said to me: "If I win a lottery some day, I'll pay for your film!" Three months later he won a lottery. But he was an anarchist and his anarchist friends said he should share out the money. But he kept his word and gave me 20,000 pesetas. It was not a gold-mine, but it was enough to pay the trip for Pierre Unik, Eli Lotar and myself. Pierre Unik was moreover paid by *Vogue*, which published a very interesting reportage, appearing in three issues.

ANDRÉ BAZIN − I heard somewhere that initially *Las Hurdes* was a film commissioned by the Spanish Government for social and educational purposes.

LUIS BUÑUEL − Absolutely not. In fact it was prohibited by the Republic as dishonourable for Spain and a denigration of the Spanish people. The authorities were furious and instructed all the Embassies to see that the film was not shown abroad, as being injurious to Spain. Thus it was only released in France in 1937, at the height of the Spanish war.

ANDRÉ BAZIN − Who wrote the commentary?

LUIS BUÑUEL − Pierre Unik. We did it together.

ANDRÉ BAZIN − Who had the idea for the music?

LUIS BUÑUEL − I did. I had special ideas about music in the cinema.

JACQUES DONIOL-VALCROZE − Had Grémillon nothing to do with it?

LUIS BUÑUEL − No; I only knew Grémillon four years later, in Spain, when I brought him there as a movie director. At that time I was a producer. He came for practically nothing because he liked Spain.

ANDRÉ BAZIN − Certain scenes were cut by the censor. In particular the cock fight.

LUIS BUÑUEL − Yes. When the film came out in France, I think in 1937, there were big protests in the Savoy papers, saying that tourism in Grenoble would be affected because the commentary suggested at the beginning of the film that there were certain parts of Europe, in Czechoslovakia, in French Savoy and in Spain, where there remained human groups of retarded civilization. Madame Picabia had told me that in Savoy there was a village like Las Hurdes, where bread was almost unknown and where there was almost total consanguinity.

ANDRÉ BAZIN − What in your view is the relation between a film like *Las Hurdes* and your previous work? How do you see the relation between Surrealism and the documentary standpoint?

LUIS BUÑUEL − I see a lot of relationship. I made *Las Hurdes* because I had a Surrealist vision and because I was interested in the problem of man. I saw reality in a different manner from the way I'd seen it before Surrealism. Pierre Unik also felt like this.

ANDRÉ BAZIN – We would like to know a few details about your ideas on music in the cinema. Particularly in relation to *Las Hurdes*.

LUIS BUÑUEL – Once I was in New York at a Congress of the Association of Documentary Film Producers, and all the most famous American composers of film music were there. *Las Hurdes* was shown, and one of them, tremendously enthusiastic, came up and asked me how I had had the marvellous idea of using the Brahms music. But truly I hadn't invented anything. It simply came to me that the general feeling of the film corresponded to the Brahms music. I took the Fourth Symphony . . . I remember that it was on four Brunswick discs. Everyone is startled by something so simple that it's almost idiotic, just because they are always looking for effects and elaboration. Personally I don't like film music. It seems to me that it is a false element, a sort of trick, except of course in certain cases. I've been amazed to find in this Festival* feature films without music. I could mention three or four which have sequences of twenty minutes or more without any music – *The Great Adventure*, for instance . . . Now that I'm deaf, I can't even hear if there's a 24-piece orchestra all the time. But it's all the same to me, and proves to me that in all events silence would be preferable.

JACQUES DONIOL-VALCROZE – In fact there's practically no music in *The Great Adventure*.

LUIS BUÑUEL – In the Japanese film *The Gate of Hell* the music is also very special. I can see, in world production, the possibility of suppressing music most of the time. Ah, silence! That is the important thing! I discovered nothing about music, but instinctively regarded it as a parasitic element which above all served to give value to scenes with no other cinematographic interest. For *Cumbres borrascosas* I put myself into the state of mind of 1930; and since at that time I was a hopeless Wagnerian, I introduced fifty minutes of Wagner.

Eli Lotar wrote a very interesting diary of the shooting which has until now remained unpublished. The cameraman was then at the peak of his career, which was afterwards cut short on account of his political intransigence. Previously he had worked on Joris Ivens' *Zuiderzee* (1930); but *Las Hurdes* remains his most notable work. Subsequently he developed a feeling for Spain, and in 1934 made a fine documentary *La canción del afilador*, shot in the province of Malaga.

Lotar used a Kinamo camera, a Debrie 120 and three silver paper reflectors

* The interview was recorded during the 1954 Cannes Film Festival.

which were utilized in the interior sequence of the mother who has just lost her child, and in the final scene. The lighting of the interiors (the pan across the bodies of the family sleeping in sexual promiscuity) and of the final scene of the old woman going through the streets asking for prayers for the dead, was done with simple torchlight, which made the work very difficult because of the excessive smoke they produced. The entire film was shot in these difficult, almost amateur conditions; so that its near perfection is the more astonishing.

Lotar felt that Buñuel should have shot more footage, and edited more ruthlessly. During shooting Buñuel maintained an almost infantile tyranny over the group. He and Unik ganged up against Lotar and Sanchez Ventura, particularly in matters relating to money. Buñuel, always so generous with his own money, was viciously mean in administering his 20,000 pesetas. According to Lotar, Buñuel used every last metre he had shot in the finished film. Such economy would be understandable in the circumstances; but in fact Buñuel accuses Lotar of exaggeration. 'On the contrary,' he told me, 'I threw away some working material which I thought unusable, even though it was extremely interesting, because at that time I did not know how much material you can use despite technical shortcomings in it. If I were to do the film today, it would be longer by those metres of celluloid which I threw away.' In fact four reels of off-cuts from the film are preserved by the Cinémathèque of Toulouse, to which it was presented by Conchita Buñuel.

The four-man crew was in Las Hurdes during April and May, with a short trip to Madrid in between. Lotar's diary records that on 28 April they were in the village of La Alberca, where they shot the scenes of the fiesta and the cock fight (cut by the French censors) and the pans and shots of rural architecture. On 20 April Lotar had been in Paris. On 24 May the crew were back in Madrid with the shooting finished.

Actual filming lasted about a month, the rest of the time being taken up in selecting locations and planning shooting. Buñuel knew Las Hurdes well. He retained his interest after the film, and in 1961, on his return to Spain, went back again. But it is one thing to go as a tourist and another to film. Although the film has all Buñuel's quality of seeming to be shot quite accidentally, with all the freshness of chance and improvisation, the preparation was meticulous. Buñuel had diligently studied the thesis by Legendre, who had been visiting Las Hurdes since 1908. He talked with scientists who had visited the region. Legendre's book had caused a commotion into which others besides Buñuel had been drawn. The scandal of the discovery of this backward and deprived region had brought other investigators to the hidden valley. Gustavo Pittaluga (father of the celebrated musician) made a trip there with Francisco Aranda, father of the present writer, to study tumours of the neck and their hereditary

Las Hurdes

factors. In 1925 Dr Marañón brought King Alfonso XIII himself there; and a short reportage now preserved in the Cinemateca Nacional in Madrid provoked no less scandal than Buñuel's film, though for different reasons. Following his visit, the King put in hand the construction of a highway from Salamanca to Las Hurdes. The work of civilizing the territory was not very rapid however; and when Buñuel made his film, it was still in the wretched state we see. In fact Las Hurdes was later transformed; though even today there are other regions, such as the Sanabria district, the Monegros and the Almería desert, which are in some respects more backward than Las Hurdes, especially in agriculture.

Undoubtedly the progress of Las Hurdes owes much to the scandal provoked by Buñuel. For those who regard him as a sadist, relishing the misery of the land with his camera instead of doing something about it, time has provided the answer. If Buñuel had practised charity in the region instead of making his film, the inhabitants would certainly have had no long-term betterment. The film effected more in Madrid than a mess of pottage would have done in Las Hurdes. The first screening took place in the Palace of the Press in Madrid in 1933, and was attended by all the capital's intellectuals. Lotar says that Buñuel was in the projection box during the show, 'seeing to the sound'. He read the written text admirably in a tone which combined insolent indifference and apparent objectivity; and used the accompaniment of

93

the Brunswick discs which formed the sound-track when the film was eventually synchronized, in Paris, early in 1937. At the end of the 27-minute projection the audience was apparently not pleased. The same Dr Marañón complained that Buñuel had ignored the beautiful architecture and the artistic traditions of the village of La Alberca. Evidently the two men thought on different lines.

The description of the film which follows is based on Freddy Buache's synopsis in *Luis Buñuel* (Premier Plan, 1960), with some additions. (The full scenario has been published by *L'Avant-scène du Cinéma*, number 36, Paris, April 1964):

Before penetrating into the land of Las Hurdes, which no road links to the outside world, the film-maker halts at the last village, La Alberca. It is a feast day: a marriage has just been celebrated and the villagers are engaged in a bizarre and barbarous ceremony which consists in pulling the feathers from the heads of cocks tied by their feet: a suitably cruel prelude to the discovery of the 'Hurdanos'. The camera pans over the streets and buildings with the apparently indifferent objectivity of any documentary. It settles on an inscription which reads: 'Blessed be the hour in which Holy Mary conceived, through the work and grace of the Holy Spirit.' The camera, descending in a vertical panoramic shot, next settles on a round-topped door from which a cow emerges. Another vertical panorama descends in close-up on a woman, showing us the gaudy decoration of her clothing, mostly charms. Then the camera carries us through a mountainous and desolate landscape in which the Carmelites first established Christianity. We see the ruins of a monastery dominating the village in a metaphysical sense. The commentary explains that there used to be monks here surrounded by young acolytes. The hamlet is made up of low houses, the walls without windows and roofs without chimneys, petrified nests of men, living in the worst conditions of physical and mental hygiene. 'In Las Hurdes,' the commentary emphasizes, 'we never heard a song.' Families live in a single room. In the street a little boy drinks from a gutter; and the camera, moving in a panoramic shot, reveals, a little higher up the street, pigs paddling in the same stream. The water in this gutter serves for all uses. Sickness abounds. Yet here, like everywhere else, the sum of the angles of a triangle is equal to two right angles; and the moral which the pupils learn in their school is the same as anywhere else: a little boy writes on the blackboard, under the supervision of the teacher: 'Respect the property of others.'

The commentary informs us that during the winter months there is no food, and in the summer the population eat green fruits, which produce fatal dysentery.

A travelling shot shows the bare feet and frail legs of the children. On the

Las Hurdes

wall of the classroom is an engraving showing a marquis in a powdered wig, accompanied by his lady in the high fashion of the eighteenth century: a confrontation of two aspects of the same society, as the symbol of aristocracy is faced with the most abject misery.

The soil being so arid, the Hurdanos do not raise domestic animals. Only the least poor among these poor people manage to raise a single pig; but they do not keep it long. They kill it as soon as it has a little flesh on it, and eat it in two days ... The hives which can be seen about the region do not belong to them, but to proprietors in Salamanca, who load them on asses and send them into town. Sometimes an ass trips and falls; the honey covers it and the bees attack the animal whose flesh is eaten by some wandering dog. (These asses have a significance similar to the putrefying ones in *Un Chien andalou*, though more concrete.)

The month of May is the hardest time of the year for the Hurdanos. Then they have nothing to eat but cherries, but they eat them while they are still green and suffer dysentery as a result ... With difficulty they collect together a little soil on the stony banks of the river; but these poor gardens produce little because the artificial soil is soon exhausted and the Hurdanos have no manure since they possess so few domestic animals. Hence they prefer to stay idly in their beds, sleeping fully clothed on heaps of fermenting rotten leaves ... When a viper bites them, the bite itself is rarely fatal, but in trying to cure it with herbs, they infect the wound and die ... Incest still further increases the degeneracy of a people in which the aged are thirty years old. There are many cripples, dwarfs, cretins ... malaria spares no one; we see a man in convulsions on the edge of an unfenced terrace. Buñuel himself approaches a little blonde girl, typically Salamancan, very beautiful, resting on a heap of stones. With his hands he opens her mouth to show that it is in a state of putrefaction. The commentary says: 'The little girl died the following day.' A long sequence is devoted to the death of a baby, whose mother, a beautiful woman, suffers silently inside a hovel. A group of bearded men come to take away the little corpse. Putting it into a basket, like Moses, they take it to the river which they cross, holding their burden aloft, on the way to the distant cemetery, the only place where there is earth. Weeds and thistles grow in a desolate field, without memorials. It is a scene of arid poetry, brutal, but of intense lyrical force. The little procession of men with the baby, the crossing of the river ('We never bathe in the same water again; all flows on') show Buñuel a poet first and a sociologist or scientist second. This scene is developed philosophically and poetically in comparable scenes in *Subida al cielo* and *El rio y la muerte*.

The final sequences show a game between cretins who might come from a painting by Velazquez, a general view of the village with the smoke rising from the cracks between the stones of the walls – a magical and hallucinating image – the people sleeping in their houses and a panoramic shot from above of an old woman ringing a bell and asking for prayers for the dead. This is the final shot of the film. The commentary ends baldly: 'After a month's stay in Las Hurdes we left the country.'

Into this enumeration of facts, each one more absurd and at the same time more severe and precise, Buñuel abruptly introduces a didactic exposition of the habits of the anopheles mosquito, with illustrations from ancient texts. The digression is not pointless, but has the same function as the commentary on scorpions, the views of Rome and certain of the titles introduced into *L'Age d'or*. This kind of presentation produces a deliberate poetry of the horrible. 'Like the abundance of objective information which is woven into the film, this brief sequence brings a weight of reality to the nightmare, forces you to look from the effect to the cause, and prevents any possibility of pity, because pity, sister of resignation ... is the principal specious alibi available to the individual who is too cowardly to engage himself in revolt. The corruption of soul and body among the Hurdanos follows a cycle of hopeless degradation. In showing it to us deprived of all pathos, Buñuel postulates that a single, final hope exists, *external* to the Hurdanos – who are to an extent ourselves, victims of themselves and of others just as we are. This is to know the world, and its mechanical cunning. To know it is already to be in a position to oppose it; and so, to wish to change it' (Freddy Buache: *Luis Buñuel*).

The intense power of *Las Hurdes* arises from its operation on three quite different and yet integrated planes. It is first a scientific documentary of anthropology and human geography, exploring with perfect scientific discipline the causes of biological sickness and degradation in a race. It is also a subversive surrealist film. Ado Kyrou has vigorously underlined this aspect of the film: 'It is in no way different from *L'Age d'or*. Its realism is the same and so is its Surrealism ... for Buñuel vision is equivalent to adopting a position; and the spectator has no alternative but to do the same ... The dramatic architecture of the film is based on the phrase "Yes, but ..."' That is to say that Buñuel presents to begin with a scene which is insupportable, then throws in some hope, but ends by the destruction of that hope. For example: bread is unknown, *but* from time to time the schoolmaster gives a slice to the children; *but* their parents are frightened of something they do not know and throw the bread away. Or again, the peasants are often bitten by vipers, *but* the bite is never fatal, *but* the peasants make it fatal in trying to cure themselves with herbs that infect the wound. Each sequence is based in this way on these three propositions, and thus the progression into horror attains limits which can only lead to revolt' (in *Luis Buñuel*, 1962). At yet another level *Las Hurdes* operates as tragedy. The tragic nature of man's destiny is glimpsed in *L'Age d'or*, and expressed palpably in *Las Hurdes*. In discussing *Los Olvidados* we shall again stress the meaning of tragedy in its individual and social aspect as it is understood in terms of contemporary materialism.

Eventually Pierre Braunberger decided to take the film for world distribution, and Buñuel added a sound track in Paris. The film achieved a commercial release much wider than simply in *cinémas d'essai*. In Spain its prohibition was ratified by the three Republican governors, including Azaña, as head of the Republic. In the United States the film was initially distributed by the Museum of Modern Art in New York, and afterwards on 16 mm by commercial companies. Today the film stands as a classic of the cinema and is constantly shown all over the world – including Spain. Buñuel has enjoyed no financial profits from his creation.

Buñuel intended to make further documentaries, but in 1933 he was obliged to return to work as a laboratory technician, as if nothing had happened. It was in this year that he first decided to film *Wuthering Heights*. His collaborator on *Las Hurdes*, Pierre Unik, who was eventually to die in a Nazi concentration camp in the U.S.S.R., helped with the adaptation. Georges Sadoul also worked for a night on the script. The choice of *Wuthering Heights* was significant. André Breton and the Surrealist group had adopted the book as one of their banners, along with their liking for the early English

'Gothick' novels. The review *Minotaure* had dedicated many pages to it, with illustrations by the best Surrealist painters of the period – illustrations which had no influence on Buñuel's eventual treatment. The scenario revealed the underlying Surrealist intention alongside an attempt to make a commercial film. It was to have been one of the first essays in popularization since the rupture between Surrealism and the Communist Party. For Buñuel there was the further intention – not a primary one – of converting himself into a director of films whose appeal would not be only to the dilettante. When everything was prepared, however, the project aborted because the studios were destroyed by fire.

In the same year Buñuel married Jeanne Rucar, a tall, dignified and very beautiful woman – a typical Lilloise, and surprisingly like Luis's mother. The following year their first son, Juan Luis was born in Paris, taking the French nationality which he still retains. At the same time Buñuel suffered a severe attack of sciatica from which he continued to suffer until 1940, and which was the origin of his habit of sleeping on a mattress laid on the ground. His marriage was happy. The man who in his work had displayed so violent a temperament and so frank a sexual obsession, enjoyed a private and marital life of model normality.

Sexuality in the work of Buñuel is part of his vision of the determining factors of life; the exaggeration of its importance is only an apparent one. The attitude of Breton and the best Surrealists was generosity, understanding and intelligence in the face of the problems deriving from sexuality. They affirmed the omnipotence of desire, and recognized – in accordance with the discoveries of Freud and his disciples – the determining importance of sexuality in all human activity. Breton and Buñuel alike fearlessly examine sexual aberrations. They see them as explanations of inexplicable phenomena, as clues in the discovery of the foundation of the human being; or at times use them deliberately to provoke mental crisis in the reader or the spectator, whom they force to recognize that the narrow limits of traditional morality are insufficient and lead to a false impression of the world. The Surrealist method of 'scandal for scandal's sake' was not by any means gratuitous.

From the point of view of bourgeois morality, Buñuel's work in the cinema is often scandalous, iconoclastic, full of sexual allusions. But only a fanatic or idiot could see as obscene, passages in which characters find themselves in situations of sado-masochism, fetishism, paranoia, schizophrenia and occasionally homosexuality (discreetly hinted in *Robinson Crusoe*, overtly treated in *Los Olvidados*). On the contrary, this is the manifestation of a spirit of exploration of man and his situation in society, which Buñuel carries to its limits. He has treated in his work, almost exclusively, exceptional human types in whom aspects of brutality, physical or social deformity or other 'disagreeable' attributes, predominate. Literature and art have always sought extreme types and situations for the sake of the discovery of man; Buñuel has honourable models in Shakespeare, the Greek tragic authors, Balzac and Dickens. Nor can we consider him any more morbid than Stroheim, Eisenstein and Kurosawa. He is certainly less so – and a good deal more moral in his intentions – than King Vidor, Lang, Von Sternberg. The personal biography of the man and the record of his works have mysterious concomitants; but they cannot be exactly and literally equated.

7. The Spanish Comedies

Buñuel's activity in the Spanish film industry in the 1930s has been kept secret by all his friends in an admirable conspiracy of silence. Buñuel prefers people not to talk about his Spanish comedies; but in a study of this sort it is not possible to leave aside his 'bad' films. In fact Buñuel's Spanish comedies were no worse than some of the Mexican ones, such as *Cuando los hijos nos juzgan* (*Una mujer sin amor*), made in 1951. Moreover the Spanish experience must be taken into account to provide the clue to a better understanding of the subsequent results of his remarkable compromise with the Mexican cinema, and the extreme speed and efficiency he showed as a commercial director. Nor were these films inconsiderable, particularly taking into account the conditions under which they were made.

In an interview with the Communist magazine *Nuestro Cinema*, in 1935, Buñuel had expressed his wish to work on a 'commercial' film, in the best sense of the word. He was invited to direct the production of the Spanish firm Filmófono, run by an old friend, Ricardo Urgoiti, son of the founder of Spain's most important newspaper *El Sol*. Buñuel accepted.

Urgoiti had established Filmófono as an importation and distribution firm. He hoped to maintain a higher level of material on the national market, thus making a contribution to popular education. He also hoped to make enough money to sustain the enterprise. However, he suffered losses with practically all the foreign films he presented, particularly with the Soviet pictures which he showed for the first time in Spain. He recovered a little of his losses with *Sous les Toits de Paris* and also, to a lesser degree, *Le Million*: but above all with the first Disney Silly Symphonies (*Skeleton Dance* and the rest) and the launching of Mickey Mouse.

To help promote his films Urgoiti decided to establish a cine-club in which he could preview them. He asked Buñuel for his help, and Buñuel accepted delightedly: he had been a founder of the Cineclub Español in 1928, but Giménez Caballero had given it too eclectic a character for Buñuel's taste. With the new cine-club he took his revenge. He gave it a more orthodox basis, politically as well as aesthetically. The club gave *L'Age d'or* its first and only showing in Spain. All Buñuel's friends gave a hand with the screening, F. García Lorca, G. de la Torre and others collecting 300 duros for the hire of the Press Palace and for the customs duties. The Count de Foxá has left a detailed account of the historic screening in his book *Madrid, de Corte a Checa* (1938).

Paradoxically, Urgoiti believed that to produce films would save him from his crisis and help out the distribution business. He counted on producing films that would be very cheap and very commercial, and again asked Buñuel to help. The director looked beyond the immediate dreams and thought that the films might give him the possibility of little by little improving the normal production standards of the country. He knew, through the experience of the *avant-garde* which he so heartily detested, that to make intelligent films for minority audiences does not greatly advance the cinema. He also began to recognize, like a certain section of cultivated Spaniards, that the regeneration of the country would not be achieved through a cultural revolution (as it was believed in the preceding decade) but through an economic revolution; and he set himself to work on realistic bases.

In his autobiography, Buñuel described this period of his life:

'I left Warner Brothers, but only because I began to produce pictures in Spain for my own country and for South America. For this purpose, I entered partnership with a young Spanish financier, Mr Urgoiti, who owned the best chain of theatres in Madrid. I was the anonymous producer of several films made by Filmófono, which was the name of the company. Although it had started, there did not yet exist in Spain the specialized work of the Hollywood studios, and I had to develop directors, writers, etc. The pictures were an economic success, the principal ones being *Don Quintín el amargao, La Hija de Juan Simón, Quién me quiere a mí?, Centinela alerta!* They are nevertheless mediocre if compared from an artistic standpoint with similar American ones, although intellectually and morally they are no worse than those the Hollywood studios produce. Our experiment was going marvellously, when the work was suddenly stopped by the Spanish Civil War on July 18, 1936.'

Buñuel had tacitly imposed one condition: his name should not appear; in the credits of the film, the name of the assistant director would appear as director. Everything was organized in a few months, with a crew of collaborators who were practically unknown. When Buñuel began to produce in the miserable CEA Studios in Madrid, everyone laughed at him, certain that nothing would come from his extravagant working system. He established a daily time-table of eight hours, observed with absolute punctuality, where normally the custom in Spanish films had been to work the whole day during shooting. The players rehearsed in advance. They would repeat their rehearsed reading on the stage, and it would then be filmed. There would be only one take. Everyone had strictly to follow the script (at that time the word was practically unknown). The unit was calm, good-humoured and to all appearances inactive in the studios. Notwithstanding, at the end of a month the film was ready. It was a revolution in Spanish film production. 'Luis was marvellous' Urgoiti has told me; 'and incredibly economical. He counted up every fraction of every minute, every metre of raw film. I had given him a ridiculous budget. I stayed in my office, waiting for him to come and ask for more money. Instead, after three weeks, he came in with the finished film and part of the money I had given him. "Take the change," he said; "Keep it for the next one." '

Other members of the unit have confirmed this. 'Buñuel did everything: contracts, casting, script (in collaboration with Ugarte), rehearsals, lighting, corrections, camera angles and, naturally, direction and editing. We were no more than humble students.' Beltrán, the cameraman, thus confirmed in an interview the activity of Buñuel as the real creative force behind the films of Filmófono.

Buñuel had chosen the technicians among his friends. Almost all confirm the admirable selection, and that Buñuel retained the same group. The director of photography, for instance, José María Beltrán, worked on all the films. Previously he had worked for five years in commercial movies and two with the documentarist Carlos Velo.* Beltrán was later to take a prize at Cannes for his Venezuelan colour film *La balandra Isabel* (1954). The sound experts, Antonio F. Roces and León Lucas de la Peña, also came from Velo's documentary unit and were among the finest Spanish sound technicians. The cutter, Eduardo G. Maroto subsequently made three two-reel 'burlescos' which were the most notable of pre-war Spanish comic shorts. One of the

---

* Velo, like Buñuel and many others, went into exile after the war; and became famous through his Mexican films *Raices* (1955) and *Torero* (1956). *Raices* appears under the signature of Benito Alazraki, though it was in fact made by a Teleproducciones unit under Velo's direction. *Torero*, on the other hand, while credited to Velo, was not a personal work but was partially shot by Hugo Butler, and later completed and edited by Velo.

assistant directors, José Luis Sáenz de Heredia, a cousin of Primo de Rivera, founder of the Fascist Party, became famous subsequently in his own right.

It was Sáenz de Heredia who revealed the paternity of the four Spanish comedies. In an article 'How and Why I Became a Film Director', published in the Madrid magazine *Radiocinema* in 1946, he denied his role as author of the two Filmófono films credited to him, declaring that he could never have been the author of anything so terrible. He related that in 1935 he went to the studios in search of work and was sent to a stage where he met señor Remacha, a friend of Buñuel's and musical director of all the films. Remacha asked him, 'Do you know anything about the job?'

'Very little. I've directed a film, but I don't know much.'

'Good. I'll be frank with you. It is true that we need a director, but more in name than in fact. The man who is really going to make the film is Buñuel.'

'I just want to learn the job, that's all. Dealing with a talent like Buñuel will be all the better.'

'Fine. Let's talk about money. How much do you want?'

'Absolutely nothing.'

'That won't do. We have to save money, but we want to pay everyone. We'll give you 1,500 pesetas.'

For the second film Sáenz de Heredia received 3,000 pesetas. In a later article he asserted that he received respectively 1,000 and 1,500 pesetas, and again insisted that he was not in any way responsible for the quality of the films signed by him. Nevertheless they made him famous, and with the experience acquired on them he went on to become the leading Spanish director of the 1940s. He could hardly complain about the tiny sum of money he received; and subsequently expressed his gratitude to Buñuel: 'I would be untruthful if I did not confess that I took my first lessons from Buñuel.' In a private interview Sáenz de Heredia has praised the efficiency of Buñuel as executive producer, and declared that it was he who directed the films of Filmófono from start to finish.

For his own part, Buñuel has admitted to his work as producer, but not as director: 'Presently I . . . began to make films as a producer. I made four of no interest whose titles I have forgotten . . .'

Don Quintín el amargao

For Filmófono's first film Buñuel decided on a *zarzuela filmada* – a native variety of the operetta film. For a quarter of a century, since the genre was invented by the Aragonese director Segundo de Chomón in 1906, the foolish plots of the *zarzuela* dominated the silent cinema; and the plague only increased with sound. Thus Buñuel settled on a genre which, however dreadful,

103

Don Quintín el amargao: Alfonso Muños and Ana Maria Custodio

was the one traditional form our cinema had produced. If it is considered further that the zarzuela originated in the single proletarian theatre with a tradition of allegory, burlesque, farce, musical interludes, stretching back for centuries, it is clear that a zarzuela by the farce writer Arniches, with popular, crude, even obscene language would attract Buñuel as much as it would horrify the bourgeoisie. (Arniches has also been the inspiration of good Spanish films by Perojo, Neville, Berlanga, Bardem and others.)

Buñuel's adaptation of *Don Quintín el amargao* was not sophisticated. It included almost all the clichés of the zarzuela filmada, the best part of it lying in its details. The story was very much to Buñuel's taste: a man who has grown old in the solitude of a hard life – bitter, brutal, unjust, an exploiter ... but capable of recovering human tenderness if he feels himself loved. Don Quintín throws out his unfaithful wife; as she leaves him she tells him that he is not the father of their little girl, María. He consequently abandons the child, who is brought up by the drunken Nicasio and his wife, along with their own daughter Jovita. Meanwhile Don Quintín, a bitter and disappointed man, becomes the proprietor of a tavern. On her deathbed his wife reveals that in fact María was his child, and he sets out to find her. By this time María has left her adopted parents to run away and marry her lover Paco. Don Quintín hires Jovita as a star, hoping that María will come and see her dance. Don Quintín by chance meets Paco; a quarrel promises to turn into a bloody fight; but in the nick of time Don Quintín learns that Paco is in fact his son-in-law. All is forgiven.

Although the story is developed with all the tricks, coincidences and shameless sentimentality of the Spanish melodrama, the screenplay reveals the hand of an expert adaptor, with an awareness of sophisticated montage possibilities as well as social sensitivity. It is worth quoting one or two extracts from the script, published anonymously in 1936:

14. María sits on a public bench. Near her a workman is eating from his lunch box. She looks at him hungrily
15. Queue of beggars at a soup kitchen. María is the third in line. Everyone except her has a bowl. The man distributing food asks:

    YOUR BOWL?
    I HAVEN'T ONE.
    NO FOOD WITHOUT A BOWL. GET SMART OR DROP DEAD. NEXT!

    The next in line waits
16. María begging in the street
17. Exterior of a night club
18. Dissolve to interior of night club. Gaming room. Clients busy at the tables. The croupier shouts:

    29. RED. NOTHING. NEXT!

In spite of the conventional situations, the comic portrait of the Spanish lower classes is penetrating, and its cinematic treatment is at once dynamic and characteristic of Buñuel as we know him from later work.

43. A road-worker's hut. Nicasio's wife is suckling two babies, one at each breast. Nicasio enters, drunk and singing:

    BURY ME IN A PUB, RIGHT INSIDE A BARREL

    His wife abuses him as she puts the babies into the bed. Travelling shot towards the bed. Close-up of the babies, dissolving very slowly, and changing to a close-up of two eighteen-year-old girls in the same bed (voices, insults). The father proceeds to beat them brutally for having neglected to heat his breakfast potatoes. The girls go out into the yard. They sit at the well, one of them holding a magazine in her hand, and complaining:

Don Quintín el amargao: José María Torres' street set

45.

WHY SHOULDN'T I CRY, SEEING WHAT MY LIFE IS LIKE ...?

The camera moves over the magazine, in which we see a full-page picture of Greta Garbo in a sophisticated pose.

The songs are ingeniously handled. In the stage version of *Don Quintín* they were performed by a non-acting chorus. Buñuel instead invents a device making use of a gramophone and radio:

55. Interior of café ... Saluqui takes the disc from its hiding place and puts it on the gramophone:

(Disc:) DON QUINTÍN IS NO RASCAL ... HE IS NO FOOL ... HE MEANS NO HARM ... THE POOR FELLOW IS JUST EMBITTERED.

56. Some of the customers begin to sing in time with the disc. Among them are two old women, a tramway conductor and his wife who is feeding a baby at her breast, a priest (...) Suddenly one of them sees Don Quintín arriving. (She gives the alarm. Saluqui has not time to remove the record, but turns on the radio in order to drown the sound of the disc. But the radio is playing the same chorus. DON QUINTÍN. This increases the general embarrassment at the point when Don Quintín enters, bringing the sequence to a climax.)

Since the first edition of this book appeared Buñuel has gone so far as to admit that this sequence, at least, is his work.

The ingenuity and accomplishment of the film amazed the critics, who were naturally unaware that its author was Buñuel. It had been advertised as 'a Madrilene burlesque with Hollywood rhythms', and the supposed director was Luis Marquina, son of a mediocre dramatic author. He was in fact director only in name. 'The song sequence is one of the best moments in the history of the Spanish cinema,' exclaimed Antonio Guzmán Merino in a 1935 review. Santiago Aguilar, after visiting the studios the same year, wrote in *Cinegrammas*: 'The street set is the best I have ever seen in the Spanish studios. The designer José María Torres has created a setting worthy of René Clair' (he might more accurately have said worthy of Lazare Meerson, in the 'lyrical realist' style he had created for Clair's sound films). 'The lighting is marvellous . . . faces admirably lit and detail clear even in the backgrounds.'

The praise was merited. The street set was outstanding. There was nothing in itself novel about the staging of the musical numbers (they were sung in the street, on the balconies, terraces and so on; and the camera jumped from one to the other of the singers by montage and other effects, since at that time there were no *moving cranes* in Spain. This kind of invention was already familiar from the work of Clair, Charell and Forst; but for Spain it was revolutionary. While the qualities of the film were surprising for the experts, the audience was able to take them in its stride. The film was excellent, but above all it had the air of being 'normal', even commonplace. The acting was as excessive as was usual in Spanish films of the period, though within its convention quite good, particularly the performance of Alfonso Muñoz – who had been the lead in Margarita Xirgú's stage company – in the title role.

A present-day critic with no prior knowledge of the Spanish cinema of the thirties would rate *Don Quintín el amargao* as a poor film with a brilliant intellect behind it. In Spain the film remains as one of the best *zarzuelas* filmed in the sound period, and Buñuel considers it the best of the four films he made for Filmófono. *Don Quintín el amargao* had a tremendous commercial success in Spain and Spanish America; and in Mexico Buñuel was asked to direct a remake, *La hija del engaño*, made in 1951. Buñuel's description of the film suggests that its quality is comparable to the Spanish version, though with certain technical gains, the organization of the studios and film industry being better in Mexico in 1951 than in Spain in 1935.* Nevertheless *La hija del engaño* appears to be a film of slight importance, shot in eighteen days on a minimal budget. It was never exported outside Spanish America. It is, says its director, 'an amusing film'.

* In fact, apart from changes of Spanish into Mexican slang words, the script and dialogue of the second version is the same as that of the first.

107

La hija de Juan Simón

For Filmófono's second production Buñuel chose the other perennial scourge of the Spanish cinema, the *españolada* – again almost certainly first created by the genius of Segundo de Chomón. If the *zarzuela filmada* was created for home consumption, the *españolada* was primarily directed at the French market; and originated when Chomón was contracted in 1905 to make co-productions for Pathé. The French public was well prepared for a type of romantic folklore pastiche originally created by Beaumarchais and carried to its most absurd limits by Prosper Merimée in his eagerness to create a pro-Spanish atmosphere at the time that Eugenia de Montijo became Empress of the French. What is incomprehensible is that this patently false image of Spain was gladly accepted by the Spanish themselves; so that to this day a large percentage of national cinema production is composed of *españoladas*.

This time, unable actually to dignify an unpardonable genre, Buñuel chose instead to exaggerate it, to accumulate its most awful conventions in order to carry the style to a kind of delirium. The scenario was based on a play which had been produced at the Alcázar Theatre in Madrid, where it was directed by the notable architect Nemesio M. Sobrevila. Urgoiti asked him to adapt the play for the screen.

Sobrevila was himself a film-maker. In 1926 he had made *El Sexto Sentido* (*The Sixth Sense*), the second Spanish *avant-garde* film, and the first of feature length to gain a public showing. Like *Don Quintín* this film had tried to use the conventions of the *zarzuela filmada* – the story-plot, acting style and atmosphere – in such a way as to dignify it by underlying Pirandellian pretensions and a technique borrowed from German Expressionism in the design, lighting and shooting. A sentimental intrigue was constantly interrupted by the appearance of the girl's father,* a magician with a strange machine which he declared to be 'the Sixth Sense' but which was actually a film projector by means of which the protagonists were shown their future on the screen. Though somewhat amateur, the film is interesting and from time to time reveals genuine cinema erudition, as for instance its pastiches of German abstract films.

Sobrevila began to direct, and two of the scenes he completed are the most Buñuelesque in the film, one of them even looking forward to the great final sequence of *Cumbres borrascosas* (*Wuthering Heights*, 1953). The opening scene is the most absurd and the most pseudo-romantic: the scene of the famous popular dance 'The Milonga' which gives the film its title. In a nocturne of exaggerated *flou* (perhaps an ironic reminiscence of Epstein's *Fall*

---

* Played by the painter Ricardo Boneja.

of the House of Usher) we see between the cypresses and jack-o'-lanterns Juan Simón at his macabre work of digging a grave, while the lush voice of Angelillo sings:

> Himself his own daughter
> He brings to the graveyard
> Himself digs the grave
> The while singing a dirge.
> And all the folk ask him:
> 'Whence come you, Juan Simón?'
> 'I am the gravedigger –
> My own heart I bury.'

Lacking experience in the studio, Sobrevila fell a week behind in the shooting. Urgoiti and Remacha begged Buñuel to take over; but he was again suffering from sciatica, and unable to involve himself at the studio. However, after Ugarte had directed a few more scenes, Buñuel agreed to take over. He was paid the same fee as for *Don Quintín el amargao*.

Sobrevila (whom Buñuel says was 'a madman') was resentful and resigned from the picture, though his work as designer remains. Though less good than those of his second and unfinished *avant-garde* film *The Madrilene Hollywood* (1928) – a sketch film which treated the *zarzuela* in futurist, expressionist, Surrealist and other styles – the decors of *La hija de Juan Simón* were outstanding among Spanish film design of the period. In 1936 Sobrevila emigrated to France, where he was assistant on *The Lost Division*, a feature directed and photographed for MGM by the Filmófono photographer Beltrán, which remained unfinished.

It was at this point that José Luis Sáenz de Heredia was taken on as nominal director. He had already directed a film, *Patricio miró a una estrella* (1934) with Antonio Vico; and despite the wretched resources available to him, had succeeded in making a film whose dynamism and intelligence already presaged the accomplishment of his best comedy, *El destino se disculpa* (1941).

The unit was the same as for *Don Quintín el amargao*; and an adequate cast was headed by Ana María Custodio. The male lead was Angelillo, a Communist flamenco singer. Buñuel was amused by his exaggerated interpretations of the songs and by his pretensions. An interviewer for the review *Films Selectos* (26 October 1936) visited Angelillo in his home and noted: 'I read the titles of Angelillo's record library and was astonished. There were Chinese, Japanese, Russian, Arabic records, Berlin-published liturgical music and many North American songs.' 'Yes,' Angelillo told him casually, 'Russian airs and liturgical music are inexhaustible founts of flamenco phrases.'

Another of Buñuel's discoveries for the film was an adolescent gypsy girl, incredibly thin and with nerves of steel. She was at that time dancing at nights on the tables of the Paralelo in Barcelona, performing with astounding vitality something which she alleged was flamenco dancing. Buñuel, in asking her to exaggerate a style that was already in itself an exaggeration, laid the foundations of the dancer Carmen Amaya, later famous. In his opinion, the sequence of her dance in the film is the best thing in all his work at Filmófono.

The whole film has the same malice in relation to the *españolada*. Enrique Herreros, who worked as Filmófono's head of publicity (later, after a brief career as a designer he became a brilliant cartoonist in a vein comparable to that of Charles Addams) has given some details about the film and its making: 'Even if filmgoers don't recognize it, the Surrealist spirit and Buñuel's own black humour are everywhere in the film. I remember that for a scene involving an accident Buñuel asked me to get a car, which had to be a 1932 Hudson. When I couldn't find one, Buñuel shifted the scene to the end of shooting, to give me another month to search for the car. Finally I found the great ostentatious machine with its flower vases and fancy handles; and we took it to the steepest and most arid spot in the Madrid mountains. He filled the car with actors playing rich people, and threw it over a precipice at a bend. (Not with the actors still actually in it, of course; it only looked that way!) A motor accident was *de rigueur* in every melodrama of the period; but *this* accident, as it was filmed, had the unmistakable cruelty of Buñuel.'

The story was typical of the *españolada* melodrama of the period. Some revelling gentlemen come to a village, and make a deep impression upon the heroine, who makes up her mind to leave the place and go to Madrid. Angelillo, a young man who is in love with her, follows. On the road he meets Carmen Amaya, dancing in an Andalusian inn. Carmen encourages him to become a flamenco singer. He follows her advice and wins a contest. Meanwhile the heroine has found work in a tavern, just managing not to stray from the strait and narrow, until a gentleman dishonours her. She has a child. An acquaintance tells Angelillo that she has died. He sings, 'Oh Carmela, my anguish is so great ...!' Carmela, in fact still alive, but now a prostitute, goes to a theatre to hear her old sweetheart who is now a celebrated flamenco performer. The star, all in black, stands on the stage with the heel of his shoe resting on the little stool which guitarists use for this purpose:

> Like that Magdalene
> Redeemed by Jesus –
> So good were you,
> Carmela of my heart.

La hija de Juan Simón: Angelillo

> The dastardly world
> One day forces you to sin
> And having thus injured you,
> This same world reviles you.

As he begins to sing, the camera draws back to the seat where the girl is sitting, framing it in the foreground with the stage and the singer – like a little insect – in the background. Laden with jewels, she weeps and nods her head, as if saying, 'How true!' The song reveals to her that he still desires her; and she rushes to be reunited with him. Her sweetheart pardons her and they all live happily ever after, not forgetting the illegitimate child.

Among other notable episodes is one in which Angelillo is imprisoned. In a corridor with cells on either side, he sings accompanied by the other prisoners. The image jumps from one to the other in the operetta convention. Angelillo sings:

> I am a little bird, born to sing –
> And so I beg my liberty.

Another voice, talking, replies: 'Will the fugitive be so kind as not to protest

La hija de Juan Simón: Angelillo singing 'I am a little bird . . .'

further?' Behind, on the walls of the cells are drawings of hammers and sickles, and political slogans directed against Azaña, the socialist minister who banned *Land Without Bread*.

Herreros advertised the film with the slogan '*La hija de Juan Simón* is like the music of de Falla or the Gypsy Romances of García Lorca – the triumph of the popular roots of culture.' The phrase was outrageous, although as we have seen there was an element of truth in it which the educated public did not by any means guess at. The 'sophisticated' public saw in the film only bad taste, when in reality it was a case of an intellectual stylization of bad taste, charged with invention and humour. Only Buñuel, in fact, could have plumbed such extravagant depths of vulgarity. Generally the critics received it very badly, though a few, without perceiving its ultimate intention, recognized its professional level. Certainly, however, no one for a moment regarded it as a sophisticated or intellectual film, even though it offended the middle classes and delighted the ordinary people in the way that the most authentic Buñuel films always do.

La hija de Juan Simón had an even bigger commercial success than *Don Quintín el amargao*. Sales of the music alone paid for the film, and the profits

La hija de Juan Simón: Angelillo and Pilar Muñoz

were abundant. It was still being shown, along with other Filmófono pictures, after the Civil War. All the films enjoyed success in Spanish America. In Spain there was even a cartoon parody with the same title, *La hija de Juan Simón*; and as late as 1958 there was an execrable remake, directed by Gonzalo Delgras, with Antonio Molina and María Cuadra.

Quién me quiere a mí?
Filmófono's third production was to have been another *zarzuela filmada* after Arniches, *La alegría del batallón*, but various circumstances required its postponement; and to fill the gap the company made *Quién me quiere a mí?* Having proved his ability in *La hija de Juan Simón*, Sáenz de Heredia was, he says, given almost complete control, with only superficial supervision by Buñuel. The film was the worst of the group, a commercially successful melodrama on a topic of current controversy, divorce, which had recently been permitted in Spain. The theme could have been important, had it been handled with more seriousness. Lina Yegros and other fashionable actors of the day went through their accustomed routines. The child of the broken marriage who has to suffer the consequences of the rupture was played by a girl who had just won a radio contest and was publicized by Herreros as 'the

113

Spanish Shirley Temple'. In fact the consequences of the family break-up did not go much further in the film than having the father feed his baby from a bottle. (Buñuel recalls with great amusement a treasured moment in *Don Quintín el amargao* also involving a baby's bottle. Don Quintin, appalled to find he has nearly killed his daughter in ignorance of her identity, weeps, leaning against a street door. A little girl passes and asks why he is crying; 'My mammy says that men who cry cannot be bad,' she says, holding up an enormous, phallic bottle.).

Centinela alerta!

With *Quién me quiere a mí?* finished in three weeks, shooting of the Arniches subject began in February 1936. Although the main reason for the choice was the popularity of the *zarzuela*, Arniches was a writer not unsympathetic to Buñuel, who will often describe some situation as 'farcical enough for Arniches'. (Another of his favourite expressions is 'good as barracks bread'.) Buñuel and Ugarte paid more attention to the scenario of this film, giving it a continuity, bizarre situations and well-defined characters, even if the treatment can hardly claim profundity. It is in the tradition of *zarzuela* and also of a type of French film farce seen at its best in Renoir's *Tire au flanc*, which also carried a discreetly anti-militarist message. Here the anti-militarism is not as violent as might be looked for from Buñuel, being limited to ridicule of the characters and an invitation not to take military glories too seriously. The atmosphere of the barracks, the smaller details of military life, the self-important soldiers and the peasant soldiery were well explored for the purposes of comedy. The cast this time was good, with Angelillo appreciably more disciplined as an actor and given good songs, and the playing of Luis Heredia notable.

Although Buñuel prefers *Don Quintín* and projects it frequently in his home in Mexico (he has 16 mm copies of all four Spanish comedies), *Centinela alerta!* was the best of Filmófono's four productions. Urgoiti considers that it could be regarded as 'good not only in the national context, but in terms of contemporary European production in general'.

Buñuel collaborated on the scenario, and discharged his duties as head of production, but was in no way responsible for the direction, except for some scenes shot in the last days, when the director Jean Grémillon fell ill. (He and Urgoiti also lent their voices to the film, dubbing two peasants who make obscene remarks when they see a naked woman emerging from the river).

The friendship of Buñuel and Grémillon dated from Paris days. Grémillon, having suffered political difficulties in France on account of his adherence to Communism, emigrated to Berlin in 1932, and the following year to Spain. Here he had made the excellent *La Dolorosa*, in an Aragonese setting, before

Buñuel entrusted him with the direction of *Centinela alerta!*, for a fee of 15,000 pesetas. Knowing that the production was not at the level of his reputation (Grémillon, who loved Spain and understood its sensibility and culture, was already considered an exceptional director), Buñuel and he decided to omit his name from the credits. The film consequently appeared without a director credit, announced simply as 'Producción Filmófono número 4'.

I talked to Grémillon (in a café on the Quai de la Seine, a little before his death in 1959) about this collaboration, and he confirmed the qualities of Buñuel as a production chief. Like Buñuel he also felt a little ashamed of the Filmófono rut. He praised the work of Daniel Montorio on the music of the film (the director was himself a good composer; and Remacha, a friend of Buñuel and himself, was a noted mediaeval musicologist and later became director of the Pamplona Conservatoire). Grémillon's hand is identifiable in certain scenes, especially the exteriors which are treated with a characteristic realist lyricism: among them the nocturnal *verbena* (saint's day vigil), shot like other scenes in little villages outside Madrid which the cinema has only recently rediscovered, is especially good.

The film was shown at the Avenida Cinema in Madrid in August 1936, after the outbreak of war. Despite its undisciplined levity, it was not prevented from being shown in the Republican zone.

Grémillon recalled that he and Buñuel set about reworking the script of *Wuthering Heights*. Among other ideas in Buñuel's mind at this time was a project for adapting literary works such as *Tirano Banderas* by Valle Inclán, another inspired by an episode in Pío Baroja's trilogy *La lucha por la vida* about the *bas fonds* of Madrid (certainly a precursor of *Los Olvidados*) and so on. He already had Galdós' *Fortunata y Jacinta** ready for immediate production. The Filmófono programme announced sixteen films for 1936–37.

All went before the wind. The war wrecked the immediate future of Buñuel and Grémillon, as it destroyed so many other things and left the careers of so many artists in suspense. Grémillon had had plans for settling permanently in Madrid and working in the Spanish cinema. With the bombardment, Buñuel managed to overcome his resistance and made him take a plane to Paris in July 1936. Thus ended the projects of Filmófono; and with them a brief era of hope for the Spanish cinema.

---

* The book was recently filmed by Angelino Fons.

8. Documentary

Buñuel's first three films form a triptych, a progressive exposition of his Surrealist ideology and a Surrealist language. They thus also represent a progressive approach to documentary. *Un Chien andalou* defines the object, reveals a passion for the study of things, their position, their sense, their disorientation, clearly declaring the realism that he has never abandoned. *L'Age d'or* applies this definition and language to a denunciation of the contemporary world. The third film, *Las Hurdes – Tierra sin pan*, applies them to a particular instance, defined concretely in space and in time. The evolution towards pure documentary is apparent.

In his second creative stage Buñuel was making commercial films, melodramas and comedies. Yet he continued to use the cinema to document our times for proletarian use. When we examine his filmography, we find few works which do not constitute a study of some determined human situation in relation to the material circumstances which condition it. *El* is an example. The psychiatric study of the protagonist, who to a certain degree derives from the hero of *L'Age d'or*, is continued in *La vida criminal de Archibaldo de la Cruz*, who presents another variation of the obsessions which result from an Oedipus complex and the bourgeois education. Robinson Crusoe in Buñuel's version is another facet of the situation – though in this case it is the father who appears as its root cause, when he is seen in Robinson's dream, reproaching his son's conduct and his rejection of 'the golden mean' of family comfort. (The father appears cleaning the back of a pig with a brush.) Far from being a story for children, *Robinson Crusoe* is a systematic study of human loneliness, its psychological and physiological consequences (madness, sexual frustration, homosexuality), as well as of the relations between men who represent two races, two civilizations, two moralities. *Los Olvidados* could almost be taken as a documentary on the abandoned children of the poor quarters. A melodrama as apparently ridiculous and disjointed as *Susana* discusses the principles on which the moral and material order of land-ownership is based, and how it can be disintegrated by a catalyst from outside. *Cela s'appelle l'Aurore, La Mort en ce jardin* and *La Fièvre monte à El Pao* together constitute another trilogy which studies in a very documentary manner contemporary political processes in Spanish America, in their social and revolutionary aspect. *Nazarín* is a serious examination of religious faith carried to its ultimate consequences, another aspect – also certainly pathological – of individual psychology. *Viridiana* and *Belle de Jour* continue these investigations, though in the female variant and in different circumstances. *The Young One* contrasts the different types of relationship which a girl establishes in the crisis of puberty with three men who present the conflict of virility, race and religion. Buñuel's is a psychological cinema above all.

'I am only interested in human relations,' he told me recently. But as we have seen, in order to enter into such relations it is necessary to know the surrounding circumstances; and in every film Buñuel introduces large sections of pure documentary, in the strict sense that the word has acquired in relation to the cinema. In order to understand the relationships of *El Bruto*, Buñuel gives an extended and minute description of the hero's work in a slaughterhouse (a cruel and bloody vision which certainly inspired Georges Franju's documentary *Le Sang des bêtes*). In order to understand the passion of the protagonists in *Cumbres borrascosas* (*Wuthering Heights*), he recreates the landscapes, the background of customs and incidents of Emily Brontë's novel, transposing it to the Mexican countryside. He also likes to introduce passages of documentary of much more oblique relevance: in *L'Age d'or* the newsreel shots of Imperial Rome are simply Surrealist *trompe-l'oeil*, while the documentary prologue on scorpions serves as a parallel metaphor. In *El* there is a sequence showing work in a mineral excavation site; and in *La Mort en ce jardin* the initial sequence shows gold prospectors at work. *Subida al cielo* provides the pretext for an exhibition of authentic Mexican folk customs; and the panorama is filled out by *El río y la muerte*, particularly in the funeral rituals (which had earlier delighted Eisenstein, in

Que Viva Mexico!) which are given their philosophical–anthropological interpretation.

Buñuel's work as a documentarist is the least studied area of his career. He himself does not like to talk about it; and in any case his memory cannot be so clear about his work – albeit immense – on so many anonymous films, as about his major works:

'When the civil war broke out, I stopped all cinematographic work and I placed myself at the disposal of the government. This sent me to Paris as attaché to the Spanish Embassy in that capital. In 1938, about eight months ago, I arrived in the U.S.A. with a diplomatic mission, and here I was surprised by the end of the war. As I could legally remain in the United States, I plan to stay here indefinitely, intensely attracted by the American naturalness and sociability.'

There the autobiography ends, though Buñuel added a few paragraphs, which are reproduced later, on his idea of documentary. The *Cahiers* interview continues the story:

'Then came the war in Spain. I thought the world was coming to an end, and that I had to think of better things than making films. I put myself at the service of the Republican government in Paris, who sent me in 1938 to Hollywood on a "diplomatic mission" to supervise, as technical adviser, two films which were to be made on the Spanish Republic. There I was taken by surprise by the end of the war, and found myself completely abandoned and without work in America. Thanks to Miss Iris Barry I obtained a job at the Museum of Modern Art. I thought that I would do great things, but it turned out to be a bureaucratic job. I had fifteen or twenty people under me. I was engaged in making versions for Latin America. I stayed there for four years.'

At the beginning of the war, Buñuel was mobilized to the service of the cinema, along with the other Spanish film-makers, regardless of their political ideas. The impetus this gave to national documentary film-making has still to be properly evaluated. All the Spanish cinéastes were engaged in documentary; and several of the productions on which foreign film-makers collaborated with Spanish artists and technicians have become classics. Buñuel recalls that he was concerned with the preservation of many films; and among others that passed through his hands was *Spanish Earth*, by Ernest Hemingway and Joris Ivens. Ivens has described his first meeting with Buñuel: 'I first met Buñuel in 1932. I had seen *L'Age d'or* which interested me a lot. I found out the address of the young director, went to his house, rang the bell and said, "I'm Ivens." That's the way I behave. At first I thought we were not going to have much in common, with his Surrealist antecedents. But no. Though our ideological positions did not appear to coincide, we found ourselves very close in conversation, and we became friends. Buñuel seems to me a man of the cinema *par excellence.* Others, one thinks, are intellectuals and artists who might have done other work. Not Buñuel. He is all cinema in his way of thinking and seeing. Although he likes to fool around and do never mind what, he is absolutely dedicated to the cinema. It is clear in his work. Good cinema, honest cinema. I met him again in Paris in those dangerous days when to make documentaries was to be a soldier in the front line; and he helped me to get safe conducts for Madrid. I could write a book on the events of these times and how much the foreigners helped me (Roman Karmen, for instance, who was shooting the basic material of his subsequent film *España*, helped me to repair my camera). Buñuel also was always helpful.'

For his part, Buñuel did not reciprocate admiration as far as all Ivens' work was concerned. Some of it seemed to him to be monotonous and of little significance from the point of view of aesthetics or content. *Spanish Earth* is one of the few which he finds interesting.

This and other evidence shows how busy Buñuel was during the conflict, gathering together film material in order to compose it into definitive compilations in Madrid and abroad. Part of the anonymous material was shot by Buñuel himself. Although meagre, there are some references to this period. Thus Henry Miller in *The Cosmological Eye* wrote: 'Buñuel seems to have been lost from view. There are rumours that he is to be found in Spain where he is quietly putting together a collection of documentaries on the revolution. Whatever may be, if Buñuel retains something of his old vigour, it promises to turn out very well . . .'

Buñuel was sent by the government to Paris in 1936 to occupy himself with the material; and was entrusted with editing a full-length film out of news footage of the war. In his office near la Madeleine he completed a four-reel compilation (he himself remembers it as being in eight reels; so perhaps it was subsequently shortened): *España 1936* or *España leal, en armas!*, a co-production with the French Communist Party. Accounts of Buñuel's role are contradictory. According to him, it was no more than a simple labour of editing together some news material of an informative character, done by Jean-Paul le Chanois under his supervision at the selection, montage and recording stages. In a letter he has said: 'It is false how much is attributed to me in relation to *España leal, en armas!* I was only involved in this film as an Embassy employee . . . I was concerned with material shot in Spain, and I commissioned a compilation film whose title I do not remember.'

Others are convinced of Buñuel's dominant role, and regard the compilation as a very personal creation in which none of the elements of the Buñuel world are absent. Fernández Cuenca, director of the Filmoteca Nacional Española which has a copy of the 9-reel version, says that the film was shown in Madrid with Buñuel credited as director, and cites such a

España leal, en armas!: the first victory of the Republic

characteristic Buñuel montage as a religious procession of suppliants to the Virgin, asking for rain, which cuts to a proletarian march demanding from the People's Commissar the construction of a dyke for the artificial irrigation of the fields. Another characteristic detail is the sequence of the sacking of churches in Barcelona, accompanied by a bland commentary which points out that 'the sculptures we are looking at are true works of art. It is possible that this one is a Montañés.' *

Despite his evasiveness ('*Don Quintín el amargao* is more mine than this film') a documentary of this sort must have attracted him. Knowing his meticulous nature, his infectious creative energy and his 'scholarly despotism' when supervising a production, and on the other hand reading his declarations about the profound effect which the conflict within his country made upon him, it is impossible to doubt that his supervision of the film was something more than a bureaucratic job. Recently Buñuel has recalled an incident in which he was not directly concerned: in 1938 his co-director and the co-author of the commentary both of this film and of *Las Hurdes*, Pierre

---

* The name of a famous Andalusian baroque sculptor. The intention of the sentence becomes more apparent if one is acquainted with the collective Surrealist text '*Au Feu!*', on the burning of churches in Spain in 1931 (in *Le Surréalisme au service de la Révolution*).

Unik, disputed Jean-Paul le Chanois's claims to author's rights in the work, before the Paris union tribunals. The decision was in favour of Unik, which officially confirms the creative supremacy of the Buñuel–Unik team over the honest but essentially journeyman work of le Chanois.*

The documentary opens with a shot which inevitably recalls an early sequence in *October*: the equestrian statue of Philip IV in the Royal Square in Madrid turns upon itself (the effect is achieved by moving the camera around it). A similar image was used by Eisenstein, also to symbolize the fall of a monarchy. The years of the Republic pass across the screen like a rhythmic montage of shot sequences: the elections of 1931, the social disorders, workers' demonstrations and the Popular Front, military parades, the Civil Guard, falangists and boys of the 'Arrow Brigades', shots of the government at work, of agrarian reforms, until the elections of 1936 in which for the first time women voted, with shots of citizens, priests and nuns voting, and the atmosphere becomes always more tense until the outbreak of hostilities.

Without falling into the clichés of war documentary, the central part of the film, with its energetic commentary, shows scenes of the war derived from the archives of both sides; continues with a montage of contrasts, with abrupt juxtapositions between shots of the battles and others from behind the lines: the siege of Madrid, the queues for food, the frantic work in the factories and fields, the devastation from the bombardment; and suddenly, political scenes from abroad which illustrate the relation of the great powers with the Spanish conflict. We return to shots of the debris, and those terrible images of women with their dead children (just as in *Las Hurdes*), mute as stones; close-ups of the corpses of girls, with their open wounds and their sexual parts, symbolizing the extinguished spring of life, and all the bloody process, ending with the collapse and the final shot of a woman rising up with a symbolic flag.

'The film, always sustained by highly dramatic images, ends in an atmosphere of tragedy. Without rhetoric, Buñuel has created thirty-five minutes of true political cinema. The images speak in a sparse and economical language, documenting the indifference of the (foreign) powers and the heroism and suffering of the Spanish people. Buñuel has said: "I want the cinema to be a witness, a reflection of the world, and to say all that is important in reality." With *España 36* he undoubtedly remains loyal to his own theoretical premises,' comments the Italian critic Corrado Morgia.

This film reveals an originality of conception comparable to that of *Las Hurdes*, or – within its formula of documentary fiction – *Los Olvidados*. It

---

* Le Chanois is credited as cutter. When asked if he did not himself supervise the cutting, since he had claimed hardly to have worked on the film, he replied: 'I am not as frivolous as that! I supervised it three times: the raw material, the mute cut and the final one with sound.'

excites the reaction of the spectator in the same subversive way by counter-pointing images of tragedy and a tone of remoteness. It is the antithesis of any vulgar notion of political propagandist cinema. Underlining the despair, con-cealing none of the seriousness of the facts, eliminating any easy philo-sophy of optimism, Buñuel and Unik achieve through their awesome images and tense montage much more than mere slogans, mere documentation.

España leal, en armas! was thought to be lost until it was rediscovered in 1966 by the historian Jay Leyda in the Staatliches Filmarchiv of East Berlin. After a thorough study Leyda reported to us, in 1967: 'The film consists of four reels (some forty minutes) and I have found both the Spanish and the French versions. The editing is the same in both, and perhaps the commen-tary too. But the music is quite different. The French version uses almost exclusively discs of the 7th and 8th Symphonies of Beethoven, in very much the way Brahms' Fourth Symphony is used in *Las Hurdes*. The music of the Spanish version is more mixed and less organized – someone other than Buñuel must have done the editing of these discs. There are no credits at the beginning of either version, and the title of the film also is missing from the Spanish version; but Buñuel has written to me that le Chanois (then called Jean-Paul Dreyfus) did the montage while Buñuel was producer (Chief of Production), supervisor and co-author of the commentary. Clearly it is more his film than le Chanois', who certainly was not its "director". Most of the actuality footage used in it is unknown to me (as to other people who have seen it) and the incidents shown in it, which start with the outgoing of the King, do not seem to go beyond the beginning of 1937. I do not believe that either photographs or frame enlargements would give any idea of the film, but would only look like news film in the worst sense . . .' *

In 1938 Buñuel was in Hollywood. There he was engaged to supervise two films about the Spanish war. One of them, *Cargo of Innocence*, about refugee children from bombed Bilbao being shipped to the U.S.S.R., was started by Metro-Goldwyn-Mayer but abandoned because of the turn of events in Spain. Consequently he found himself in New York without work. He had the good fortune to meet Iris Barry of the Museum of Modern Art Film Department, who not only offered him work, but gave him hospitality in her home; and a great friendship grew out of this contact.† From 1939 to 1941 he worked at the Museum. Characteristically he says that his job was 'purely bureaucratic'; but the composer Gustavo Pittaluga, one of the distinguished artists under his command in the Spanish section, has said, 'Buñuel should not be so modest about his secondary works, and ignore his activities at the Museum of

---

* The rediscovered film was first shown publicly in Vienna in April 1969 as part of a retrospective of Buñuel's films presented by the Austrian national film archive.

† Charles Laughton and his wife Elsa Lanchester were also at the Museum for a while.

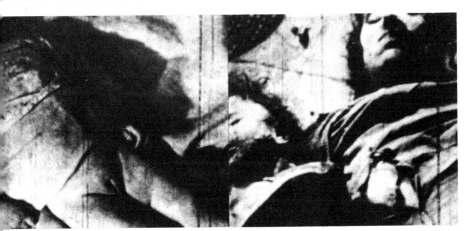

España leal, en armas!: the elections of 1936; parade of fascist children; dead children after the bombardment of Madrid; banner of the Republic; fall of Madrid

Modern Art. The fact is that Luis created maybe 2,000 remarkable works. We were sent anodyne documentaries, often extremely feeble primary materials, which the Museum team turned into marvellous films. And not just Spanish versions, but also Portuguese, French and English. Through his reconstruction of the material, cutting or extending scenes, creating dialogue and sound track, he would *create* a good documentary through editing.' Pittaluga, a friend of Buñuel, is expansive and inclined to speak in hyperbole; but I am more persuaded by his opinion than by Buñuel's excessive modesty. Iris Barry, for many years director of the Museum's Film Department and to a large extent influential on the notable expansion of American documentary in those years, confirmed Pittaluga's view. Even so, extensive research over several years has failed to reveal the titles of films of this period identifiable as Buñuel's own work; essentially he operated as part of a team.

His commission was to choose documentaries suitable for South America, and afterwards to supervise the dubbing, re-editing, commentary and music. One instance was a British documentary, produced by John Grierson, *High Over the Border*. Buñuel's is not one of the dozen great names of the cinema that appear on the credits, though Iris Barry, Pittaluga and others have assured me that this beautiful film in the form that it emerged from the Museum's documentary centre, owes something to him. Buñuel remembers the film very well, but insists that his work consisted only in arranging the Spanish version. (The original director of the film, John Fernhoult (Ferno) confirms that Buñuel's contribution was all made in the laboratory.) In a letter from the Museum of Modern Art, Lothar Wolff, chief editor of the series, bears witness to 'the admirable work of Luis Buñuel in the elaboration of the Spanish American version' of another film, *El Vaticano de Pio XII*, the second part of an extraordinary four-part film, *The History of the Vatican*, in Louis de Rochemont's *March of Time* series. In the course of the film we see the Pope bang his fist with all his might on his despatch table.

Buñuel will claim only one work of montage as his personal creation. 'I made a film, *Triumph of the Will*. For this I reduced the original twelve reels of Leni Riefenstahl's 1933 film *Triumph of the Will*, plus the other twelve of *Baptism of Fire*' ('What a dreadful title!' Buñuel adds; the phrase cannot fail to shock a Surrealist sensibility). Riefenstahl's film on the Nuremberg Rally with its Nazi speeches, though it aimed to be a work of Hitlerian propaganda, was in the outcome a terrible indictment of Germany and the criminal fanatics who ruled it. *Baptism of Fire*, a long actuality compilation showing the systematic *Vernichtung* (a scientific process of destruction and massacre) of Poland in 1939, was designed to be shown to European countries as a nakedly brutal warning of what would happen if they did not show themselves sympathetic to Hitler. It was assembled in 1939 by Hans Bertram.

'Although I shortened most of the material, I left nine uninterrupted minutes of soldiers marching in goose-step. In making a parallel montage between the two films I showed what Nazi propaganda promised and what the Nazis actually did, a few years later. My film was intended for the Congress in Washington, who had at that time no idea what political propaganda for the cinema was like. I think it was very important for them, although it never had any public showing.'

Either directly or indirectly linked to the documentary group at the Museum were people like Robert Flaherty, Willard Van Dyke, Pare Lorenz, John Fernhoult (Ferno), Joris Ivens, John Grierson, Josef von Sternberg, and Jay Leyda; later Frank Capra, John Ford, John Huston, William Wyler and other Hollywood directors were to be mobilized to war service in documentary. The movement created around the Museum, linked with – but independent of – a more official governmental department existing in New York, constituted a deployment of culture and art to the service of a social and political end without parallel in the story of the American cinema and – save for the Soviet school – in the whole of world cinema. Georges Sadoul, the French historian, considered the American documentary of this period as more valuable and significant than the British documentary school of the thirties. Its full story has still to be written; when it is, it will no doubt reveal the political intrigue and the obscurantism relating to a proto-McCarthyist attitude which grew up after Roosevelt's death in 1944 and reached its apogee after the war ended, and which led to the destruction of this remarkable cultural movement.

I have received very reserved replies from people I have questioned about these events. Forty employees left the Museum on account of their political beliefs. The Museum of Modern Art is supported by a subvention from the Rockefeller Foundation; and the Film Department was constituted by the 'Film Officers for the Rockefeller Committee on Panamerican affairs'. The expulsion was not a mass affair; people left one by one, at different junctures, over the course of a year, as they were denounced. Buñuel gave his own explanation of his dismissal in the *Cahiers* interview:

BUÑUEL: In 1942 I was obliged to resign because I was the author of *L'Age d'or*. Miss Iris Barry accepted my resignation with tears in her eyes. It was the day of Mers-el-Kebir; the atmosphere was dramatic. Journalists came to see me but I refused to give any interviews. It seemed to me that at this moment it was not important whether Mr Buñuel was in or out of the Museum. Still I was very sad, penniless, and spent the following months as best as I could manage . . .

DONIOL-VALCROZE: Did your leaving the Museum have a direct relation to

Dalí's book? It was through him that it was discovered that you had made *L'Age d'or*?

BUÑUEL: Yes.

The explanation of Buñuel's dismissal does not seem to have been merely his association with *L'Age d'or*, however. In fact the Rockefeller Trustees seem to have been alarmed by Dalí's information that Buñuel was a member of the French Communist Party. This *had* in fact been true. In 1926–27, when *La Révolution Surréaliste* changed its title to *Le Surréalisme au service de la Révolution*, the main Surrealist group declared their adherence to Communism and loyally paid up their subscriptions. In 1933, after seeing the Soviet film *The Road to Life* (directed by Nikolai Ekk) with its antipathetic moral of regeneration through labour, there was a profound schism between those who remained Surrealists but not Communists, and those who remained Communists but not officially Surrealists. The second group included Breton and Buñuel. Buñuel's subscription to the Communist Party lapsed after he came to America in 1937.

Recently (1972) a reliable and privileged member of the Museum staff has recalled, 'One day Iris came into the restaurant in a terrible state, almost in tears. She had just been visited in her office by the Archbishop of New York, the future Cardinal Spellman, who accused her angrily: "Are you aware that you are harbouring in this Museum the Antichrist, the man who made a blasphemous film *L'Age d'or*?" He threatened the most dreadful consequences unless Buñuel was removed, and left Iris no alternative at all but to ask for his resignation.'

Buñuel again returned to Hollywood, perhaps hopefully taking with him some of his scripts, such as *La duquesa de Alba*. But in those critical times all doors were closed. The old friendships of 1930 were of little service, since most of the people he had known had left a Hollywood which had lost its freedom and inspiration. According to Jay Leyda, he found Los Angeles a much more ugly and detestable city than New York, which had its fascination, and where he could live modestly but in a stimulating intellectual atmosphere. At this time he relied on some small financial help from his mother; and he sold some gags to Chaplin, who was preparing *The Great Dictator*.

The entry of the United States into the war briefly provided him with the job of commentator on some army documentaries.

'I spoke in my "beautiful voice" for fifteen or twenty films about explosives, aeroplane parts and so on ... for Spanish versions.'

But the idea of realizing personal works was not far from his mind. Like many others of his New York colleagues he wanted to make documentaries; and the autobiography which we have quoted was primarily a 'curriculum vitae' presented to solicit the Museum to give him the chance to do just this. We can only guess what the results would have been had he been given his opportunity:

'MY PRESENT PLANS

'I have already said that my cinematographic activities were completely interrupted by the Spanish conflict, and it has been exactly three years since I have practised my profession. Both because of a spiritual, as well as a material urge, I must return to work, the latter reason emphasized by the fact that I am married and have a son.*

'One of the avenues suggested to me is to look for a position in the Hollywood cinematography, a thing, if not impossible, at least difficult in view of present conditions in the industry.

'Another field is independent production. And I call it independent in the artistic sense, as the so-called independent productions here are perhaps more dependent than the others on commercial routine and demands. Well and good: this type of independent film to which I refer has disappeared almost completely because of the great cost of production.

'I believe that the most interesting experiments which are made today are to be found in documental films, which are in reality the successors to the aforementioned "independent productions".

'To my mind there exist two different types of documental films: one which can be called DESCRIPTIVE, and in which the material is limited to the transcription of a natural or social phenomenon. For example: industrial manufacture, the construction of a road or the operations of some aviation line, etc. Another type, much less frequent, is one which, while both descriptive and objective, tries to interpret reality. It can, for this reason, appeal to the artistic emotions of the spectator and express love, sorrow and humour. Such a documental film is much more complete, because, besides illustrating, it is moving.

'Although there are themes which lend themselves more readily than others to such a purpose, none are excluded *a priori* from this emotional possibility. The banal action of building a road or showing a new aviation line to which we referred before, can, according to its interpretation, become dramatic, comic or subversive.

'Documental films generally bore a public, not versed in that understanding. More material than necessary is used to bring out details whose value is solely visual or dynamic. The great majority of documental films lack psychological value.

'Thus beside the DESCRIPTIVE documental film, is the PSYCHOLOGICAL one.

'I should like the making of documental films of a psychological nature. I have a plan, which I shall now put forth, but the uncertainty of not knowing whether it could ever be financed kept me from greatly elaborating my ideas which require much preparation before they can be transferred to the screen. Even though it may not be mine, I am enthusiastic about the realization of any idea pertaining to this type of film.'

* This was written in 1939; a second son, Raphael, was born in New York in 1940; he remains an American citizen.

9. The Dark Times

'After this,' Buñuel told *Cahiers du Cinéma*, 'I was taken to Hollywood by Warner Brothers, who had an idea for the production of Spanish versions. I warned them that I was lazy, but that when I worked I worked well. I was hired as a producer, and well paid, but this production of Spanish versions never got under way, and once again I was employed as a dubbing expert. I spent two years in Hollywood from 1944 to 1946.'

During this period, too, he strove to make films of his own. He apparently suggested that they let him direct a gangster film. Later Buñuel provided some ideas for a horror film that was being prepared – *The Beast with Five Fingers*, directed by Robert Florey with Peter Lorre in the leading role. The producer entrusted Buñuel with the sequence of the hallucinating dream; but it was rejected from the script as being too strong. However in the final shooting Florey retained some of Buñuel's original images alongside the others. What might have been just a routine horror picture attracted the attention of observant French critics who were unaware of Buñuel's collaboration on the film. In particular the Surrealist group (in *L'Age du cinéma*, etc.) acclaimed it as one of the most interesting films to have come out of Hollywood in those years, particularly for the sequence – certainly Buñuel's – of the severed hand which approaches Lorre in his office, menacing him and forcing him to certain acts. Although vaguely recalling *The Hands of Orlac*, this hand goes much further than the expressionist film, and becomes a hallucinatory and onanistic Surrealist vision, such as we see in *Un Chien andalou* and *El ángel exterminador*.

In Los Angeles he met an acquaintance from Surrealist Paris days, Man Ray; and together they planned a scenario, *The Sewer of Los Angeles*, whose action took place on a mountain of excrement close to a highway and a dust desert. The scheme was abortive; but later Man Ray managed to collaborate on a Surrealist film *Dreams that Money Can Buy*. Two synopses by Buñuel are deposited in the Museum of Modern Art. Of *Goya and the Duchess of Alba* (a project which he had cherished since as early as 1928) Buñuel has written to me that 'it seems the worst to me: I wrote it in the hope of selling it to Paramount'. The comment indicates that the idea of making commercial films was in his mind. It would have been a spectacular film in the best sense, with enough action and intrigue to be commercial. As in his subsequent films, the scenario contains much interesting and valuable material, though in dilution. The characters are defined in a historical, social and political situation. The idea of *l'amour fou* is embodied in the figures of Goya and the Duchess. Shoe fetishism, so often a feature of his films, surfaces in a member of the family of Charles IV, who has a habit of stealing shoes and hoarding them in an enormous cupboard. (This detail does not in fact appear in the synopsis reprinted in the Appendix to this book, but according to Jay Leyda was part of the original script.) There are also autobiographical allusions in the portrait of Goya, who was born close to Buñuel's village, and was of a comparable physical type. The dramatic scene in which Goya first realizes his deafness is significant, for instance: Buñuel began to recognize the first symptoms of his own deafness over a period of several years, after he had been present at a shooting competition held in a tunnel in Zaragoza. The echo produced extreme pain. Some doctors however say that the deafness is largely of nervous origin.

The other treatment, *Ilegible, hijo de Flauta*, was a Surrealist subject. Evidently Buñuel also hoped for American finance, since this too is in English. The scenario was written by Juan Larrea, the author of the original text dating from 1929, and scripted by Buñuel. Clearly the idea of making a new Surrealist film was frequently in Buñuel's mind, though he would not be able to realize it until 1962.

In 1946 Buñuel left Warners. His resignation was voluntary, but it coincided with the period of depression in Hollywood due to the dual crisis of the McCarthyist purges and the development of television. Fifty per cent of cinema employees were dismissed; others suffered salary cuts – a proposal to which Buñuel would not agree. 'As I was relatively well paid in Hollywood, I could save enough to realize my ideal – to do nothing for a year. However, I had no money left by 1947 when Denise Tual persuaded me to go to Mexico. She wanted me to do a film in France. I was delighted, and thought that there was at last a break in the clouds. The subject was *La casa de Bernarda Alba*; but finally I was unable to do it because Garcia Lorca's family had already sold the rights. However, I met Oscar Dancigers in Mexico, and he asked me to make a film for him. I did so; and remained in Mexico.'

The year of inactivity in Los Angeles was one of those dead points in a man's life which must end either in collapse or some important reaction. Happily, for Buñuel it was the latter. During the Californian period he lived comfortably in a bungalow, ran a car, and while his children went to the beach (which he detested), would go to Antelope Valley, a hunting ground, to rest and meet such American contemporaries as Aldous Huxley and Alexander Calder, whose house he had rented for a while.

Jay Leyda has described Buñuel at the moment of his crucial decision: 'The last time we met in California was just after his definitive parting from Hollywood and his little bungalow there. He was not certain that it would be possible for him to make films in Mexico City, but at least he felt happier with the Spanish colony there, particularly with those old friends who had been living there since 1939. He made believe that he was not worried: "I shall find *something* to do there," he said.'

The simple fact of going to Mexico was decisive in Buñuel's rediscovery of his road. Not only the idiom and the race, but the physical types, the dry and dusty landscape, the impassioned speech, the attitudes to life and death, the religious problem, the social structure which he attacked, all combined to restore him to conditions in which he could be himself. From the very first film his personality and his *Spanishness* were engaged, while he observed, understood and analysed the idiosyncrasy of the Mexican people with a greater profundity than any of the cinéastes who had preceded him. Like many other Spanish exiles, he definitively adopted Mexican nationality.

Gran Casino

For his first film Buñuel was poorly paid and given a very inferior subject by Oscar Dancigers. But he was loyal to his contract, gave himself wholeheartedly to the work and wrote a good script, in collaboration with Michel Weber. 'It was . . . a film with songs. They sang tangos and goodness knows what else . . . in any event a great deal. It was called *Gran Casino*. The story took place in Tampico in the oil era. The script was not bad, but the film had in it the two best singers of Mexico and Argentina, Jorge Negrete and Libertad Lamarque, so that I kept them singing all the time – a competition,

Gran Casino

a championship. The film was a flop, and I remained another two years out of work.'

Tampico in the oil era could have provided an interesting scenario. The late thirties had seen a reawakening of 'national consciousness' in Mexico, vividly expressed in culture as well as politics. It was a period of great mural paintings, of landscape painting celebrating the national scene, of novels of regional customs and realistic treatment of proletarian themes. The new regard for things Mexican extended to the decorative arts, music, dance and theatre. Politically, the Indian began in 1940 to enjoy in reality the rights of equality with the whites he had theoretically possessed since 1910.* As is often the case the origins of this cultural and moral revaluation were economic, the most significant step being the expropriation of the petrol industry from the North Americans by the Governor of Cárdenas, on 18 March 1938. This action, with the consequent violence and bloodshed, took place at Tampico. Although he was forced to reduce it to a bare musical comedy, Buñuel's film had this background. For Max Aub it was 'a perfect one and Buñuel's best film form'.

* See the present writer's article 'The Rise of Mexican Film' in *Films and Filming*, London, July 1960.

In some countries *Gran Casino* is in fact known as *Tampico*; and it is possible to speculate what film Buñuel might have made on the theme, given his opportunities. In the outcome it remains just one of the general run of musical comedies, except to the Buñuel *aficionado*, for whom there are occasional glimpses of the authentic artist. He had fun with the songs. One of them for instance featured Libertad Lamarque rehearsing beside a piano in a Western-style saloon. The scene begins in normal medium shot; but then cuts to a long-shot, viewed from the far end of the saloon, twenty metres away, so that the singer looks like an ant, gesticulating in the distance. Critics of the time who did not know Buñuel often failed to see the joke, and reckoned it simply technical inadequacy. A comic montage effect was employed to emphasize the singing 'championship' to which Buñuel refers; the film would cut between vast close-ups of the stout Negrete – the camera apparently being on the verge of entering his mouth – to very distant shots of the wretched Lamarque singing his feeble tangos. (Typical titles of the songs are *Duena de mi corazon, Vles cursi, Adios, pampa mia, La nortena, El choca, Loca, El reflector del amor*.)

From time to time the film betrays clearly the presence of Buñuel. A scene of a fist-fight is observed subjectively by a camera which seems always to be seeking shelter in the corners of the room, bewildered at the brutality before it. One of the fighters bumps into a cupboard (cupboards frequently figure in Buñuel's films); and the doors open up like two arms about him. The sequence closes as one of the combatants loses consciousness, and the image becomes a whirlpool, dissolving and fading. My own memory of this scene has been confirmed by Jay Leyda who has seen the film more recently: 'For me it is a scene of absolute poetry, and a denunciation of violence done without rhetoric and with passion; and this was at a time when Hollywood treated scenes of brutality with total sadism.'

A love scene is also memorable. A fixed camera reveals a public bench standing in the middle of a muddy area; behind are oil derricks. The lovers enter; a gentle breeze flutters her light dress. A longer shot shows an enormous 'parchment moon' (in Lorca's words) in the background. The hero approaches to kiss the girl; but Buñuel, who hates the conventionalism of kisses on the screen, does not register the kiss: instead the camera slowly pans down the two bodies towards the ground. The man is stirring the oily mud with a walking-stick, causing a little whirlpool. He dips his stick two or three times in the middle of this, and when he lifts it out, two drops of mud slide down and fall off. The camera returns, upwards the length of the bodies, and arrives at their faces just at the moment they have ended their kiss. The man's action recalls the eroticism of the cane in *Un Chien andalou*.

These details, lasting only a few seconds, went more or less unnoticed in

El gran calavera: Fernando Soler (centre)

what seemed at the time a perfectly conventional musical. Indeed, its very ordinariness makes it hard to understand its failure; superficially its main difference from the run of Mexican films of the period was its more fluid technique, its distinctive rhythm and the use of very fashionable players. However, the consequences of failure were two more years without work. Buñuel must have been near despair.

El gran calavera

Buñuel's next opportunity came when Fernando Soler, an elderly star, asked him to direct a film intended as a vehicle for himself. Soler, in fact, really wanted to direct himself, employing Buñuel as a superior technician. Buñuel accepted the job. The scenario was adapted from an indifferent comedy by Adolfo Torrado. The film opens with the release of a drunk from the police lock-up. We discover that he is in fact Don Ramiro, a millionaire who has taken to drink since the death of his wife, and is disastrously neglecting his business affairs. His family, in an attempt to lay hands on his money, convince him that he is in fact ruined, move to a poor quarter of town and take to hard and humble employment, in the hope of setting him a good

El gran calavera: the opening sequence

example. The plan misfires; Don Ramiro attempts suicide, and as a result discovers the plot. He thereupon turns the tables and convinces the family that he really is ruined. Believing that they now have to earn their living in earnest, they grow to discover happiness in honest labour.

The film is very uneven. The scenes with Soler tend to be slow; but Buñuel had more rein on the days he was shooting the scenes in which the old man did not appear. Certain scenes are memorable. Buñuel himself says that the opening scene is the only good thing in the film: a close-up shows a tangle of legs. Their shoes reveal that they belong to people of very varied social conditions. A hand begins to grope about among the legs. The camera slowly draws back to provide the solution to the puzzle: the legs belong to a group of drunks locked up in a cell together.

Don Ramiro's daughter Virginia is in love with a workman, Pablo, who earns a little extra money by doing street publicity from a car on which he has installed a couple of loudspeakers. From the top of a skyscraper we see the street below, seething with tiny figures, and with the car as small as an insect driving about, issuing forth announcements that sound like Surrealist phrases: 'Go to bed ugly and get up beautiful with Sin of Syria Cream' and the like. In medium shot we see Virginia meet Pablo, all dressed up, and get into the car. He alternates his microphone speeches with amorous conversation which is broadcast through the streets of the city. They get out and he buys her an ice-cream. With the door open, they sit on the running board of the car (it is a shot which occurs again in *Subida al cielo* and *La ilusión viaja en tranvía*, and is clearly related to Buñuel's use of open cupboards elsewhere in his work). The declaration of love which results – not at all like conventional cinema formulas – is expressed with subtle eroticism by the way she happily licks away at the ball of her ice, while he nervously nibbles.

The final sequence takes place in a Mexican church – baroque, ridiculous, the altar decorated with flowers and candles. The organ plays honeyed music; the congregation of stout and haughty ladies watches the arrival of the bride and groom. Virginia has been forced into marriage with a man of her father's class. The priest, all in gold and lace, solemnly celebrates the mass. He turns to the congregation to recite the epistle of St Paul ... At that moment Pablo arrives at the church door with his loudspeaker car. The priest begins: 'My children!' The car explodes: 'Best ham!' In the duel between sermon and speaker which ensues there is a chaotic abundance of intermingled and superimposed phrases. Sometimes the juxtaposition of phrases is casual and senseless (though always irreverent); sometimes it is comically explosive: 'The chastity of marriage ...' '... is only possible with Sigh of Venus Stockings ...' The effect here is something much more subtle than the joke of the amorous conversation in the car. Buñuel has invented a sound *collage* which develops the old Surrealist technique of Max Ernst, carrying it to an ultimate and delicious richness.

The wedding guests are disturbed, scandalized, turn indecisively from the altar to the street door. But if the noises from outside seem infernal to them and the priest, for the bride they are like the bells of heaven. Suddenly gathering up her train, she runs out of the dark and musty building into the light, and enters the car with the man she loves. The guests, as in a Keystone comedy, hurl themselves to the door of the church, in their anxiety to stop her determined gesture of liberation. But the car is already far away. In vain they run after it, clutching their hats, disappearing up the highway with dignity thrown to the winds, in pursuit of the couple liberated by *l'amour fou*.

El gran calavera was a vulgar commercial film; but it was funny, with a much more rapid and assured rhythm than the Mexican cinema was accustomed to. It had a huge success throughout Spanish America and was shown also in Spain and Portugal. This time Buñuel's personal inventions did not pass unnoticed; and the film's success was finally to give him the chance to make a film to his own taste. He explained it in the *Cahiers* interview:

JACQUES DONIOL-VALCROZE – Oscar Dancigers was always your producer there?

LUIS BUÑUEL – Yes. I owe a lot to him. Thanks to him I was able to stay in Mexico and make films.

ANDRÉ BAZIN – It is often said that you worked in very 'commercial' conditions in Mexico. Did Dancigers plan his production in such a way that you were obliged to make melodramas of very facile subjects?

LUIS BUÑUEL – Yes; and I always agreed.

ANDRÉ BAZIN – But *Los Olvidados*?

LUIS BUÑUEL – With *Los Olvidados* it was different. After the failure of *Gran Casino* and two years of inactivity, Dancigers asked me to suggest a treatment for a film for children. I timidly proposed the scenario of *Los Olvidados*, which I had already written with my friend Luis Alcoriza. He liked it and set me to work. Meanwhile there was an opportunity to make a commercial comedy, and Dancigers asked me to make this first, in exchange for which he guaranteed me a degree of freedom for *Los Olvidados*. So I made *El gran calavera* in sixteen days, and it enjoyed a tremendous success, and I was able to start work on *Los Olvidados*.

10. Los Olvidados

'During the three years I was without work (1947–49) I was able to explore Mexico City from one end to the other; and I was very struck by the wretchedness in which many of its inhabitants lived. I decided to base *Los Olvidados* on the life of abandoned children; and in researching the film I patiently consulted the archives of a reformatory. My story is entirely based on real cases. I tried to expose the wretched condition of the poor in real terms, because I loathe films that make the poor romantic and sweet.

'*Los Olvidados* is, perhaps, my favourite film. If I had had all the facilities I wanted, it could have been a masterpiece' (Buñuel in *Nuevo Cine*).

Buñuel told *Cahiers du Cinéma*, '*Los Olvidados* was made with relative freedom. Of course Dancigers asked me to take out a lot of things which I wanted to put in the film, but he left me fairly free.'

ANDRÉ BAZIN – What kind of things?

LUIS BUÑUEL – All the things I took out were of purely symbolic interest. I wanted to introduce crazy, completely mad elements into the most realistic scenes; for instance, when Jaibo goes to beat up and kill the other boy, the camera pans across a huge eleven-storey building in process of construction in the background; and I would have liked to put a hundred-piece orchestra into it. It would have only been glimpsed, vaguely and fleetingly.

I wanted to include lots of elements of this kind, but I was absolutely forbidden.

ANDRÉ BAZIN – What you're saying is very important, especially to the extent to which *Los Olvidados* could be taken as a social or pedagogical film, in the tradition of *The Road to Life*, *Boys' Town* or *Prison Without Bars*. What you've just told us could seem to contradict the social realism which some people have chosen to emphasize in the film. It would be important to know the extent to which the realism is necessary, or if, on the contrary, it is there as an excuse for the real poetic message of the film.

LUIS BUÑUEL – For me *Los Olvidados* is effectively a film of social argument. To be honest with myself I had to make a film of a social type. I know that this is the way I see things. Apart from this, though, I did not want in any respect to make a thesis film. I had seen things which had distressed me very much, and I wanted to put them on the screen, but always with the sort of love I have for the instinctive and irrational that you can find everywhere. I've always been attracted by the strange and unknown, which fascinated me without my being able to say why.

JACQUES DONIOL-VALCROZE – You had Figueroa as photographer, but you used him in a completely different way from his usual style. Did you prevent him from making beautiful images?

LUIS BUÑUEL – Naturally, inasmuch as the film did not lend itself to them.

JACQUES DONIOL-VALCROZE – He must have felt very miserable.

LUIS BUÑUEL – Very miserable ... It's true. I have to say that I didn't behave with him like a dictator conceding favours in terms of 'Come then, my friend, since you are so eager to do it ...' But the essentials are true. After eleven days shooting, Figueroa asked Dancigers why they had chosen him to do a film which any newsreel cameraman could have done. He was told: 'Because you're a very quick and very commercial cameraman.' It's true. Figueroa is fantastically quick and very good. It's a guarantee. At the start he was terrified of working with me. We could never agree. But I think he developed a lot, and we became very good friends.

Figueroa's camerawork is the principal element of surprise for the Buñuel connoisseur. For the first time the spectator is startled by the aesthetic quality of the photography. Buñuel did everything in his power to prevent the audience from experiencing any agreeable aesthetic impressions; but for all that the hand of a studio craftsman – meticulous and baroque – is evident. Figueroa was to work again with Buñuel on *El*, but there the director has complete dominance: the contrasty blacks and whites of the photography have none of the rich, pearly-grey range of *Los Olvidados*.

The budget for the film was a mere 450,000 pesos – very much less than

Los Olvidados: the opening sequence

even the cheapest of the 'artistic' films then being made by Emilio Fernandez. Buñuel was paid very little, but he worked conscientiously, recognizing that his one chance of re-entering the cinema was being gambled on this film. The marvellous collection of local characters was not played entirely by non-professional actors, as is often asserted. Estella India was a famous Mexican actress. Roberto Cobo had a lot of experience in music-hall, though this was his first film. Even the unnamed ten-year-old who plays the little girl had acted before. Indeed, Miguel Inclán's creation of the blind man, impressive though it is, has too much professionalism about it. Buñuel rehearsed a great deal with his actors; and according to Cobo the director made nineteen takes of the scene in which, as Jaibo, he seduces his friend's mother. (Buñuel says this is not true.) Inevitably, *Los Olvidados* has not the formal spontaneity of preceding films.

The story is set in Mexico City, but the director was concerned to give the impression that it could equally happen in any other city. He explains how social conditions, lack of affection and poverty make a child into a criminal. The film is a record which offers no solution to the stated problem since as Buñuel declares in the foreword to the film: 'The task of finding a solution lies with the forces of progress.'

139

Los Olvidados: Roberto Cobo and Estella India

As the film opens, a young boy is waiting in the market place while his father, up from the country, goes about his business. He waits for hours, until someone tells him: 'Don't wait for him, because he won't be coming back.' With this confirmation of his terrible despair begins a dark story, an accumulation of violent events. The boy, just as in *El Lazarillo de Tormes*, is taken off by a blind beggar, old, vicious and miserly, who treats him with extreme cruelty. A gang of street-boys, led by Jaibo who has just come out of a reformatory, attempt to rob the blind man, stoning him brutally. One of them, Pedro, witnesses Jaibo's savage murder of a boy whose evidence sent him to the reformatory. From this moment a silent complicity grows up between them: Pedro fears the older boy at the same time as he is fascinated by him; and Jaibo makes use of this. Eventually Jaibo seduces Pedro's mother. In the seduction scene, Buñuel marvellously captures the idiom of popular Mexican speech:

'How great it must be to have a mother! Just think: I never even knew mine. When I was very little I used to have bad fits. One time, when I came to, I saw a lady, like this, very close. She looked very pretty and she was crying; so I think it was my mama . . .' (he laughs).

'And was she beautiful?'

'Like the Queen of an Altar.'

This technique seduces the woman, who is forty, still handsome and abandoned by her husband; and she is already looking longingly at the boy's muscles when her son enters:

'Ma! The police are looking for you!'

Somewhat later, Pedro is sleeping in the filthy room in which his mother also sleeps, after she has told him that there is no supper. Buñuel introduces an Oedipal dream: the mother floats from her bed (an effect achieved by soft focus and slow motion) and approaches him like an angel. Suddenly she offers him an enormous lump of meat, dripping with blood and sinew; and the boy wakes with a scream of horror ... Only Buñuel could conceive such a scene. The unbridled eroticism, the underlying Freudian and Surrealist references which give it intellectual weight and exclude any pornographic interpretation; the way in which such a scene is interwoven with banal incidents, show that after twenty years of comparative inactivity, Buñuel remained completely himself.

Pedro is sent to a reformatory for the theft of a knife. His first action is to seize a cudgel and kill the chickens in a compound where he has been put to work. The other boys are stunned; some are angry; others feel tempted to unite with him in the act of anarchic rebellion. Pedro is punished; but later the director, a typical liberal figure, determines to test him. He sends him out of the reformatory on an errand. Pedro is about to return, when Jaibo meets him in the street, discovers he has money on him, and kills him in a moment of frenzy. Buñuel's criticism of the gesture of the liberal director reflects sentiments about the 'soft' policies of the Spanish Republic which resulted in Civil War. Don Lope, in *Tristana*, is one of several characters who illustrate Buñuel's conviction that liberalism is a disastrous error in contemporary circumstances.

Jaibo is discovered and surrounded in a yard by the police. It is a leaden grey evening and a suburban train passes slowly by. He is shot. As he lies on the ground, struggling with his agony, he still endeavours to escape. His head moves mechanically from side to side; he cannot breathe. His voice is heard although his lips do not move. It is the *voice off* of his mortal delirium, to which the voice of his mother replies.

'I am falling into the great black pit ... I am alone, alone ...'

'As always, my little one, as always ... Sleep ... Sleep!'

'I am alone ... (*superimposed is the image of a ravening dog, the symbol of his death, approaching him*) ... The mangy dog! I am alone, alone, alone ...'

Jaibo dies, remaining still, with his eyes open. At first we do not realize why the image is so terrible: the camera is not now filming Jaibo, but a still photograph of him. The difference between a filmed image of a motionless person and a still photograph is the difference between an image in which time passes and one which is intemporal, between life and death. Truffaut used the effect for the final scene of *Les Quatre Cents Coups*. The 'freeze' is now an all-too-familiar device. Its first appearance was in *Los Olvidados*.

The death of Jaibo is treated with neither more nor less charity than that of the boy who represents the sympathetic character. The body of Pedro is taken by Jaibo's grandfather, who puts it in a sack before the police can trace it, loads it on a donkey and takes it to a sewer, rolling it down the slope into a filthy gutter where pigs water. The camera follows the descent of the bundle, then slowly moves up the hillside again, in an oblique pan so as to frame the horizon, with a vine silhouetted against a brilliant Western sky over which is superimposed the word 'FIN'.

The film went to the Cannes Festival of 1951 against the wishes of its director, who was as always nervous about his work. He confided to the Cinémathèque Française that he feared the critical reaction after his earlier, Surrealist work. He was reappearing twenty years after with a dramatic story film – having always in the past condemned the story form in works of art; with a Mexican instead of a French film; with a film that was popular and of social content. He feared that people would feel he had betrayed his earlier work and Surrealist allegiances (which, in fact, some critics did). The people at the Cinémathèque (who subsequently helped to arrange distribution for the film in France) talked him out of his fears: 'The point is that all those Surrealists are now linked by one great beard; and you have none.'

The Cannes Festival gave him the prize for best direction, while the FIPRESCI (International Press) jury gave him an award in recognition of his total *oeuvre*. The critics were enthusiastic. The resurrection of this new Buñuel was a kind of miracle; never in the history of cinema had a director re-emerged after so many years of silence.

Los Olvidados demonstrated that the theories and the dialectic of Buñuel's first period were still valid. Though the manner and method of the film were not in any respect *avant-garde*, the film raised new questions. It was concerned with reviewing the essential validity of many aspects of Surrealism, and examining to what point they remained applicable to present contingencies. Buñuel was to continue this process in his subsequent films. Thus he influenced the renascence of the Surrealist movement. Breton was at that time still alive in Paris, and incorruptible like Buñuel who had already said that so long as Breton was alive, Surrealism could not die. Since 1951 a revaluation of Surrealism has been evident in France, Switzerland, Poland, England, Spain, South America and elsewhere. All this is secondary to the significance that a man of the stature and integrity of Buñuel had never succumbed. This consideration undoubtedly influenced the success of *Los Olvidados*, added to the shock-power of the film. It was, moreover, an important discovery for Europe, to learn that Mexico had another cultural aspect than the vapid folk-lore drama which was familiar through the films of Emilio Fernandez.

Los Olvidados has been Buñuel's most praised and discussed film since *L'Age d'or*, and has sometimes been regarded as his masterpiece. In 1960 the director himself considered it one of his favourite films, along with *L'Age d'or*, *El*, *Cela s'appelle l'Aurore* and *Nazarín*, and rated it higher than *Robinson Crusoe* or *Subida al cielo*. His personal affection for the film is understandable, considering that it was possibly the most crucial and anxious undertaking of his career. In retrospect the intrinsic value of the film has perhaps been overrated. The compromise between his personal world and the social content of the film was sincere, but an effort. Buñuel has told me that the reformatory sequences gave him pleasure to do, because they fitted logically into the development of the story; yet these are the scenes which have in particular been charged with a demagogic and artificial optimism, quite alien to Buñuel. Many critics have regarded them as a concession. (In fairness it cannot be said that he offers any solution with the reformatory, even though its warden is so notably liberal. Buñuel was presenting one of the directions in which reclaimed children may drift. In his next film, *Susana*, he makes very clear his feelings on those institutions whose mission is more to rid society of uncomfortable anti-social elements than actually to do anything to help them.)

The violence, always present in Buñuel, here seems at times to be pitched to a forced note. The astonishing brutalities shock us with a regularity that becomes predictable. The dynamism of Buñuel's films comes from the succession of actions ('I do not comment, I describe,' said Stendhal). His films are full of incidents; and there are no contemplative sequences or restful scenes, except when he wants to present effects of contrast, or he insists on the 'rehabilitation of daily reality'. In *Los Olvidados* the accumulation of episodes becomes monotonous, perhaps because it does not respond to the interior necessity of the creator, undermining a novel-like unity. The same defect is found in *La Mort en ce jardin* and *Nazarín*. In any event, the artifice would not be apparent if it were not that each of the incidents is treated as a similar crescendo in the whole dramatic ellipsis. Our defensive mechanism at the violence tends to negate the latent sentimentality of the episode. Freddy Buache comments that 'This unbalance between the too-vivid explosiveness of the narrative and the muted greyishness of the (social) criticism caused Georges Franju to say on leaving the projection of *Los Olvidados*: "This film is not a violent work; it is simply at times *brutal*." '

Even so the film exists on a totally different level from all other films about juvenile delinquency. For the first time the theme is treated without any of the automatic 'tics' of traditional morality. For this reason it is altogether preferable to *The Road to Life* – admirable though Nikolai Ekk's film still appears. For Buñuel it was naturally impossible to treat the theme as the Soviet film had done, by offering solutions. He has told me: 'The artificial optimism of recent Soviet films is as reactionary as bourgeois ideals of religion, country and family.'

When we call *Los Olvidados* a melodrama, the word is not used in a pejorative sense. The sociologist Edgar Morin has written with reference to the Mexican cinema in general and Buñuel in particular: 'In the Mexican cinema there is a rawness in the treatment of death and sexuality which makes us feel the fleshliness of man.' He adds also: 'Those who condemn the melodramatic structures of the traditional popular novel forget that they are the same as those of Greek tragedy and Elizabethan drama.' The Mexican poet Octavio Paz pinpoints the tragic essence of *Los Olvidados*: 'Jaibo ... dies, but he brings about his own death. The collision between human consciousness and external fatality is the essence of tragedy. Buñuel has rediscovered this fundamental ambiguity: without human complicity cestiny is not accomplished, and tragedy is impossible. Fate unmasks freedom, and is the mask of destiny. The old conception of fate continues to function, though deprived of its supernatural attributes: now we confront a social and psychological fate.'

Los Olvidados belongs to the total *oeuvre* of Buñuel. Its originality consists in treating the tragic sentiment in popular language. It is one hundred per cent Mexican in idiom. Buñuel had assimilated the national tradition of the Mexican cinema as rapidly as he had assimilated those of France and Spain. Arriving in Mexico at a moment when the national cinema was divided between works destined for museum habitués and an immense bulk of mediocre popular films, Buñuel chose, as he had in Spain, to identify himself with the second category. Melodrama and popular film comedy have better antecedents in Mexico than in Spain: there is the excellent tradition of Bustillo Oro, dating back to 1928, and since 1938, of Julio Bracho and Blas Galindo. Buñuel followed this line; and treated a national problem in language that was utterly simple, with incidents that were equally banal, scenes that were quite childish in appearance. But he gave to all this profundity, sincerity and grandeur.

Characters in Buñuel's films behave quite differently from other directors' creations. They do not evolve like phantoms out of nothing, nor do they make those gestures or hand movements, or say the words which we are used to hearing from the screen. When Robinson Crusoe swims to the island beach, he does not leap up from the ground at once, but stays there a long time, exhausted, as he might well do in real life. When, in *La Mort en ce jardin*, a brave man is going to be shot, he does not pose in front of the firing squad like Marlene Dietrich in *Dishonoured*, but has to be set on a chair, fainting with fear, and tied so that he does not fall off. Such scenes mingle with the banalities of daily life to which we have already referred (Viridiana peels an orange in spirals; The Young One casually kills an insect in passing). Together they convey the strange sense of truth which is unique to Buñuel. Buñuel's whole vision of reality is based on this kind of observation: 'I like the moments when nothing is happening: a man who says "Give me a match." This kind of thing interests me a lot. "Give me a match" interests me enormously ... "What do you want to eat?" "What time is it?" I made *Subida al cielo* a bit in this spirit.' (Interview with *Cahiers du Cinéma*.)

Los Olvidados is, like *Las Hurdes*, a tragic poem on man, who fascinates Buñuel both by his intrinsic beauty and his immense horror. The world is a kind of inferno, with no way out. The human being, like a homunculus, bears his destiny. Man cannot modify himself. Evil is intrinsic to man and child, as witness the dream of Pedro and the death of Jaibo.

From this film we can trace a slow evolution towards a greater confidence in life (which progressed along with his personal rehabilitation). *Susana* was also to be about the force of unrestrained evil, but would mark an advance from *Los Olvidados*. To a point both works are optimistic, since their negativism comes only from the absence of favourable conditions for betterment. The children in *Los Olvidados* or *Susana* are bad because they are without love, and can survive only by doing ill. By creating a society which is not criminal, we shall ourselves cease to be criminal. ('Dans une société criminelle,' wrote the Marquis de Sade, 'il faut être criminel.') This is the degree of optimism implicit in Buñuel, which is not utopian but humanist. Only Buñuel can see no escape. His lack of faith in any political credo or progressive ideal brings him to a blind alley. The young ones of *Los Olvidados* are all alone; so is Susana. She, however, seeks the companionship of love. In *El Bruto* the men walk like the blind through the steam coming from the boiling blood on the floor of the slaughter-house. They search in the labyrinth. Thus men search for one another, uniting against evil (in this case represented by their boss). *El Bruto* first announces Buñuel's hope of finding in human and social solidarity the solution to his apparently indeterminable conflict. All the subsequent films express these ideas. Without seeking to please, or looking for easy solutions, every film asserts the need for salvation through solidarity, through love, through human dignity which will submit to neither slavery nor humiliation. From *Robinson Crusoe*, the cinema of Buñuel arrives at an admirable serenity. *Nazarín*, with all its ambiguity, discovers the only solution for Father Nazarín – to live with other men like himself, defying the abstract principles that separate him from them.

Difficult, full of contradictions and dramatic recantations, all Buñuel's work is the reflection of the man. The reflection is faithful, because Buñuel can no more deceive other people than he can himself. 'His struggle between beauty and rebellion is transmitted to his films. Every image is a sort of desperate invocation to the law which he is seeking. This invocation has often the character of a magic sign rather than of argument, rationalization or explanation. The films are not answers, but questions. It is an *oeuvre* created from instinctive, primary *Anschauungen*' (Max Lautenegge and Mario Gerteis, *Luis Buñuel*, Zurich). This is true; but at how many other times does Buñuel invoke common sense, the dialectic practice of scientific precision, *morality*? He has said: 'To have a code of laws is for most people stupid, but not for me.' 'Sociologically it is clear that madness, for Buñuel, lies always in characters whose surroundings and ideals are based on beliefs and traditional morality. For him the mad and the good bourgeois are two extreme instances of the same social type: the parasite' (Lautenegge and Gerteis, op. cit).

For more than thirty years Buñuel composed, with means exclusively cinematographic, the precise image of his vision of the world, until he succeeded in resolving the conflicts and finding the tranquillity which becomes evident after 1961. The process was not intellectual but intuitive, spontaneous, connected with mental associations which must not be confused with symbols, the error of many of Buñuel's critics. *Los Olvidados* marks the culmination of the conflict. In it we find the popular language inherent to a mass spectacle like the cinema, through which he is able to explain things not only to others, but to himself.

It is an error to regard the Mexican films as a decline from the excellence of his early work into commercialism and compromise. In these films, modest as they are, Buñuel totally realized himself as a man and as an artist. In spite of their technical imperfections, their formal shortcomings, the dead weight of story and melodrama which has often to be supported, it was these films in which his genius matured, in which he affirmed himself as the creator of an *oeuvre* which is continuous, original, sincere and explosive in its lyrical force. In the first seventy-five years of cinema he stands as one of the three or four greatest figures. In Spanish culture, so high in moral philosophers, though not in pure philosophy, he comes near to Quevedo, Gracián or Goya as an example of the sensibility of a race and as a thinker. I have avoided calling Buñuel an artist, because his intention is not to create works of art with his cinema in the sense the word is understood in the usage of non-materialist aesthetics. He is an artist in the sense that he transposes one world – our world – into the different laws of another, the cinema.

11. From Susana to Archibaldo

Los Olvidados still did not give Buñuel full freedom of action; for several more years he was obliged to accept commercial chores, apparently conventional Mexican melodramas. His greatest merit has been precisely to know how to submit himself to such work without betraying himself. His achievement was not altogether novel; throughout history the major part of great works of art were made to order. The limitations of expression within which the artist works are almost always limitations imposed by the patron: the work finished in a fixed time, with a certain limit of money, with a particular size, illustrating a concrete theme. Beyond the strict limits of the commission, transcending it, the artist expresses his own vision of the world. It seems to be a condition of creation to demand transpositions and limitations. Paradoxical as it may seem, the independent and rebellious Buñuel achieved in the restrictive circumstances of his Mexican films, works as complex as those he had made in France. Nor is it always the films with the biggest budgets and best technical facilities which in the outcome were the best of his Mexican works.

Susana
Susana is a characteristic case – a sort of prototype, even a caricature, of the series of 'commercial' films. In it Buñuel, so concerned in his first Surrealist

Susana: Luis López Somoza, Matilde Paláu, María Gentil Arcos

work to destroy conventional aesthetic conventions, reveals deep respect for the established traditions of narrative, structure and form. *Susana* observes the conventions of Spanish and Mexican melodrama with such reverence that the extreme abuse with which Spanish critics loaded the film is understandable. Discerning critics however recognized it as one of his most fascinating creations, working through a sort of code, introducing all the familiar Buñuel themes in cypher. In the course of the *Cahiers du Cinéma* interview André Bazin asked: 'Do you also rate *Susana* or *Subida al cielo* as little commercial films in which you managed from time to time to introduce something personal? For us they are much more important than you seem to admit them to be, and we find them very rich. Are they exclusively commercial chores as far as you are concerned?

LUIS BUÑUEL – No. I watch them with the pleasure that I felt in doing them. *Susana* would have been more interesting if I could have given it another ending. It is a film which I made in twenty days. But time does not count. Five months or two days doesn't really matter. What counts is the content, the expression.

Buñuel often gives his films a little prologue which provides a key to the action. *Susana* begins with the protagonist being dragged off screaming to the punishment cell of a 'State House of Correction'. Darkness, thunderstorm, bats ... Susana, terrified, asks for God's help. A flash of lightning casts a shadow from the grating window of her cell, forming a cross. Susana kneels; and when she is about to kiss the cross, a hairy spider runs from the centre. Horrified, she hurls herself at the bars, which give way, permitting her to escape. With a concentration which reaches the point of the ridiculous, Buñuel has introduced the elements of the conventional drama, but he has also inserted into them a distinctly personal image (the spider on the cross). And the solid barred window that gives way causes us to doubt whether we are in the dominion of reality or dream. Is it melodramatic convention or – as good Christians would suppose – a miracle, seeing that God always helps the bad when they invoke his aid? Buñuel is already teasing and mystifying. Beneath the foolish little anecdote of a femme fatale devouring men, the serious Buñuel describes an eternal tragedy of causes and effects.

She flees through the storm and finds herself at a ranch where the rich landowners – as good Christians – offer her shelter. Susana sets about a systematic programme of seduction, passing from the foreman, Jésus, to the son of the family, and finally to the father Don Guadelupe. Don Guadelupe's wife, Dona Carmen, wants to turn the temptress out, but Jésus has meanwhile solved their shared problem by ratting to the police, who take Susana back to prison. Life resumes its old calm; everyone retires behind his former mask of hypocrisy.

The *huis clos* provided by the ranch is a microcosm of society. The landlords are surrounded by their servants. The capitalist structure secures this condition in which some serve and others are served. Outside in the street there is unemployment, hunger. The logic is simple: if the landlords are not well served, they threaten to throw the servants into the street. Based on this system of terror everything works admirably, almost idyllically. Until, that is, someone who will not conform to this order escapes from the prison which the landlords have created and erupts into this world, whereupon the whole apparent equilibrium collapses. This is what happens in *Susana*. The foreman threatens the workers with dismissal when they annoy him with proofs of his lechery. The son of the landlord threatens the foreman. The landlord threatens his son. The system of threats is so interdependent that when Susana – incarnating beauty, carnal desire, rebellion for love – comes along to catalyse it, there is a chain reaction. Then it is as if the process were reversed, so that at the end of the film Susana arrives once more at the gaol where she was at the beginning and everything is restored to its original order, miraculously, and all are once more 'happy'. As if nothing had happened; as if the disinfecting presence of Susana had not taken off all the masks. The wife has seen that her conjugal life was not based on love. The landlord kisses his wife with desire; and the deliciously comic bedroom scene ends with his exclamation, 'Ah! women!' and her 'Ah! men!' This one kiss has in it a noteworthy violence and obscenity – though in fact it is the only one in the film hallowed by the sacrament of matrimony. We guess, though, that the man has not kissed his wife in this way for many years, and that he does it now only impelled by his awakened desire for Susana. The husband, for his part, has clearly seen the hypocrisy of the wife. Five minutes before this final scene, all the characters were prepared for murder.

In a world where order is maintained by imposing respect for false values and the benevolent absolution of misdeeds, such a regression is possible: it is the 'happy end' recognized by this society. In the last three minutes of the film everything is put right, and it ends with a retrospective travelling shot which shows the sunny estate, complete with lambs and ducklings. The voice of a servant is heard announcing that the mare (who throughout the film was on the point of being killed to avoid a bad birth) has borne a beautiful foal to enrich the wealth of the estate. The good Lord accomplishes all things, once the forces of the Devil have been destroyed. This marvellous ending is at the same time the most extreme form of childish melodrama. Buñuel's comment in the interview shows that he was dissatisfied with the ending; and when I praised it to him, he replied: 'You have recognized the true feeling, certainly. If I say it was unsatisfactory, it is because it was not sufficiently emphatic. In the cinema it is essential to make things absolutely clearly understood; and if they are not, they lose all their value. For that ending to be good, it had to be perceptible to all the audience, and not just a few like yourself.'

If we are not to be misled by the absurdities of the melodramatic convention, it is necessary to make the effort to recognize – in this as in all Buñuel's Mexican films – the traditions of the *genre*; the rules of the game which the author is proposing to us. Buñuel assists us at every moment, maintaining the tone. The decoration of the house and the yard of the estate, suggested by actual country houses of Mexico and Spain, seems to be swallowed up in a devouring light. The system of doors giving out from the house on to the yard is knowingly calculated to facilitate the incessant transit of the characters. The movement of these within the frame is equally clever. The lecherous Susana never pauses. No sooner has she finished seducing one man than another falls into the field of her intentions. As the film progresses, the action becomes more rapid, the entrances and exits more torrential. Nor does the camera wait. It goes ahead to seek out the characters. A slight lateral pan (rather like Dreyer) and there is the next one! Here is a fresh victim! At the climax of the film, when all the characters make their way by night to Susana's apartment, hoping to have their chance to quench her erotic fever, the camera seeks out the people as they lurk in nooks, measuring the distance between them, or from them and Susana's apartment, in rapid, almost hysterical sweeps. Never was Buñuel's camera so active. The director has abandoned his habitual near-static camera and his Russian-style montage; and for this film about the decay of occidental society, he uses the most decadent Hollywood techniques.

Such technical artifices facilitate entry into the dramaturgical mechanics of *Susana*. But these mechanics have their material causes and practical justification. Susana is the character of melodrama who represents, in bold outline, 'evil'. But she is also the human being sacrificed by a social order. What, finally, is this unhappy creature seeking? The same thing the very Christian lady of the house enjoys and guards – first with gestures of charity; afterwards asking God to put things in order. ('I ask nothing for myself, but for the home,' she prays to the crucifix; but what is 'the home' but the personal universe of the bourgeois lady?) And when God does not help her, the lady uses other means, attacking whip in hand in a frenzy of sadistic pleasure. In order to get a home, Susana on the other hand, has to struggle, deceive, lie, prostitute herself: her every action will engender the necessity of new acts of evil-doing. If in the end the tragedy represents the force of evil which spreads by geometrical progression, the determinist sense represents the endless and hopeless struggle of a human being, involved in a social condition whose structure does not permit him or her to live without humiliation. What has this creature done that, while still only a girl, she should be locked up and tortured in a prison? It could be argued that a corrective institution for minors is a benevolent institution set up for the good of the children themselves. But if we analyse a film by Buñuel we have to begin by casting aside all hypocrisy. Moreover the author dissipates any doubts in the opening scene of the film. The first two phrases we hear are spoken by the gaolers who are locking Susana in the punishment cell: 'You'll learn to be good here.' 'Oh yeah? Since she first came here two years ago she's just got worse all the time.'

Elsewhere the conventions and vocabulary of the melodrama are respected. The maid, commentating events with instinctive common sense, is the 'Gracioso', the 'Celestina', the 'Sancho Panza' of Spanish literature. The wife – one of Buñuel's most entertaining creations, representing the force of the established world against anyone who attempts to resist the destructive turns of destiny – is the grotesque personage of the drama, treated by Buñuel as mercilessly as other 'mothers' throughout his films. The passive, cowardly object of the tragic forces is, ironically, the lord and master of the group.

The actors who play these characters have each an extremely limited repertory of signs, with which he expresses essential and primary reactions. The more limited the vocabulary, the freer the language. Susana herself does not know much more than to pull down the shoulders of her dress to increase the *décolleté*. Throughout the film she does this incessantly to resolve every situation. Anyone who accuses the director of a failure of imagination here, has not understood the magic property of repetition, the feeling of totemic ritual which is provided by the repetition of a gesture (*El ángel exterminador* confirmed and underlined this). It is the basis of all oriental theatre. Setting aside this value, though, could poor Susana resort to better means to make her way than to demonstrate her fine breasts? Buñuel has often spoken of the priority of the flesh; and Susana's repeated gesture recalls the character in Henry Miller: 'When I want to make an erotic conquest, I don't waste time in strategy: I take my prick out and there you are.'

The dialogue, too, is made out of clichés, or rather old proverbs whose wisdom and sense no one questions. One character will contradict another with a proverb which annuls the one before. 'Old folk don't get measles,' the landowner tells his wife to convince her that it is impossible that he could fall in love with Susana. Of course he has done so. 'Do good to others without looking who you do it to', says the saintly woman to the maid, who counters: 'But it is better to do it with one eye open and the other closed.' And she adds, 'Like the priest does.' *Susana* and *Tristana* both enrich Spanish idiom with their use of proverbs.

The conventions do not preclude a Surrealist vocabulary as well. The amorous meetings take place among ruins. The son of the house falls into temptation from the woman at the bottom of a well. Kissing Susana by force, his trousers are still stained with egg from having crushed a basket which she was carrying from the chicken-house. The landowner falls in love while hunting birds, with a gun in his hands. The women argue hotly while they rhythmically work the treadle of a sewing machine. But the essential surrealism of *Susana* lies in the spectator's experience of finding himself little by little taking the side of 'evil'. Are we, in communion with Buñuel, sinners possessed by the devil, perverse beings by nature? Or is it that Buñuel has made us see that if we put ourselves on the side of the lubricious Susana and against these good Christians, it is because the spirit of justice is awakened in us, because finally he makes us discover where the positive values, and the truth, lie?

La hija del engaño

Despite some changes of character names, *La hija del engaño* does not differ materially from the original Spanish version of *Don Quintín el amargao*, made sixteen years earlier with the same script, either in the quality of the realization or the intention. It would be curious to see them together. In both versions, Buñuel's tactic is to take the melodrama to the point of burlesque, retaining the breakneck, patently false dénouement and happy end. Arniches' flowing burlesque offered better opportunities than *El gran calavera*, where Buñuel in any case had to proceed with caution and dissimulation so that the producer–actor should not be aware of the transformation from bourgeois comedy into Buñuel's own special kind of *guignol*.

Buache points out a scene with Marta, Don Quintín's long-lost child, in the house of her adopted father Lencho. 'During a long sequence in darkness, nothing is heard but the noise of a spanking which the drunkard is administering to the girl. When the blackout ends and the image reappears, Marta is already a young woman; we learn from the dialogue that Lencho continues to spank her, but the significance of the corporal punishment is not quite the same: there is a clear feeling of an erotic flagellation. Thus we move imperceptibly from novelette psychology (wicked adopted parent and poor abandoned child) to the phenomenological description of a passionate relationship established on a reciprocal, instinctive and dominant will for pleasure. Throughout the story the film-maker forces the dreadful sentimentality to the point where it reaches irony or comedy in order to turn it inside out like a glove, and by a paraphysical logic, the trivial moralizing suddenly declares his own demystifying criticism.'

Cuando los hijos nos juzgan (Una mujer sin amor)

Cuando los hijos nos juzgan was based on de Maupassant's story *Pierre et Jean*, about an old antique dealer whose young wife deceives him with an engineer, but still will not abandon her ailing husband. Family attitudes and loyalties are gravely strained twenty-five years on when the couple's son is left a fortune by a mysterious rich Argentinian. The film was in essence characteristic of a whole group of shoestring and virtually unplanned productions made in Mexico at the period, all based on good novels. On this film Buñuel enjoyed the comparative luxury of a twenty-day shooting schedule instead of the sixteen days allowed him on *La hija del engaño* (which was shot in such haste that all the shots of a staircase had to be identically lined up so as not to reveal that there had not been time to finish the set). Buñuel uses the drama to show family relationships carried to the limit of exasperation, insult, violence, Latin sadism, the demystification of the Christian concept of the holy and abnegating mother; and he found opportunities for brief, delightful sketches in the course of knocking off the muddled melodramatic narrative.

Subida al cielo

Another acquaintance from Buñuel's days in the Residencia, the poet Manuel Altolaguirre, also exiled in Mexico and occasionally himself a Surrealist, produced *Subida al cielo* as well as providing its flimsy picaresque

Subida al cielo: Oliverio on the bus . . .

plot. Oliverio, about to be married, has to postpone the ceremony in order to make a two-day journey to get his dying mother's will ratified. On the way, the bus and its passengers encounter a variety of adventures and delays. They are stranded in a storm, get stuck in a river; a woman has a premature delivery; the bus stops at the driver's home to celebrate his birthday; Oliverio is vamped by the local tart, and – more from irritation than actual desire – sleeps with her, during a torrential storm on top of the mountain called Subida al Cielo (Ascent to Heaven). He finally returns home to find his mother already dead, but he is able to carry out her testamentary wishes by pressing her thumbs on to the document. Beneath the stock characters and the surface jollity, there are elements that are profound and poetic in the record of birth and love and death (not only the mother, but also the tiny girl who on the outward journey leads the oxen and the bus out of the water and on the return is lying dead in her coffin, the victim of a viper bite). There is much and disturbing eroticism, and two dream sequences to match those of *Los Olvidados*. In one, Oliverio dreams that his mother, raised on a pedestal, calmly knits, while he is drawn along an endless umbilical cord to the tart, the whole fantasy taking place in a bus that is transformed into a tropical garden.

... is vamped by the local tart

A film deliberately shaped as a minor work, it is one of Buñuel's (and Mexico's) most delightful comedies, with its own easy elegance and none of the routines of a 'folklore' movie.

El Bruto

El Bruto was made in eighteen days. It 'could have been good', Buñuel said in his *Cahiers* interview: 'The scenario I did with Alcoriza was interesting, but they made me change everything from top to bottom. Now it's just any film, without anything remarkable.' The 'Brute' of the title is Pedro, a young butcher and the strong-arm man of Cabrera, a property-owner who engages him at the suggestion of his wife Paloma. With his great strength, Pedro kills the tenants' spokesman, Carmelo. Thrilled by this display of violence, Paloma becomes his mistress. The tenants, however, determine on vengeance, and give chase to Pedro after having wounded him. He takes refuge with Meche, the daughter of his victim, who is unaware of the identity of the murderer. Living with her, he softens, regrets his former actions and becomes sympathetic to the plight of the tenants whom Cabrera exploits. But Paloma, jealous, sets her husband against Pedro, and tells Meche the truth about him. When

155

Meche rejects him, Pedro kills Cabrera. Paloma denounces him to the police, who kill him, as Meche forgives him.

Ado Kyrou has described *El Bruto* as: 'One of the best-made films of Buñuel ... A sublime melodrama ... All the elements of the old melodrama accumulate; but they are transformed by Buñuel's social grasp of the subject, and the vision which constantly opens up into Surrealism despite its realist appearances: the senile grandfather gets up in the night to steal chocolates, the abattoirs are protected by an image of the Virgin Mary ... love as pure as in *L'Age d'or* changes the destiny of men and makes them rediscover life.' In his own unique fashion Buñuel manages to blend melodrama, neo-realism and Surrealism. The central figure of the Brute, admirably played by Pedro Armendariz, is one of the figures who seem particularly to fascinate Buñuel (compare the gamekeepers in *L'Age d'or* and *The Young One* and the butlers in *El ángel exterminador* and *Le Journal d'une femme de chambre*): the proletarian who becomes the willing agent of the bourgeoisie.

Las aventuras de Robinson Crusoe

'What interested me in the story was the solitude of Robinson and his new meeting with a man. It is a commercial film ... the book never interested me. ... Anyway, I don't know the film (my last sight of it was in the cutting room) and I don't know what music they adapted to it.' Although in fact there was probably some front-office cutting of the film, Buñuel's modesty is unjustified: quite apart from all its other merits, it is a model of interpretative adaptation.

Buñuel follows Defoe's flat documentary style in recording the day-to-day routines and struggles of Robinson's life; but there are resounding philosophical and moral overtones. In the first half he deals with solitude, 'looking into the heart of the man to see there the desolation and anguish of someone isolated from all human contact' (Tony Richardson). Robinson is deprived of all his ordinary social and moral and religious supports; and must find his resources in himself alone. In a moment of despair he cries to God ... and hears only the echo of his own voice in reply. Buñuel records the stages of solitude: the initial struggles for mere physical survival; the tormenting drunken vision of his old comrades; the agonies of sexual deprivation when he gazes at the scarecrow he has dressed in a woman's gown (the film is profoundly erotic, even though the first half is a solo performance and there is no female character); the vision of his father, an old man in an enormous red hat, upbraiding him and advising him not to go to sea but to be content with his station in life. Buache has described the 'cruel and tender song of solitude': 'The days pass, his beard grows, the castaway little by little organizes his existence. He talks to his dog, is touched when his cat has kittens. His crops

El Bruto: Pedro Armendariz, Katy Jurado; Rosita Arenas, Pedro Armendariz

Las aventuras de Robinson Crusoe: Dan O'Herlihy and Jaime Fernandez

ripen, but the birds threaten them. Robinson makes a scarecrow with a woman's dress; he suddenly experiences sharp nostalgia of love and desire. He learns to light a fire, to knead dough, to bake bread ... He has to fight against death, sickness, fever, the grief of losing his dog. He reads the Bible: the Scriptures have no longer any meaning.' Finally reconciled to his life and master of his fate, he becomes an odd, insect-like figure, neglecting his home, his animals and his appearance, trotting crazily along the beach under his goatskin umbrella, chattering to himself.

The second part of the film deals with his renewal of relationship with mankind, in the shape of Friday. Suddenly, with the arrival of this second person, he seems to forget all he has learned. There is a resurgence of all the old social prejudices and principles. Buache continues: 'The civilized man is reborn, with all his trail of moral *partis pris*, his defensive reflex being only an alibi; at once Robinson becomes a colonialist, and can conceive no other sort of relationship with Friday than that of master and slave ("I had at last a servant ... With my musket I taught him respect ...") He puts him in shackles, and later teaches him Christian theology. But Friday replies with disconcerting sense, which Buñuel compares with the reply of the dying man to the priest, as described by de Sade: "Thus your God makes everything

Las aventuras de Robinson Crusoe

awry simply to test or try his creature; does he not know his creature? Can't he guess the result?"' The last scene is a bitter and characteristic joke. As they set out on their return journey to England, Crusoe is wearing a resplendent officer's uniform; while Friday is dressed as a seaman. 'Like all great dramatic poets', wrote another film-maker, Tony Richardson, 'Buñuel has created out of a character motivated with strict psychological accuracy an immense and powerful symbol of our own times.'*

El

El is a scientific study of a psychopath. It is some tribute to its accuracy as a psychiatric document that it was shown by Professor Jacques Lacar to his students at the School of Psychotherapy, Hospital Sainte Anne, Paris. 'It is one of my favourites,' Buñuel has said, 'I like it particularly because it is a true documentary on a pathological case. But all the minute, detailed, documented exposition of the psychopathic progress of the character is improbable in the eyes of the ordinary public, who generally laugh during the screening of the film. This confirms my feeling that the traditional commercial

* *Sight and Sound*, January–March 1954.

Two scenes from *El*: the beginnings of obsession in the church (above); and a crisis of paranoia (below)

cinema has cultivated a great fondness in the public for the conventional, the superficial, the false commonplaces of sentiment.

'I would have liked to suppress the melodramatic part which precedes the marriage of the hero and which is no more than an amorous intrigue between the girl he is to marry, her fiancé and the paranoiac himself.

'The film's final intention is humorous rather than anti-clerical. The character is certainly pathetic. I am touched by this man possessed by such jealousy, such solitude and interior anguish, such exterior violence. I studied him like an insect.' (Interview in *Nuevo Cine*.)

The protagonist, Francisco, a rich, forty-year-old virgin, lives alone in his oppressively opulent villa. His sense of moral rectitude is illustrated by his dismissal of a maid when he catches her being kissed by his manservant, and his dismissal of his lawyer for too great leniency to his tenants. One day he is bewitched by the feet of a girl he glimpses in church, pursues her and seduces her away from her fiancé. Half-fascinated and half-repelled by this strange man, the girl, Gloria, agrees to become his bride. After the wedding (and a wedding night which recalls the garden scene in *L'Age d'or* in its frustrations), Francisco becomes more and more insanely jealous, until one night he comes to her room bearing menacing instruments: rope, needle and thread, scissors, cotton wool, antiseptic. The girl flees, but her mother, confessor and ex-fiancé all disbelieve her stories. Finally Francisco runs amok in church and tries to strangle the priest. In an epilogue Gloria, with her new husband and son, visit Francisco in the monastery where he has sought refuge. He assures them that he is now happy and well. As he walks away from her he pursues a crazed, zig-zag course along the path.

Tony Richardson, one of the earliest European critics to value these Mexican films of Buñuel's, wrote of the film on its first appearance: 'Relentlessly Buñuel watches, as if it were a snake, the paranoia unwind its fascinating coils; he gloats in the incidental comedy of its writhings (as when Cordova jabs a knitting-needle into a key-hole through which he imagines someone to be spying). Sometimes, though, one feels that Buñuel himself twists the tail of the snake to produce fascinating wriggles for their own sake. This is accentuated by the inadequacy of the players, neither of whose personalities is interesting enough to encompass the range and subtlety of characterization demanded. But the failure lies deeper. The conventional, commonplace script has only been partly assimilated by Buñuel. The ruthlessness of his study of the paranoiac sits uneasily with the elements of comedy-of-situation in the script: it called, perhaps, for the hand of a Sturges. There are signs, too, of production difficulties and confusions in the narration.

'Buñuel's personality is most evident in the blasting anti-Catholicism of the film – a subject to which he always reacts in his grandest, most authoritative

Abismos de pasión: Alejandro (Jorge Mistral) in the tomb

manner. The paranoiac is portrayed as deeply religious, and it is at a ceremony for the initiation of young priests, at which he is a lay official, that he first sees the girl. This magnificent sequence presents the heavy, oppressively ornamented setting, the strain on the blanched faces of the boys, the weary ritual of the bishop, and Cordova's desperate attempt to keep his attention on the solemnity of the occasion while, despite himself, it wanders on to the legs of the spectators. The climax of the film provides a further opportunity. Cordova, desperate and exhausted, has gone into a church; in a rapidly mounting cross-cutting sequence, all the congregation, the altar boy, the priest himself, seem to him to be cat-calling, pulling faces, thumbing noses.'

Abismos de pasión (Cumbres borrascosas)

'It's a film I wanted to make at the time of *L'Age d'or*. It's a key work for Surrealists. I think it was Georges Sadoul who translated it. They liked the side of the book that elevates *l'amour fou* above everything – and naturally as I was in the group I had the same ideas about love and found it a great novel. But I never found a backer, the film languished among my papers and was made in Hollywood eight or nine years later.* I hadn't thought about it

---

* By William Wyler, in 1939.

any more until Dancigers, who had two stars under contract, Mistral and Irasema Dilian, both very well known in Spain, asked me to make a film from a script I didn't like. Then he reminded me that I'd once mentioned my adaptation of *Wuthering Heights*, and I showed it to him. He accepted it. Really, I was no longer interested in making this film, and I didn't try any innovations. It remains the film I conceived in 1930, a 24-year-old film, but I think it's faithful to the spirit of Emily Brontë. It's a very harsh film, without concessions, and it respects the novel's attitude to love.'

Abismos de pasión (*Cumbres borrascosas*) is visceral. Buñuel changed the story only to be the more faithful to the spirit of the book. He side-steps the bad actors, using them as he uses the skeletal trees in the dark and jagged landscape, as objects in a composition in which the camera and the editing are the true protagonists. By faithfully realizing his project of twenty years earlier (it seems more likely that the Buñuel–Unik scenario was prepared after *Las Hurdes* rather than at the time of *L'Age d'or* as Buñuel suggests) he achieved an anachronistic quality, a little like some old film by Dmitri Kirsanov, which only adds to the fascination of the work. For the present writer it is a masterwork from start to finish, though the last three reels, unanimously admired by Buñuel's critics, are undoubtedly the most powerful. From the death of Katy–Cathy and the blasphemous invocation of Alejandro–Heathcliff, asking God to send him to hell where she will be waiting for him, to the final profanation of her tomb, trying (finally!) to sleep with her, the action has a feverish lyricism equivalent to the best passages in Emily Brontë. The close of the final scene is magnificent. As Ricardo–Hindley enters with the shot-gun with which he is about to kill Alejandro, the passionate lover sees in the figure, silhouetted in the doorway of the tomb, the image of Katy, robed in white, and beckoning.

Buñuel was dissatisfied with the actors: 'Irasema Dilian, with her Polish accent and Mistral with his Spanish accent ... introduced an element of undesirable – because uncontrollable – unreality.' He confesses also that he still blushes at the music of the film. 'It was my own fault. My negligence. I went to Europe, to Cannes, and left the composer to add the musical accompaniment; and he put music throughout the film. A real disaster. I intended to use Wagner just at the end, in order to give the film a romantic aura, precisely the characteristic sick imagination of Wagner. Still, I think that my version reflects the spirit of the novel much better than the one made by Hollywood.' It is impossible not to agree.

La ilusión viaja en tranvía

In the same year as this intense romantic melodrama, Buñuel made a light comedy, patently intended for the home market, full of Andalusian wit and, he

La illusión viaja en tranvía: the shot repeated from *Subida al cielo*

said, 'with a final reel of good cinema'. *La ilusión viaja en tranvía* is an apparently superficial picaresque comedy, in which the improbable happens at every turn, transforming the everyday into miracle. A couple of tramway workers decide, one day of holiday, to take their old tramcar, condemned to be broken up for scrap, on a last jaunt. As it rattles on its journey, outrageous and extraordinary episodes accumulate: characters reveal their essential natures. The people who get on to the tramcar are disturbed because there is no fare to pay, and an American tourist suspects she smells Communism near at hand. An orphan is persuaded that the actress who passes by on the pavement is his long-lost mother. A couple of little old ladies exploit a statue of the scourged Christ, living very well off the money they blackmail out of good believers. The vehicle becomes a transport for the workers from a slaughterhouse; and the heads of bleeding carcasses dangle from the luggage racks – a fine Surrealist image. Few Latin comedies can boast the invention and the infectious *pasodoble* rhythm of this merry caravan of smiling denunciations and cruel jests. As a comedy it is a worthy rival to *Subida al cielo*; one of its best and most characteristic sequences is the performance in a

La ilusión viaja en tranvía: a hoard of black market corn is discovered by the hungry populace

popular theatre, with Biblical episodes in which Buñuel cheerily parodies himself.

Asked about the apparent connections of this film with the Italian neo-realist work *Molti sogni per la strada* (1948, directed by Mario Camerini), Buñuel said that he had never seen it, but 'I am ideologically opposed to the neo-realist tendency. Neo-realism introduced some enrichments to cinematographic expression, but nothing more. Neo-realist reality is partial, official, above all reasonable; but poetry, mystery, are absolutely lacking in it. Neo-realism confuses ironical fantasy with black humour . . .' Conceiving the film Buñuel may rather have recalled the time in 1931 when the Andalusian Surrealist group hired a tram in Seville, filled it up with friends, a brass band and a movie actress, and spent the day merrily driving round the town and engineering many strange incidents.

El rio y la muerte

'In this film there are seven deaths, four burials and I don't know how many funeral wakes.' *El rio y la muerte* is Buñuel's commentary on the Mexican

El rio y la muerte

way of death, a kind of local variant on the 'vengeance' Western. The hero is a young doctor working in a modern hospital on the outskirts of Mexico City. When his father dies he returns to his village to look after his mother; and discovers that his father has been the latest victim of an old vendetta. The rest of the film is concerned with his efforts to break the chain of killing, against the wishes of the traditionalist mother who expects him to defend the family honour with the gun.

The film was more expensive and ambitious than Buñuel's previous Mexican productions, and at times its pictorial qualities and its depiction of Mexican folklore recall the glossy films of such contemporaries as Emilio Fernandez, Gavaldón or Crevenna. The overt tone of liberal morality and the condemnation of Mexican *machismo*,* rural feuds and their consequent retaliatory deaths is at odds with the marginal irony as well as with a brutality that sometimes approaches the grotesque. There is a certain black humour in the depiction of the social recovery effected by the enlightened young doctor; and there are Buñuelesque touches in phrases like 'the Lord has his reasons'

* The Mexican myth of virility; 'in Mexico they are so virile that even the women are manly'.

166

which commentate the killings. Overall however it is uncharacteristic. A film clearly intended for the Mexicans, with their traditional concept of the imminence and gratuitousness of death, it is distinguished from Buñuel's *oeuvre* in general by its preoccupation with *recherché* plastic effects. J.-A. Fieschi, in *Cahiers du Cinéma*, described the film as 'the least ambiguous, the least wicked and, by the same token, the least fascinating and characteristic of Buñuel's films'. Buñuel concurred: 'I hate its educative pretensions. It is a failure.' Ironically, the producers, bowing to pressure from the authorities, submitted *El rio y la muerte* to the 1954 Venice Festival, in place of *Robinson Crusoe*. It was the only film by Buñuel shown there without success.

Ensayo de un crimen (The criminal life of Archibaldo de la Cruz)

The vein of black comedy in *Ensayo de un crimen* is (or at least was, before Buñuel) comparatively rare in Latin-American cinema; and finds its nearest equivalents in English literature. A kind of prologue introduces the infant Archibaldo, a spoilt, rich child who, with his delight in hiding in the wardrobe where his mother's clothes hang, promises to become as neurotic as Francisco in *El* – to whom, in fact, he has distinct resemblances. One day his mother gives him a musical box surmounted by a twirling ballet girl. As it starts to play, a stray bullet from a revolution in the street outside kills his governess, thereby convincing the child of the magical properties with which the toy has been credited. He gazes round-eyed at a trail of bright blood running down her smooth thighs as she lies on the floor, her skirts pulled up in her death fall.

The child is father of the man. Years later, the grown-up Archibaldo, a distinguished ceramist, is delighted to rediscover the musical box in an antique shop. The music brings back the image of the blood on the thighs; henceforth his erotic desires will be identified with a megalomaniac desire to kill. But poor Archibaldo is constantly frustrated: his intended victims always die by other means before he has the chance to kill them. Thus a nun, nursing him during a breakdown, falls down a lift-shaft before he can cut her throat with a razor; a whore is killed by her protector; his unfaithful fiancée is shot by her lover. The only intended victim who escapes completely is Lavinia, an independent, teasing, amoral (as opposed to his religious nature) girl whom he has selected for her resemblance to a wax mannequin to which he is bizarrely attached. He plans to burn Lavinia, like Joan of Arc, in his ceramic kiln; but when she eludes him is reduced – in the most disturbing and truly Surreal scene in the film – to embracing the wax figure, and then consigning it to the ovens, where its limbs curl and writhe obscenely.

Archibaldo, constantly frustrated (the impotence symbolism is obvious) finally attempts to give himself up to the police; but the commissioner laughs

Luis Buñuel

Ensayo de un crimen: Archibaldo (Ernesto Alonso) with intended victim . . . and mannequin substitute

at him: 'If we imprisoned everybody who ever wanted to kill someone . . .!'
Archibaldo meets Lavinia again; and throws his magic music box into the
lake, where the little dancer seems to stand for an instant on the surface of the
water. Unlike Francisco, Archibaldo is clearly cured, as we see him finally
walking off in company with Lavinia. He sees an insect on the path, and
draws back from killing it with his stick.

The absurd story is developed parallel with a precise psychological definition of the central character, and with marvellous and characteristic details.
'The film', said Buñuel in an interview for *Nuevo Cine*, 'is a joke, a *divertisse-
ment*. My intention was to create a happy situation at the end as absurd as
the preceding tragic situations of the film. The final scene was imposed neither
by the producer nor the censorship. Absolutely not. It is in my original script.
I wanted it myself. Ado Kyrou has written that it is the result of a commercial
compromise, a happy ending. It is no such thing. The arbitrary ending was
my own idea. It is a *scherzo*.' He was delighted when in 1972 the critic
Antonio Castro called *Archibaldo* the most pornographic film he had seen.
'*All* my films are pornographic,' he boasted; and a little later declared the
same to a reporter for *Paris-Soir*.

12. Severe and Serene

Following *Archibaldo*, Buñuel was offered the opportunity to work in France. This return to the country which had understood him best and helped him most was significant: it marked the end of Buñuel's exile, and his recognition as a director of international stature. Now his interpretation of the world could be expressed in a clear dialectic. The three co-productions – *Cela s'appelle l'Aurore* was a Franco-Italian production; *La Mort en ce jardin* and *La Fièvre monte à El Pao* were Franco-Mexican – form a loose triptych on the principle and practice of revolution under fascist dictatorships with clear allusions to the régimes of several Latin-American states, and to Spain herself.

For *Cela s'appelle l'Aurore* Buñuel was given the opportunity to adapt a very good book, by Emmanuel Robles. Jean Genet was commissioned to do the script, but failed to deliver, though he had been paid. Consequently Buñuel wrote the scenario in collaboration with Jean Ferry. Gorzone rules his industrial empire on a Mediterranean island with a rod of iron. A good Christian and a good family man (apart from a little adultery) he exploits his workers without mercy. In this evil microcosmic capitalism, the art-loving commissioner of police and the humane doctor Valerio represent opposite poles. Valerio's wife Angela cannot understand why her husband will not

Cela s'appelle l'Aurore: the killing of the dictator (above) and the death of Sandro (below)

leave the wretched island for a fashionable practice in Nice. While she goes off on holiday without him, he falls in love with a rich young widow, Clara.

His sympathy with Sandro, a worker dismissed by Gorzone, is turned to active involvement when Sandro, whose tubercular wife has died, kills the dictator and seeks sanctuary in the doctor's house. When Angela returns home and finds Sandro there, she leaves her husband without a word. Valerio refuses to betray Sandro to the police chief. Sandro flees, and shoots himself to avoid arrest. In the last shot Valerio walks along the beach hand in hand with Clara, and closely followed by three comrades of Sandro's. Valerio has earned both love and friendship.

Few of Buñuel's films have more divided his admirers. Raymond Durgnat considers that 'From what is, perhaps, his most schematic scenario, Buñuel wrings a film whose beauty is all the more poignant for its severity. In its intransigence it is almost the humanist equivalent of a Calvinist proposition. This intransigence comes from the remarkable purity of the script, which allows its characters certain Machiavellian compromises, but no sentimental or selfish one.'

Ado Kyrou, writing as a committed Surrealist, has seen the film as at once a progress – towards greater clarity of style and socio-moral ideas – and a regression: 'The regression is more complex. Seeing this film which moves me practically to tears, I have still the impression that Luis wants to prove to the French that it is wrong to class him as incoherent, crazy. While retaining his virulence, he loses his violence. The calm which is identifiable in his last Mexican films here becomes a calm of "logic". Is it a return to traditional logic? True there is no lack of Buñuelian sequences (the image of Christ with the electric wires . . . the cop who reads Claudel and decorates his desk with a Dali Christ, etc.) but the novelty of *L'Age d'or*, of *El*, of *Archibaldo de la Cruz* was the way of presenting a violent story, the Surrealist viewpoint. Here the subject is Surrealist (revolution and *amour fou*) but the film is not. Any one of a dozen other directors could have made *Cela s'appelle l'Aurore* as well as Buñuel. No one else could have made *Archibaldo* for instance, or even *Susana . . .*'

The film develops a violent story in the most direct realist tradition. Examined objectively it is a compact, decent work; and if it has about it something of the pamphlet, it must be acknowledged that it is a very worthy pamphlet. 'It is one of the films I find most satisfying. It is such a perfectly pure story . . .'

La Mort en ce jardin

The second film of the trilogy was based on the novel by José-André Lacour. As it finally turned out, the film is some way from Buñuel's original concep-

La Mort en ce jardin: Georges Marchal, Michel Piccoli

tion, for the scenario was considerably modified by the French producers; and a work which might have been great is in fact somewhat muddled. The action takes place in a diamond field in an unnamed South American state. The adventurer–prospectors are served, according to their various ways, by a priest, Father Lizzardi, a prostitute, Gin, and a trader, Chenko. Chenko, having bribed the local governor, confronts the miners with a decree ordering the nationalization of their claims. The miners attempt protest; and a professed anarchist manages to organize them and resist the police chief's order to disarm. Meanwhile Lizzardi counsels Christian resignation and peaceful submission. A natural revolutionary appears in the shape of Chark, who after being arrested and escaping by blowing up the police post, leads a little band of refugees towards freedom. In their terrible journey Chark, the positive, active man battles for leadership with Lizzardi, with his Christian philosophy of patient submission. Each compromises. Lizzardi, burning his prayer-book to light a fire, approaches the practical lessons learnt by Nazarín and Viridiana; Chark is forced to abandon his anarchist stand. As the arrival of Friday caused Crusoe to revert to his former attitudes and prejudices, so does the party's discovery of a crashed aeroplane stuffed with food, jewels and corpses.

173

The film falls into two clearly defined sections: the revolution in the village, with its impressive scenes of the revolution and the confrontation between establishment and proletariat; and the second, the journey through the forest, which defines the complex character of Father Lizzardi, a figure with so many facets that he can be regarded as one of the most interesting figures in all Buñuel's work. The film culminates in a final sequence which is a strange compromise between realism and magic. Raymond Durgnat has written: 'From the moment Chark's band enters the jungle, the film has an atmosphere of dream, as it prepares the inner disintegration of the characters. The starving fugitives stumble on a snake, and while we are still startled by the threat it conventionally represents, Chark has killed it for food. But before a fire can be lit, the snake is "animated" by ants. The fugitives come across a postcard of Paris which seems to promise help until Castin recognizes it as his own "fetish"; it animates before his delirious eyes. The aeroplane saves them, yet all but Chark and Maria are destroyed by it. The film has the nightmarish "Yes, but" structure, a structure which (as in *Las Hurdes*) is also a form of dialectic. The intricate gunplay of the first half is treated with a speed, a cerebrality, that abstract it into a series of syllogisms in the logic of power.'

La Fièvre monte à El Pao

It is convenient to treat the third of the co-production 'trilogy' here, though in fact it followed *Nazarín*. Again the script was modified, and the film fell short of the masterpiece that might have resulted. It dissected human conduct in an imaginary fascist state, the hypocrisy of non-intervention, the useless sacrifices of individual activity in the face of the dictatorship. The story is based on a novel by Henri Castillou, which Buñuel had long wanted to film. The hero, Ramon (Gérard Philipe) is a high-minded but cowardly official in a little Latin-American republic, whose President is using the murder of a local Governor as the excuse for political oppressions. Ramon's love for the Governor's widow, Inés (María Félix), secures his promotion, but his lofty and liberal principles almost bring about his ruin. He is eventually saved by weakness, when Inés is able to persuade him to betray a rival, and to turn a bloody revolt to his personal advantage. Finally, though, this same cowardice destroys Inés; and as the film ends, we see that Ramon will in turn be destroyed by the resurgence of his own feeble idealism.

The story was totally sympathetic to Buñuel – iconoclastic, sceptical of authority, exact in its analysis of the moral and psychological fallibility of the protagonist. The paradox that motives are not by any means always related to effects, too, is dear to him; and Ramon is to a degree a prototype of the Nazarín whose Christian charity invariably results in disaster and bloodshed.

La Fièvre monte à El Pao: Buñuel directing María Félix and Jean Servais

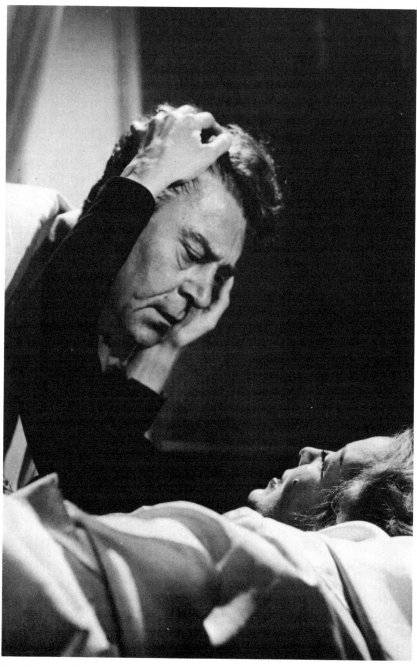

La Fièvre monte à El Pao: Jean Servais, María Félix

So it is surprising that much of the film is flat and wayward in its handling: perhaps Gérard Philipe's fatal illness – in the film he already looks frail and tired – took its toll of the production.

Nazarín

Nazarín must be accounted a predecessor of the series of Buñuel's masterworks. It is a fairly faithful adaptation of the story and character created by Galdós. Buñuel for the most part simply added three short sequences to illuminate the central themes: humanism opposed to religion; the failure of a purely Christian attitude in a world as imperfect as ours; the observation of the collapse of the principles of faith and morality in a priest. The setting is Mexico in 1900, during the rule of the dictator Porfirio Díaz, supported by a land-owning class, a military clique and a conservative clergy. The synopsis which accompanied the film's original release summarized the story as follows:

The slum-house of Señora Chanfa (Ofelia Guilmain) is a court of miracles: craftsmen, beggars, whores, muleteers, thieves. The humble priest Nazarín (Francisco Rabal) lives there. His mainstay is alms: he asks nothing of his fellow men, but is mocked by them. Nazarín, in his daily life, only obeys the lesson of Christ: compassion, love and forgiveness.

Near him, in the same slum, the destinies of two women are being woven. Beatriz (Marga López), a victim of hysteria and a sense of guilt, has been abandoned by 'Pinto' (Noé Murayama), the man she at once desires and rejects. She fails in an attempt to commit suicide; and in Nazarín's sweet regard she finds new reason for devotion and surrender. Andara (Rita Macedo) is a whore whose primitive kindliness is lost under the flashy colours of her trade. She kills another woman in a brawl and hides herself, wounded, in the priest's shabby room.

The lives of Nazarín and the two women meet. Andara flees from the police; Beatriz, from herself. Both decide to follow Nazarín on the road. The priest has been reprimanded for protecting Andara and deprived of his clerical garb. He takes to the fields, believing – like Don Quixote – that only in pilgrimage, among the nameless poor, can he fulfil his ideal of the good. Once more, the errant knight goes off to undo the wrongs of others. What does he find on the way? In a rail junction, the workmen who repel him because the priest accepts to work for food instead of a salary: Nazarín's humility creates a row between the workers and the foreman; there are shots and several dead. In a village, the religious hysteria of the ignorant women who believe Nazarín is capable of doing miracles: while the priest heals a sick child, the women scream, tear their clothes and treat

Buñuel directing *Nazarín*

Nazarín as a witch-doctor. In a town struck by cholera, two lovers who, in the throes of death, grasp at their sexual passion and refuse religious comfort. In another lost hamlet, a humiliated dwarf in whom love and humanity are but the caricature of the divine likeness. And in all his travels, he finds an unjust society which will not be moved by the example of pure Christianity. Such are Nazarín's windmills. But it is hard to conquer him. His words, again and again, will be of pity for the sinner, wrath for the pharisee and brotherhood for the humble.

Justice pursues the fugitive whore and the priest who has protected her. And in a forgotten village, justice finally catches up with them. Nazarín, Beatriz and Andara walk with the chain-gang of criminals, who mock them, speculating whether the priest who travels in company with two sinful women is a rogue or fool. In prison Nazarín is struck and derided by a parricide (Luis Aceves Castañeda) and defended by a church-thief (Ignacio López Tarso). He feels in his own flesh what insult and injury mean. The images of failure cloud the priest's eyes when the church-thief says: 'What's your life worth? You're on the good path; I am on the bad path ... We're both useless.' Doubt sinks deeply into Nazarín. What can

Nazarín

the lonely Quixote oppose to human evil? But perhaps Andara and Beatriz have been changed ... Nazarín will discover that neither his words nor his example will change the world. All has been in vain.

He walks in shackles, wounded and spat upon. Doubt becomes stronger than faith. Men laugh at the good and ridiculous man; but in Nazarín's ears their jeers resound like the drums for an execution. He doubts. And because he doubts he accepts his destiny and his failure with a new statement, no longer humble but rebellious, of his moral conviction. He stops and once more receives alms. The path of the good man, of the moral hero, opens before him: the path that leads to the scaffold reserved by society for rebels.

Perhaps the best critique of *Nazarín* was that of the Mexican writer Octavio Paz: 'Sometimes an artist surpasses the limits of his art and offers us a work which has its equivalents in a freer and ampler sphere. Some of Buñuel's pictures – *L'Age d'or*, *Los Olvidados*, *Robinson Crusoe* and now *Nazarín* – without losing their cinematic quality, carry us to other provinces of the spirit; certain drawings by Goya, a poem by Quevedo or Péret, a chapter by the Marquis de Sade, a short play by Valle Inclán, an episode by Cervantes.

... Buñuel's films may be seen, and judged, as cinema, but also as works pertaining to the broader and more permanent universe of those masterpieces which both reveal the human condition and show us a way to surpass it. In spite of the obstacles our world opposes to such undertakings, Buñuel's film unfolds under the double arch of beauty and rebellion.

'*Nazarín* belongs to the great tradition of the Spanish Fool, inaugurated by Cervantes. His folly consists in taking the great ideas and the great words seriously and trying to live according to them. Don Quixote saw Dulcinea as a peasant woman. Nazarín, beyond the monstrous features of Andara and Ujo, sees the helpless image of the "fallen men"; behind the sexual delirium of Beatriz, he finds the echo of divine love ...

'The picture abounds in scenes of the best and most terrible Buñuel: his fury, more concentrated, is the more explosive. Scene after scene, we are taken through the "cure" – that is, the torture – of the fool. All those he approaches reject him. The powerful and satisfied, because they consider him a dangerous and antisocial individual. The victims and the persecuted, because they need *another*, more effective, kind of consolation. Even the feelings of the women who follow him – a blend of Sancho Panza and Mary Magdalene – are mixed. In prison, among thieves and murderers, comes the final revelation: both the "good" of Nazarín and the "evil" of the church-thief are useless in a world where "efficiency" is the supreme value. Faithful to the tradition of the Spanish madman, Buñuel tells us the story of a disenchantment. In Don Quixote, the illusion was the spirit of chivalry. In Nazarín, it is Christianity. But there is something else. As Nazarín's pilgrimage takes him through hills and hamlets, the image of Christ pales in his conscience, and the image of man begins to illuminate it. That is: Buñuel gradually takes us, in a series of exemplary episodes, through a double process: the illusion of divinity fades out, the reality of man is discovered. The supernatural gives way to something marvellous: human nature and its powers. This revelation is embodied in two unforgettable scenes: when Nazarín offers the "comforts of the other world" to the dying lover, and she answers, fixed to the image of her love, with these *truly* perturbing words, "cielo no, Juan sí" ("No heaven; but Juan"); and at the end, when Nazarín refuses alms and after a moment of doubt, accepts it not as charity, but as a sign of friendship. Nazarín, the lonely one, is no longer alone: he has lost God, but he has found love and fraternity.'

The Young One

The action of *The Young One* is set on a swamp island somewhere off the Southern States. Fleeing from the mainland where he has been accused of raping a white woman, Travers, a Negro, arrives on the island in a motorboat. The island is inhabited by three people: Miller the gamewarden, Pee-

Nazarín

The Young One: Zachary Scott, Bernie Hamilton, Crahan Denton and Kay Meersman

Wee his old assistant, and Pee-Wee's granddaughter Evalyn (Evvie). Pee-Wee dies, but Evvie goes blithely and unselfconsciously about the daily tasks of life.

While Miller is absent from the island, Travers takes supplies and one of his guns, and makes friends with Evvie. When Miller returns and discovers Travers has been at his cabin, he angrily sets out with a gun in pursuit of him, but gives up when he is convinced that Travers has been killed. That night, however, Travers surprises Miller and takes all his firearms, leaving him defenceless. Miller is obliged to make truce with Travers, who sets about repairing his boat, intending to escape from the island. Travers accepts employment as Miller's assistant, in place of the dead Pee-Wee. While the Negro sleeps in Pee-Wee's shack, Evvie moves in with Miller, who seduces her.

Next day a preacher arrives from town, brought by Jackson the brutish ferryman. Jackson brings news that a Negro is being sought for rape, and Miller, realizing that the man is Travers, joins Jackson in a merciless manhunt. Jackson wants to take him alive, but Miller says 'If I clap eyes on him, I'm going to shoot.'

Meanwhile the priest has discovered that Evvie has not been baptized, and announces that he will rectify this. He stays the night in Pee-Wee's hut. A declared anti-racialist, he still insists on turning over the mattress on which Travers has slept. When the priest baptizes Evvie, her innocent scepticism (she asks to see the 'golden key' he has promised her) recalls that of Man Friday in *Robinson Crusoe*.

Miller and Jackson capture Travers, who declares his innocence. When they tie him to a stake, Evvie surreptitiously releases him. The priest has meanwhile discovered that Miller has 'deflowered' Evvie, and blackmails him with the knowledge: he will keep silent if Miller will allow the Negro to escape, and subsequently marry Evvie. The priest and Evvie start for the landing stage where they believe Jackson waits for them at the launch. But Jackson has managed to ambush Travers, intending to kill him. In the combat that ensues, Travers gets the upper hand, but with his knife at Jackson's throat, refuses to kill him and thereby give the mob on the mainland another reason for lynching him.

Evvie, the priest and Jackson leave for the mainland in the launch, with Jackson still intent on returning for Travers with the law. But farther down the beach, Miller helps Travers into his boat, sees him start the motor and head for another part of the mainland and a chance for escape.

'So it is,' writes Freddy Buache, 'that Miller's love for a nymphet leads him to question his own racial prejudices, i.e. his whole conception of life, the world and society. His previous moral code had seemed straightforward enough: two and two make four, one does not make love to little girls, one respects other people's property, Negroes are subhuman, and good is all on one side, with evil all on the other. But in fact nothing to do with mankind can be so simple or so natural. Our acts and our thoughts are above all distinguished by ambiguity, which does not of course mean that on the level of collective and individual praxis there is not the Right and the Left, the baddies and the non-baddies. I do not see any contradiction in these two statements because they do not work on the same level: a moral system based on ambiguity does not mean that unambiguous judgments may not be passed on men's actions, on the intentions that determine them and on the honesty that makes them authentic.'

This Mexican–U.S. co-production possesses a clarity of action, a fluidity and a unity of time, place and action not very frequent in Buñuel. *Nazarín* discovered its power in the theme, aesthetic and structure. By comparison, *The Young One* is all spontaneity and freshness. Buñuel has told me that the film was made 'with one stroke', and that he likes it very much. 'All the people changed, underwent an evolution during the shooting ... as is evident, the whites are not always as bad as one imagines' (*Nuevo Cine*).

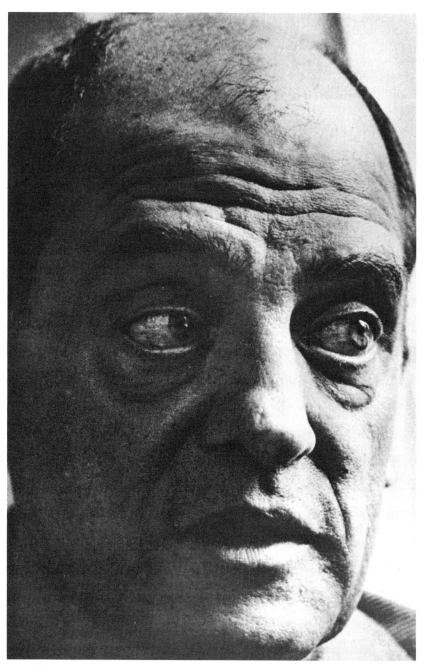

Luis Buñuel

Shortly after finishing the film, Buñuel told Derek Prouse, 'with something like grim mirth', that he had almost cancelled the whole project after the first week because of the girl's and other actors' inability to perform the simplest actions with any semblance of naturalism. He had to ask Zachary Scott, who plays Miller, to overact in order to impose some sort of unity on the playing. 'But finally I'd still prefer to work with someone like her than with any star. The chances of capturing something real are so much greater.' In the outcome the portrayal of the thirteen-year-old Evvie is a triumph, in her pagan innocence putting the shoes on her dead grandfather's feet and then eating a slice of bread and butter before going outside, squashing a spider and then tending her beehives among the flowers; or hopping along the landing-stage, in the final scene, in comically inappropriate over-size high-heel shoes.

In the publicity hand-out for the film, the distributors quoted Buñuel's reply to a question put to him for *Film: Book One* (Grove Press): 'What kind of pictures would you make if the limitations forced upon film-makers such as financing, censorship, etc., were non-existent?'

'If it were possible for me, I would make films which, apart from entertaining the audience, would convey to them the absolute certainty that they DO NOT LIVE IN THE BEST OF ALL POSSIBLE WORLDS. And in doing this I believe that my intentions would be highly constructive. Movies today, including the so-called neo-realist, are dedicated to tasks contrary to this. How is it possible to hope for an improvement in the audience – and consequently in the producers – when every day we are told in these films, even in our most insipid comedies, that our social institutions, our concepts of Country, Religion, Love, etc., etc., are, while perhaps imperfect, UNIQUE AND NECESSARY? The true "opium of the audience" is conformity; and the entire, gigantic film world is dedicated to the propagation of this comfortable feeling, wrapped though it is at times in the insidious disguise of art.'

From 1950 Buñuel's biography is very much that of his films. The periods between production were spent at home. He entertained very little, went to the cinema three or four times a year and sometimes met the Spaniards he knew in Mexico. As well as Buñuel there were Carlos Velo (supervisor of productions for Barbachano who produced *Nazarín*); Julio Alejandro (adaptor of *Nazarín*); Luis Alcoriza, Buñuel's collaborator on some of the best scenarios and a personal friend; Manuel Altolaguirre who produced and co-scripted *Subida al cielo* and wrote and directed a film of originality and poetic merit, *El cantar de los cantares*; the Spanish critic Alvaro Custodio; Garcia Ascott, scenarist, collaborator of Barbachano and a director of documentaries in Cuba; the Spanish writer Max Aub, who also wrote a number of scripts for the Mexican cinema; Pittaluga and Eduardo Ugarte, who had followed him from New York.

Reunion with his mother at the 'LAragon' café in Pau

Buñuel bought a little house in Cerrada Félix Cuevas, in the Colonia del Valle, near Mexico City – simple and convenient with a little garden and a garage. Not until after the French co-productions did his economic situation improve so that he could reasonably look forward to an old age free from penury. 'To be poor is worrying, above all,' he told me; 'but to be rich is even worse.'

His son Juan Luis has given some details of his family life: 'At home, when he has had money he has spent it on good living. We have always eaten wholesome food. At home we have beefsteaks ten centimetres thick. There is always good wine in the cellar, and whisky, which father drinks. My parents have been very good. Mother is very calm, understands my father very well, and knows how to cope with his nervous moods. Father was always very attentive and gave us an extraordinary amount of his time. I never recall him smacking us or punishing us severely. He did everything needful to give us the best possible education. He sent me to a good college in Ohio and afterwards sent me and my brother Rafael to the University of California, where I studied English literature. My younger brother had an equally careful education. I must mention that the decision to go into films was entirely mine and not in any way influenced by my father. When Orson Welles came to Mexico I went to him with no recommendation and asked him to let me be his assistant director on the film of *Don Quixote* he was making for television. Later my father took me as assistant on *Nazarín*.'

Buñuel was not very interested in travelling, or in how his films did at foreign festivals. *Subida al cielo*, *Los Olvidados*, *El rio y la muerte*, *The Young One* and *Viridiana* all went to Cannes without his authorization, sent by the producers. When a French company invited him to make a film in Europe it was his first journey there since before the war. He did not want to return to Spain at that time. His family came from Zaragoza to meet him at Pau, near the Pyrenean frontier. There, after twenty years of exile, he saw his mother, his brothers and the snow-capped mountains of the Spanish frontier; and the experience moved him. This was at the time he was making *Cela s'appelle l'Aurore*. Other French producers wanted to employ him; there were discussions about making *Thérèse Etienne* in Switzerland; there were talks about *La Femme et le pantin*. Subsequently the producer involved in the last project told the press, with evident irritation, that he could not accept Buñuel's treatment. 'I asked for an adaptation of the Pierre Louys novel, and he turned me in something that was pure Buñuel from start to finish.' In consequence the film was assigned to Julien Duvivier, who made a character-istically mediocre commercial piece of it. Buñuel returned from Mexico with a contract to make *La Mort en ce jardin*.

In 1959 he attended the Cannes Festival to present *The Young One*: and from that time his public life has become progressively more active. The private man at this period has been best described by J. J. García Ascott, a young Spanish cinéaste of the Mexican colony:

'Something from the dolmen, a monolith from the cave of Altamira. From that image of a highwayman–seducer of fiction, glimpsed sharpening a razor in the opening of *Un Chien andalou* we have passed to the monolith. Among the tourist sites of eternal Spain, along with Cuenca and the Escurial, there is the face of Luis Buñuel. Like the faces of other Spanish artists – Picasso – there is in it something of the bull. Weather-beaten skin. Eyes whose fixed gaze is an assault. A latent, contained force, an enormous power economically irradiated, defensively protected. At times, a brief, tense anger bursts out. Or, rather, a flashing reflection of the deep anger which in Buñuel must be seismic and final.

'Apart from this, he is at once unquiet and calm. Probing with his inter-locutory eyes. Fixed and attentive – and a little deaf – in every theme, every discussion. Buñuel takes life seriously.

'And within life, humour. On the one hand Buñuel has a childish delight in simple and uncomplicated jokes, repeated time and time again with slight modification, seeking in them a new meaning and a more profound perfection, applying them to new aspects of the conversation, expressing all their marrow with a full and broad satisfaction. And sometimes, days and weeks later, at some point in the talk, the joke which everyone else has forgotten will resurface, having revolved within Buñuel, like a stone polished by the waves,

187

drawing out at every movement new, intimate and forgotten satisfactions. On the other hand, linked to this childish and elemental pleasure, Buñuel has a keen vision of "black humour", a vision which is free and profoundly healthy and which permits him – and us – to benefit by one of its forms most replete with non-conformism and rebellion. Because Buñuel is a non-conformist and rebel with the same complete naturalness with which other people are vegetarians. Everything in him implies the idea of absolute spiritual purity. And, within this humour, there never comes to his lips the hint of an expression which is coarse or insolent, never anything off-colour, obscene or pornographic.

'For there is something of the monk in Buñuel. A solitary house, a monastic room, scorn for the superficial or decorative aesthetic. He is only exacting about eating and drinking – but even then, simple food, wine and good whisky. That is all. In his library are three main sections: Galdós, some Surrealists and precursors, and Fabre's *Souvenirs Entomologiques*.

'In his cell, Buñuel collects arms. He regularly cleans and polishes shotguns and Winchester carbines, rare Mausers and Lugers. Smith and Wessons, little Astras and ancient duelling pistols as dainty as greyhounds. And in his little crucible, with the ritual gestures of Crusoe, he moulds lead shot.

'But he neither uses them, nor hunts. His fondness for arms is also something anthropological. In them Luis Buñuel's endless love for the object finds its most defined form. Cleaning guns, immaculate ramrods, grey steel smoothly shining, constitute a true domestic ontology.

'And in truth everything in the house and in the person of Buñuel evokes "the actuality of the object itself". There is no alternative, there seem to exist no other possibilities or divergences. This applies very specially to his wife, the extraordinary Jeanne, a Lilloise as Luis is a Spaniard, as much a piece as a woman as her husband is as a man. If there is any case of the perfect meeting of "the other half", it is indeed, without doubt, this.

'And from these two halves, two sons. Monumental. Two towers . . . two mastiffs, full of rare gentleness and sweetness. In the house are juxtaposed a portrait of Buñuel by Dalí, a painting by Leonora Carrington, a map of the Paris Métro, a little upright piano. Upstairs the noise of a sewing machine. Everything produces a perfect sense of equilibrium. "The actuality of the object itself": things complement one another with silence and grave harmony. Not even the fleeting appearance of an incredible rat-coloured and frowning dog, a strange and marginal mutation in the zoological process, is capable of altering an order which rests on the simple truth of existence.

'Buñuel practically never goes out. Only a meeting with his friends is able to take him from his interior domestic life. And even so, an early leave-taking allows him to maintain the rhythm of a life which sends him to bed before ten at night in order to begin the day before sunrise.

'Buñuel rarely goes to the cinema. Two or three times a year, and without reference to the reviews. He is rarely pleased. Among the exceptions I remember – recently – hearing him mention *Un Condamné à mort s'est échappé, Twelve Angry Men, Wild Strawberries, The Cranes are Flying, Les Amants*. But he is never unfair, and as a professional he can admire technique when it is deserving of admiration.

'And here we touch on a point rarely mentioned by his commentators and analysts. For beyond the essential aspects of his work, which do not concern us here, Luis Buñuel is a director of admirable technique, expert in its most hidden corners, and able to solve spontaneously its hardest problems. When he is filming, invariably dressed in a combination of open-necked shirt, sweater and khaki trousers with huge pockets – with the single variation for exteriors of an impressive *salakof* – Buñuel is a fast and efficient director. Not a single gesture of "genius", not a single pose is detectable in his controlled and thoughtful behaviour. He establishes a good and correct relationship with his crew, and when working with actors never uses a single shout or a single artifice of seduction while breaking them in and convincing them. Few and very precise instructions. And when it seems that there has been some carelessness in the preparation for filming of a scene, the hoarse voice interrupts, always timely, always opportune, to recall the particular detail. But at the same time there is no excess of sketches and notes. Before dawn, Buñuel has thought out his scenes. After that it is a formal improvisation, on the set, with the scenario and actors before him, in full presence and vision of what he has to create.

'When the labour is done, Buñuel does not give much further time to the finished work. Already he is concerned, privately or officially, with something new. Once back at home, in his centre of gravity – as the filming is the centre of action – he resumes his day-to-day life.

'And so we leave him, sitting in an armchair with a cigarette between his fingers, cleaning his weapons solicitously, lining them up in shelves and racks.

'Luis Buñuel, the man in whom non-conformism is virtue, the protest rectitude, and rebellion a high, grave and deep *morality*.'

(J. J. García Ascott: *Portrait of Luis Buñuel*, in *Universidad de Mexico*, Vol XIII, No 4, December 1958.)

13. Viridiana

The biography of Buñuel does not end, however, with this amiable portrait of a man withdrawn to his Mexican retreat, adapted, Americanized, in permanent exile. He is too Spanish and too much a rebel not to strike a blow to assert his lasting ties to his fatherland. Slight as it is, Buñuel's Spanish production was our only cinema worthy of the name. Consisting of the two Surrealist films made in France, the two documentaries and the four unsigned comedies, this little group was nevertheless enough to indicate the possible triple direction of a Spanish cinema.

At the 1960 Cannes Film Festival, a group of Spaniards, among them the young Carlos Saura, director of *Los golfos* – a production of Films 59 which was Spain's official Festival entry – met with Buñuel and discussed the importance from every point of view of his returning to make a film in his native country. He would find the fundamental themes, the landscapes, the people and the problems of his country, to which he had always remained faithful in his work. The key to Buñuel remained his *Spanishness*, in the sight of the world. His return would be of special significance for those inside Spain who were struggling to give the cinema a national character. Spain still had an abundant production; but it had not yet found a national personality. To find a tradition was, in the Spanish idiom, like looking for three feet on a cat. Our culture has hardly ever maintained a logical character or continuity. It has been created in leaps, by sporadic feats of genius. Today, as so often in the past, we had to build a bridge over the post-war hiatus, cultural and therefore moral. The generation of 1960 had to create its own continuity with the second and third decades of the century. It is easy enough to do this with the wealth of works of exile literature, essay and thought that have been left to us; but in the cinema we have little but Buñuel. This was the gist of our discussions in Cannes. Buñuel said to me at that time, 'I know that as a good patriot I have to return to Spain and help; but maybe I am not a good patriot. I am tired and too old to begin something else there.' Such a pessimistic expression is in him no more than the reflection of a momentary depression in a man who is all energy. A few months later a correspondence began between him and his producers, which ultimately led to the production of *Viridiana*. In a letter to Pedro Portabella, of Films 59 (who were eventually only nominally co-producers of the film; the effective producer was UNINCI), Buñuel talked about the script of the film, which he had to prepare in principle as a Mexican production. He thought it suitable for Spain, since 'it could pass for a white film, although I must say it is full of darker intentions'. He summarized the story in a few words, and, professional as always, predicted that the audience would burst into applause in the sequence of the beggars' orgy, brilliant and effective as it would be.

By December 1960 Buñuel was installed in the capital, on the seventeenth floor of the Torre de Madrid. He was very happy. In Cannes he had said that he feared to come back to 'his city' to find it empty of the friends he had known, with the cafés and their marble tables replaced by self-service cafeterias, and everything changed. He did not, however, remain defeated by nostalgia. He told me that he thought Madrid splendid, much better than before. He still found his old cafés and his old friends. In Calle Victor Pradera, in the Café Viena, he became the centre of a circle, with a happy mixture of the survivors of his generation, those who like him had come back (the composer Pittaluga, José Bergamín, the essayist and maker of entomological films Guillermo Zuniga, the actor Francisco Rabal and others) and the people of the new generation, of whom he strongly approved. After Cannes he had written to his family, 'If Spanish youth is like those I have met here, then Spain is getting better.' In Madrid he gave no press interviews, but was at pains to receive, with rapt attention, the young independent critics, students of the cinema school, debutant directors.

For two months he did nothing but rest, and quietly plan the technical and artistic personnel of the film and the exterior locations. Buñuel knows admirably how to 'waste' time. We helped him to instal his Christmas 'Crib' in the apartment of the modern block. A bright and vulgar 'crib', such as a devout Madrilene might have, but full of anachronisms and inappropriate figures, creating shocking scenes (the 'dislocation of place' characteristic of Spanish Surrealism). His sister Conchita looked after him until his wife and Juan Luis arrived. He visited Zaragoza, to see his family, Las Hurdes, 'his' Toledo which he had loved from student days, when he had visited it every Saturday. He celebrated a very Spanish Christmas: 'It is a festival which I like a great deal, like all traditional festivals, with its intimacy, its fire and its other symbols.'

Shooting of *Viridiana* began on 4 February 1961. 'It is the first time I have had such freedom since I made *L'Age d'or*,' he told me in an interview for my correspondent's notes in *Sight and Sound*. 'Do you know', he added, not without irony, 'that *Viridiana* is the story of an Italian saint of the sixteenth century?' Effectively, Buñuel had unlimited freedom for the realization of his script. Economically, naturally, he was restricted. The budget of five million or so pesetas (finally the film cost six million) did not seem a great deal when compared with the 480 million for *King of Kings*, which was then shooting in the Spanish studios; but it was a very large sum compared with anything that Buñuel was accustomed to. 'If you had the millions of *King of Kings*,' he was asked, 'how many good films could you make?' 'If I had all that money, I would throw Franco out of Spain,' he replied. Awareness of his own value

Directing *Viridiana*; Aguayo at the camera

does not prevent almost comic gestures of sincere modesty. 'Imagine,' he said, with no touch of sarcasm; 'Nicholas Ray (the director of *King of Kings*) came to see me at home and told me that he admired my work a lot. Such an important man, and so rich! I say to myself, so I'm worth something after all!'

Viridiana progressed rapidly. The crew was partly composed of the same young technicians as *Los golfos* – a well-made film, though nothing indicated it as coming from the same group as *Viridiana*. Buñuel won from the actors interpretations not only superior to anything being done in Spain – and in most other countries for that matter. He did not seek stars; 'Stars are always horrible,' he told me. With the ability which every good director has for mimicry, he gave me a humorous impression of Simone Signoret, perhaps the most intelligent and sympathetic star in all his career. 'As we were shooting, she called me to her side and said in a very low voice: "Don Luis, how would it be if, to demonstrate my impatience, I tapped with my foot on the leg of the table, like this?" "Yes, my dear: do it as you like." ' Silvia Pinal, an actress popular in Mexico, particularly in comedy, and the wife of Gustavo Alatriste, a Mexican who gave money to the young Spanish companies, proved to be a remarkably docile and accommodating actress in the role of Viridiana. The group of beggars composed one of the most picturesque and pathetically human conglomerations the cinema had ever seen. Buñuel cast them one by one: two of them were non-professionals, an authentic beggar and a dwarf vendor of lottery tickets. Never has the atmosphere of a film been more cordial. I cannot resist introducing a personal note: a witnessed day of shooting on *Viridiana*.

23 March 1961

At 8.15 in the morning I met Buñuel at the Plaza Cafetería. Luis told me to be punctual; if I arrived late he would leave without me. When I arrived, Luis, his wife and his son were already waiting there.

Buñuel seemed very fresh, more so than in the evenings. He was full of energy. No one would guess his sicknesses due to sugar deficiency, or his age – 61 years and 24 days.

It was drizzling. Very worried I asked Juan Luis if it would spoil the plan.

'We shoot despite the rain,' he answered. 'Didn't you notice the rain scene in the false miracle sequence of *La Dolce Vita*? The ground was completely dry; the impression of the rain was given by the movement of the mass and some drops of water falling in front of the camera. The contrary can happen. With a couple of good lights, and the actors behaving normally under the rain, nobody believes that it is raining. That is the suggestive power of the cinema. In the scene of the labour conflict in *Nazarín* we began in sun and finished in rain. No one in the audience has ever noticed.

'It is true that the sequence looks greyer. But people think that is an intentional dramatic effect. There are a lot of things in the cinema like that.'

Buñuel finished his breakfast. We got into a hire car which took us all. We went towards Cienpozuelos. It was the last day of locations. The following day there were three takes to be done in Toledo. After that the shooting would be finished.

In the car Buñuel told me how he had bought old clothes in the flea market and had bargained with some gypsies under a bridge at Manzanares, offering them new clothes in exchange for the ones they were wearing, and then disinfecting the garments and putting them on the actors . . .

Buñuel's wife is still very beautiful. Now more than fifty, she keeps that surpassing simplicity of a French woman of character. On this occasion she was as happy as a girl. I asked her if being the wife of Luis Buñuel had not placed her in strange situations sometimes, as the wife of an artist whose films revealed so much violence, cruelty, aberration and sadism.

'Oh yes, often. During the shooting of *Los Olvidados* the Mexicans clustered round me, gazing compassionately. "Poor soul!" they said.'

We arrived at the village. The plaza, the old two-storey buildings, the square, rudimentary arcades. Spain is full of undiscovered marvels. I asked how they had found the place.

'I travelled about in this car for five days', said Buñuel, 'and took notes on the villages which I saw between here and Alicante. Then I made the selection of images which best framed the action. The exteriors of the estate of Viridiana's uncle were filmed at La Moraleja, an estate belonging to the Marquès de Usia; and there were two days shooting at El Pardo, only a kilometre from the palace of Generalissimo Franco.'

We got out of the car at the Plaza Mayor. It was full of bearded men who looked at us curiously. No doubt they already knew that we had come to shoot there. As it was raining, the country people had all morning free to be spectators . . . and they hoped to earn ten duros by being extras.

The production manager, Quintana, selected thirty of them rapidly – 'Buñuel types'.

'How hideous these men are!' exclaimed Buñuel's wife.

'Compared with Mexicans they are beauties,' replied Buñuel. 'In Mexico I have seen the ugliest men in the world. These have interesting heads, and above all, eyes.'

Buñuel's precise observation is the observation of an anthropologist rather than an aesthete.

He had meanwhile left us, and was looking at the square from different angles. His decision is very rapid. For Buñuel, to find the angle and the framing is one of the fundamental tasks of direction. It is very rarely a problem to him. He is one of the privileged directors who can discover the most expressive composition from simple good sense.

Two lorries arrived with the lights, electrical gear and such accessories as a very modern camera. Then a bus loaded with thirty technical personnel.

A little later, Silvia Pinal. As she got out of the car, so dainty, pale and blonde, the villagers at once identified her as the star. She went with the make-up artists to an old decaying building which was in fact the seat of the Falange Espanola Tradicionalista and of the JONS. The make-up people put a base on and Silvia, with an assistant hairdresser, finished her own very simple make-up. Buñuel does not camouflage his artists; and neither Silvia nor her lips were painted. The other characters had no make-up at all. The crew, extremely disciplined, had rapidly positioned the lights, one on a tower, and set the rails for the dolly within the arcade. Already they were trying the lights. Everything seemed extremely simple. The villagers evidently were beginning to feel cheated.

'This must be a very bad and very cheap film,' one of the more knowing country people told me. 'You should have seen when the *King of Kings* Americans came. They really had some apparatus. And they took more than a thousand people from the fields and gave us thirty duros a day for four days just for putting on some short skirts and watching the passion of Our Lord.'

Juan Luis, very active, was finishing off details. Aguayo, the director of photography, was trying out a travelling shot with Silvia Pinal, who impassively obeyed, munching an anchovy sandwich the while. Buñuel, sitting in the director's chair, was concentrating hard and not talking to anyone. A wretched bus, like the one in *Bienvenido Mr Marshall!*, arrived, depositing eight village 'extras', laden with baskets, as well as the driver and Mrs Buñuel, who had crept inside with the driver because she was cold outside. Thus she is immortalized in the film!

They began to shoot. Today's scene seemed simple. There were two shots. In the first, Viridiana goes to catch the bus in the Plaza Mayor of the village, buys a ticket and is just about to enter when ... In the second shot a policeman and two civil guards are seen looking for her to tell her of the death of her uncle and to take her off with them ...

Buñuel mounted the dolly and tried out the travelling shot before the camera. Then he sat in the director's chair and ordered them to film the scene. He had given no instruction or rehearsal to the actress. I supposed that the instructions had been given in advance. On the other hand, he had occupied himself very diligently with the framing and the movement of the camera. This is characteristic of the director. This apparently very simple shot was, in reality, very complicated. It was astonishing how, almost without effort, it was finished. The shot begins with the camera arranged at the distance of a medium shot over the actress, who is looking out on to the square from

Luis Buñuel

Directing the 'simple shot' for *Viridiana*

behind a column of the portico. She frowns when she sees the bus coming; then takes her bag and begins to go forward. Thus Buñuel has given us in a very cinematic – that is, elliptical – form, the arrival of the bus. After this very beautiful shot (it has the function of a close-up) the camera recedes, showing the upper half of Viridiana, and effecting the travelling shot. This too is clever because the spectator first sees an advance of the protagonist, emphasized by the columns which recede behind her. The travelling shot ends, and the camera, fixed, shoots the actress withdrawing from it to enter the bus. Thus we get an impression of 'going away', of departure. Moreover in these seconds there is something of performance: during the travelling shot, the actress's way of walking and the sorrowful expression of her face reveal the gravity of the moment through which she is passing. Now we are also given a hint of her fragility and her defencelessness; as she goes down the step with her wide skirts and pathetic gestures, so pale and blonde, she gives the impression of taking a step into an abyss. A man comes into the shot and helps her down this step; then she faces the conductor, has a brief conversation with him and buys her ticket. The shot was taken silent. In the studio the dialogue would be dubbed on, no doubt: 'How much is a ticket?' Reply: 'So much.'

At this moment, Buñuel, a metre away, called 'Cut!' And he added: 'The dialogue was too long.' The take was made again, exactly as before, with this ending a little shortened. The script-girl noted in her book '27 metres'. It was the total film that had been used. We saw the ease and economy with which the shot had been done. Given its complexity, a script and direction less skilled would have made endless shots and takes. Buñuel controlled the filming precisely, despite his apparent inaction; and was exigent over each detail. The legends about his indifference, and that he only makes single takes are total misapprehensions. No doubt he makes only a single take for the majority of his shots – a notably better ratio than most directors. Yet in quite a different mood from the hysteria of many Hollywood directors, Buñuel is quite capable of repeating a shot many times (cf. the take of Cobo in *Los Olvidados* already mentioned).

In the nearby tavern Buñuel answered my queries: 'Well, these shots are quite uncomplicated. They don't call for any worry.'

Later Quintana came in. 'This man is great. Every day of shooting makes me more aware of it. He simplifies everything to mathematical precision. Where other directors would get into a great muddle, shouting and making all sorts of scenes, he resolves the problem with no fuss; and, moreover, films exactly what has to be filmed. Out of a thousand possibilities, he infallibly chooses the best.'

This recalls a critical observation by Basil Wright, writing in *Sight and Sound*: 'Buñuel does not choose the best angle; he chooses the obvious one and the only one.'

The next take confirmed this. The police, followed by the civil guards, approach Viridiana. Naturally this take does not repeat the previous travelling shot, even though the movement of the characters through the portico is similar. The camera takes them from a position in which it was left at the end of the previous set-up, where it has filmed the movement of the protagonist from inside the portico – pan – to the bus. Only the placing has been moved two or three metres further outside. From this point it shoots them arriving, like the bullfighter waiting for the bull.

Now we could understand the director's point in interrupting the over-long dialogue at the bus: it was in anticipation of the transition. The police whom we see come from behind the heavy columns, come towards Viridiana and have a brief dialogue with her. They take her back, and they all return by exactly the same route as she came. In the first take the camera was placed within the portico, so that we see the protagonist approaching us, rounding the rural architecture, going out into the square to the open air, preparing to depart in the bus. Plastically, it gives the impression of *departure*. On the other hand, in the second take, linked by the transition, the framing is the opposite. From the *outside*, in the square and the open air, we see the police arrive from the shadowy interior. The columns which previously provided a background for the woman, are now in front of the men. She had light behind her, they darkness. All this gives a certain impression of sinister contrast. Seeing them return the way they came, we have the impression of a routine. Shooting from the rear and withdrawing from the backs gives the finality of the shot (very marked because it is the end of the sequence) a pathos already classic in the cinema: Chaplin used the effect frequently. The civil guards with their cloaks and shiny tricornes, taking off the protagonist and seen from the rear, compose a very Spanish image, recalling García Lorca. This admirable montage contrast vindicates Eisenstein's view: 'The maximum pathetic effect is obtained by giving a leap in the opposite direction.' Here it is achieved with a simple change of camera position and lights. Finally, the modest use of extras in the scene is treated in a very sensitive manner – it is not too much to say poetically. In the first shot we see in the distance behind Viridiana, at the far end of the square, a couple of groups of people, gossiping interminably, very characteristic of Spanish villages. This static element reinforces the dramatic action. They remain while she departs. In the second shot, a little boy reads a comic, leaning against a pillar behind which the police pass. When they are taking Viridiana away a self-contented country couple pass, walking quietly by with their shopping basket. The audience doesn't even notice all this (the whole scene lasts a matter of fifty seconds); nevertheless it reinforces the dramatic composition in the spectator's subconscious.

The scene was finished, everything packed up in a moment, everyone paid and the unit on its way home. The locals dispersed. It was three hours since we had arrived. The rest of the day was free. The rain had slacked off. The sun was beginning to break through. Buñuel had the whole afternoon to himself, with his family, and an Italian novel he had begun. He can give the impression of a lazy life which the great creators often manage to convey. No one would have guessed that he had filmed a scene for a film which would become history.

The plot of the film gives no idea of the deep subversion latent in its expression in images, as realized by Buñuel. This is why the script was approved without any problems. Thus we reprint below the original synopsis as it was printed in the publicity leaflet issued by UNINCI for the Cannes Film Festival. The reader who wants a fuller account can read the complete script with its marvellous dialogue, although the scenes of the beggars have inevitably lost much in translation. (See Bibliography):

Don Jaime, an old Spanish *hidalgo*, has lived in retirement on an abandoned farm since the death of his wife thirty years ago on their wedding night. He is visited by his niece Viridiana, a novice in a convent, who bears an extraordinary resemblance to his wife. She has come to take her final farewell of her uncle before taking the veil. In face of the resemblance, Don Jaime falls passionately in love with Viridiana, but neither his prayers nor his proposals of marriage can persuade her to stay with him. One night, the last before her departure, Don Jaime persuades Viridiana to put on her aunt's wedding dress, and with the collusion of Ramona, the servant, pours a drug into her coffee and tries to ravish her; but at the last moment stops himself. The next day he admits to Viridiana what has happened, and she leaves, horrified. As she is catching the bus which will take her back to the convent, she learns that her uncle has just hanged himself from a tree . . .

Viridiana returns to the farm of Don Jaime; for the moment she will not return to the convent. She feels she is to blame for the death of her uncle, and wants to make expiation. In the farm there is also Jorge, Don Jaime's natural son, and Lucia, the woman with whom he lives. Viridiana devotes herself to charitable works, welcoming beggars and installing them in the house. Jorge wants to organize everything, so that the farm can become productive and life resume its course. There are soon differences between them because of their different ways of life. Jorge would like to throw out the beggars; he finds all this useless and absurd, while Viridiana welcomes them more and more and increases the sacrifices of her hermit's existence. The relationship between them is distant, strange.

Lucia, faced with Jorge's behaviour, leaves him, vaguely jealous of Viridiana.

One day Jorge and Viridiana have to go to town on business. The beggars, believing that they will not return till morning, take the house by storm and organize a great feast. They eat, drink, dance, make love . . . The wedding veil of Don Jaime's bride serves as fancy dress for one of them, the cupboards are empty, the house becomes an incredible orgy . . . Jorge and Viridiana return unexpectedly, and the beggars flee to the village. Two remain, however, and while Ramona goes to seek help, try to rape Viridiana, after having overpowered Jorge. Jorge asks one of the beggars to kill the other, offering him money to do so; and thus succeeds in saving Viridiana.

Peace restored, Jorge plays cards with Ramona, with whom he is having an affair. Viridiana tries, in vain, to resume her life of prayer and sacrifice. She goes into Jorge's room, afraid and distressed. Ramona wants to go away, to leave them alone together, but Jorge will not let her. He invites Viridiana to sit down with them, and all three resume the interrupted game of cards.

Viridiana beside 'the crown of thorns, the nails and the hammer of the Crucifixion ...'

Viridiana proved to be one of Buñuel's most brilliant and graceful films. Its plot has the same melodrama characteristics and the same multiplicity of episodes as the Mexican films: although his producers gave him total freedom for the first time since *L'Age d'or*, Buñuel did not launch himself on a radically different style. There is nothing anti-commercial about the film, though of course its realization is more successful than that of the Mexican films as Buñuel has been able to take particular care in his *mise en scène*. Canet's art direction shows a great advance over *El*: the settings of Don Jaime's mansion are costly, heavy, lugubrious, *fin-de-siècle*, mouldy, pretentious – in short bourgeois – and play the same important psychological role as the hero's house in *El*. The sound-track uses a lot of music, though Buñuel has not broken with his determination not to use 'background' music. Everything we hear belongs to the action, played by the actors on a harmonium or on a gramophone.

An unusual technique for Buñuel is the use of an artificial montage in the style of the Soviet silent cinema: shots of Viridiana and the beggars kneeling in the fields and orating the Angelus alternate with shots of workmen labouring to pull a cart of gravel, chopping wood and so on. A scene in no way blasphemous in itself, it produces a profound shock in the conventionally

Don Jaime with his fetish – his dead wife's wedding trousseau

devout; and its intention is very clear to anyone who knows the significance for the Surrealists of Millet's 'The Oration of the Angelus'.

The '*leitmotif* object', which has always been prominent in Surrealism and in Buñuel's cinema, is particularly stressed in *Viridiana*. An example is the skipping rope, with its wooden handles of clearly phallic allusion. In Surrealist terms it would be called an 'object of multiple uses': the child skips in the garden with the rope which old Don Jaime has given her, so that he can admire her erotically; later Don Jaime commits suicide with it, finding in death the substitute for his frustrated libido; the child returns to skipping with it, beneath the hanging tree, even though she is told that it will bring bad luck and shows a lack of respect for the dead. (In spite of superstition, ignoring death, the rhythm of life continues.) The beggar who attempts to rape Viridiana uses the rope as a belt. *Viridiana* is of all the films richest in such details. Viridiana peels an apple, obsessively letting the peel fall in a spiral: the tics, the details without any apparent sense of significance, because always it is necessary to seek these in the subconscious, help to fill the films of Buñuel with a sense of mystery, of vague fatality, of empty spaces, of enigmas which no other director would accommodate, but which are at bottom Buñuel's causative truths.

We are in a world that is obsessive and obsessed: Don Jaime, the rich

Viridiana: the beggars' Last Supper . . .

landowner ruled by his inhibitions, trapped by the sexual tabu to which the death of his bride on his wedding night delivered him – a prototype of bourgeois convention, like the protagonist of *El*, though his neurosis is less grave and more amiable; Viridiana with her Christian ideals and her chastity carried like a burden, sleepwalking, burning her knitting in ritual gestures as the protagonist of *L'Age d'or* plucks feathers. But *Viridiana* has two faces. The strange and the aberrant are confronted by the implacable logic of the film itself. Buñuel continues to be above all a Surrealist.

The second part of the film is dominated by the twelve beggars, in whom the duality is elaborated. They are normal with respect to one another; but in other respects monstrous. Physically they are grotesque, socially they are destitute, psychologically they are deceived and exploited. Hence their ill faith, their mistrust, their pride. It is pure Buñuel that during their party they compose a plastic image which caricatures Leonardo's 'Last Supper', which a female beggar 'photographs' with an obscene gesture. That they dance *sevillanas* is inevitable; that they dance them with the only available gramophone record in the house, Handel's *Messiah*, is also logical – and also Buñuel. In the most natural way in the course of the merrymaking, the old beggar puts on the bridal veil, taken from a cupboard, without any of the sexual sym-

... is 'photographed'

bolism of the moment earlier in the film when Don Jaime put it on to excite himself before a mirror, remembering his dead bride.

With this delirious film Buñuel has given the Spanish cinema the equivalent of Quevedo's *El Buscón* and *Los Sueños*, of the picaresque, of Galdós. It is not the only Spain that he shows us, but it is one of the authentic faces of the country. Buñuel intended no more than to present his vision of Spain. He aims neither to dogmatize nor to generalize; and it takes ill faith to read the film in such a way. Every work of the imagination has ultimately to be based on real fact. To make his nightmare of Spain, *Viridiana*, he had to take a particular type of woman which abounds in our country; an uncle who owns vast estates which lie unproductive – as there certainly are in Spain: it is one of our grave problems; some beggars, who again are for ever with us; some irreverences and blasphemies such as are spoken every day among us. All this is not criticism, but observation – just as is the notorious knife in the form of a crucifix, which was at one time mass-produced in Albacete (see the letter to José Bello reprinted in the Appendix).

The double sense that these things can have in Buñuel is something different again. He discovers the double meaning through the associations of the gymnastic Surrealist mind. Much more than malice or deliberate

blasphemy, it is a matter of an imagination keenly sensitive to the paradoxes of objects, beings and situations, which can acquire unexpected,
irreverent or scandalous significances. The quality is already evident in *Un
Chien andalou*, a film innocent of abstract propositions. The profoundly
revolutionary aspect of *Viridiana* is that it too is an innocent film.

It is necessary to emphasize this point because of the scandal that the film
occasioned in Spain. Buñuel set out simply to make a commercial film in
Spain. He had his own initial doubts: '. . . at best they will ban it', he told me;
'or put it on for half a week in an out-of-the-way fleapit where it will achieve
neither glory nor blame'. I told him that a worse danger was that the film
might be reclassified in the Third Category, which means that it loses the
rights of exhibition in good cinemas, and export. This used to happen with
pictures of very low artistic quality or of unusual content, or which were in
any way not agreeable to the government. Buñuel was alarmed by the
suggestion; but the next day came to tell me that the censorship had stressed
that there was no danger of this happening.

The Director of Cinema and Theatre was eager that the film should
represent Spain at the Cannes Film Festival. When the Festival had actually
begun, the film was still being finished. Buñuel had taken a copy, with the
separate sound-tracks, to Paris to do the mixing there, since this is one of the
technical aspects in which our cinema industry is inadequate. The producers
promised to do everything possible to have the film ready in time. Mixing was
finished five days before the end of the Festival. The producers explained
quite honestly that there was no time to send the film to Madrid for viewing
by the Selection Committee for Festivals and afterwards reach Cannes in
time. The authorities, who had approved the script almost without objection
and who had selected the film for Cannes, after a viewing without dialogue or
sound, decided, without seeing the final version, to authorize sending
Viridiana directly to the Festival. It was the official Spanish entry. Buñuel
remained in Paris and warned the present writer not to go to Cannes. The
Director of Cinema and Theatre went up on stage to collect the awards won
by Spain, of which there were four: for *Fuego en Castilla*, a Surrealist film by
Val del Omar, for Leopoldo Torre Nilsson's *La mano en la trampa*, another
UNINCI film; and the French critics' prize of the French press, as well as the
'Palme d'or' for *Viridiana*.

The copy shown was the integral version of the scenario approved by the
censorship, which had been modified in one important point from the version
initially submitted. Viridiana's final decision to renounce her metaphysical
ideals and go to the room of Jorge (the prototype of the normal man and
therefore without interest) to give herself up to him, was changed to have
Viridiana enter the room where he and the maid (now his mistress) were

playing cards, and have Viridiana join the game. This modification was made in consequence of suggestions made by the Direction of the Censorship. Buñuel adopted it with delight: 'It is a magnificent ending; much better than the original crude one.' In fact the international critics praised Buñuel for the subtlety and irony of this ending, of which he is not the true author.

It seems possible that the Censorship also wished Buñuel to convert Don Jaime's suicide into a heart attack. Buñuel himself proposed to soften a couple of scenes for the Spanish version: Viridiana praying beside the crown of thorns, the nails and the hammer of the Crucifixion; the attempted rape of the heroine. Other scenes, including that of the little girl snatching the crown of thorns from the fire and watching with innocent delight while it burns, were to be suppressed. These emendations did not however take place, because the film was not – and still has not been – shown in Spain. For a time it was forbidden for journalists and critics even to mention the existence of the film. The copies and materials in Spain were blocked; and the copy deposited with the Cannes Festival, which subsequently went on to Venice and Locarno, was used to dupe all the copies that have since been sold or shown.

Spanish reports of the Cannes Festival made no mention of the Palme d'or, the first major prize ever obtained by the Spanish cinema. The Director of Cinema and Theatre was dismissed, and the twenty members of the official Spanish delegation to the Cannes Festival were punished. Meanwhile the fact that Gustavo Alatriste had put up most of the money for the production made it possible legally to claim Mexican nationality for the film; and as such it was shown all over the world, excepting always Spain. Critics everywhere exalted the film, though the scandals surrounding it continued. In January 1963 copies of the film were seized by the Rome and Milan police under article 402 of the Italian penal code which provides sanctions against works which 'condemn the official religion'. The Italian critics protested, and the film was granted the impunity due to a work of art; but *L'Osservatore Romana* resumed the virulent attacks it had opened when the film was initially shown. In England, Surrey banned its showing.

Meanwhile *Viridiana* had turned Buñuel, finally, into a director of popular celebrity and 'box-office'. The huge profits were deposited in a Swiss bank to await the judicial untangling of the rights of the Spanish producers and of Alatriste, whose investments were in the ratio of one to five; Alatriste had put in some five million pesetas of the budget, and subsequently put it into circulation.

Buñuel returned to Mexico somewhat perplexed. Once he had sought scandal and found it. Now he found it without seeking it. This, according to some of the fanatics, is what had brought *Viridiana* to perfection: to be something in essence, and not by seeking.

14. The Great Films of Maturity: I

El ángel exterminador

'The producer Gustavo Alatriste', Buñuel told me, 'is the man who has given most liberty to any author in the history of the cinema. When I returned from Spain after *Viridiana* he gave me another film, and didn't even ask to see the script that I prepared. When the film was finished, he screened it and said: "I don't understand a thing in it. It's marvellous."

'The production was more difficult and took much more work than *Viridiana*, and cost three million pesetas more. For the new film to be a success it would have to be done over twice. That's how films should be made: once your ideas are developed in the first realization, it should be done all over again. But this privilege which is normal for poets or musicians is prohibitive in an art as costly as the cinema. There have been very few films which have been made like this – among them Max Ophuls' marvellous *Letter to an Unknown Woman*, which David O. Selznick produced. To have made the film as I would have liked I would have had to shoot it in London, for a start. I would have chosen elegant actors. But I am accustomed to resigning myself where secondary details are involved. It is the price of freedom. Even so I would *prefer* to work in better conditions. The people who think that I make films in the way I prefer are wrong. I am one of the people who admire

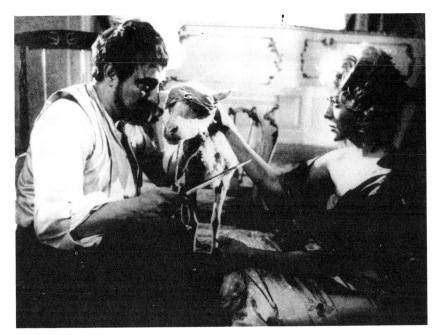

El ángel exterminador: Bourgeois sensibility – sheep blindfolded for slaughter

Visconti, for example. What impeccable technique! What beauty! Do you remember the scene in the box in the theatre, in *Senso*? I like this kind of refinement and I would love to have the talent and the money necessary to do such lovely things. Where I have insisted, though, is in not compromising where essential moral considerations are involved. Alatriste, financing the films out of his private resources (he is not a rich man, by the way, but he earns a lot every year and spends it) and leaving me to do as I pleased, was sensational. He did not even interfere when I gave his wife a secondary rôle in the film. (Silvia Pinal plays one of the guests at the party.)

'I always follow the law of the least exertion. So when Alatriste gave me work, I said to myself, "Since I have to do another film, and since I can choose, I will take this old impossible screenplay." Originally, in 1952, it was only a subject for a two-reeler, a short intended for the Barbachano series, under the general direction of Carlos Velo. There only the basic situation would have been expounded. The original title was *Los Náufragos de la calle Providencia*; but José Bergamín suggested the new one, for which I paid him royalties. Afterwards, as you know, I extended the scenario to six reels, but I felt that once the situation was established it would repeat itself. Now in making the plan for the feature film, I enriched it and added the abrupt finale

GUSTAVO ALATRISTE
presenta

EL
ANGEL
EXTERMINADOR
de BUÑUEL

Valdés Leal's painting (above) and the poster for the film

of the church sequence. I also added the sheep in the salon. And the gag of the party, where the people are sitting at table and the host announces an exquisite dish brought from Persia; and the servant, entering with the tray and falling down, scatters the food all over the floor to the contained fury of the guests who politely pretend to the host: "How charming, what a delicious joke you have prepared for us" . . . This scene came to my mind recollecting a party of rich people in New York, when the millionaire host offered his guests meat brought specially by aeroplane from Argentina for the supper. Iris Barry told me about it when we were working at the Museum of Modern Art in New York.'

The film came to be called *El ángel exterminador*, like the great painting by Valdés Leal in the Seville Museum, which was adapted for the publicity of the film. The angel in the picture wears high boots as he floats on air, wielding a six-thonged whip.

The story of the film begins with a dinner party at the palatial mansion of Mr and Mrs Nobile, to which a score of people of the highest society are invited after the opera. There is something strange in the air, however. Before the party starts, all the servants except one leave the house under various inconsequential pretexts. The party begins to take bizarre turns; and when the guests make as if to leave in the small hours, none of them can actually do so. Indeed, no one seems able to cross the threshold of the salon in which they are assembled. Hours lengthen into days, and the outside world begins to make rescue attempts. All is in vain; an invisible and impenetrable wall separates the two worlds.

Camping like ship-wrecked travellers in their one room, the guests soon begin to suffer from thirst and hunger. Some fall ill; one dies; and two young lovers kill themselves. The rest degenerate to the most primitive passions and superstitions as all the restraints of education and social training collapse. When their situation seems extreme, the guests are unexpectedly succoured by a flock of lambs – the only living creatures who seem able to pass unscathed through the magic barrier. A little later they suddenly chance upon the magic charm that breaks the spell and releases them.

Some days later the survivors come together to give thanks in the local cathedral. The service ends and everyone makes for the door – but no one is able to cross the threshold. As over the villa, a yellow flag is hoisted over the cathedral; and soon a flock of lambs is seen making for the church door, while in the square outside the police disperse crowds of rioting demonstrators.

The resulting masterwork was comparable only to *L'Age d'or*. What the years had taken from Surrealist vocabulary in terms of strident and scandalous anger, *El ángel exterminador* compensated with a refinement of technique and image, a serenity and balance which only make the underlying

El ángel exterminador

subversion more pointed and profound. The restraint and the air of everyday normality which surround the events of the film make the images even more surprising than in the old masterpiece. But essentially we are in the presence of the same' man and the same preoccupations. The story of *Los Náufragos*, with its concern with sociology and the destiny of man is now only the basis on which Buñuel constructs his marvellous, delirious personal world. It would be absurd to suppose that the theme, simple as it is, of the guests who cannot leave the house and have to remain for days and weeks, suffering various physical degradations, is only the excuse to mount a thesis work, and that all that appears extemporaneously in the film has a symbolic value. On the contrary, Buñuel, working with a 'psychic automatism' gave joyous freedom to the caprices of his imagination, adding a whole world of images in the course of the shooting. In its language *El ángel exterminador* still remains the most distinctly and completely Surrealist film since *L'Age d'or*, and, in the writer's opinion, is second only to that film in Buñuel's whole *oeuvre*.

The 'enrichments' of the script in its penultimate version are innumerable: scenes or shots which are repeated from another angle in another part of the film; the irruption of the flock of sheep into the salon where the guests are shipwrecked; the appearance of a bear, roaming absently through the deserted halls outside their confines; the fabulous retreat improvised in the room behind a folding screen; a Chinese vase which provides the only recourse for the prisoners, and in the bottom of which, if they look, they see a beautiful landscape. (This scene, absent from the released film, is a direct recollection of the privies of the hill-side town of Cuenca. Juan Luis Buñuel told David Robinson: 'Cuenca is built on the side of cliffs, and the lavatories are also built on the side of these cliffs, so that when you look down through the hole of the lavatory you really do see below you rivers and eagles flying. And my Aunt was telling me the other day that one of these lavatories was a roosting place of white pigeons; and you went in there and they would be flying below you and inside with you . . .')

In the original scenario the story ended with the arrival of the police to rescue the imprisoned guests – but inevitably too late – a bomb planted by the mob explodes as they arrive. Buñuel devised a brilliant alternative solution. Now the guests decide to return to the exact positions they were in when they first noticed that they could not leave. They sit in chairs in identical postures, and one of them, 'The Valkyrie' (Silvia Pinal), plays the same Paradisi sonata on the piano. At once they are free to leave. The film cuts suddenly to the interior of the cathedral, where the guests have gathered for their thanksgiving. They are all restored once more to their former dignity and pride, as if nothing had happened, as if they had not been on the edge of despair, in a regression to the most primitive brutality and cannibalism. Then the priests make to leave by the door of the cathedral . . . and the spell has begun all over again.

The film was coolly received at Cannes, where it received no prize apart from that of FIPRESCI. It was, certainly, a very personal and complex film, not easy to understand at first sight: only the habitués of Buñuel's cinema could follow it without being disturbed. The thousand majestic *trouvailles* in the course of its subtle narrative can only delight those who are capable of abstracting themselves from the world of cartesian logic which dominates man, the cinema spectator. True, the actors were not good enough; but the overall force of the work, the rich invention, the technical quality (the film is impeccably photographed by Figueroa), the subterranean cataract of accusation against a society in process of decomposition reach to the least sensitive spectator, and contribute to making *El ángel exterminador* one of the most singular and important films in the whole history of the cinema.

'I have not introduced a single symbol into the film, and those who hope for a thesis work from me, a work with a message, may keep on hoping! It is open to doubt whether *El ángel exterminador* is capable of interpretation. Everyone

El ángel exterminador

has the right to interpret it as he wishes. There are some who give it an interpretation that is solely erotico-sexual, others political. I would give it rather a historico-social interpretation. But when the critics at the Cannes press conference asked Juan Luis why there is a bear in the film, wandering through a smart party, he answered, "Because my father likes bears." It's true. There are those who interpret the bear as the Soviet Union about to devour the bourgeoisie. That is nonsense. Then they asked him what was the meaning of the repetitions of shots in the film. I had anticipated this and told Juan Luis: "Answer that when I finished the film I decided it was still short, so to lengthen it . . ." People always want an explanation of everything. It is the consequence of centuries of bourgeois education. And for everything for which they cannot find an explanation, they resort in the last instance to God. But what is the use of that to them? Eventually they have to explain God.

'There are some very intelligent people who believe in God. Why not, after all? It is human nature to seek hope. As for me, I must remain as I am. I have not received the Grace which comes from faith. I am interested in a life with ambiguities and contradictions. Mystery is beautiful. To die and disappear for ever does not seem to me horrible, but perfect. On the other hand the possibility of being eternal does horrify me. Look: if my best friend, long ago dead, were to appear to me, touch my ear with his fingers and burn it instantaneously, I would still not believe that he came from Hell. Nor would I believe as a result either in God, or the Immaculate Conception, or that the Virgin could help me in examinations. I would only think: "Luis, here you have another mystery which you don't understand."

'One must be sincere about these things. A few days ago I received a visit from a Dominican father (you know that the Dominicans are not only in favour of *Nazarín*, but are also for *Viridiana*?). And he asked me what I thought about Christ as a human being, leaving aside his divinity. "An idiot," I replied. The priest looked very surprised and asked me, how could I have such an opinion about a man who had said things like "Love thy neighbour as thyself." I replied: "Give me a ball-pen, and in fifteen minutes I'll write you ten sentences like that. What's the use?" '

(Conversations with J. F. Aranda, in *Kosmorama* (Copenhagen, February 1963) and *Filmkritik* (Munich, June 1963).)

Projects

In October 1962 Buñuel returned to Madrid, and again installed himself in the Torre de Madrid, where he had lived during the shooting of *Viridiana*. He resumed his dawn walks through the Casa de Campo, his domestic circle with Gustavo Pittaluga (who had settled in Spain two years before) receiving a few privileged friends. The only interruptions to his three-month stay were a holiday in Galicia and some trips to Toledo. Sometimes in the evenings he would eat with his friends in good but secluded restaurants. Almost all the day was spent in his hideaway, reading, looking at the panorama of the city bathed in the brilliant autumn light.

'It is my summer holiday. You know how much I like the cold. This wonderful Madrid air! Look how clearly and how far you can see from here!'

Buñuel repeated that idleness is the perfect state for him. 'In fact I am preparing a film and I want to do it in Madrid. I am too deaf now to work in countries where they don't speak Spanish. A French producer is pressing me to direct *Le Journal d'une femme de chambre* for him. I would like to do it; but no.'

I asked him if he knew the version by Jean Renoir, which seemed to me very stylish. 'This tends to be the besetting danger of artists who grow old. The terrible thing is that we don't notice it ourselves. It is the others who tell us. Each time you are better or worse. No, I have not seen Renoir's film. I believe that he used only one episode out of Mirbeau's book; and I can imagine which: the best. I would emphasise the maid's relationship with her seven bosses. What troubles me most is to prepare a film in this way, with long conferences round a table. Afterwards, once you are in the studios, the work is easy. I'm getting old and I only want to make films in Mexico and Spain.'

I was in fact astonished to see Buñuel in Spain again, after the *Viridiana* scandal. We had all thought he would have twenty-five more years of exile. 'On the contrary, in Mexico they gave me every sort of security to come, and here they promise me freedom and facilities to make a film. They say that the government has a new look, that the censorship is "democratized" and so on. There are people in the Cinema Department now who actually like the cinema; and that is already something.'

'Are they nice?'

'I asked myself what they were after,' grunted Buñuel. 'They were all being *very* nice.'

'And what are you after?'

'The same as always: to make a good film. Now more than ever. After *Viridiana* and *El ángel exterminador* I have to choose a film with much care. Something which responds to my actual needs and expresses what I am today.'

'In that case might we not have another masterpiece, but also another scandal and another prohibition?'

'Let what will be; we can't help it. I never sought to create a scandal except with *L'Age d'or*. If I make a film in Spain it is so that the Spaniards can see it; and I want to respond loyally to the offer which they have made to me and to the producer. Still, I am beginning to think that *Viridiana* need not have been a scandal. Do you recall what I told you at the time? The natural subversion of the film cannot be denied; but what is seen in the images is accurate. It could have remained a nice rosy tale if the censorship had made three or four cuts and substituted three scenes for which I had in any case shot alternatives. By banning the film, the censors played a bad hand. Not as far as the film is concerned of course. It would have been shown without attracting praise or blame and abroad it would have attracted much less notoriety and fame.'

Buñuel was looking for a subject. Friends in Spain and abroad had sent him numerous scripts, which he kept, either skimming or reading them attentively, always having a friendly word or two for the author. I suspected that he would end by choosing his own subject and writing his own screenplay as usual. He rejected a project to film *Divinas palabras* which had just been revived in the Madrid theatre to a sensational reception. 'It has a vicious blind man and an idiot, and the public would say that it duplicated characters from *Viridiana*.' From Valle Inclán he would have preferred *Tirano Banderas*, a project of 1936, and closer to Surrealism; but 'it has too much action and too many characters, and is dangerous. It could turn into an actors' film. The modern cinema demands all the time more concentrated action and fewer characters.' *Romance de lobos* was also examined. 'I admire Valle Inclán for his language, his goldsmith's precision. In the cinema this does not count.'

He also considered *The Everlasting Husband*, by Dostoievski, and Huysmans' *A Rebours* – 'suppressing some episodes, like that of the black mass'. He was most tempted by a project for a collection of stories linked by a common bond of mystery: 'three, or better, four mysteries: one metaphysical, another realistic, another of "things as they are", another grotesque. It would be a joke to give the episodes the titles Painful, Jocose, Glorious, Joyful and Mysterious, parodying the Mysteries of the Catholic rosary. But that is a *boutade*. I would certainly consider a title which has nothing to do with anything, as I did with *El ángel exterminador*.

'First I have taken a story by the stupendous Mexican writer Carlos Fuentes, who is 34 years old. It is metaphysical, expressed through the story of the relationships of a man and a woman and a third person who has died. Then *Las Ménades* by Julio Cortázar. This would be crazy and very amusing. It is just a concerto, a normal concerto in which there is something like Brahms' Fourth Symphony. The public is very excited. Imagine a provincial city, like Zaragoza, and the arrival of an orchestra of world celebrity. The bourgeois element of the "philharmonic society" or something of the sort, is carried into ecstasies by the music. At the end the applause is clamorous; it is more; the public in its excitement invades the stage to embrace the musicians. Its enthusiastic fury grows overwhelming; it ends by breaking the violins, destroying everything, leaving the municipal theatre in ruins. (*Vide* also Appendix: *Instrumentation*.) Finally, *La Gradiva*, a marvellous novel by the Austrian writer Jensen. Do you know the book? It was almost the Bible of the Surrealists in 1930, and Freud published it with a long psychoanalytical commentary.'

'Would you use this commentary?'

'No, only the novel. But it is important that Freud liked the book. Freud was one of the three greatest men of this century, with Lenin and Einstein. And the three most repugnant were Truman, Cardinal Spellman and Adenauer. To return to *Misterios*. As the action takes place in Pompeii, I would have to do all the exteriors there. The final episode is one of corrosive humour and the most subversive of all. It is one of my own stories, something about the abduction of a little girl. I'm going to spend Christmas in Mexico and then I shall start to make the script. I hope to be in Madrid in March to prepare the film.'

This project was not in fact to be the definitive one. Meanwhile Buñuel was free to make a film without Alatriste. Among his contacts in Madrid he arrived at an agreement with Epoca Films, a young producer who had been responsible, among other minor films, for *Los Chicos*, the second film of

Marco Ferreri. Buñuel was also eager to contact a French or Italian producer so that in the event of things turning out as with *Viridiana*, the foreign producer could demand his negative and copies and so avert the risk of destruction which a film could run in Spain. The Spanish producers found that the last episode of *Misterios* would be unacceptable to the censorship, and proposed to cut it out. Buñuel had spoken of making three mysteries, and, should the film remain too short, four. He knew that it would not be a short film but he wanted to put in his own episode. He had also mentioned that in the last resort each story might be shown separately, or alternating, with the omission of one or another episode – a method which Buñuel in the outcome would never have accepted.

During the subsequent readjustments to the scenario, Buñuel suggested including, as a brief episode, *Ilegible, hijo de flauta*, the script which he had written years before with Juan Larrea, and published in *Nuevo Cine* in Mexico; and also a delightful story suggested by the actor Fernando Rey. This related how a Spanish Jew descended from those who were expelled by the old Catholic kings, comes to Spain as a tourist. These Jews still keep the keys of their ancient houses. Our man tries his in the locks of all the houses of Toledo. He enters one; it is now a church and he sees on the altar a crucified boy. In the fifteenth century the Jews were accused of crucifying a Christian boy every year on the evening of Holy Thursday. Various episodes follow, until at the end, the Jew, on his way home, is stopped on the highway by the Civil Guard. 'Who is that boy in your car?' 'Oh, I found him lost on the road and I am taking him into town.' The police apologize. 'It is just that we are looking for a boy who has been abducted.' They continue to inspect the car. 'And this hammer, nails and crown of thorns?' 'Just a souvenir . . .' They let the car continue on its journey. On his return to Constantinople, the Jew is asked by his wife: 'Did you accomplish your mission in Spain?' 'Yes,' replies the Jew, and gives his wife a box of Toledo marzipan.

Actually this was the abduction episode in *Misterios* to which Buñuel referred. In any event, the project was discarded, and he returned to *The Everlasting Husband*. Buñuel frequently changes his mind. Today he is no longer interested in making this film or attempting a theme of jealousies of little actual importance. A new film based on Galdós, the author of *Nazarín*, was suggested. An enthusiastic Galdós reader in his youth, Buñuel had always clearly visualized *Nazarín*, and, to a point, *Angel Guerra* and *Doña Perfecta*. But the work finally chosen was a little-known Galdós story, *Tristana*.

According to Galdós, *Tristana* is the story of a Don Juan in decay – a man who is generous, sympathetic, the classic *hidalgo*. There comes a moment when he has to help a couple who have a child. The mother dies, then the father, and their protector ends by taking in their child. On reaching adolescence, like Evvie in *The Young One*, she becomes his mistress.

Coming of age, already a little withered and an Ibsenish figure, she falls in love. Tristana practises music and painting, wants to be an actress; but she returns to Don Juan, who is the one who really helps her. Meanwhile the gentleman's relations insist that the strange situation be regularized by a marriage. As an incentive they offer Don Juan an estate. Don Juan recognizes that to marry is logical, and Tristana accepts, becoming a bourgeois wife who plays the violin in church at *novenas* and so on. She makes exquisite puddings for her delighted husband, who eats them ravenously.

Buñuel recognized the démodé side of the nineteenth-century tale: the relationship of Tristana with the young painter with whom she falls in love. All this part was reduced; and Buñuel added brief sequences of his own which brought the problem up to date, in the same way as he had done with *Nazarín*. Hence *Tristana* became a more demoralizing work, but with an up-to-date humanist base. It is an analysis of the process, often studied by Buñuel, of the changes which circumstances can produce in a human being, until finally he is transformed to a mere scrap of flesh. Submission to routine and other degradations can be lucidly examined in the story, along with the way a decaying society still imposes its scale of values tyrannically on the individual.

The scenario was prepared in collaboration with Julio Alejandro, Buñuel's co-writer on *Viridiana*. The unit was partially hired. Locations were sought in Salamanca, but Buñuel finally decided that the Madrid suburbs of Puento de Toledo would do as well, and would save him from having to leave his convenient apartment. The studios were hired, and the censorship seemed to promise no difficulties. Yet though Buñuel's honest intentions were evident, after so long away from a Spain that was now transformed, it was harder for him to assess the subtle evolutions of the criteria of the Spanish censorship. In May, just when everything was ready to begin production, the prohibition arrived, saying that the script contravened one specific article of the new censorship code, which forbade incitement to a duel ... The censorship had its revenge; Buñuel realized that he would be unable to make films in Spain; although 'if I was offered another contract, I would still accept, taking a cash advance of course. I am only a modest professional'.

Buñuel's spirits were unaffected; and when I lamented that such promising works were consigned to the rubbish bin, he exclaimed: 'What does one story or another matter? It is the script that is interesting. You know, I could make the life of Christ into a Buddhist film. My next one will extend the theme of all my films, eroticism and religion. *Tristana* was a pretext. It gave me an opportunity to deal with some aspects of Spanish life. That apart, like all my

Buñuel in Toledo, November 1962

films it would contain no social criticism or condemnation of this or that. No thought of it. I limit myself always to showing things without taking positions for or against. People know that, particularly the producers. There are half a dozen admirable producers in Spain. The producers read my script and compared it word by word with the censorship code. The censors asked for nine copies of the script instead of the usual three, in order to examine them; and after this they approved my script in the pre-censorship stage. I think even the Ministry doorman examined it. But as you see this did not stop them from banning it on the second censorship examination. It is a hardship, because now that I begin to be old myself I feel inspired by this work about old age and decrepitude. Everything in the film would be ugly, out-of-date. The secondary characters, the old people, would be very important. And the deaf-mute boy. I treat all my characters with love. The critics say that I am not a humanist, because I put disagreeable figures into my films. They do not understand me, because for me they are human beings, and I love them, all of them, the boys in *Los Olvidados*, the paranoiac in *El*, the beggars of *Viridiana*.'

Talking about his projects at this time he spoke with enthusiasm of a film in two or three reels about Semana Santa which he wanted to make in Calanda.

'I went back there this Easter. Everything was just as it was in my youth. I would start by studying the village – its solitary shepherds, its poor labourers, a whole description of the region. I see myself as a child going for a walk with my father, who wears his straw hat and carries his shooting-stick. Suddenly we come upon the putrid flesh of a putrid dog. This is my earliest memory of the presence of death. Then the drums start, and the mediaeval Mystery with a music of unidentified origin which they preserve there, the terrible procession. Juan Luis ruined his hands by beating the drums for the whole three days of the procession. I played them too, but only for a few hours. It is very savage. The ear trembles with the vibration. The men seem possessed. People cannot speak in the houses, because the noise in the streets is so loud. It is much better at Calanda than at Alcañiz, twelve kilometres away, and where the tourists all go. There they wear fancy clothes and have good German drums. In Calanda it is primitive and authentic, much more so than in Andalusia.

'The film would not need a script. I would put a couple of boom operators and a professional tape-recorder to take the images and sound, and I would shoot from above the march. I would take the material abroad, edit it and sell it to a distributor for next to nothing; and he would make a million out of it. It would bring all the tourists from Alcañiz to Calanda. Photographing the procession I would take care to show in the background houses with signs saying "Hotel. Hot and Cold Water. Every comfort." When the tourists arrived, of course, they would find only a broken-down inn where they would have to sleep alongside the pigsty!'

Buñuel was not to realize this project either; but his son did, in 1965, with a small French crew. Buñuel told me that the film was well received at private previews in Paris and New York – the only showings it had had up to that time – and that it was very good. 'Quite different from the way I would have done it. It is a documentary.' Juan Luis's excellent documentary, with its touches of excellent humour, won him a first prize at the Tours Festival.

In the spring, Carlos Saura asked Buñuel to appear as an actor in the film he was then shooting, *Llanto por un bandido*. He was delighted at the idea, and one afternoon in Colmena de Oreja, they shot the exteriors of the opening sequence, over which the titles were to appear, the execution of some bandits in a public square. Buñuel, stocky, phlegmatic, dressed like a Goyaesque peasant, is the executioner, who mounts the scaffold, carefully checks his 'garrottes', and when the condemned men arrive, surrounded by police and officials, kneels before each in turn, asking pardon 'for what he is about to do', according to the old degrading ritual; then executes them one by one with an energetic movement of the arm. The censorship cut out almost all the sequence, even though it would have been concealed by the title; and in the released version Buñuel is merely seen kneeling and crossing himself, nothing more.

Buñuel as the executioner in Carlos Saura's *Llanto por un bandido*

It was the first time he had appeared on the screen since the prologue to *Un Chien andalou* and he acted very well. 'Now I'll be overwhelmed with Hollywood contracts to be a character actor,' he joked. Later, in 1965, he again appeared as an actor, playing a priest in *En este pueblo no hay ladrones*, a film from the group of young experimental film-makers which had grown up in Mexico in reaction against the general catastrophe of the cinema there. Buñuel appeared preaching from St Paul's Epistle.

Le Journal d'une femme de chambre
Buñuel was by this time at work with the French scenarist Jean-Claude Carrière, preparing *Le Journal d'une femme de chambre*, which he had finally decided to accept after innumerable telegrams from the French producer. The film was finished by the autumn. Like Buñuel's other French films up to that time, it emerged with little éclat and not much commercial success. A comparison with Renoir's version is almost irrelevant: they are completely different works. Buñuel's adaptation is concise, and marvellously concise the use of the image. Brusque cuts in the editing carry us rapidly from one scene to another, carrying to its limits the progressive film language of the French *nouvelle vague* which had found inspiration in Buñuel and to whom he now

returned homage. The last sequence is a model: a fascist demonstration appears at the bottom of a Paris street; there are black clouds overhead. Cut. The demonstration half way down the street. Cut. The demonstration in the foreground, with its placards declaring 'Down with the Republic'. Thunder. Cut. End.

'Given the fact that the action is set in 1930, this is a brilliantly ominous evocation, not only of the imminent rise of Hitler, but of the reverberations which still smoulder under the surface today.

'But it can also be read in another way, as a barbed private joke. For as the chanting demonstrators file past him, Joseph starts a cry of "Vive Chiappe! Vive Chiappe!" which the demonstrators take up blindly; and Chiappe, of course, was the prefect of Police who, in 1930, banned *L'Age d'or*. By cutting into and thus speeding up the footage of the "Vive Chiappe-ists" marching away, Buñuel turns them into absurd automata, literally whisks them out of sight, then lifts his camera to call on that avenging blast of lightning. Here Buñuel is at his brilliant best, and yet the sequence leaves one a trifle uneasy, as though someone apparently aiming at a range target had instead killed a passing bird. "Only connect..." *Le Journal d'une femme de chambre* is a beautiful film, impeccably photographed, impeccably acted, impeccably directed; yet somewhere, its connections grow hazy.

'The trouble seems to lie partly in an awkward indecisiveness about the character of Celestine, whose ambiguity tends to shadow the film, and partly in the fact that Octave Mirbeau's novel is almost *too* tailor-made for Buñuel. Jokingly, when it was announced that he was to make this film – and remembering bizarre details like the skewered goose and slaughtered squirrel from Renoir's version – one said that he was going to have the time of his life. And he has. Buñueliana (mostly culled from Mirbeau) abounds in the film, from the elderly foot fetishist to the lady with the bathroom full of test-tubes and syringes, from the ants crawling over the greenhouse frame to the snails crawling over the murdered child's leg, the butterfly being blown to pieces by a bullet, the absurd priest toddling along the street, or that same slowly and painfully skewered goose. Buñuel himself has remarked *a propos* of *Viridiana* that he originally intended Don Jaime's son (the character played by Francisco Rabal) to be a dwarf, but changed his mind because people would have said it was "too Buñuel". One's complaint in *Le Journal d'une femme de chambre* is not so much that it is too Buñuel, as that most of the Buñueliana is simply superb decoration...

'It is possible, of course, to see the film as a masterpiece in a minor genre, simply as a collection of sharply incisive sketches illustrating the corruptions and perversions of the French bourgeoisie. On this level it certainly works beautifully. "La campagne, c'est toujours un peu triste," says Celestine almost

Le Journal d'une femme de chambre: Jeanne Moreau with Jean Ozenne (above) and with Françoise Lugagne and Georges Géret

as soon as she arrives at La Prieure, and Roger Fellous' camera records a beautiful, mournful landscape of fields, parks and forests from which life seems to be alien, to have retreated into warmly foetid burrows like the gloomy Monteil mansion, stuffed to bursting point with objets d'art, and with a grand salon where visitors are obliged to take off their shoes in case they spoil it. It is against this grey, joyless background that Buñuel unfolds his tableau of decadence and depravity, which is perfect of its kind: in a room where a massive bible stands open on a lectern and a Pre-Raphaelite angel simpers from a wall, old M. Rabour leafs through his album of Victorian girlie postcards; the frigid Madame Monteil interviews a fascinated curé about the theological implications of "certaines caresses", or concocts weird potions in the privacy of the bathroom which Celestine is forbidden to clean; and an elderly, virginal and tolerably hideous kitchen-maid weeps with tearful joy when coaxed into the steamy damp of her laundry by the furtively desperate M. Monteil. Buñuel, however, has tried to push a little further, not entirely successfully, through the character of Celestine herself.' (Tom Milne in *Sight and Sound*, Autumn 1964.)

Simón del desierto

In Mexico, Alatriste paid Buñuel almost five million pesetas to maintain his exclusive services. *Simeón el estilita*, which was the idea that resulted in *Simón del desierto*, was begun for him. When the money ran out, Buñuel offered to extend the film to a showable length at his own expense, provided that the film was not presented at the Venice Festival. Originally conceiving it as a feature film of eleven reels, Buñuel succeeded in leaving it sufficiently realized in only five, though the forced solution of creating an improvised epilogue before all the consequences of them have been explored remains apparent. Even so, *Simón* remains an important and very personal work, though its awkward length of 42 minutes limits its commercial showings.

The film is surprising and profound, serious and entertaining, full of gags and of clear Surrealist inspiration. Simón is one of the innumerable stylites who proliferated in Egypt at the beginning of the Christian era, holy men or ascetics who pray in the middle of the desert, perched on top of a column. Believers gather at his feet to hear his preaching. Fourteen years pass. Food is sent up to him in a basket on the end of a rope. (St Simeón was a stock theme for discussion and private jokes in the Residencia, where Surrealist comedy was built around his situation and arrangements. García Lorca was a master at this kind of improvisation, and invented fables and fantastic episodes around the mystical figure, describing for example how 'his excrements glide down the column as beautifully as wax falling from a candle'.)

Simón del desierto: Claudio Brook and Jesús Fernández

In the film, Simón moves to a new and bigger column which a believer has constructed for him. He has diverting conversations with the monks; performs miracles, in face of the total indifference of those who do not revere them; talks with a dwarf; struggles against the temptations of the devil who appears to him in the form of a beautiful woman and then in the form of the Good Shepherd (both metamorphoses are played by Silvia Pinal), who is subsequently transformed into a goat-bearded figure who kicks the Pascal Lamb grazing near by; blesses everything in sight, good and bad, including the insects. In the Epilogue, Satan translates him to the New York of our own times, where Simón regards night clubs with people dancing rock and roll. *'Vade retro!'* he murmurs, to drive away Satan; with no effect. Buñuel, in his apocalyptic vision, appears to see no escape for the saint any more than there was for Nazarín or for Viridiana (who was also exposed to rock and roll at the end). 'The basic structure is the same,' commented Ulrich Gregor (*Filmkritik*, Munich, No 19, 1965). 'Christian ideas crumble anyway before reality without the ability to change, and the saint will end overwhelmed with doubt, under the form of an allegorical epilogue. Otherwise the film is presented on the surface as pure comedy. Although Buñuel takes his saint seriously, he sees him in an ironic perspective. He shows the division between the exalted prophet and the blind idolatry of the believer, from which many-faceted and comic contrasts result; but behind every gag, every irony, every Surrealist image of the film, is concealed a philosophic intention.'

Belle de Jour

Parting from Alatriste, Buñuel returned to Spain at Christmas 1965. He was deeply impressed by the *Breviario y Santoral* by Brother Justo Pérez de Urbel which had just been published in Madrid. He was fascinated by the account of the discipline of the old monasteries, in one of which, for arriving two minutes late in the refectory, a friar was whipped on the table before starting his meal. This led Buñuel to study the monastic scholars and alchemists of the middle ages, and to concoct a script out of Matthew Gregory Lewis's *The Monk*. Written by a Protestant, this Gothick novel was very dear to the Surrealists. It proved to be one of his best scripts. In Buñuel's version a sixteenth-century scholar of the church, the Prior of a Convent of Calle Montera, Madrid, comes, from excessive study of theological mysteries, to suffer a madness, like a new Don Quixote. He can no longer distinguish good from evil, which occasions terrible confusions. His behaviour becomes chaotic, and frequently sacrilegious. His sickness, as often in real life, becomes mixed up with sado-masochistic obsessions and perversions. An infernal woman poses as a novice monk and tries to convert him through sex to Satanism; yet the monk always retains a dreadful consciousness of sin. The

Belle de Jour: Catherine Deneuve, Geneviève Page

French producers were delighted with the script, but after a few months the company failed, and Buñuel had to accept another offer: an adaptation of Joseph Kessel's *Belle de Jour*. *The Monk* now exists: Buñuel gave the script, free of royalties, to Ado Kyrou, who directed it in 1972.

In July 1966, Buñuel, who was clearly disappointed not to do *The Monk*, which would have complemented *Simón del desierto* as a serious work of investigation into problems of religious belief, said: '*Belle de Jour* is a period book, very *démodé* nowadays; and I have had to modify it rather. (He had just finished the script with Jean-Claude Carrière.) Happily the character of the protagonist is well defined, and pathologically precise and exact. She alone interests me rather. But I am tired and old. I have had enough of cinema, enough of stars and actresses.' In fact physically he was still full of energy and humour. His ironies, jokes, little comedies with his sister Conchita and everyone who visited him, were endless. Such weariness as he betrayed seemed the direct result of having to make this film. 'After this I shall make one or two more, and then retire.' (He has several times already announced his 'last film'.) 'This novel of the twenties, of the period of Paul Morand, done in a realist style, is about the masochistic impulses of a woman who, fearing that she is frigid, ends by working in brothels. I hope I can save such a stale

Belle de Jour: Séverine with her first client

subject by mixing indiscriminately and without warning in the montage the things that actually happen to the heroine, and the fantasies and morbid impulses which she imagines. As the film proceeds, I am going to increase the frequency of these interpolations, and at the end, in the final sequence, the audience will not be able to know if what is happening to her is actual or the heroine's subjective world – reality or nightmare. Catherine Deneuve is contracted, and the producers are Paris Films (Robert and Raymond Hakim). Shooting will start at the end of the summer and I hope to shoot it in two months. Then I am going to Zaragoza for a couple of days to see my mother, and afterwards returning to Paris.'

This is exactly how things went; and the finished film was the French selection at the Venice Film Festival, where it won the Golden Lion of St Mark by a five to two vote of the international jury. It also received a prize from a group of the independent press which wanted to declare its disagreement with FIPRESCI. The public at Venice was distinctly mixed in its response. In France the opposite phenomenon was observed. The public received the film with great enthusiasm (as they were later to do in Britain, Germany and elsewhere) while the press remained to a degree reticent, if generally favourable. *Paris Match* praised the tact and the director's restraint in treating 'a subject as daring as might be' so chastely. *L'Express* rhapsodized in the terms which have become usual when French critics write about Buñuel; Pierre Billard wrote (29 May–4 June 1967): 'In evoking with that un-hypocritical modesty that is so much his own, the dreams of Séverine, and giving them the ordinariness of reality, Buñuel explores the character, explains her, and at the same time introduces without any friction her own obsessions: Séverine as a child molested by a workman in the voluptuous terror of a deserted corridor; Séverine whipped and violated by servants or covered in mud by her husband: such are the images which haunt *Belle de Jour* and reveal its masochism. But in Buñuel the aesthetic progression is always conditioned by a moral position. These cords, these chains, these whips, these boots with which the film is packed, are not the stock-in-trade of a fairground showman. They constitute the painter's arsenal, collected with a humour which is often misunderstood by his admirers ("Why don't audiences laugh more at my films?" Buñuel asks) by a man who is obsessed by all the mutilations of the human being. Like those of Providence, the ways of Buñuel are impenetrable; but they always lead to the full expansion of man and to the affirmation of his right to happiness.'

The author himself, Joseph Kessel, wrote to a friend after the first showing of the film: 'I was nervous about going to this screening. I came out of it full of gratitude. Buñuel's genius has surpassed all that I could have hoped. It is at one and the same time the book and not the book. We are in another dimension: that of the subconscious, of dreams and secret instincts suddenly laid bare. And what formal beauty in the images! And beneath the severity, the most contained and most moving pit.'

Buñuel, as he intended, succeeded in saving a story which was not on his own level, by transposing much of the psychological definition and even the narrative to the plane of erotic dream. For Surrealism, reality and dream are one. As to the 'chaste' style of the director, it must be pointed out that the French censors helped him here, by prescribing three cuts at the end of the sequences of the meetings of Séverine with three of the odd clients of the house of assignation where she goes to appease her masochism. In the first (the professor of gynaecology who dresses as a servant and requires to be ill-treated by the prostitute) the censor cut the conclusion in which the woman repeatedly pricked the client's servile behind. There are no cuts as some believe in the episode of the fat Chinaman who explains with such insistence in his native tongue the significance of a mysterious box. We do not see what actually happens when they go into the bedroom. Only at the end, we see Séverine, half fainting on the bed, as the camera sweeps smoothly up her body and into a close-up of a towel stained with very red blood. Buñuel was irritated by the pruning of this shot. Very little was cut from the most Buñuelesque and absurd episode involving the necrophile who mourns and recites conventional funereal phrases over the coffin in which Séverine lies naked beneath a transparent black chiffon négligée. The client gets under the coffin; there is mysterious vibration; and finally the servant enters and asks if he should release the cats that have been prepared. Buñuel says of the cuts in this sequence: 'The ambiguity is established by the landau, which is the symbol of the irrational. When the landau comes, it is a signal that you do not know whether what is seen is actual or not. After one of these landau shots the gentleman makes an assignation with Séverine. The next shot was a religious mass in the chapel of the castle, in front of Grünewald's Christ, which I like very much. The priest (played by Jean-Claude Carrière) is consecrating the holy wine. This scene was cut by the French censorship. The second cut is where the butler is stripping Deneuve. The third is when the butler puts her in the coffin. There are no more cuts in the sequence.'

For me, *Belle de Jour* is something less than we might have looked for from Buñuel's maturity. It touches only distantly on the religious and social problems which he follows in his best work. According to the Surrealist canon, acceptance of erotic liberty is almost the realization of the liberty of man; and only in this sense is *Belle de Jour* a significant link in Buñuel's work. From a formal point of view, it was the best-made film of his career to date (it was also the one for which he had most means), even though stylistically there are elements which trace directly back to *Un Chien andalou*. The uncritical admiration of many critics in face of this film indicated that they either did not know Buñuel very well, or had not troubled to take him seriously until now. The lovely autumn colours, dominating the film, the beautiful interiors, clothes and elegant photography of vibrant mists, all contribute to the enchantment of the film. However, we would not be logical if we overrated the film on these grounds after having insisted so often in the course of this book on the quality and absolute values of the 'badly made' films of his difficult years. *Belle de Jour* leaves us with the impression of the work of an old master who is in total control, avoids all dangers, maintains his youthful vigour and sustains his themes, but is somewhat tired in face of the commercial impositions of the producers.

La Voie Lactée

The disproportionate success of *Belle de Jour* (which on one occasion Buñuel, with his drastic humility, told me had no more merit than Columbus's egg) placed him in a position where he was free to select his own story. Possible subjects seemed to be *Los Misterios*, *The Monk* or a long-cherished idea of a life of Christ shown according to the traditional iconography, but 'always walking quickly'. Sequences from this project which he had from time to time described indicated that it would have been the exact antithesis of the *Life of Christ* which Carl Th. Dreyer dreamed of making and which (to judge from a reading by the director in Copenhagen in 1956) would have expressed the metaphysics and social implications of the story in enervating ritual slowness. Buñuel reckoned that this idea, nurtured since the twenties, was not enough to justify a whole film. Since a film on the life of Christ did not strike him as being worth the trouble, he had the idea of combining the theme with the *Misterios*. What better mysteries than those of dogma? Withdrawing to La Cazorla, a tourist hotel in the Andalusian sierra, in 1968, he classified with the help of his current co-writer, Jean-Claude Carrière, the six great mysteries of the Christian religion and studied all the heresies that rise from each of them. He started to sketch the new scenario. The script was completed in Mexico; and thus originated the first film in the whole history of the cinema whose sole content is religion. For though there are many films with religious themes or motivations, there is none whose material is exclusively abstract thought, the dogmas of faith.

That Buñuel should create such a film (he would have been capable of making it long before) is less surprising – miraculous indeed – than that he should have found a producer and above all a distributor for it. The historical importance of this film, which opens up the way to a speculative, essayist cinema, has yet to be fully realized. After Buñuel, films based on thought concepts, on a conceptual Weltanschauung, are possible. (Eisenstein planned

La Voie Lactée: Buñuel directing Claudio Brook in the 'Doctrine of the Trinity' sequence

a feature-length film on *Das Kapital*, but was never able to make it.) This is the true importance of the film.

The closing title of the film says: 'Everything in this film which concerns Catholicism and the heresies to which it has given rise, in particular from the dogmatic point of view, is rigorously exact.

'The texts and citations are taken either from the Scriptures or from ancient and modern works of theology.'

'The original script, it appears,' wrote David Robinson (*Financial Times*, 24 October 1969), 'indicated a similar title at the commencement of the film, but including the words: "Throughout the film all the apparitions, miracles, or stories of miracles are treated entirely seriously and in conformity with traditional representations given by the Church, without any spirit of derision." Perhaps such a statement begged too many questions, taking into account both the nature of dogma and of Buñuel's comic vision.

'The film takes the form of a picaresque adventure, moving quite freely through time and space. Two shabby men, one elderly (Paul Frankeur) and one younger (Laurent Terzieff) are on pilgrimage to the shrine of Santiago de Compostela ... They tramp, beg, steal, hitchhike. Either in their imaginations or on their journeyings, there are encounters and adventures which seem to take place anywhere – in Bethlehem or Spain, in the first century or the seventeenth. They are never surprised by marvels or very much discountenanced by misfortune. Buñuel treats them quite freely and casually. When he wants to leave them for a while, he does so; and they disappear entirely from the closing scenes of the film.

'The connection of their adventures is heresy. Each of the sketches – they follow rather like numbers in a revue – has as its theme the heresies which attach to the six major dogmas of the Catholic religion. This fact presents a certain difficulty for audiences in a non-Catholic country like our own. It is no positive obstacle to enjoyment of the film; but a great deal must seem more pointed to spectators living in a Catholic atmosphere and more keenly aware both of the fact that a heretic is above all a believer who deviates from the orthodox belief in one detail only; and of the passionate debate that for 2,000 years has surrounded dogmatism.

'(There may be readers who like me need to be reminded what the major heresy-exciting dogmas are: (1) The nature of Jesus Christ; He is at once both God and Man; (2) The Trinity: one God in three substances; (3) Transsubstantiation; the communion bread and wine *become* the body and blood of Our Lord; (4) The Immaculate Conception; (5) Men have Free Will, while God has prescience of all their actions; (6) The Origins of Evil; Since God is Good he cannot Himself have created Evil.)

'Of course Buñuel is not interested in these specific questions *per se* but only in the effect of their discussion upon the lives and nature of men. What fascinates and appals him is how over the centuries people have been prepared to wage war, to suffer or die – or conversely to torture and kill – in defence of some small argument or article of faith which might seem to the uncommitted spectator a good deal less significant than the dispute of the Big – and Little – Enders.

'Perhaps a better parallel than Swift is *Alice*. Buñuel has a Jansenist and a Jesuit fighting a duel over the question of free will. When they stop their fight as suddenly as they began and march off in cheerful conversation, you are irresistibly put in mind of Tweedledum and Tweedledee, even though a broken rattle constitutes a much more substantial cause of war than these theological questions. Practically all the dogmatic discussion takes on the marvellous circular quality of *Alice*:

' "If I wasn't real", Alice said . . . "I shouldn't be able to cry."

' "I hope you don't suppose those are real tears?" Tweedledee interrupted in a tone of great contempt . . .

'It is worth remembering that *Alice* has always been a major text for Surrealists; so that though the resemblances of the film are more likely to be the result of unconscious influence than simple coincidence, Buñuel's two heroes wander through the wonderland of dogma and heresy very much as Alice explored a fantasy world in which all the objects and people and arguments and ideas were queerly distorted reflections of Victorian life and thought, belief and society.

'Buñuel of course has more ends in view than writing for infant girl-friends. His argument, if it is not by then already clear, is summed up in the last scene, where Jesus appears to tell his disciples, "I am not come upon the earth to bring peace, but the sword. For I am come to set the father against the son, the daughter against the mother. Who loves his son and his daughter more than Me is not worthy of Me . . ." This is the Christ created by men and by the arrogant vanity with which we will defend our ideas just because they are ours: my religion – or country or race – right or wrong.

'*La Voie Lactée* is like all Buñuel films, a serious film and full of references. But it is not a solemn film. Buñuel is the most hilarious chronicler of the human tragedy . . .'

The acceptance of the film by the distributors and by the public indicates the extent to which Buñuel had dominated the market, how he had been able to create 'his coterie' in vast numbers of a specialized public – or rather a public initiated in his line of visual ideas. Apart from his own name, firmly established after *Belle de Jour*, there was a good deal of skill and not a few precautions involved in making the film readily available to the audience. In the first place the writers wove a linking narrative for the film, in the story of

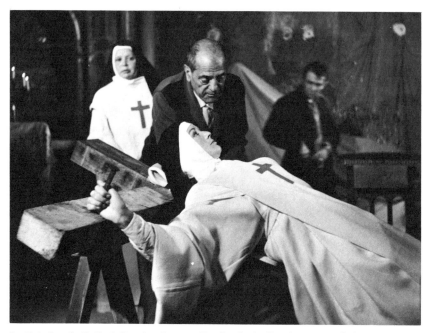

La Voie Lactée: Buñuel directing Augusta Carrière in the 'Jesuit vs. Jansenist' sequence . . .

the two pilgrims (really two beggars) who encounter varied adventures in the manner of the traditional Spanish narrative from *Don Quixote* throughout all the picaresque novels. The episodes are presented with a total absence of logical or temporal order, as in dreams; and paradoxically his Surrealist structure makes the film much more acceptable than if it were planned as a naturalistic narrative. Finally each 'sketch' is treated with a clear stylistic definition of comedy, sometimes carried to a point of burlesque.

For Buñuel this film is the major act of his creative power. 'My career is a bridge spanning from *L'Age d'or* to *La Voie Lactée*,' he tells us, though it must be said that *Simón del desierto* could quite easily have made one of the episodes of this last film. Inevitably it is a difficult and controversial film. Again we are in the presence of a work which is both more and less profound than appears. More: in the sense that Buñuel, as we have said, is opening the door towards a conceptual cinema, and includes the intention of adding fuel to the flames lit by the Second Vatican Council. Less: in that *La Voie Lactée* is not a film about the theological questions nor a film about religion, although it is concerned solely *with* religion. Religion becomes 'working material' for an essentially Surrealist work; and nothing pejorative will be

... 'The wedding at Cana': Edith Scob, Bernard Verley

found in this by anyone who understands the nobility with which writers on art such as Foncillon invest the term 'working material'. As a trivial example: a Surrealist may make a collage in which he sticks nymphs, tritons and so forth on a print showing an anarchist throwing a bomb at the royal carriage; and will produce an unexpected plastic composition. Would he intend to exalt or denigrate the royal figure? Neither: he is indifferent. Which does not exclude the subversion of the final result of his composition, since if not subversive it would be neither Surrealist nor a good picture.

There are moments when, for someone familiar with his work, Buñuel seems to be amusing himself with the unconsciousness and purity of a little boy. At other moments we suspect that it has all been a pretext for him to display his collection of obsessions and his repertory of 'rustic anecdotes' (the term is used with the respect due to every popular expression impregnated with atavistic wisdom). With a work like *La Voie Lactée*, however, it is impossible to apply the canons of traditional criticism, to question the fragmented structure, the lack of formal 'dramatic build-up', the prolixity and lack of definition in the characters, the situations which begin and are interrupted without formal conclusion. In its own way the film is strictly constructed, measured and weighed almost with fanaticism. Nor does it lack its

La Voie Lactée: Bernard Verley with (r.) Jean Clarieux

own fluidity nor a rhythm of sonata tempo. Buñuel, as he has confessed, always longs for elegance, an aesthetic.

Here, supremely, is Buñuel the entomologist, once more considering the mystery of man's cerebral mechanism, the absurdity which believers will accept and which, once believers themselves, they will impose on others by fire and sword. Here is the pessimism of a humanist observing violence, cruelty, folly; the conduct of man seen in this case through his most expansive social activity in history, religion.

L'Age d'or is all sensuality and fresh inspiration; *La Voie Lactée* is mature, heavily charged with reflection and study. The critics treated the new film with the respect due to a classic. *L'Unità* of Rome (8 March 1969), after singling out the splendid sound-track and Christian Matras' photography (far from the charm of the soft colours of Vierny in *Belle de Jour*, and filmed like a tourist taking snaps of Holy Week with his Kodak), affirmed: 'Buñuel's style has achieved the maximum sobriety, purity, an extraordinary candour born of the serenity of art; of this grace (with a small letter) found in the culmination of a career of forty years, other precious fruits may be born.' *Il Corriere della Sera* of Milan, naturally more reticent, observed that: 'The fatigue of being an atheist, of resisting throughout a whole lifetime the temptations of faith, has a high price. *La Voie Lactée* is an embroidery of inventions of a more youthful aggressiveness and amiability than we might have hoped for from Buñuel, who has not always shone by his rational lucidity (sic!), and closer to the debate on the theology of violence and other themes of today. The grotesque tone of the film, the liveliness of the sarcasm which colours it, are not a sign of blasphemy so much as a spirit of irony with which Buñuel tries to protect his old age' (5 March 1969). And *Stampa Sera* of Turin (1 March 1969): 'Buñuel has achieved a serenity and imperturbability which put him almost outside time. Unlike the prophets, he neither exalts nor condemns.'

Invited to the Festival of Cinema of Religious and Human Values at Valladolid, the film aroused controversy. The Jesuit father Staehlin (a specialist in cinema matters, who years before had fearlessly launched Bergman on our screens, and a member of the Spanish censorship) resigned from the organizing committee because he considered the film unacceptable. A doctor of theology, José Jiménez Lozano (in *El Norte de Castilla*, 11 May 1969) protested violently against the film, carrying his susceptibilities so far as to feel himself offended by the visual treatment of the Blessed Virgin, which no other critic had found disrespectful. Yet another Jesuit, Father Arteta, in various numbers of a Saragossan review, *Dichos y Hechos*, was deeply concerned with the artistic and moral personality of the author and with what might be termed 'his existential anguish'. The Rome distributor, Medusa Film, says that though the Italian government was prepared to prohibit the film, the Holy See itself intervened in its favour. All we can say, the connoisseurs of Buñuel, is that he could have made a film many times more aggressive. In this sense, Buñuel's present restraint and wisdom becomes almost irksome for some of his friends.

15. The Great Films of Maturity: II Tristana and Le Charme Discret de la Bourgeoisie

A few months after his return to Mexico, the Spanish producers for whom Buñuel had prepared *Tristana* contacted him. Now they were sure that the film was viable. On the one hand Buñuel needed no persuasion; he had always been dominated by a desire to film in Spain; on the other he began work unwillingly. He has always to conquer a desire for inactivity; less from laziness than from an existential terror at the prospect of returning to creation which is common among artists. 'Why more films?' he would say; 'There are enough already'; and 'Movies are as big a nuisance to make as they are to see.' In the case of *Tristana* there were other reasons for his attitude. The scenario no longer attracted him. Since this old project he had been able to create very personal works which had given him an international status. He had conceived *Tristana* with the aim of continuing his activity in the Spanish cinema after *Viridiana*, correcting his tactical error with the censorship (or, rather, the censors' own error). Now it did not interest him. When the producers visited him in Mexico to tell him that finally the production of the seven-year-old project was feasible, the director must have been disconcerted. He accepted, largely out of faith with the young producers who had expended much hope, money and work on the enterprise; partly because he had taken an advance of 30,000 dollars, which the producers would not accept back, since they insisted on the clause in the old contract which provided for resumption of the film in the event of conditions permitting it.

He arrived in Madrid in Spring 1969. Things were still not easy, and the permission to shoot was only granted in September. Buñuel's nerves seem to be one of the causes of his deafness, which grew worse in these months. The circumstances of a costly production, always tedious, tried his patience. Among other things, the French co-producer had insisted on Catherine Deneuve for the title role. France also brought an assistant director and a pair of minor technicians, as well as giving the actress an excessive salary in order to bring more capital and receive more from advance guarantees. Although the publicity did not hesitate to describe Deneuve as the director's favourite actress, quoting the success of *Belle de Jour*, Buñuel in fact detested her as much as he did any other star. 'The awful thing about actors is that actor face,' he would say. Probing deeper into his hidden psyche, Buñuel has an instinctive and ill-dissimulated aversion for the woman-fetish, through the mechanism of the 'mother-complex' examined by Freud. Not that this prevented Buñuel from having an impeccable taste for a fragile and fleeting female beauty which is exactly the antithesis of the type of the women he has personally loved: his mother, wife, sister and so on. In fact Catherine Deneuve irritated him and, joking, he said that at the end of the film he made her 'worse than the script provided for her to be', to annoy her. But after the shooting was finished he said that 'she was a good actress' and considered taking her for the next film. Deneuve had been a model of professionalism and docility, an attitude which was no doubt helped by the salary of some fifteen millions which she earned in a month's work.

The Italian co-producers had sent a fashionable juvenile lead, Franco Nero, rather unsuited to the role of the provincial Spanish painter. The Italians also wanted to send the celebrated photographic virtuoso who had made a great impression with his work on *Fellini-Satyricon*; but here Buñuel was adamant. 'Let them send a sound recordist if they must.' He grumbled too 'I'm weak; I end up doing what other people want'; and chose Aguayo, the cameraman of *Viridiana*, an excellent craftsman but recognized as very conservative. Buñuel was aiming in this way to make *Tristana* a film that would be one hundred per cent Spanish. He also recognized that this kind of camera work was the kind of plastic style called for by the theme of *Tristana*.

Buñuel took much care over the character of Don Lope, and was delighted with the work of Fernando Rey, with whom he had found himself very much in sympathy on *Viridiana* and the proposed episode for *Los Misterios*; both appreciated the same dark humour.

The first script, done with Julio Alejandro, was then in its fourth revision. A comparison of the different versions reveals a process of schematization,

Tristana: Catherine Deneuve

whose object would become apparent once the film was made. The author was leaving as a pure sketch the evolution of the spinsterish Tristana towards a masochist perversion tinged with religiosity, a development instinctively sympathetic to Buñuel. Asked why he had suppressed the scene of the confession – in which the priest warns Tristana against so much haircloth and self-flagellation, which might well become devotion to snares of the devil and the sin of pride – Buñuel replied that 'the theme was very clear and became obvious. I will no longer indulge in scenes like this when not necessary.' 'Obvious' is a key word. *Tristana* was to be an exercise in the presentation of obvious facts in which the development was not obvious. Buñuel withdrew to more recondite complicities with the spectator.

Admirably organized and with one of the best crews that could be put together in Spain, the production consisted of a month of exteriors in Toledo and twenty days in the Siena studios which had just been opened in the Carretera de Colmenar Viejo. Without achieving the high polish of *Belle de Jour*, the *mise en scène* was excellent. Quite different from *Belle de Jour*, *Tristana* mixed violent colours or sepias, and the many exteriors of the imperial city were ugly. Since Buñuel always has personal motives, there may be in this an element of revenge against the city he so much loved in his youth and which is now deprived of its old mystery and intimacy. In an interview for French television he had already protested when his old feeling for the city was recalled: 'I don't like Toledo: it is old and stinks of piss', he answered.

During the shooting, Buñuel as usual altered and added details. He worked with great economy, but still suppressed a good deal in the editing. An example is the meeting of Tristana with the two deaf-mutes, the ascent of the cathedral tower and the scene in the belfry. Aguayo did a panoramic shot from the cloisters to pick up Saturno. ('This is very vulgar,' said Buñuel, talking to himself; and immediately, with the grimace of a *nouveau riche* in a cinema without financial privation, 'But it's nice. Cut it!' At once his instinctive sense of economy called him to order: 'I'll be able to use it somewhere else ...' He never did.) Saturno looks for Tristana, and meets his deaf-mute friend. Tristana arrives: the two boys rush to kiss her cheek, which she avoids, and makes to bang their heads together. Tristana leaves the scene and is heard laughing as she goes off towards the bell-tower. The camera tracks in, and then moves away from the boys to pan to the top, at the same time as a travelling movement leaves the arch of the cloister which has framed the image, to settle on the view of the tower, as if indicating that the next sequence would be centred there.

This extremely condensed structure is still further abbreviated in the editing. The whole work, take by take, was to undergo drastic reduction, resulting in extreme concentration of effect. Many things considered indispensable for traditional film language are missing. Buñuel had begun to suppress these conventionalities as early as 1928; and today's new cinemas have without exception followed him.

If we discuss details of syntax, the reader is already aware that it is not from a wish to define an 'aesthetic' for Buñuel. It is because *Tristana* is, essentially, *language*. It is through this that Buñuel transcends himself. There is no craving for elegance in him, rather a discipline, formed in the asceticism which was important in Spanish conceptualist literature of the Conterreform. It is certain that the career of every artist leads to a process of purification, synthesis, except in the rare cases of enrichment through a baroque rhetoricism (as happened with Eisenstein); also it is true that Buñuel, at the expense of avoiding becoming a stylist, has arrived at being one: as much through the Surrealist fear in face of the trap of aestheticism, as through fear of revealing his intrinsic poverty in some aspects of film-making (*Belle de Jour* is a case in point); but in *Tristana* the condensation of the structure is so aggressive as to be evidently the true key to the film.

The work has not a single scene of brilliance. Hence the quiet, discreet tone, just as demanded by the needs of Spanish production, becomes suspect for an audience (or a censor). At the same time, and by the same reason, every

Tristana: Fernando Rey and Catherine Deneuve

millimetre of this grey film acquires importance, because Buñuel alone has given us the structure. This is not much to give in an entertainment! The narrative destruction of *Tristana* is that of *Un Chien andalou*. Permitting the spectator no complacency creates a total distantiation, more advanced in some respects than that of Brecht. *Tristana* becomes revolutionary, not because it incites us to change the world, as Marx demanded, or to change life as Rimbaud wished, or even to seek for truth: *Tristana is* the truth. A truth nowhere ranked or mixed with subjective visions, for example, as happens in reality and in the Surrealist dream. Things are thus: Spain, the provinces, Don Lope, the Church, woman, and so on, under a particular weight of history and customs, produce a given result, like laboratory chemistry. The consternation is as unprovided with liberty as with hope. From a naturalist novel by Galdós, charged with quiet liberal ideals, Buñuel derives a work which can qualify as politico-scientific cinema.

'*Tristana* has forty per cent of Galdós's dialogue, but the film will be as much mine,' Buñuel told us during shooting. Likewise it has this same percentage of the peripetia, the critical lucidity and the precision in establishing ambience and atmosphere of the novelist. It is the most Spanish film of Buñuel; and a public used to a cosmopolitan cinema which hardly exists as

'Spanish' at all, was astonished by the accumulation of local detail – the eating scenes with 'cocido', 'acelgas', 'migas'; the priest who watches over the family morals and so on. It is above all Spanish by the study of characteristic national situations and characters: from the time and the locales of Galdós, but transmuted by Buñuel to a provincial city in the twenties (as in *Le Journal d'une femme de chambre*) and still quite identifiable in 1970. This means that a moment in time becomes a constant of historical causality, and a dialectic analysis of broad scope.

The progressive degradation of the illusions and the purity of Tristana can be taken as typical of all human life advancing towards maturity. The means of defence and compensation used by each of us in the face of these phenomena vary greatly, and those of Tristana were anagonic to those chosen by Buñuel. Don Lope has the characteristics of 'Don Juanism' common in Spain, particularly in the generation which preceded ours, of whom he can be considered one of the representative types of Spaniard. Sexually he is what Buñuel himself has not been, has not been able to be and, as an intelligent man, has not wished to be. The bourgeois legacy of Don Lope, of parasitism surviving off unearned income, is that which Buñuel in his youth knew by the name of 'señorito', used pejoratively; a class from which, as we have seen, he released himself forcibly. The sense of honour, which Buñuel ridicules, follows from his class; so does the demand for unilateral fidelity applicable only to the woman, while Buñuel only recognizes the moral honesty of bilaterality; so also involvement in duels, a custom extremely comic to the Surrealist, and so fascinating as to make him into a collector of pistols.

The liberal and progressive ideas of the bourgeois of the old school incarnated in Don Lope (boasting of being a freethinker and anticlerical, anarchical defender of the thief and detractor of military authoritarianism) are, as Buñuel has told me 'those which reigned among the "intelligentsia" of the Sorbonne when I arrived in Paris'. Buñuel, already initiated into this current of ideas in Madrid, continued in them in France and – what is important – submitted them to a rigorous critical analysis which led him to reject them, submitting himself to the Surrealist discipline. As to the final scenes of Don Lope offering refreshments in his home to a group of priest friends, it is a demonstration of what can frequently happen to such Spanish gentlemen in their old age. It is a demonstration full of irony, which obliges us to re-examine the certainty of our braggart youthful positions. In this respect Buñuel will sometimes tell his friends, with morbid complacency, that when his death becomes imminent he will call a priest to his bed. Thus will he disturb his friends with the doubt whether he will thus have crowned his existence with a cold posthumous sacrilege, or whether he intends to assure his entry into Heaven! One more demonstration of Buñuel's black humour, with its consequent taste for the creation of ambiguity and transcendent doubts, which does not spare even himself. The end of *Tristana* is no more than the visualization of this terrible jest.

Le Charme discret de la bourgeoisie

Buñuel returned to Madrid in January 1972. 'I'm not thinking of making any more films,' he told me, as he had already said to the press. All the same he had under his arm the script, which he had finished with Jean-Claude Carrière, for *Le Charme discret de la bourgeoisie*. Like a small boy making excuses, he said: 'It's just that I got bored in all that time in Mexico so I got to writing.' This was a little surprising in a man who has always insisted that he never gets bored; but clearly it was only a pretext. The fact is that after a month's rest he went to Paris to see Silberman, whose friendship with Buñuel, and his ability to persuade him, are enormous. The idea of the film had already been discussed with the producer. This concerned the repeated frustration of a dinner party, because of mistaken appointments. From this the director was able to develop all the nightmare of the bourgeois party in search of a dinner through the whole length of a film, with marginal episodes inserted.

Silberman liked the script and invited Buñuel to start at once. 'He was marvellous to me, giving me the "monitor", which allowed me to frame up the shots without hanging about the camera.' It was the first time that anyone in France had used the new electronic device which will in future be an essential tool for directors.

'In France the director really is boss, not like in Hollywood. Everything was very convenient. I hate a film unit, the lorries with generators and lights, the cables, the stars; but when I start to work I throw myself into it altogether and forget myself. I'm very nice, never raise my voice, and everyone's happy.' Fernando Rey said on television that at the party at the finish of the shooting, there is always someone who cries. The expansive atmosphere which Buñuel creates with his ironic humour keeps the unit happy.

Edward Landler, who was present at the shooting, wrote to me on 1 August 1972: 'Don Luis was in the office checking the costumes when I arrived. He seemed in excellent health and very good spirits. I was sometimes allowed to be present at the shooting, and learned a lot. Buñuel taught me the value of the extreme close-up as a sign of narrative importance and of the subconscious. Don Luis had a new plaything (the monitor, a television screen connected to the camera) and felt himself in the place of command and directed looking at the television screen. He often seemed tired, but was very well and very lively.

'Towards the end of the shooting, all the same, the arrogance of the French crew produced a certain friction. There was some professional antagonism between the different nationalities involved, and this was not always very friendly, though it all settled itself.'

There was also a labour dispute, a threat of strike by part of the crew who refused to work on Saturdays. René Clément fought this claim, forgetting his left-wing sympathies. Buñuel finally settled the question by declaring that *he* wouldn't work on Saturdays. This gesture earned him a letter of thanks from the French union of which he has been a member, as a 'Frenchman', since his Paris days. All the same the producer couldn't grumble: the shooting lasted a little less than the six weeks planned, and cost 800,000 dollars, while Clément's venture cost 1,600,000 for a film which turned out to be quite mediocre. *Le Charme discret*, on the other hand, was to have an unprecedented financial success. In the United States, where Buñuel was until recently almost unknown, the film took many times the millions earned by *Tristana*. Silberman offered to give Buñuel ten per cent of the profits, but on principle he refused.*

The shooting had begun on 15 May 1972, and the film was finished in a little over two months. Buñuel's own assistants remarked on the rhythm and humour which he brought to the film. He had never felt so free to improvise; an example was reported by Diego Galáin, *Triunfo* (Madrid, 8 August 1972):

'Bulle Ogier has a practically silent role. Buñuel, in the course of shooting, adds phrases and actions to it:

' "Bulle, when you enter this scene, say something about cyclists."

' "What, for example?"

' "Ask if there are any cyclists here. No, better, say: We passed a cyclist." '

(The scene is where the Thévenots arrive at the Sénéchals' flat for a meal which is, of course, frustrated.)

' "No, no" (laughing). "Better say: We passed a dozen cyclists."

'Finally the phrase used by Bulle Ogier is: We passed two hundred or two hundred and fifty cyclists . . .'

The film was rapturously received by critics in every country. In an extended analysis of the film in *Sight and Sound* (Winter 1972–73) Jonathan Rosenbaum wrote: 'If *Le Charme discret de la bourgeoisie* registers as the funniest Buñuel film since *L'Age d'or*, probably the most relaxed *and* controlled film he has ever made, and arguably the first global masterpiece to have come from France in the seventies, this is chiefly because he has arrived

* Information given in conversation by Buñuel.

Le Charme discret de la bourgeoisie: The Ambassador (Fernando Rey) shoots the Colonel . . .

at a form that covers his full range, permits him to say anything – a form that literally and figuratively lets him get away with murder. One cannot exactly call his new work a bolt from the blue. But its remarkable achievement is to weld together an assortment of his favourite themes, images and parlour tricks into a discourse that is essentially new. Luring us into the deceptive charms of narrative as well as those of his characters, he undermines the stability of both attractions by turning interruption into the basis of his art, keeping us aloft on the sheer exuberance of his amusement . . .

'Every dream and interpolated story in the film carries some threat, knowledge or certainty of death – the central fact that all six characters ignore, and their charm and elegance seek to camouflage. Ghosts of murder victims and other phantoms of guilt parade through these inserted tales, but the discreet style of the bourgeoisie, boxing them in dreams and dinner anecdotes, holds them for ever in check. To some extent, Buñuel shares this discretion in his failure to allude to his native Spain even once in the dialogue, although the pomp and brutality of the Franco regime are frequently evoked. (The recurrent gag of a siren, jet plane or other disturbance covering up a political declaration – a device familiar from Godard's *Made in U.S.A.* – acknowledges this sort of suppression.) But the secret of Buñuel's achieved style is

... Fernando Rey, Delphine Seyrig, Bulle Ögier, Paul Frankeur, Jean-Pierre Cassel

balance, and for that he must lean more on irony – an expedient tactic of the bourgeoisie – than on the aggressions of the rebel classes; when he sought imbalance in *L'Age d'or*, the revolutionary forces had the upper edge. An essential part of his method is to pitch the dialogue and acting somewhere between naturalism and parody, so that no gag is merely a gag, and each commonplace line or gesture becomes a potential gag. Absurdity and elegance, charm and hypocrisy become indistinguishably fused.'

Le Charme discret de la bourgeoisie is filled with amusing sequences whose roots go back into the beautiful psychic automatism of the Surrealists; but the sheer quantity becomes excessive. Its flow, well as it is linked in an oniric context, can become monotonous. The work is full of magnificent situations; but the bourgeois audience do not attack the screen, as they did for *L'Age d'or*, but leave the cinema smiling, thinking that the money spent at the box-office has been well worth while: the artist whom the Surrealists emancipated with the rebellion of disagreeable and ill-made works, has worked well in the service of the rich. But the fact that some of the dreams become reality in the eventual sequences of the film confirm that it is really a wooden horse in the city of the bourgeois. There are no lame truths, but there is less urge to

247

disturb. The proof is the good reception of the film by all audiences, including those of North America. Buñuel, at 72, was entering with a firm step on a phase in which he wanted to embrace a majority of the audience, coinciding in this with the 'divulgent' phase of Surrealism proper, which was on the point of celebrating the fiftieth anniversary of its 'Revolution'. *Le Charme* is for the writer a good film, well integrated into an historic moment, the present. It is not a landmark, as *El ángel exterminador* was.

The success of the production inevitably brought a shower of prizes and offers. 'Gustavo Alatriste wrote to me and offered me 300,000 dollars to make whatever I wanted,' Buñuel told me. 'Alatriste is a good friend, to whom I owe *Viridiana, Simón* and *El ángel.* I replied regretting that I could not accept his offer, which as far as he was concerned was an extremely generous one. Still . . .' Still . . . Hollywood or Silberman (or better, both together) were going to offer him much more, no doubt. The reaction of Hollywood was the classic one: absorption of the European artist who was starting to show incontestable box-office receipts. In December a special dinner was organized in Buñuel's honour, with 200 guests. Buñuel made an appearance, but refused the dinner, on the pretext of his deafness, etc. Under pressure he accepted an intimate dinner 'with four or five people', which became a dozen of the old great ones of the local art, who can be recognized in the photograph published at the time. Hitchcock called him the best director in the world. King Vidor, at 78, drank to 'the best and most modest of us all'. Buñuel was not accompanied by a member of his family, but by his producer, Silberman, and his writer, Jean-Claude Carrière. Seeing them all together in George Cukor's beautiful house, it is hard to avoid the feeling that it looks more like a business lunch than a *hommage*. The Hollywood invitations continued on successive evenings, at the house of William Wyler (whose *The Collector* Buñuel admires) and so on. The reader may be tempted to suppose the dreams of *The Discreet Charm* transformed into reality.

The old great ones of Hollywood are also leading lights of the Academy. Buñuel himself had already been elected a member, with all the appropriate honours, three years before. From the time of his election, Buñuel has voted for the Oscar awards. On 28 March 1973 he himself received the Academy Award for the best foreign film screened in the USA during the previous year. As he himself has said: 'The vote is perfectly democratic and the outcome unforeseeable, since it is a vote which includes 2,500 idiots, including for example the assistant dress designer of the studio who, as a member, has the right to vote.'

Before this Buñuel had received the prize for the best film and the best director awarded by the U.S. Critics' Association, in New York. 'Much more important, since the Oscars are the worst prizes that exist . . . though for my own part I don't care tuppence for any prize,' he commented. The rebel Surrealist would have refused the Oscar in 1930 and even in 1950, but 'a gesture which was then an antisocial act has become a publicity stunt today; and I'm no Marlon Brando'.

It is impossible not to recall Buñuel's joy when Sartre refused the Nobel prize, including the considerable sum of money that went with the award. He sent the philosopher a telegram of congratulations; and told us: 'I would love to receive the Nobel Prize for Peace or Literature (the Science Prizes are more respectable) or the Oscar, just to be able to refuse it.'

In January 1973 Buñuel returned to Spain, as was now usual, and stayed in the Monastery of Paular, a lovely spot near Madrid, in the Somosierra, with an excellent hotel. There he was joined by Jean-Claude Carrière and sketched out the scenario of the next film, for Silberman in co-production with Hollywood, and to be shot in Paris. The title aims at the most immediate socio-political reality of contemporary North America:

The Fantasm of Liberty

'The idea is very good, or very bad, depending on how you look at it. It's about a decaying lineage. An action begins and the situation at once goes off into something different. Thousands of things happen, but there is no story to tell, and certainly no unifying thesis. In short, it's going to be my most Surrealist film.'

After a few days in the Torre de Madrid, a medical examination for a slight intestinal disorder, and three weeks in Zaragoza to see his family, Buñuel went on to Paris (where he met his producer, full of the new scenario) and to the Cannes Festival, 'where I saw no films but had some lovely drinks'. After this he returned to Madrid, presumably to work on the dialogue of *The Fantasm of Liberty* with Carrière – a comparatively light task since the dialogue of a Buñuel film is as functional as is implicit in the scenario. At the time that this edition was in preparation, he had returned to Mexico and it remained uncertain when he would commence shooting.

This book ends on a present of a promise and optimism which few creative artists well past seventy can ever have known. Beginning at the period when its protagonist was the doubtful taste of specialized minorities, we leave him with a world popularity, accepted as the major living figure in the history of the cinema, for his uncompromised honesty and integrity, the depth and originality of his creation. Rarely can the biographer of a living subject have felt more rewarded.

It remains to be seen what place posterity will reserve for Buñuel. Our own opinion is implicit in the text: we see him as a man representative both of an historical era and of a particular Spanish generation. This is the primordial and imperishable value of the man and the artist. It may yet be that his work will further transcend the coordinates of history and time in the sense of that kind of universality which the work of an artist like Shakespeare acquires. It is clearly something possible, given Buñuel's intrinsic quality of genius: his very personal poetry, born of a terror and attraction towards crudity, violence, the contradictions of reality, the constant transition in the human mind between the real and the unreal.

As an artist he aspires to exceed his epoch, escaping from the bounds of any academic aesthetic. His language employs tradition and conservative methods, with simple functionalism. As he has succeeded in almost all his work in expressing himself acceptably with this synthesis, the language will remain valid. Certainly he will not be recorded in the history of the cinema as one of its stylists, creators of visual vocabulary, or most refined technicians. But this is not important.

Thirty or even twenty years ago new plastic or theatrical currents invaded the world, demanding general adhesion. Buñuel might well have seemed to the victims of these diseases as antiquated as White Russians to Marxist art. Today too many of these 'isms' have fallen into discredit for there to be any continuing interest in forms of expression justified only by an aesthetic which is based on metaphysical principles and not on the needs of reality. The mentality of Buñuel is exemplified by his attitude to Surrealism. Already in 1929 he abandoned such aesthetic as this movement had – and which today is without value – retaining that which was to contribute to future culture: the incorporation of the materialism of scientific investigation arising out of psychoanalysis and other aspects of Freudian or post-Freudian phenomenology, and its philosophical implications: the benefit of its riches of poetry and fantasy, arising from the pre-conscious activity of man.

Among Spanish thinkers, Buñuel has been one of those most distant from the Eternal; but his work seeks the permanent values of *Man*: *L'Age d'or*, *El ángel exterminador*, *Simón del desierto*, *La Voie Lactée*. They are films of engagement; and as such launch conflicts with the social structure which still exists; but at the same time they launch conflicts inherent in human nature, and sometimes inherent in the social structure, which seem to be far from disappearing, even today. For this reason the work of Buñuel may prove important for the future, not only through its quality of testimony to our own times.

We have a creator of 75 years old, in his prime, and from whom we can look forward to ever more perfect films. Buñuel will continue his implacable labour of disorienting and bringing despair to those who for very good reasons detest him; and of keeping faith with those who, like himself, love.

Anthology

Instrumentation (1922)
for Adolfo Salazar

Violins
Affected ladies of the orchestra, insufferable and pedantic, sawers of sound.

Violas
Violins arrived at menopause. These old maids still keep in good voice, within their little range.

Violoncellos
Rumblings of sea and jungle. Serenity. Deep eyes. They have the persuasiveness and the grandeur of Jesus's speeches in the desert.

Contrabasses
Diplodocus of instruments. The day that they decide to give forth their great roar, frightening the spectators out of their wits and away! Now we see them sway and growl contentedly because of the way the contrabassists scratch their bellies.

Piccolo
Ants'-nest of sound.

Flute
The flute is the most nostalgic of instruments. That which in the hands of Pan was the trembling voice of meadow and wood, sees himself in the hands of a fat, bald gentleman ... ! But even so, she remains the Princess of instruments.

Clarinet
A hypertrophied flute. Sometimes, poor thing, it sounds well.

Oboe

A sheep's baa-ing transformed to wood. His waves, deep, mysterious, lyrical. The oboe was the twin brother of Verlaine.

English Horn

A middle-aged oboe, with experience. He has travelled. His exquisite temperament has become more grave, more genial. Just as the oboe is fifteen years old, the horn is thirty.

Bassoon

The bassoons are the fakirs of the orchestra. Sometimes they look at the enormous reptile in their hands, showing its forked tongue. Once hypnotized, they cradle them in their arms and remain ecstatic.

Contra-bassoon

The bassoon of the Tertiary Earth.

Xylophone

Children's game. Water of wood. Princesses embroidering tapestry in the garden, moon-beams.

Muted trumpets

Clown of the orchestra. Contortion. Pirouette. Grimaces.

French horns

Climb to a peak. Sunrise. Annunciation. Oh! The day when they unroll like a carnival squeaker . . . !

Trombones

Rather a German temperament. Voice. Choir masters of old cathedral with ivy and rusty weather-vane.

Tuba

Legendary dragon. Its hoarse subterranean voice makes all the other instruments tremble with fear, asking themselves when the prince in shining armour will arrive to free them.

Cymbals

Shattered light.

Triangle

Silver streetcar for the orchestra.

Drum

Slight stage thunder. 'Somewhat' menacing.

Bass Drum

Prophetic. Stubbornness. Rudeness. Boom. Boom. Boom.

Kettle-drums

Leather olive-baskets.

(published in Pedro Garfias's review, *Horizonte* No 2, 30 November 1922)

NOTE: Apparently Buñuel's first published literary text, this is clearly a homage to Ramón Gómez de la Serna, father of the twenties *avant-garde* groups, including Surrealism. He had invented this kind of absurdist metaphor, which he called 'Gregorias' and which became very popular in Spain. An example, later than Buñuel's text, is 'Cymbals are the sneeze of the orchestra'. The comparison is interesting; de la Serna's image is essentially literary, Buñuel's visual.

The text combines Buñuel's interests in music, natural sciences, and his view of the orchestra as a bourgeois monopoly and therefore to be despised and destroyed. (Cf. comparable references in *L'Age d'or*, the projected scene in *Los Olvidados* discussed on p. 137, the destruction of the cello in *El ángel exterminador* and the 'Las Menadas' episode in the *Misterios* script. In *Le Charme discret de la bourgeoisie*, one of the characters chatting in a tea-room says, 'Cellos are going out of fashion. They are sacking them from the orchestras.')

Downright Treachery (1922)

For a year now I have been labouring on my work, on my great work. Every day I invest five, six, ten hours on this climactic work which the best literary reviews of the world are already discussing. The furniture, the parquet, the books of my apartment are delighted to see me working on this work of genius. The moment they heard, the table, the library and the bed crowded around me chirping happily. The library especially came closer, on tiptoe, and arched its book-loins in an expectant attitude. A spider who was working on a big construction project in a corner always descended from his scaffold by the pulley, and assented with his legs.

My only enemy, inciting and bronchial, was the wind. Almost every night, before entering my apartment, I left him whistling cheerily intertwined with the cables of the street or amusing himself playing with the papers which were grazing on the pavement. But I was scarcely undressed, and the accommodating armchair struck itself, opening its cordial arms to receive me, when the wind began to give the window violent blows on its back, seeking to creep in by some chink or intent on opening it by force; but *my* window resolutely crossed its two stout and only fingers and mocked the wind. The latter, in revenge, nimbly rustled the waving walls, whistling noisily, and flung handfuls of dust and stones against the glass. But I, in spite of everything, stayed calm and continued to work.

One night, in the end, he swore to me that if I let him come in, to admire my work, he would stop annoying me, and on the contrary would bring me all sorts of perfumes and music to lull my great task.

Enchanted by this proposal and, moreover, it must be admitted, by a certain feeling of legitimate pride that so important a personage should interest himself in my work, I decided to accede. The wind, yelling with joy, uprooted a couple of trees, gave a 25° turn to a few houses, and chimed all the bells of the city in a triumphal band. Not content with this, he boasted a bit of necromancy. Three priests sneaking through the streets were transformed into as many upside-down umbrellas; he turned the streets and the houses into Himalayas capped with clouds, and by his magic made the cafe tables sprout with rags, scarecrows, straw and other objects from the Great Dunghill Jewelry Store.

Finally I decided to receive him, taking into account his concern to please me, and opened the window.

The wind, grotesque, threw himself in and sniffed about everywhere. Where he caused a true terror was in the basket of papers; they were resting quietly, but on discovering the presence of the monster, terrified, maddened, they jumped over one another, herded together and fled in all directions to hide themselves in the bucket and under the wardrobe; because the wind is the cat of papers.

Frankly: I was irritated by his informality and the little interest he showed in seeing *my* work, and consequently I admonished him severely. Then, feigning great attentiveness, he looked through the thousands of leaves, making them sound like a conjuror with a pack of cards; but all of a sudden, with a single gesture, he flung them into space through the stupefied window which opened its great mouth in terror and threw itself behind him.

I was thunderstruck, insensible, unbound for ever. He had carried off *my* work, *my* definitive work, which now flew converted into seagulls on the horizon.

I swore instant vengeance. I at once conceived a way. When I saw him sleeping on the roof, where the chimneys yawned, also sent to sleep by his snoring, I put another window which scarcely fitted, which at times became unhinged. And he fell into the trap.

As usual, when he woke he flung himself against it, but found himself caught, conquered, defeated by the crannies.

For years now he has groaned sadly and begged his liberty. Inflexible, I keep him there exposed with the chinks of the window, always locked and safe from himself. *He does not play with me.*

(*Ultra*, Year 2, No 23, 1 February 1922)

Luis Buñuel

Suburbs (1923)

Suburbs, outskirts, last houses of the city. This essay is about this crazy conglomeration of mud-walls, hillocks, dried up beetles, etc.

They are not the great suburbs of a London: rowdy, seedy, but full of feverish movement. They are those others of the little provincial capital, where poor and idle people live, 'things of shreds and tatters'.

These suburbs have the anodine and expressive complexity of the garret. They are like the junk-room of the city. There is all that is mothy or useless.

In that absurd aesthetic which so much characterizes the suburb, everything is askew, symbolized by the object which crosses our path: the empty tin can, the ravening dog, the burst-bellied mouse or the bent and dusty gas lamp.

All its psychological and material perspective – hostile and sad – remains in our final spiritual plane. The soul of the suburb strangles anything within it that can possess life and movement. In the watercolour which we paint at once with the palette of our senses, we use no more than one colour: grey.

All the racket and shrieking which emerges from the great mouth of the city here becomes obsessing and is united in the monotony which smears the atmosphere of the suburb. Happiness hangs like rags from the eaves, scarcely ever stirred by the breeze of children's voices; the voices of the children who are seen through the dungheaps and to whom no one tells stories.

Our gaze is wounded from time to time – our gaze which has for the suburb the egoist 'God forgive you, brother' of fallen things – by the sign 'TAVERN' in degenerate letters, sick to the core, and which here loses even the proud and vibrant quality which, like wine, this title has everywhere else.

Sheltering under the walls of some little yard, we see at times the earth hills cohabiting with these hundred vague and useless objects – because already one hundred hands have taken all their vitality – and which bury our imagination as in a grave. These little yards suffer nostalgia for bleating, and in the groin of their ochre walls are jewels of vervaine, filthy and forgotten.

In the subjective observation of the suburb the twilight is lit by the evening oil lamp, and then everything is made more rendingly inert. Our soul is lugubriously whipped by the rag hanged by the electric cable or the cries which drift through the air like bats. Far-off the weak lantern wings the eye of sunset, and the rag-dressed shadows take shelter, stretching out their silent and imploring hands.

The endless yawn of the suburb, its fringed and withered eyes, are always the huge maleficence of the city. Even when day dances gaily through the nearby rooftops, it is immediately seized by the snare of the endless sadness of the suburb, which is the black brush-stroke upon the riotous gaiety of the town. These lethargic quarters belong to the land of the incurable, the doomed. Their emotion is the emotion of dried trees. The inhabitants have become victims of the rabid bite which the soul of the suburb produces. This suburbophobia has no cure other than the premature injection of some sacks of gold.

Among the grace of the words figures that of the suburb, dressed in rags, stained with grease, and on its face the brand of the gulf which sleeps in the entries of the houses.

(in *Horizonte*, No 4, January 1923)

NOTE: Written under the influence of the 'realistic' literature of B. P. Galdós and Pío Baroja, this essay already evinces the near-Surrealist vision of an 'aesthetic of the absurd'. Almost every image of this early text was realized in *Los Olvidados*, twenty-seven years later.

Palace of Ice (1927)

The puddles formed a decapitated domino of buildings, one of which is the turret of which they told me in my childhood, with only a single window, as high as the eyes of a mother when she leans over the cradle.

Near the window is suspended a hanged man who swings over the abyss surrounded by eternity, howled at by space. IT IS I. It is my skeleton of which nothing remains but the eyes. At one moment they smile, at another they cross, at another moment THEY GO TO EAT A CRUMB OF BREAD IN THE INTERIOR OF THE BRAIN. The window is opened and a woman appears, polishing her nails. When she considers they are sufficiently filed, she takes out my eyes and flings them into the street. There my eye-holes remain, lonely, without sight, without desires, without sea, without baby chicks, without anything.

A nurse comes to sit by my side at the café table. She unfolds a newspaper of 1856 and she reads, in an emotional voice:

'When Napoleon's troops invaded Zaragoza, VILE ZARAGOZA, they found nothing except wind in the desert streets. Only in a puddle the eyes of Luis Buñuel were croaking. Napoleon's troops finished them off with bayonets.'

(from the unpublished book *El perro andaluz*, 1927; published in *La Gaceta literaria*, 1928)

Redentora (1929)

I found myself in the snow-covered garden of a convent. I was watched curiously from a nearby cloister by a Benedictine monk who held a great red mastiff on a chain. I sensed that the friar was waiting to set it on to me, so full of fear I began to dance upon the snow. At first, gently. Then as the hatred grew in the eyes of my spectator, with fury, like a madman, like someone possessed. The blood flowed to my head, making me see red before my eyes, a red just like that of the mastiff. The friar disappeared finally, and the snow melted. The red butcher had vanished in an immense field of poppies. Amid the corn, bathed in spring light, came my sister, dressed in white, carrying a dove of peace in her raised hands. It was precisely midday, the moment when all the priests of the earth raise the host over the corn.

I received my sister with my arms crossed, completely liberated, in the midst of a silence as august and white as the host.

(in *La Gaceta literaria*, No 50, January 1929)

NOTE: This fragment was published together with *Bacanal*. The strongly anti-religious and Surrealist dream contains a few remembrances of the shooting of *Mauprat*. The sister is evidently Conchita.

The Rainbow and the Mustard Plaster (1927)

How many priests * can you get on a bridge?
Four or five?
How many quavers has a *tenorio*? †
1,230,424
These questions are easy.

* The word used is '*maristas*' – Mary-ist priests.
† A play of words between *tenor* and *tenorio* (= a Don Juan) is lost in translation.

Is a piano-key a bedbug?
Will I catch cold in the thighs of my lover?
Will the Pope excommunicate pregnant women?
Does a policeman know how to sing?
Are hippopotami happy?
Are pederasts sailors?
And are these questions also easy?

In a moment there will come along the street
Two gobs of spit holding hands,
leading a college of deaf-mute children.

Would it be impolite if I were to vomit a piano
Over my balcony, to them?

(from the unpublished book *El perro andaluz*, 1927)

NOTE: Certain images are persistent throughout all Buñuel's work. The priests on the bridge appear in *L'Age d'or*, where also objects are thrown over a balcony. Pianos figure particularly in *Un Chien andalou* and *The Exterminating Angel*.

Project for a Story (1927)

It is about a soiree which I give in my house and which ends catastrophically. I am forced to go to the house of a wise friend of mine, where terrible things happen. Thence I fall into the Hospital de Afuera in Toledo, where also things happen. Finally I die, without having made my will – and what a will! – and, finally . . .

All said and done, I had scarcely time to die decently. Four gravediggers snatched my body, taking me to the nearby church to bury me. They raised the foul lid of the tomb of Cardinal Tavera, and taking out his putrid flesh, which they had to throw into a mule cemetery, *because not even the poor wanted it*, they laid me there for ever.

REST IN PEACE THE CACHESEXE!!!

NOTE: This unpublished fragment is an example of the almost 'automatic' oniric text, along with Buñuel's fascination with death and sex. The tomb mentioned is the one over which Catherine Deneuve leans in close-up in *Tristana*.

A Proper Story (1927)

Carmencita was very obedient. Carmencita's innocence was proverbial. Her mother watched over her night and day, and by her vigilance created a barricade between her daughter and the temptations of the world. When Carmencita arrived at the age of twelve years, her mother became very worried. 'The day that my daughter menstruates *for the first time*,' she thought, 'goodbye to her golden innocence.' But she managed to solve the problem. When she saw Carmencita grow pale *for the first time*, she rushed out into the street like a mad thing and came back in a little while with a large bouquet of red flowers. 'Take these, my child; take them; now you begin to become a woman.' And Carmencita, delighted and deluded with these marvellous red flowers, forgot to menstruate. Each month, twelve times a year, for many years, Carmencita was thus beguiled and preserved from the dreadful truth. With the warning rings about the eyes, on the 30th of each month, her mother put the red flowers into her hands.

Carmencita, though everyone else named her Doña Carmela. At this age, one month it happened that the rings no longer appeared around her eyes; and then her mother gave her a bouquet of white flowers. 'Take them, my daughter; it is the last bunch I shall give you; you have already ceased to be a woman.' Carmencita protested. 'But mamma, I was never told that I had been one.' To which the mother replied: 'So much the worse for you my child.' It was this white bouquet, already withered, leafless, shaken and dry, which they put in Carmencita's coffin.

An Improper Story (1927)

When Mariquita arrived at the critical age, her mother wanted to do the same with her as she had done with Carmencita, and when she saw her become hollow-eyed and pale, gave her a bouquet of red roses. But Mariquita was much saucier than Carmencita. She took the bouquet, opened the window, threw the flowers out of it and proceeded to menstruate.

(unpublished)

The Comfortable Watchword of St Huesca

A question followed by a cannon shot.
'I haven't uttered it yet,' said the Governor.
'Well that's up to you, and to make sure, look.'
The Governor administrates himself, and sees the following:
Two hours afterwards, between the carretera de San Feliu and San Quixols, walks a lump of roast meat, weighing about two kilos, fat and quite blackened. Still I see it and without remorse can cry 'Son of a bitch'. But it neither stirs, nor argues, nor vomits; it does not care.
The road disappears on the horizon in an obstinate straight line, dusty, lit by the summer's hottest sun. Seeing it evokes certain opera performances at the moment in which a lady in a box puts her lorgnettes to her eyes.
Meanwhile the roast meat continues on its way without thinking anything of interest. Only a little cloud of dust betrays his passage. Suddenly an immense crowd, attracted by the sun, springs from the earth, a million million little tailors of which the tallest is less than a millimetre tall. Some jump a metre in the air, others persecute a lost peasant woman, others burn like candle-wicks, others beg an offertory.
The lump of meat, disturbed, vomiting, starts a quick helter-skelter, knocking over all the tailors in his path. Half an hour later the road is only an enormous marsh; each tailor dissolves into a drop of urine, dishevelled, sobbing, and before melting in the dust, desperately grasping the telegraph poles along the way. Amid all this chaos, through all the spaces of the horizon, come echoes of organs, of prayers, of hymns from far-off cathedrals.
The lump of meat has started on a rapid career. In a bend on the road two peasants of Aragón grow upon his ears. At the next bend is a split cypress which stops in front of the meat. The lump of meat halts and watches.
Exactly one metre from the base of the cypress he sees a bundle, which at once becomes defensive. The lump of meat knows that this can influence the life of the city. It is an ordinary tic-tac which now jumps, now enquires, now concentrates on fencing against a book or now overturns a tramcar which was at the head of the crowds. He has nothing to do with agonies or with history. After all he goes where all the people go.
The lump of meat continues on, watching.
The allegations of the cypress are few. Its chambers are covered in steel valves, vegetable coloured, and their yard is of jellied meat, which makes such a mighty racket that the birds flee from the roofs. The racket is not heard because it is less than a black cat and as silent.

The lump of meat thinks that this is a unique occasion. However it waits for the sunset in order to go into action.

Meanwhile the tic-tac, leaning bowed against the earth, distends and throws itself vertically into space. As it goes up it swells and becomes spherical. Soon it is nothing more than a cotton cover spread over the most miserable of beds.

It is eight o'clock and a student is getting ready for class.

Beside the holy water stoup, the lump of meat offers the sacred liquor to the first women bigots. In the afternoon all the mules of the town were to appear dead in the stables. The populace, mutinying, meet at the ciborium and destroy it with hatchet blows. Somebody is going to soak it in petrol. Suddenly a cry of horror: five hundred consecrated hosts, with their members erect, are trampling the lump of roast meat, which, relaxed, does not realize what is happening, nor cares, nor puts itself beyond the horizon flying round the sun. One of the public approaches the lump of meat, and while the rest of them drive them away with blows, introduces his hand through the washbowl of the lump of meat. After much trouble, he manages to take off a fat book with oblique corners. On the cover in golden letters appears the title

LIFE OF SAINT HUESCA

Soon after a sacristan loads a donkey with pitchers at the ruins of the church. In each pitcher is hidden a bandit who, on arriving at the wood, will jump out of his hiding place and together with his companions, will construct a hut. In the hut will be a whore. The whore will go to a cypress. One windy day the cypress will attract the virgins, who will offer it their arses. The arses of the virgins will be trampled by the lump of meat, who will sing while trampling, and the psalm of the lump of meat will be like the glug glug glug of the water which will return the sight to the blind. 'Glory to the Lord of Space.'

The Governor is now standing, attending the passing of St Huesca, who walks to martyrdom with a bowed head. Her hand fences with a palm. Behind her, half crushed by the hail of stones, creeps a black and deafening cat.

On the cross where they have crucified St Huesca, hangs indifferent, sheeplike, converted into a reader, the lump of roast meat.

INSCRIPTION FOR THE TOMBSTONE OF THE LUMP OF MEAT

'Two boys went through a belfry without thinking of the advantage of their obligations, when suddenly they seemed to hear all that went on in the Institute. Then, climbing a cypress, they were able to see what followed: two Marist priests, resolved to gamble their lives, entered a tram. At the first stop, they dismounted and again got into another tramcar, full of beehives. The bees made a fine racket and the Marists lay down in their coffins, ready to stake everything. One of them said in a low voice: "Are you sure that the Bologna sausage is made for the blind men as Péret has said?" The other replied: "We are already at the bridge." Below the bridge, in the middle of the water, half green, half putrid, they could see a tombstone which said: "Las Normas." Around it hundreds of people were celebrating the New Year.'

This was the stone which the lump of meat was to have for 364 days of the year and 365 in leap years.

(unpublished)

Letter to José Bello in Answer to his Best Wishes on the Feast of San Valero, Patron Saint of Zaragoza (1927)

My dear Pepin, How touched I was to read your letter, and to see the modesty with which you recall the unforgettable day of the 29th, the day on which San Valero of the Wind passes with an arched window over his head along the pavement of Cecilia Gasca! You have always been very good and remembered this day of the 29th. I, on the other hand, have decided to auscultate myself on the day of San Valero. I am not well. I become weaker every day. When the doctor began to examine me, a great windstorm blew up outside, so violently that it tore away the wickets of the balcony as if they had been arms. The dust in the street was so thick that you could not even see the priests passing. Amidst the dust, rapidly turning, emerging from it to glitter for an instant before once more disappearing into nothingness, an infinity of sewing machines, sticks, funnel-shaped basins and little Formosan islands surrounded by tunny-fish.

Neither my father nor the doctor understood anything of this. My good father objected that this squall represented a dangerous peril in his life and that he would not for a moment tolerate so indecent a diagnosis. The doctor said that it was very likely so, but that my ancestor had always been more than a match for him and that for such a veteran as he believed himself, he, the doctor, was taller and more brief, another bone for the other dog.

My father took me by the hand and led me into the street. The violence of the wind was at its height. What an odour of wax! A despicable row deafened us and great and powerful squalls prevented us from advancing. The tornado flung in our faces, until we were almost overwhelmed, hundreds of half-naked priests. I noticed that all of them, as they hit our noses, started to sing the same song, between their teeth. It was something like this motet:

> Lassie, lassie, pretty lassie,
> You just don't know what it is, the sea;
> If you knew, my life, my puss,
> You would start at once to turn and spin.

The morality of it might seem light, but it is enough to recall to me the time when I was a waiter, when my poor father used to come and bring me couscous to the café, a little before midday, upon an unforgettable golden platter which he always left three or four kilometres from the tables.

All the time the priests crashing against our noses became more numerous. The song became a murmuring, almost unintelligible, which made me realize that there was a not very respectful allusion to my absent mother. But tell me, Pepin, who is offended that the capitals cease to be of such or such a style? Hey, tell me . . . To hell with it!

Finally the moustache of one of the priests was caught in the white and venerable moustache of my father. The priest stayed there, ready for everything, like all good folk. He took advantage of the situation, to my great regret, to deliver the following philippic:

'In truth I say to you, my son, San Valero never ceased to respect the code. The art of his era – and I speak without bitterness – consisted of exiling noises, parasites of the great naves of churches where alone the battlesmoke can rise. There, wandering breasts, wings of stone, sad furrows, sweet repasts on tombstones, incests, the disembodied phrases that are heard only in the night and the hills of wood raised by the hands of children!

'So then, San Valero, seated opposite the casket, interfered with nothing. He never wanted for a penny. He, his father, his grandfather, all were accountants, and more than accountants, engineers. Pity that the son of San Valero, also called San Valero, had not the wherewithal to pay for his studies. But that belongs to the next chapter.'

With these final words, the night fell. The priest fell silent and, with skill and love, he began to gather his straying fish, and having reformed the flock, made it adventure down the steep slope which descended to the valley.

VERY IMPORTANT

The valley led to a valley which I could not pass. Ten enormous priests with mighty scimitars barred my way. On the resplendent blades of the arms I could read the following inscription: 'The valley led to a v . . .' The last word, half obliterated, was hard to interpret. Could it say valley, or perhaps vigil? Perhaps neither valley nor vigil, and it was a photograph of the Last Supper, in which the guests would have been replaced by ciboria and where the ciborium seated in the place of Christ gives a drink to the ciborium which leans its head on his shoulders, and the last ciborium – the one which represents Judas – has a cart in his hand.

I become angry:

'Are you priests or idolators? If the first, let us fight; if not, may the Lord pay you.'

But already the nightfall, the valley, the vigil, the scimitars have become no more than the drumming of a typewriter, operated by the chief of technocrats himself. He takes the paper off the carriage, puts it into an envelope and, by hand, addresses it in pencil:

Señor D. Alaticio Pantaléon

Palatino Pudibundo

Panticosa

Write me,

LUIS

REALISTIC DETAILS

My sister observed that this San Valero's Day was very strange in Zaragoza. 'In San Pablo street you meet unaccustomed people, baronesses, countesses, those of Parellada with enormous hats! Then, to enter the church of San Pablo, you have to descend some steps and in the interior, on an altar, was San Valero who is a swarthy saint with one finger raised and a tart such as one eats on the vigil. Finally, at home, we eat an S.V. made of sugar and everybody is very jolly and very sad. Perhaps because it was the day when our grandfather died.'

(Text written in 1928 and addressed to José, or Pepin, Bello who was a friend of Buñuel at this time. Rediscovered by the author it was first published in *Positif*, November 1959)

On Love (1929)

I. What kind of hope do you have in love?

L.B. If I love, all hope. If I do not love, none.

II. How do you envisage the step from *the idea of love* to *the fact of love*?

Would you, voluntarily or not, sacrifice your liberty to love?

Have you done so? If it was necessary in your eyes would you consent to the sacrifice of a cause to which until then you had felt committed, in order not to be unworthy of love? Would you settle not to become what you might have been, if this is the price of enjoying fully the certainty of love? How would you judge a man who went so far as to betray his convictions to please the woman he loves? Could you ask such a thing, could you obtain it?

L.B. 1. For me there exists only the fact of loving.

2. I would willingly sacrifice my liberty for love. I have already done it.

3. I would sacrifice a cause for love, but that would have to be decided by cases.

4. Yes.

5. I would judge him very well. But despite that I would ask this man not to betray his convictions. I would even demand it of him.

III. Would you acknowledge the right to deprive yourself sometimes of the presence of the loved one, knowing how exalting absence can be to love, but recognizing the seediness of such a calculation?

L.B. I would never separate myself from the loved one. At any price.

IV. Do you believe in the victory of admirable love over sordid life or of sordid life over admirable love?

L.B. I don't know.

(Surrealist enquiry, *La Révolution Surréaliste*, No 12, 15 December 1929).

Bird of Anguish (1929)

A pleniosaur slept between my eyes
While the music burned in a lamp
And the landscape felt a passion of Tristan and Isolde.

Your body moulded itself to mine
As a hand moulds to the thing it wants to hide;
Skinned
You show me your muscles of wood
And the bouquets of luxury
That could be made with your veins.

A stampede of bisons in heat was heard
Between our breasts, trembling like the leaves of a garden.

All love dialogues are alike
All have the same delirious chords
But the breast crushed
By a music of secular recollections;

Then comes the prayer and the wind,
The wind that weaves sounds in sharp points
With a sweetness of blood
Of howls, made into flesh;

What eagerness, what desires of broken seas
Converted into nickel
Or into an ecumenical song of what could have been tragedy,
Will be born, as the birds of our mouths are joined
While death enters us by the feet?

One o'clock struck, extended like a bridge of kisses
Two o'clock flew off with hands crossed over his breast.
Three o'clock could be heard more distant than death.
Four o'clock already trembled with dawn.
Five o'clock rhythmically traced the day's transmitting circle.

At six o'clock were heard the little goats of the Alps,
Led by the monks, to the altar.

(from *Helix*, No 4, May 1929)

Luis Buñuel

A Giraffe (1933)

This giraffe, of life size, is an ordinary piece of wood cut out in the form of a giraffe, and with one feature which distinguishes it from the rest of the animals of the same type made of wood. Each spot on its hide, which from a distance of three or four yards looks perfectly normal, is in reality formed either by a little cover which any spectator can very easily open by turning it on a little invisible hinge placed on one side of it, or by an object, or by a hole which lets the light through – the giraffe is only a few centimetres thick – or by a concavity containing the various objects detailed in the list below.

It should be noted that this giraffe only takes on its full sense when it is entirely realized, that is to say when each of its spots fulfils the function to which it is destined. If this realization is *very costly*, it does not remain on that account any less possible.

EVERYTHING CAN BE REALIZED

To conceal the objects which must be placed behind the animal, it is necessary to stand it in front of a black wall ten metres high by forty long. The surface of the wall must be unblemished. In front of this wall must be arranged a garden of wild daffodils, of dimensions similar to the wall.

WHAT MUST BE FOUND IN EACH OF THE GIRAFFE'S SPOTS

In the first: The interior of the spot is made up of a rather complicated little mechanism very like that of a watch. In the middle of the movement of toothed wheels a little screw spins dizzily. The whole gives off a faint corpse smell. After leaving the spot, take an album which is to be found on the ground at the giraffe's feet. Sit in a corner of the garden and leaf through this album, which presents dozens of photographs of very small and very wretched little desert places. These are ancient Castillian towns: Alba de Tormes, Soria, Madrigal de las Altas Torres, Orgaz, Burgo de Osma, Tordesillas, Simancas, Sigüenza, Cadalso de los Vidrios and above all Toledo.

In the second: So long as this is opened at midday according to the instructions on the outside, you will find yourself in the presence of a cow's eye in orbit, with its lids and lashes. The spectator's image is reflected in the eye. The lid is to fall suddenly, putting an end to the contemplation.

In the third: On opening this spot is read, on a background of red velvet, these two words:

AMERICO CASTRO*

The letters being detachable, they may be rearranged in all possible combinations.

In the fourth: There is a little grille, like that of a prison. Through it can be heard the sounds of an actual 100-piece orchestra, playing the Overture to the *Mastersingers*.

In the fifth: Two billiard balls fall out of the opening of the spot with a great crash. All that is left inside, standing on its end, is a rolled parchment, tied with string; unroll it in order to read this poem:

TO RICHARD COEUR DE LION

From the choir to the cellar, from the cellar to the hill, from the hill to hell, to the winter sabbath of agonies.

From the choir to the sex of the she-wolf fleeing in the timeless mediaeval forest.

Verba vedeta sunt fodido en culo et puto gafo, this was the taboo of the first hut built in the

* The name of a professor at the University of Madrid who was also ex-Ambassador to Berlin.

infinite forest, it was the tabu of the dejection of the she-goat whence emerged the crowds who raised the cathedrals.

Blasphemies floated in the marshes, the rabble trembled beneath the ship of bishops of mutilated marble, the sex of women were used to mould toads.

With time the nuns bloomed again, growing green branches out of their dry old sides, the incubi making eyes at them while soldiers pissed in the convent walls and the ages stirred in the wounds of lepers.

From the windows hung clusters of dry nuns who produced, with the help of the mild spring wind, a sweet murmur of prayer.

In the sixth: The spot moves from part to part of the giraffe. Then a landscape is seen through the hole; ten metres away my mother, Madame Buñuel, dressed as a laundress, is kneeling beside a little stream washing linen. Some cows behind her.

In the seventh: A simple curtain of old sack-cloth dirtied with plaster.

In the eighth: This spot is slightly concave and is covered with very fine, curly, blonde hairs, taken from the pubics of a young Danish adolescent with very clear blue eyes, a plump body, tanned skin, all innocence and candour. The spectator must gently breathe on the hairs.

In the ninth: Instead of the spot is discovered a fat dark moth with a death's-head on his wings.

In the tenth: Inside the spot an appreciable quantity of dough. One is tempted to knead it with the fingers. Razor blades very well concealed tear the hands of the spectator.

In the eleventh: A pig's bladder membrane replaces the spot. Nothing more. Take the giraffe and take it to Spain, to place it in the place called 'Masada del Vicario', seven kilometres from Calanda in the south of Aragón, its head pointing north. Break the membrane with one blow and look through the hole. You will see a very wretched little house, lime-washed, in the midst of a desert landscape. A fig-tree stands some metres from the door, in front. Behind bald and olive-covered mountains. An old labourer probably will come out of the house at that moment, with bare feet.

In the twelfth: A very beautiful photograph of the head of Christ crowned with thorns, but LAUGHING UPROARIOUSLY.

In the thirteenth: In the depths of the spot, a very beautiful rose made, life-size, out of apple peel. The male sex organ of the flower is in bloody meat. This rose will become black some hours later. Next day, it will rot. Three days later, a legion of worms will appear on the remains.

In the fourteenth: A black hole. This dialogue is heard, whispered with great anguish:

WOMAN'S VOICE: No, I beg you. Do not freeze.

MAN'S VOICE: Yes, I must. I could not look you in the face. (A noise of rain is heard.)

WOMAN'S VOICE: I love you all the same, I will always love you, but do not freeze. *Do . . . not . . . freeze.* (Pause.)

MAN'S VOICE (very low and sweet): My little corpse. (Pause. A stifled laugh is heard.)

A very bright light suddenly shines from the interior of the hole. In this light are seen some marauding chickens.

In the fifteenth: A little window with two leaves made in perfect imitation of a big one. Out of it suddenly comes a thick puff of white smoke, followed a few seconds later by a far-off explosion. (Smoke and explosion must be like those of a cannon, seen and heard at some kilometres distance.)

In the sixteenth: On opening the spot there is seen two or three metres away an 'Annunciation' by Fra Angélico, very well framed and lit, but in deplorable condition: slit with knife blows, sticky with pitch, the face of the virgin carefully messed up with shit, the eyes dug out with needles, the sky bearing in very crude letters the inscription: 'DOWN WITH THE TURK'S MOTHER'.

In the seventeenth: A very powerful jet of steam bursts out of the spot the moment it is opened, and will blind the spectator frightfully.

In the eighteenth: The opening of the spot brings about the alarming collapse of the following objects: needles, thread, a thimble, bits of material, two empty match boxes, a piece of candle, a very old card game, some buttons, empty bottles, a square watch, a door handle, a broken pipe, two letters, orthopaedic instruments and some living spiders. The whole lot scattered in the most distressing fashion. (This spot is the only one which symbolizes death.)

In the nineteenth: A model less than one metre square behind the spot, representing the Sahara desert under a brutal light. Covering the sand, one hundred thousand little Marist priests made of wax, their white aprons standing out from their cassocks. In the heat, the Marists gradually melt. (It will be necessary to have several million Marists in reserve.)

In the twentieth: This spot is to be opened. Ranged on four shelves are seen twelve little terra cotta busts, representing Madame . . .,* marvellously well executed and life-like, despite being barely two centimetres. By means of a magnifying glass it can be established that the teeth are made of ivory. The last little bust has all its teeth pulled out.

(from Le Surréalisme au service de la Révolution, No 6, 15 May 1933)

NOTE: Buñuel recalls: 'the Giraffe was in fact made, except for the things seen in its interior. Instead of cupboards, the spots were posters with texts. Instead of seeing things, you read them. This enormous giraffe was finally installed in the hall of the Vicomte de Noailles, and visitors were obliged to climb a step-ladder to take off the covers and read the messages underneath. After only a few days it was installed in the garden, with other works of art.'

---

* I am unable to reveal this name.

II. BUÑUEL AS CRITIC

A Night at the 'Studio des Ursulines'

Tonight's programme begins by promising ten minutes of pre-war cinema. The lights go down. Spiritualism? Mouldering ghosts return to a luminous second existence. A whirlwind of old memories. Tsar Nicholas approaches, surrounded by pompous priests. How pathetic seems the smile he gives as he passes in front of the camera! Some of the Russians in the cinema weep to see his smile from beyond the grave. Then a primitive Renault, from which dismounts M. Poincaré, makes us more sensitive to the beauty of the latest Packard or Isotta-Franchini. Then comes the tango *milonga*. The man's moustache is much longer than his partner is tall. With the most serious air in the world the couple abandon themselves to the most absurd movements, and the audience's laughter continues without respite to the end of the reel, because immediately after this there follows the fashion news.

A natural history lesson in hats. The models strut like hens. From before, from behind, from the sides, demonstrating the fit, the hang, the materials, the percales. We manage to compose our gravity. We, too, think that our own epoch is a model of good taste . . . and simplicity. Perhaps by force of elaboration. These pre-war actualities are the resumé of the contemporary age. And the finale almost chokes us with laughter. The projection culminates with the showing of a primitive drama. Photographed theatre. The lens, immobile, simply records. Its only virtue consists in silence: happily we do not hear the words which accompany the action. To compensate, of course, the actors gesticulate wildly in the midst of their disastrous scenery. Three or four grand gestures of the bearded protagonist and with them the end of the film and our laughter.

Rapid evolution of the cinema. And alarming. It might seem – leaving aside the infinite possibilities of three dimensions and colour – to have arrived if not at the end, to the limits of its technical evolution. And yet might not the film which now seems to us so excellent, within a few years make us laugh in just the same way? It is one of the most serious objections which can be presented to the cinema. If the true work of art resists the passage of the centuries, keeping its pristine beauty always intact and fresh, why does the film, a victim of time, arrive at such harmful senescence? Clearly the primitive cinema had not yet discovered its proper language, its characteristic means of expression. None of the four great pillars which support the temple of photogeny had yet been created: neither the individual shot, nor the camera angle, nor lighting, nor the strongest and most definitive, of montage or composition. The film, like the work of the theatre, exists in space and time. In the film however, both remain fixed and for ever, without the possibility of evolution, while in the theatre, fashion and taste bring about corresponding variations. Hence theatrical adaptation. So, then, the taste of every epoch, powerless before the definitive character of the film, will deprecate its aesthetic values. It has been said that stylizing costumes, architecture and so on might avoid such a tragic end. But would not the playing, by the same process, still make them old-fashioned? We must return to this very important theme.

Coordinations and combination of its light rays, we take n as the film of the *avant-guerre*. Cavalcanti now demonstrates to us that when we take $n + 10$ it gives the *avant-garde*, the purest expression of our times.

We know Alberto Cavalcanti as the designer of *Feu Mathias Pascal*. Since then, as a director, he has realized a scenario by Louis Delluc, *Le Train sans yeux*. Today he reveals himself as one of the great hopes of the French cinema, to whose most youthful and sensitive forces he belongs.

Rien que les heures. Neither loves, nor hatreds, nor *dénouement* sealed with a kiss. The blind rotation of the hands of a clock, passing twenty-four times through the hours. The ideal passage of the city's day towards the future. Cavalcanti begins by showing us how painters see Paris more in the fashion of the rue de la Boetie. Instantly, the city seen by a camera lens. Character: a clock.

Dawn. A yawn and the raising of a Venetian blind. First wispy smoke from the morning chimneys. The sepulchral portals of a metro station are passed; the daily resurrections begin. Baskets of vegetables and fruit. Through a street, *en plongeon*, an old woman drags her rags and her – drunkenness or sorrow? A retail market. Motors. The morning moves into a crescendo. Wheels, pulleys; work and traffic in major key. Midday. A worker sleeps in the one o'clock sun. Gliding trains. First editions of the newspapers and evening sun. The feet of a workman leaving work go on tiptoe so that lips may kiss. Feverish and manufacturing *rallentando*. People are taking supper. An illuminated sign. Hotel. An apache. Accordeon and *bal musette*. A tart and an American marine, like colts through the steep streets. Love and money. A crime. The old woman – strange and touching *leit-motiv* – ends her peregrination near the Seine, over whose waters the first glimmerings of the day reflect. The clock begins its revolution again. Why? The film ends.

It is one of the most accomplished films of the group called 'Without scenario'. Visual music, the two rhythms of the cinema provide the necessary nexus between the images. Subjective cinema. The spectator has to contribute his sensibility and acquired cinematic education. If anyone dared show this picture to a non specialist public, he would hear it reviled. Most anger when there is most impotence of comprehension.

The last film in the programme is Erich von Stroheim's *Greed*. This alone would merit a much more extended article than the present one. We shall limit ourselves to sketching some of its most surpassing qualities.

The film is among the most unusual, audacious and brilliant works which the cinema has created.

Seeing it, no one could remain indifferent: it will be judged as a model film or alternatively it might be thought that its author has intended to ridicule the rules and laws of the cinema and even of his epoch. But Stroheim would not have continued to work on it for years, just for ridicule. He filmed more than 100,000 metres of film, of which he used 40,000 in his final cut. It was necessary to get a specialist editor to reduce its length to 3,000 and hash up what now exists. It is said that Stroheim cried and stamped like a child. For months 'he suffered from this amputation as if it had been one of his own limbs'. With the most extreme naturalism are presented depressed figures, repulsive scenes in which base and primary passions are faultlessly realized. Such mastery in the visualization of the lowest, ugliest, vilest and most corrupt of men repels us and forces our admiration at the same time. Complete scorn and indifference for cinematographic tricks, but the greatest exaltation in the lighting. There are no stars, but there are characters carved in granite. At a blow, this new film puts the Stroheim 'type' on a level with the Zola 'type'. Neither in literature nor in the cinema does naturalism interest us. Yet the film of Stroheim is magnificent, repellently magnificent.

Metropolis

Metropolis is not one film, *Metropolis* is two films joined by the belly, but with divergent, indeed extremely antagonistic, spiritual needs. Those who consider the cinema as a discreet teller of tales, will suffer a profound disillusion with *Metropolis*. What it tells us is trivial, pretentious, pedantic, hackneyed romanticism. But if we put before the story the plastic-photogenic basis of the film, then *Metropolis* will come up to any standards, will overwhelm us as the most marvellous picture book imaginable. Imagine, then, two antipodean elements held under the same sign, in the zones of our sensibility. The first of them, which we might call pure-lyrical, is excellent; the other, the anecdotal or human, is ultimately irritating. Both, simultaneously, successively, compose the latest creation of Fritz Lang. It is not the first time that we have noted such a disconcerting dualism in the works of Lang. For example: in the ineffable poem *Destiny* are interpolated disastrous scenes of a refined bad taste. Even though we must admit that Fritz Lang is an accomplice, we hereby denounce as the presumed author of these eclectic essays and of this hazardous syncretism his wife, the scenarist Thea von Harbou.

A film, like a cathedral, should be anonymous. People of all classes, artists of all kinds have contributed to raising this monstrous cathedral of the modern cinema. All trades, all the engineers, crowds, actors, writers; Karl Freund, the ace of German cameramen with a pleiade of collaborators, Ruttmann, creator of the 'absolute' film. At the head of the architects is the name of Otto Hunte: it is to him and to Ruttmann in fact that we owe the most striking visualizations in *Metropolis*. The scenic artist, last of the theatre's legacies to the cinema, scarcely plays a part here. We sense his hand only in the worst of *Metropolis*, in the emphatically named 'Eternal gardens' with their lunatic baroque and striking bad taste. The architect will henceforth for ever replace the designer. The cinema will be the faithful interpreter of the boldest dreams of architecture.

In *Metropolis* the clock has only ten hours, which are those of work, and the life of the whole inner city moves to this compass of two times. The free men of *Metropolis* tyrannize the workers, nibelungs of the city, who work in an endless electric day in the depths of the earth. All that is lacking is the simple gearing of the Republic, the heart, the sentiment that is able to unite such extreme enemies. And in the dénouement we see the son of the director of *Metropolis* (Heart) unite in an eternal embrace his father (Head) and the general overseer (The Arm). Mix these symbolic ingredients with a good dose of bloodcurdling scenes, with stylized theatrical playing. Shake the mixture well and we have arrived at the content of *Metropolis*.

Yet on the other hand . . . What a captivating symphony of movement! How the engines sing amidst wonderful transparent triumphal arches formed by electric charges! All the glass shops in the world romantically melted into reflected light could nestle over the modern canon of the cinema. Every most furious glint of swords, the rhythmic succession of wheels, pistons, of uncreated mechanical forms is an admirable ode, a new poetry to our eyes. Physics and chemistry are miraculously transformed into rhythm. Not a moment of retardation. Even the titles, already rising and falling, revolving, hazy, melting by and by in light or disintegrating into shadows, unite in the general movement and themselves become images. In our judgment the capital defect of the film rests in the author's failure to follow the line shaped by Eisenstein in his *Potemkin*, which presented us with one actor alone, but full of novelty and possibilities: the mass. The matter of *Metropolis* calls for it. But instead we suffer a series of characters, full of arbitrary and vulgar passions, charged with a symbolism to which they in no way respond. This is not to say that there are no crowds in *Metropolis*; but they seem to respond more to a decorative need, to a gigantic ballet; they aim to delight us with their admirable and admired movement rather than to show us their soul, their exact obedience to more human, more objective motives. Even so there are moments – Babel, the workers' revolution, the final persecution of the automaton – in which both extremes are admirably accomplished.

Otto Hunte astounds us with his vision of the city of the year 2000. It might be mistaken, even antiquated in relation to the latest theories about the city of the future, but, from the photogenic point of view, its emotive force, its remarkable and surprising beauty are unparalleled; of such technical perfection that it can be studied minutely without the possibility of recognizing the *maquette*.

Metropolis cost ten million gold marks to make; with actors and extras, some 40,000 people took part in the production. The actual length of the film is 5,000 metres, but some two million metres were shot. The day of its premiere in Berlin stalls cost eighty gold marks each. Is it not demoralizing, taking into account such extraordinary resources, that the film did not turn out a model of perfection? From the comparison of *Metropolis* and *Napoleon*, the two biggest films which the modern cinema has produced, with other much humbler but also more perfect and purer works, comes the useful lesson that money is not the essential of modern cinema production. Compare *Rien que les heures*, which cost a mere 35,000 francs, and *Metropolis*. Sensitivity, paramount; intelligence, paramount, and everything else, including money, comes after.

Carl Dreyer's Jeanne d'Arc

Certainly the most original and interesting film of the new cinema season. Based on an original scenario by Delteil, it begins at the moment when Jeanne appears before her tribunal, and ends with the stake.

Based on extreme close-ups, the director very rarely if at all uses two-shots or even medium close-ups. Each of them is composed with such attention and art that often it remains a 'frame' without being a 'shot'. Unusual angles with violent foreshortening, and frequent tilting of the camera.

None of the actors wears make-up; in the pitiful geography of their faces – pores like wells – the life of flesh and blood is the more evident. At times the whole screen is the naked white of a cell, and in a corner the malicious visage of a friar. Its storms can be anticipated with meteorological exactitude. Nerves, eyes, lips which explode like bombs, tonsures, forefingers launched against the innocent breast of the maid. She replies or weeps, or, weeping, is distracted like a child, by her fingers, by a button, by the fly that settles on the nose of the friar.

The actors had to shave their heads and let their beards grow, because crêpe hair was definitively relegated to the theatre, and the genius of Dreyer lies in his direction of his players. In this respect the cinema has given us nothing comparable. The humanity of the people overflows the screen and fills the cinema. We all feel such truth in our throats and the marrow of our bones. Antidote against snake bite and against histrionism! The playing of Jannings compared with that of the least of the friars of Jeanne d'Arc appears as flabby as lard and as theatrical – though not as great – as that of Ludmila Pitoëff.

And the humanity of the Maid in Dreyer's work transcends that of any other interpretation we know. We all feel the urge to prescribe her a whipping so that we can give her a sweet afterwards. To take away her dessert from her, to punish her childlike integrity, her transparent obstinacy, yes; but, why burn her? Lit by tears, purified by flames, head shaved, grubby as a little girl, yet for a moment she stops crying to watch some pigeons settle on the spire of the church. Then, she dies.

We have kept one of her little tears, which wandered our way, in a little celluloid box. An odourless, tasteless, transparent tear, a droplet from the purest fountain.

Camille (1927)

Forgotten in a garret of the literary mansion, the last of the *midinettes* has till now remained undisturbed. It was anomalous that the young and traumaturgical hands should not have adopted a resurrectionary attitude over this corpse when so many had been successfully resuscitated. Before anyone else could beat him to it, Fred Niblo, the daring creator of *Ben Hur*, with his tools over his shoulder, set out into the garden of love where Marguerite Gautier had her regions, antipodes to our sensibility. A bold journey – he had to travel through hostile country, very well guarded and almost inaccessible to the camera. But with the grace of a conjuror or a poet, he has breathed into the perilous novel an emotion and vigour that it never possessed. Now he has us, in the face of this film, a little *midinette* ourselves. Does not something like this happen in face of the latest films of Chaplin, with their romantic and sentimental themes? (Remember the Christmas Eve sequence in *The Gold Rush*. In this sense Buster Keaton is superior. Through such obstacles, André Suares, the great enemy of the seventh art, has come to speak of the '*ignoble* heart of Chaplin'.)

From the cinematic point of view, this would be the one culpable defect; but on the other hand, we venture to assert that Fred Niblo's film can be numbered among the most perfect which the screen has produced. The strange fact is that from beginning to end, the film-maker follows the original work circumstantially.

One more proof of the advance, of the excellent maturity to which cinema technique has attained, is the illumination and ennoblement which the Dumas novel has undergone in the transposition.

Here it happens differently than with the fine arts and literature. A cinedrama, well realized, fully achieved, is more novel, more extraordinary than a film of the so-called 'visual symphony' class. That admirable trilogy of films, *Lady Windermere's Fan, The Merry Widow, Camille*, have to overcome severe difficulties in order to excite, above everything else, a peculiarly cinematic emotion: the trivial theme, the restricted action, the difficult visualization of mediocre elements and a literary excess: the suggestive power of the image tears us from our cinema seat and hurls us at a blow among the personages on the screen. We feel that they possess a very familiar soul, we come to know our own soul in the eyes which regard us from the screen in close-up, and if we really feel ourselves affected, it is because the author has been affected before us.

News From Hollywood (Latest)

We have spoken with Menjou, who vigorously denies his participation in the adultery of his delightful friend Greta Nissen.

'But it is said that you . . .'

Menjou smiles, enigmatic. He takes from his jacket a magnificent gold cigarette case, a gift from the ex-Kaiser, opens it and offers it to us, full of moustaches. We accept one, thanking him very cordially, then continue to insist:

'They say that you were seen . . .'

Menjou expresses sincere surprise.

'I was seen; so who knows? It is quite possible. I'm getting very absent-minded these days.'

The scandal the other day in Collidge's Bar, the busiest place in Hollywood, was the strange attack suffered by Clara Bow who suddenly started to cry out, calling for her mother. Everyone rose up appalled by such effrontery, and some, like Douglas Fairbanks, even called it shocking. For two hours she continued crying to the female author of her days without so much as a remembrance of her progenitor, and it was this that they could not pardon. In consequence of the event, little Clara Bow has continued to belong to Metro and thirty-two stars have immediately demanded divorce as a sign of solidarity with their friend and with respectable mothers.

Many readers have written to us in alarm to be reassured regarding the dentifrice used by Mary Pickford. They may be reassured that there is no cause for alarm. What happened was that through not finding the kind she is accustomed to use, in the shop, she found herself obliged to buy a tube of 'Sot' paste. But since yesterday the delightful Mary has gone back to using her old paste. Admirers of the gentle Mary are delighted.

Bertran y Massens has finished his portrait of John Gilbert. It is almost better done than a photograph, and many visitors have confused it with the original and offered it cigarettes. As a curious detail we offer the fact that in the costume in which the well-known actor played Henry VIII of England, are encrusted 10,000 dollars' worth of jewels. Yesterday John Gilbert organized a party in honour of the distinguished painter, a worthy successor to Velazquez, among the guests at which was Mr Nicholson, Professor of Art at the University of Pennsylvania. He was asked his opinion on the portrait. After a moment's reflection he replied: 'A magnificent portrait. It seems as if it's about to speak.'

There was much discussion of this sentence, and subsequently rumours that Mr Nicholson was preparing a new apparatus which would make possible conversation with paintings.

The father of Jannings is not called Emil, but Andrew. Telegrams to this effect have already been dispatched to all parts of the world.

There are rumours that the Ministry of Public Instruction is in future to impede every kind of cinematographic information, and even, it is said, magazines dedicated to the seventh art. Apparently the Ministry regards such things as pornographic, brutalizing public taste, encouraging the stupid triviality of the fans, a continuous assault upon the intelligence of the masses. The Ministry has imposed heavy fines on important periodicals, because, it says, given the serious character in which they glory, the insertion of such file cinema pages has immoral results. To corroborate this news, yesterday we heard that Baltasar Fernández had been detained under house arrest. We protest vigorously against these draconian measures and refer those who are not initiated in this column to that of any professional review or that of a cinema column in any of our press. The reader will judge the injustice of the ministerial measures.

Variations Upon the Moustache of Menjou

Of all the phantasms of flesh and blood upon the screen, Menjou would seem to be the one with the greatest harmony between his private life and that reflection of the quintessential life which is the film. Contemplating him in whichever of these realities, we see in Menjou the most extraordinary Menjou which art, literature and cinema can give us. In a word: Menjou is the most Menjou of all the Menjous. And by this reason alone, by having so integrally created this type, less bound with literature but much more photogenic quality than Don Juan, we feel all our admiration flooding to him. Who, moreover, is not aware that, like the syrens of song, his immense menjouesque force irradiates from his moustache, that wonderful black moustache of the films. It is usual to assert that the eyes are the best way to arrive at the depths of a personality. Moustaches like his can be so equally. So many times inclined above our heads in close-up, what can his eyes have told us that his moustaches have not said already? Under the dark magic of the moustache, the trivial gesture or the ghost of a smile acquires an extraordinary expressiveness; a page of Proust realized on the upper lip; a silent but complete lesson in irony; if he had not taken care, copyrighting his moustaches, irony would have been standardized to the use of the most modest faces.

Menjou's moustaches, which so much incarnate the cinema and his era, will replace in the showcases of the future that horrible and inexpressive hat of Napoleon's.

We have seen them, in a close-up of a kiss, alight like some rare summer insect on lips sensitive as mimosa, and devour them complete, coleopterus of love. We have seen his smile, ambushed in his moustache, spring like a tiger, lean and agile, to fall upon its prey, to subdue the gaze of his *partenaire*. The latest poll on Menjou's moustache, taken in New York among the movie stars, has been unanimous; all have said the same:

'His moustache is, perhaps, the only one which does not prick when he kisses us. On the contrary, it produces a delicious and outrageous tickling, very much appreciated among us.'

Adolphe Menjou's trip to Paris has sufficed to fill us with still more confusion. As he himself has said, he does not like the painting of Bertran Marse, which is as good as to say that he does not like painting. The sensitivity and attention of a contemporary man can apply itself to a thousand other things besides painting, can possess exquisite taste, without having necessarily to resort to the old topic of the arts, and Menjou in almost all his films shows himself as a man of today of a refined and original temperament; recall among others his happy axiom in *Monsieur Albert*, representative of the genre: 'To make a salad, the ingredients are the least important thing; it is genius that matters.' Nor has our disappointment been motivated by what in any other vulgar man could constitute a sign of cretinism or a severe obsession, that Adolphe Menjou possesses 372 neckties, a quarter of a tie more than the well-loved fingers of his bride Miss Cathryn Barver have knitted.

What is intolerable in Menjou, what we are disgusted to credit, as if it were a case of an actual impossibility, is that his moustache, his remarkable moustache, is not black, as we have always thought, but reddish, saffron-colour, shamelessly earthy.

'Like the calloused hands of a workman, this moustache is a sign of honour – black before, now discoloured by the sweat of my brow under the African sun of the floodlights,' the accused has said.

But the excuse will not do, if his moustache is not black it is as a lack in him, and without the positive and defined part of his personality, Menjou is changed into something less than a Menjou.

Adolphe Menjou was a humble man, a minor theatrical writer; Menjou was a poor shaven man. One day it occurred to him to grow the moustache. All great inventions are due to hazard. On another occasion finding himself with Chaplin, it happened that he lit a cigarette, and from this moment began his great cinema career. Because an action so trivial, so insignificant, but so difficult of realization, acquires on the screen overwhelming proportions, and it was this that such a man as Chaplin could not ignore. No melodramatic gestures, no expressions in the style of Jannings; neither archetypal terror nor fear; enough to know how to raise an eyebrow with timing and rhythm; the mummers of the classical theatre lower their eyes in shame before the expression of a Menjou exhaling his first mouthful of smoke. By the mode of opening an umbrella or calling a taxi, we can distinguish among a crowd the person best gifted to act in a film. The film actor is born, not made. The film, in the last analysis, is composed of segments, fragments, attitudes, which taken thus, separate and arbitrarily, are archi-trivial, deprived of logical significance, of psychology, of literary transcendence. In literature, a lion or an eagle can represent many things, but on the screen they will be only two beasts, and that is all and no more, even though for Abel Gance they can represent ferocity, valour or imperialism. Hence the terror of so many judicious people, the dismal 'taste for art', which whines against the superficiality of the American cinema, without taking into account that it was the first to realize that cinematic truths do not form a common denominator with those of literature or theatre. Why persist in demanding metaphysics from the cinema, and not recognize that in a well-made film the fact of opening a door or seeing a hand – great monster – taking possession of an object, is capable of enshrining an authentic and unexpected beauty? This unchangeable scenario which the Americans give us is what seems always newest. Admirable miracle of the loaves and fishes! All its photogenic value lies in the methods, in the form; and from today this can remain as a fundamental and no longer exclusive truth of the cinema.

Napoleon Bonaparte by Abel Gance

It seems to me that the art of cinema is inherent to the Northern races and that we Latins, weighed down with tradition, mysticism, culture, ecstacy – sensitive as we are to other forms of art – are powerless to assimilate that of the cinema. Each one of our attempts further confirms the superiority of young races over the rest of us.

Generally the triviality of American films has been criticized. But any one of them, even the most modest, always contains a primitive ingenuousness, a total photogenic attraction, an absolutely cinematographic rhythm.

The Americans allow us to see the essence of the drama – this is only secondary – and when they make some discovery, they never abuse it. They never show it off too much, because their whole way of being always leads them further onwards.

It is incontestable that they possess the sense of cinema to a much greater degree than ourselves.

It is certain that many people of the 'élite' have a certain inhibition against the seventh art. But it is equally certain, that, drawn by the current of the times, they could be disposed to open their arms to any worthwhile attempt. For that it would be necessary to create the film proper to initiate them into the innumerable possibilities of the cinema. No doubt trusting to the assurances of the most esteemed critics, the unbelievers have come to see *Napoleon*, and what have they deduced from it?

Gentlemen, we tell them, this is not cinema. This turns its back on the cinema. Better go and see *The Ingenue*, an American film about the amazon in love, whose finale is a discreet kiss; because it is at least light, fresh, full of rhythmical images, made with an intuition that is authentically cinematic.

The Way of All Flesh
directed by Victor Fleming

Technique is a quality necessary for a film as for every other work of art or for an industrial product. It must not however be thought that this quality determines the excellence of a film. There are qualities in a film which can be more interesting than technique. It must be said that the spectator never loses time analysing the technical means of a film: most often he demands of a film only that it affects his emotions. But 'emotion' is not to be confused with 'sentimentality'. Deprived of authentic emotion, V. Fleming's film is, in the end, a failure. Technically excellent, the film shares with many other films the privilege of addressing itself more to our tear-ducts than to our sensibility. You can hear the tears splashing on the floor of the cinema. Everyone finds a store of tears in himself faced with the spectacle: *The Way of All Flesh*.

Why are not films habitually submitted, before their public screenings, to a very minute microscopic analysis? This should be the instrument most properly indicated for the examination of films. Had it been used in this case, it would certainly have been discovered that Fleming's cinedrama was saturated with melodrama germs, infested with sentimental typhus, mixed with romantic and naturalistic bacilli.

We had believed that our times and our cinema had rid themselves totally of such a wretched epidemic.

But you have to go to poison by poison and to film by film.

Buster Keaton's College

Here is Buster Keaton, with his latest and admirable film, *College*. Asepsia. Disinfection. Liberated from tradition, our outlook is rejuvenated in the youthful and temperate world of Buster, the great specialist against all sentimental infection. The film is beautiful as a bathroom, vital as a Hispano. Buster never tries to make us cry, because he knows that easy tears are valueless. Yet he is not a clown who makes us laugh belly laughs. We never for a moment stop smiling, not at him but from ourselves, the smile of health and olympian force.

In cinema we would always prefer the monochord expression of a Keaton to the variety of a Jannings. Film-makers abuse this last, multiplying to the power n the least contraction of his facial muscles. With Jannings sorrow is a hundred-faced prism. This is why he is capable of acting on a great fifty-metre close-up and if he's asked for 'Still more!' he would show that with nothing but his face you could make a film called *Jannings' Expression, or the permutations of M wrinkles raised n to the power n.*

With Buster Keaton the expression is as modest as that of a bottle for example: although around the round, clear circuit of his pupils dances his aseptic soul. But the bottle and the face of Buster have their viewpoints in infinity.

There are rare souls who are able to accomplish their destiny in the rhythmic and architectonic gearing of the film. Montage – the golden key of the film – is what combines, comments and unifies all those elements. Can one aspire to greater cinematographic virtue? There are those who have sought to believe Buster the 'anti-virtuoso', inferior to Chaplin, to reckon it some sort of a disadvantage, a kind of stigmata in him, what the rest of us reckon a virtue, that Keaton arrives at comedy through direct harmony with objects, situations and the other means of his work. Keaton is full of humanity: but of an actual and not a synthetic humanity . . .

Much is said about the technique of films like *Metropolis, Napoleon* . . . No one ever talks about the technique of films like *College* and it is because it is so indissolubly mingled with the other elements, that no one even notices, just as if you live in a house you do not take note of the calculated resistance of the materials which compose it. Superfilms serve to give lessons to technicians; those of Keaton to give lessons to reality itself, with or without the technique of reality.

School of Jannings: European school: sentimentalism, prejudices of art, literature, tradition etc. John Barrymore, Veidt, Mosjoukine, etc.

School of Buster Keaton: American school: vitality, photogeny, no culture and new tradition: Monte Blue, Laura la Plante, Bebe Daniels, Tom Moore, Menjou, Harry Langdon, etc.

Cinema, Instrument of Poetry

The group of young people who form the Dirección de Difusión Cultural approached me to ask me to give a lecture. Although duly grateful for the attention, my reply was negative: I have none of the qualities which a lecturer requires and have a special bashfulness about speaking in public. Fatally, the speaker attracts the collective attention of his listeners, only to feel intimidated by their gaze. In my case I cannot avoid a certain embarrassment in face of the dread of what can make me somewhat, let us say, exhibitionist. Although this idea of mine about the lecturer may be exaggerated or false, the fact of feeling it as true obliges me to ask that my period of exhibition will be as brief as possible, and I propose the constitution of a Round Table, in which as a number of friends belonging to distinct artistic and intellectual activities, we can discuss *en famille* the problems pertaining to the so-called seventh art: hence it is agreed that the theme shall be 'The Cinema as Artistic Expression', or more concretely, as an instrument of poetry, with all that that word can imply of the sense of liberation, of subversion of reality, of the threshold of the marvellous world of the subconscious, of nonconformity with the limited society that surrounds us.

Octavio Paz has said: 'An imprisoned man has only to close his eyes to be able to blow up the world.' I would add, in paraphrase: it would suffice for the white pupil of the cinema screen to reflect the light which is proper to it, to blow up the universe. But for the moment we can sleep in peace, because the cinematographic light is carefully drugged and imprisoned. None of the traditional arts reveals so massive a disproportion between the possibilities it offers and its achievements. Because it acts in a direct manner upon the spectator in presenting to him concrete people and objects, because it isolates him by virtue of the silence and darkness from what might be called his 'psychic habitat', the cinema is capable of putting him into a state of ecstasy more effectively than any other mode of human expression. But more effectively than any other, it is capable of brutalizing him. And unhappily the great part of present-day cinema production seems to have no other mission: the screens rejoice in the moral and intellectual emptiness in which the cinema prospers; in effect it limits itself to imitating the novel or the theatre with the difference that its means are less rich to express psychology: it repeats to satiety the same stories which the nineteenth century was already tired of telling and which still continue in contemporary fiction.

A moderately cultivated individual would reject with scorn any book with one of the arguments that serve the film. However, sitting comfortably in a dark room, dazzled by the light and the movement which exert a quasi-hypnotic power over him, fascinated by the interest of human faces and the rapid changes of place, this same almost cultivated individual placidly accepts the most appalling themes.

The cinema spectator, through this kind of hypnotic inhibition, loses an important percentage of his intellectual capacity. I will give a concrete example, the film called *Detective Story*. The structure of its subject is perfect, the director excellent, the actors extraordinary, the realization brilliant, etc. But all this talent, all this ability, all the complications which the making of a film involve, have been put at the service of an idiotic story, of a remarkable moral wretchedness. This reminds me of the extraordinary machine of *Opus 11*, a vast machine made of the best steel, with a thousand complex gears, with tubes, manometres, dials, precise as a watch as big as a liner, whose sole use was to gum postage-stamps.

Mystery, the essential element of every work of art, is in general lacking in films. Authors, directors and producers are at pains not to disturb our peace, by leaving the window on to the liberating world of poetry tightly closed. They prefer to make the screen reflect subjects which could compose the normal continuation of our daily life, to repeat a thousand times the same drama or to make us forget the painful hours of daily work. And all this naturally sanctioned by habitual morality, government, and international censorship, religion, dominated by good taste and enlivened by white humour and other prosaic imperatives of reality.

If we hope to see good cinema, we shall rarely achieve it through big productions and those which are accompanied by the sanction of the critics and the approval of the public. The private story, the individual drama cannot, in my view, interest anyone worthy of living in his times; if the spectator shares the joys, the sorrows, the anxieties of a personage on the screen, this can be only because he sees reflected in it the joys, sorrows, anxieties of a whole society, and therefore his own. Strikes, social insecurity, fear of war, etc., are the things which affect everyone today, and also affect the spectator; but that Mr X. is unhappy at home and seeks a girl-friend to console him, and finally abandons her to return to his wife all penitent, is no doubt very moral and edifying, but leaves us completely indifferent.

Sometimes the essence of cinema spurts unexpectedly from an anodine film, from a farce or a crude novelette. Man Ray said something very significant: 'The worst films which I have seen, those which send me into a deep sleep, always contain five marvellous minutes, while the best films, the most praised, have scarcely more than five worth-while minutes.' This is to say that in all films, good or bad, beyond and despite the intentions of the makers, cinema poetry struggles to come to the surface and manifest itself.

The cinema is a magnificent and perilous weapon when wielded by a free spirit. It is the best instrument to express the world of dreams, of emotions, of instinct. The creative mechanism of cinema images, through its manner of functioning, is among all the means of human expression, the one which comes nearest to the mind of man, or, even more, which best imitates the functioning of the mind in the state of dreaming. Jacques B. Brunius has pointed out that the night which bit by bit invades the cinema is equivalent to closing the eyes. Then begins, on the screen and within the man, the incursion into the night of the unconscious; the images, as in dream, appear and disappear through 'dissolves' and fade-outs; time and space become flexible, retrace or extend at will; chronological order and relative values of duration no longer respond to reality; cyclic action is accomplished in a few minutes or in several centuries; movements accelerate their speed.

The cinema seems to have been invented to express the subconscious life, whose roots penetrate so deeply into poetry; but it is almost never used for that end. Among modern tendencies of cinema, (1) the best known is what is called 'neo-realism'. Its films present to the eyes of the spectator slices of real life, with people taken from the street, and with real buildings and exteriors. With a few exceptions, among which I would especially instance *Bicycle Thieves*, neo-realism has done nothing to produce in its films what is proper to the cinema, that is to say, the mysterious and fantastic. What use is all this visual drapery if the situations, the motives which animate the people, their reactions, the very subjects are taken from the most sentimental and conformist literature? The one interesting innovation, not of neo-realism but of Zavattini personally, is to have elevated the anodine action to the status of dramatic action. In *Umberto D*, one of the most interesting products of neo-realism, an entire reel of ten minutes shows a little maid performing actions which, a little while before, would have appeared unworthy of the screen. We see the servant enter the kitchen, light the stove, put a pan on the gas, throw water on a line of ants who advance on the wall in indian file, give the thermometer to an old man who feels feverish and so on. Despite the trivial nature of the situation, these activities are followed with interest and there is even a certain 'suspense'.

Neo-realism has introduced into cinematographic expression certain elements which enrich its language, but nothing more. The reality of neo-realism is incomplete, official and above all rational; but poetry, mystery, all that completes and enlarges tangible reality, is completely lacking in its working. It confuses ironic fantasy with the fantastic and black humour.

'What is most admirable in the fantastic,' André Breton has said, 'is that the fantastic doesn't exist; all is real.' In a conversation with Zavattini, I explained to him a few months ago my disagreement with neo-realism. As we dined together the first example which offered itself to me was that of the glass of wine. For a neo-realist, I said to him, a glass is a glass and nothing more; you see it taken from the sideboard, filled with drink, taken to the kitchen where the maid washes it and perhaps breaks it, which will result in its return or otherwise, etc. But this same glass, contemplated by different beings, can be a thousand different things, because each one charges what he sees with *affectivity*; no one sees things as they are, but as his desires and his state of soul make him see. I fight for the cinema which will show me this kind of glass, because this cinema will give me an integral vision of reality, will broaden my knowledge of things and people, will open up to me the marvellous world of the unknown, of all that which I find neither in the newspaper nor in the street.

Don't think from what I have just said that I am for a cinema consecrated solely to the fantastic and to mystery, for a cinema which, fleeing or scorning daily reality, would aim to plunge us into the unconscious world of the dream. Although I have just now indicated very briefly the capital importance which I attach to the film which treats the fundamental problems of a modern man, I do not consider man in isolation, as a particular case, but in his relationship to other men. I take for mine the words of Engels, who defined the function of the novelist (understood in this case as that of the film-maker): 'The novelist will have accomplished his task honourably when, through a faithful depiction of authentic social relations, he will have destroyed the conventional representation of the nature of these relations, shaken the optimism of the bourgeois world and obliged the reader to question the permanence of the existing order, even if he does not directly propose a conclusion to us, even if he does not openly take sides.'

Luis Buñuel

III. SCENARIOS

La Duquesa de Alba y Goya

NOTE: The synopsis that follows is Buñuel's original text, written in English.

The Duchess of Alba and Goya
by Luis Buñuel

The year 1788.

The flaming spirit of revolution has reared its head in France, but the people of Spain, docile and pleasure-loving, are more servile than ever towards the crown. Bull fights and fiestas and glorious Spanish sunshine are more to their liking than politics, making them indifferent to their uneasy ministers who brush aside all inclinations towards a liberal policy.

Soon there will be a new king. Charles IV, a huge, blustering dolt who knows virtually nothing about affairs of state, and whose chief concerns are hunting rabbits and gorging himself with wine and rich food.

Charles is called to the bedside of his father who is enduring his last illness. The feeble old man tells him about the responsibility of governing a people. Then, somewhat contemptuously, he adds:

'Let me warn you about your wife, Maria Louise, who will bring indignity on your name. She's little better than a common harlot, and right under your nose, too.'

Charles' stupid countenance darkens in bewilderment. 'Why, that's impossible,' he blurts out, 'It's hard for women of royal rank to commit adultery. There are so few people of equal rank that they have little opportunity . . .'

'What an ass you are, Carlos,' sighs the old man in disgust.

Disquieted by his father's words, Charles hastens to Maria Louise of whose disposition he is in mortal terror. She is far from beautiful, yet the piercing gaze in her lean pinched features inspires fear and respect. Now she is exasperated before the quailing Charles.

'What!' she exclaims, 'Will you accept accusations from a dying old man in his delirium? How dare you suspect my fidelity?'

Charles is both convinced and alarmed. 'I'll grant you any favour,' he says, 'if you will only calm yourself.'

'Very well,' she says haughtily, 'come here by the window.'

Maria Louise points to the courtyard where a very handsome young lieutenant of the guards is parading. He is tall, virile, only 18.

'A very talented young man who loves his king and queen,' she says softly. 'His name is Godoy. I want him as my secretary.'

The gullible Charles promises. 'As soon as I am made king,' he says. More confused than ever, he quits the chamber, leaving the princess standing by the window, her eyes feasting on her next prize.

Now the Duchess of Alba enters the chamber. She is of startling beauty, vivacious, bold, with a wealth of raven tresses framing a delicately carved oval face. 'It's tonight,' she laughs, 'Remember . . . our escapade?'

Maria Louise enjoins her to speak more quietly. Like conspirators they discuss their anticipated adventure. Disguised as ordinary shopwomen, they will saunter into the streets and mingle with the gay throngs that are celebrating a holiday on the outskirts of Madrid. Maybe they can pick up a couple of men . . .

Several hours later, the two women are lost in the crowd of merrymakers. There is gaiety everywhere, with shouting and singing in the festively decorated grove, with men playing flutes, walking on stilts, flirting with all the women within reach. The irrepressible Duchess begins to sing, and two *majos*, young toughs of Madrid, begin to flirt with her. Maria Louise is annoyed because she is receiving so little attention. She pretends to be indifferent, even after one of the *majos* grasps her arm. Then the two couples saunter off, headed for a dance hall.

They reach a dark street. The wailing voice of a monk reaches them and they stop to listen. It is someone from the monastic order of Brothers of Mortal Sin, preaching salvation. More quietly now, the party proceeds on its way.

Suddenly they are stopped by a patrol of the *ronda* watchmen. The *majos*, blustering more than ever, are furious, refuse to be questioned. They insult the watchmen, draw their swords, and the terrified ladies flee in opposite directions, with the clash of the swords ringing in their ears.

After a short chase, Maria Louise is caught, and the furious watchman, mistaking her for a woman of the streets, heaps violent abuse upon her. 'Who are you?' he demands. Maria Louise tries to conceal her face behind her mantilla, but the watchman rudely tears it away and holds his lantern to her face. Then he steps back in amazement. 'The princess!' he mutters, falling at her feet. 'Forgive me.' Hard glittering eyes are turned on the unhappy man. 'You shall pay,' she tells him as she turns away.

Meanwhile, in another direction, the Duchess is hotly pursued by another watchman of the *ronda*. He is about to seize her when a sword comes hurtling between his legs, tripping him. The terrified Duchess finds herself being led through the darkness by a kindly, burly figure who is holding her arm. They walk quickly with hardly a word between them, until the man opens the door of a house and leads her in.

'This is my home,' he says, 'You will be safe here.'

The Duchess is still catching her breath. 'Oh, no,' she pants. 'I won't remain here.'

'You must,' the man says gently, 'at least for a little while. They may still be in the neighbourhood.' Then he asks, 'Were you alone?' 'Yes,' says the Duchess quickly, anxious not to involve Maria Louise. 'But I must go now, really.'

The man smiles, caresses her hair as the Duchess coquettishly pretends to draw away. 'You needn't remain very long,' he promises, stealing one arm over her shoulder.

The impetuous Goya tries all the tricks of gallantry to win over this charming creature who laughingly persists in behaving like a wary schoolgirl. Though his efforts are seeking in vain, Goya is very pleased. Alba laughs, draws away. For half an hour they fence, with the painter pleading, 'Come, at least you ought to be interested in seeing my paintings ... in the next room.'

With his arm still around her he leads her into the atelier where the walls are covered with paintings that are famous all through Spain. The Duchess regards them in amazement. 'You are Goya!' she exclaims. He nods. The Duchess hastily covers her face in alarm, utters a startled cry and rushes out into the street. Goya tries to pursue her but the night has swallowed his beautiful, mysterious visitor ...

The following day finds the vindictive Maria Louise true to type. She hasn't forgotten the misadventure of the previous night, and she hasn't forgotten the watchman who had insulted her. Losing little time, she trumps up a false charge against the unhappy man and has him thrown into prison. 'He robbed a poor woman of her purse,' she tells the chief justice.

To Charles she tells a different story, a true version except that she substitutes the name of the Duchess for her own. 'You know how wild the Duchess is,' she says sweetly. 'She shouldn't indulge in such foolish escapades, but of course, no one else must know.' Charles, completely taken in, urges her not to become too friendly with such an irresponsible woman.

Meanwhile the romantic Goya, in whose nostrils still lingers the perfume of the woman who had so strangely moved him, searches all Madrid for her. He has become restless, forgetting everything but the beauty of that woman. As he searches for her, he hears the tolling of church bells proclaiming to the people that the old king is dead.

With traditional ceremony, a new king and queen are crowned. There is grand pomp, wild celebration in the streets of Madrid. Bells ring, games are held, people cavort and shout in glee. In the Royal palace there is much ado, with everyone pleased, especially Maria Louise, who has just commanded that Godoy be sent to her as secretary.

Entering her royal presence, the youth is bewildered, awestruck. Dropping to his knees, he is as embarrassed as a schoolboy, murmurs to the queen that he has had no training for the job he is to fulfil. 'You'll do,' says the queen very quietly; 'you will learn,' she says as the youth continues to protest his inexperience. Unable longer to restrain herself, the queen lets her fingers steal over his hair while a sigh issues from her lips. Now a subtle change comes over the youth, who is far from stupid. The humble look in his eyes gives way to one of cunning. Raising his head, he is electrified by the enamored look on the face of the queen, and with sudden boldness he springs to his feet and crushes her in his arms . . .

There is a ceremony in court. Among those present is Goya, the great court painter who rose from a peasant's rank. He is a large man, warm, passionate, yet retaining the peasant's virtues of simplicity and sincerity. He has just come in, with the Infante Don Luis at his side. Many beautiful women cast their smiles at Goya, as if trying to win his favour.

'You rarely attend these functions,' chides Don Luis, 'But you should. You must meet the great ladies. First I'll introduce you to the charming Duchess of Alba.'

Painter and lady recognize each other instantly, but both are discreet. The Duchess regards him haughtily. 'You must come to my castle and paint me one day,' she says quite formally. Goya, with equal formality, thanks her for the honour and walks off, though his heart is bursting with emotion . . .

Nearly all the great ladies want to be painted by the famous Goya. Legends have sprung up about him, about his appeal to women, about his facility with the brush, how he is able to do a complete portrait in one hour. Even the royal family dotes on him. And in the ante-room of his atelier there are always six or seven ladies waiting patiently for their turn. Often he is obliged to send most of them away.

We see him in his studio, besieged by a marquis and his wife, who is a lady of outstanding beauty. 'Please, Goya,' begs the marquis, 'you must paint my wife today. She has already made several appointments with you.'

'I regret e ceedingly that I cannot paint her today,' the artist says. 'I haven't the time, your excellency.'

But the marquis is determined. Seizing the key, he rushes outside and locks them in. 'Now you are my prisoner!' he shouts through the door. 'I'll be waiting here for two hours and I won't let you out until the job is finished.'

When the two hours are up, the marquis opens the door. 'Have you finished your job?' he asks. 'I have, your excellency,' Goya replies, glancing at the lovely marquesa whose face is slightly flushed, while a curious smile hovers about her lips. The marquis looks at the finished portrait. 'You have done your job well,' he says. 'I have, your excellency,' replies Goya, very quietly.

Several days go by. Goya hasn't forgotten his promise to paint the Duchess of Alba. Strangely elated, he has his servants carry his equipment to her castle.

Arriving in the grand domicile, he finds her more elusive than ever. Her smile, as he sets up his easel, is ambiguous, both an invitation and a mockery. There they are, the peasant and the lady, with the yawning chasm of tradition and blood between them.

Goya is startled when she cries to him, 'No, not that!' She is laughing softly, showing her small white teeth. 'I didn't want you to paint my portrait now,' she says to him. 'I merely invited you up here to paint make-up on my face.'

Goya, whose fury when aroused is notorious, clenches his fists and bows respectfully. The Duchess, still laughing, fixes him with her eyes, as if daring him to display a temper. But the artist is in control of himself now. Bowing again, he approaches her to perform the humble duty she has asked of him.

At length the Duchess looks into her mirror, smiles in satisfaction. 'Marvellous,' she says. 'What is your price?' Goya takes her roughly in his arms, kisses her mouth and cheeks with such contemptuous dispatch that the rouge is smeared all over her face. Standing erect with the quiet dignity of which he is capable, Goya laughs in his turn. 'That is my price,' he says. 'So sorry I had to spoil my work.' Then he stalks out, leaving the Duchess staring ruefully after him, her ego sharply deflated.

The turbulent spirit of war is in the air, and soldiers are being recruited to fight against the French revolutionaries. Louis XVI, a cousin of King Charles, has been beheaded in France, and a wave of fear has swept over the thrones in Europe. The Spanish people, lovers of tradition, are still loyal to the crown, but at any time their sympathies might change.

Godoy, elevated by degrees, is now Prime Minister of Spain. He is preoccupied and worried. He goes to his mistress, the queen, and tells her he wants to discuss affairs of state. 'That can wait,' she says. 'Come with me, I want to show you something.'

Taking his hand, which she fondles, she leads him to her wardrobe chamber.

'Look,' she says, 'a work of genius. A most special creation from Paris. A dress that will be the envy of everyone, especially that conceited Alba. I am wearing it at her party.'

Godoy, unceremoniously, flops on a chair and shrugs his shoulder.

The Duchess of Alba's receptions are a byword in Madrid. Now the great ballroom is lavishly festooned and brilliantly illuminated while a small army of servants deftly move about to care for the guests. On a platform off to one side, members of the orchestra are pompously taking their places waiting for their cue to begin. Alba looks gayer and lovelier than ever, and when she beholds Maria Louise arriving in her new gown she exclaims in delight:

'How stunning! How perfectly ravishing it is!'

Others present, not to be outdone, echo her praises, while the queen with a glint of triumph in her eyes, appears anxious to treat everyone with a glimpse of her gown.

Then Alba signals for the ladies-in-waiting, who come marching in with their trays of refreshments. As they enter, a murmur of amazement sweeps through the ballroom; then all are deathly silent. All the servant girls are wearing exact replicas of the queen's gown!

Maria Louise looks at Alba, her piercing eyes glowing with rage. 'It is only a coincidence,' she tries to explain. The queen, without uttering a word, storms out of the palace. The other guests don't dare remain. Mumbling their excuses, they begin to depart. Alba is left standing alone in the centre of the room. Her eye falls on the sumptuous food that has been spread on the tables, at the members of the orchestra sitting as if transfixed, at the servants who look embarrassed. Goya crosses the gilded floor to where she is standing. She regards him for a moment, her eyes filled with wonder. Then she reaches out and takes his hand. 'You are always around when I am in trouble, my friend,' she says simply.

She leads him to the garden where scented air is stirred by a gentle breeze. Here, beneath the moonlight, as they sit near a plashing fountain, the artist raises her hands to his lips. 'I shall always be around when you need me,' he says, 'but you tempt the queen too much. Why did you do it?'

'The queen and I,' Alba replies, 'understand each other – with hatred. She hates me because I am young and attractive, and I hate her for being so mean and vindictive.'

Drawn irresistibly to him, Alba rests her head on Goya's broad chest. A look of tenderness comes over his face as he tells her, 'I will not let you suffer alone.'

Alba's smile is wistful. 'You are like a great bear,' she whispers, 'great and lovable. I am sorry if I was ever rude to you. You should be rude to me – you, a man of genius.' She sighs.

'Why do you sigh?' he asks.

'I was very rash,' Alba tells him, 'the queen will answer the insult I gave her.'

Goya's arm tightens around her frail body, as if to protect her. Trembling in his embrace, she looks up at him, her eyes wild with love. She is about to fling her arms about his neck when the air is pierced with a cry, 'Fire!'

They spring to their feet. Flames are leaping from one corner of the castle as servants pour on it bucket after bucket of water.

'There is her answer!' cries the Duchess, as she and Goya watch the vanquishing of the flames.

Meanwhile, from another castle, the queen leans out from her balcony window, beholding the spectacle of the flames. 'That,' she says slyly to Godoy who is standing over her, 'is probably the judgment of God.' Godoy grins understandingly. 'Tomorrow,' continues the queen, 'she will receive my judgment.'

The vindictive queen is true to her word. On the following morning the Duchess of Alba is condemned to exile. She is ordered to depart immediately for her castle in Andalusia. The servants are tearful, but Alba as usual is very brave, comforting those who commiserate with her. At last the coach starts, and as it proceeds down the road, she looks back longingly at her beloved Madrid.

The journey is uncomfortable, the road is very bad, mercilessly joggling the Duchess. Hour after hour she is subjected to this discomfort until finally, towards dusk, an axle is broken. Coming out of the coach, the Duchess finds that the air is very cold. She shivers as her servants tell her that they might not get help before morning. Two of them go on ahead in search of a blacksmith.

Suddenly Alba utters a shout of joy. She sees coming towards her a solitary horseman – Goya. Leaping from his mount, he cries out to her, 'I couldn't let you make this trip alone, my Duchess. I'll go into exile with you!' 'But your career,' she says, 'what about your career.' Goya whispers fervently, 'You will be my career. I'll paint so many portraits of you that all the world will ring of your beauty!'

Alba enjoins him to walk with her a short distance, away from the prying ears of the servants. Forgetting the cold and the hours as they pass, the lady and the peasant at last yield utterly to the passion that draws them together. Locked in each other's embrace they swear eternal love, love that will transcend all barriers, even the one of social caste. Her protestations of love are as vehement as his own; she assures him that she loved him from the very first moment of their meeting even though she had not previously dared to acknowledge it. At last Goya realizes that she is shivering with cold.

'You cannot stay here. You must go on. And I with you,' he laughs.

'We shall never be parted again, my Francisco,' she tells him, 'but we cannot go on yet. The axle . . .'

Goya grunts masterfully. 'You rest in the coach where it is warm,' he says, 'I'll fix the axle and we will go on.'

While the Duchess, exhausted now, sleeps in the coach, Goya sets about to repair the axle. Pulling off his coat, he builds a fire and improvises a forge. Hour after hour he works, ignoring the chill that is creeping through his perspiring skin.

But he labours in vain. Overcome with fatigue and the frigid cold, he approaches the

Duchess in the coach, discovers she is asleep. Several heavy blankets cover her delicate body but Goya refuses to touch them. His chilled hands fish under the coach for a thin bit of canvas. This he takes to cover himself as he lies down to sleep near the fire.

A storm comes up. Rain beats down on Goya and extinguishes the fire. Huddled under his canvas he spends a miserable night trying to sleep.

Morning. The Duchess, rousing herself, calls to Goya, but he does not reply. Hurrying over to him she calls again, receives no response, and discovers to her horror that he is deaf. Exposure has made him quite ill. He is feverish, delirious.

The Duchess is frantic. Then she receives another shock. Five horsemen come galloping up and seize the sick man.

'King's orders,' says the captain gruffly. 'Goya is needed in Madrid as court painter.'

'You cannot take him,' Alba says fiercely. 'I forbid it.'

'Sorry,' says the captain more politely. 'I am powerless. It's the King's orders.'

The Duchess is beside herself. 'King's orders! The queen, you mean. That lustful old witch! She'll do anything to make me miserable.'

But she is powerless. Left alone now, she screams, 'Francisco! I love you! Come back to me!'

It is a love-maddened, sullen Goya that the doting court has now to contend with. Though still respectful to the royalty who are keeping him from his love, his manner is almost that of a hurt child. Even Godoy is moved.

He has just finished a portrait of Godoy.

'Wonderful' says the Prime Minister. 'You may have any price you ask.'

As he speaks we see Goya watching his lips, for the painter is partially deaf.

'Any price,' he repeats slowly. 'Would the pardon of the Duchess be asking too much?'

Goday is very sympathetic. He places his hand on Goya's shoulder.

'I wish I could,' he says sincerely. 'But it's the queen who sent her away, and only the queen can pardon her.'

Goya is in despair. Even the prospect of the greatest commission of his career, the painting of the entire royal family, doesn't seem to interest him. He knows the vanity of his royal patrons, how each of them will crowd for a favorable position on the canvas. Even Maria Louise is excited about the work he has commenced.

All the court is discussing its progress. Day after day his subjects go to their places with the eager interest of schoolchildren. Goya becomes animated again, is actually cheerful.

At last the painting is finished, all but the faces.

'When will you paint in the faces,' the king and queen want to know.

There is a cunning gleam in Goya's eye, even though his manner is more respectful than ever.

'Oh, tomorrow, probably, your majesties,' he says. 'But first I would like to speak to you if you will permit it.'

They wait for him to speak. His manner has become crafty.

'You know, your majesties,' he says very humbly, 'that the mind and hand of an artist must be free of all obsessions if he is to do full justice to his art.'

They regard him uncomprehendingly.

'My spirit would have the freedom it needs if my mind were no longer disturbed about one thing,' he goes on, '– the pardon of the Duchess of Alba.'

The queen glares at him, while the face of Charles is blank as ever.

'And,' continues Goya, 'without that pardon the portrait might suffer. There is good reason to believe that I might not even be able to go on with it at all.'

'That's impudent,' exclaims the queen.

'That's art, your majesty,' Goya replies. 'An artist is often imprisoned by his emotions.' He gestures helplessly.

'You speak of imprisonment,' snaps the exasperated queen. 'I'll show you the inside of a real prison, one that has no art.'

'If you imprison me, your majesty,' says Goya intrepidly, 'posterity will not profit by the picture of your great family.'

The queen is furious.

At last Charles asserts himself. 'We must have the painting,' he says to the queen. 'Why, it's nearly finished. Anyway, you've punished Alba enough.'

'I won't pardon that woman,' snaps the queen.

The vain Charles glances again at the painting that is nearly completed. Over his stupid face there suddenly comes a look of resolution. Even the queen is impressed. 'You want that painting as much as I do,' he says with some force. 'Alba will be pardoned.'

'She will not!' screams Maria Louise.

Charles puffs himself up, speaks from his great height. 'I am still the king. She will be pardoned.' The queen knows she's beaten, and shrugs her shoulders.

We see Charles signing the pardon and handing it to Goya. Then he calls him aside. 'After you finish this picture,' he says greedily, 'will you paint one of me alone, a big one in my best uniform? You'll do that, eh?'

Goya is overjoyed. 'I'll paint three of them,' he assures Charles.

The family portrait is finished. With the writ of pardon secure on his person, Goya starts out for Andalusia. Off to his beloved Duchess he goes, the memory of their last passionate meeting still fresh in his memory. He spurs on his horses, an artist-lover hurrying to his greatest glory.

He arrives at the castle in Andalusia. Alba's greeting puzzles him. She is cordial, but hardly more than that. When Goya arrives, she is sitting in her garden with a small party of aristocrats and bull fighters. And she seems very attentive to one of the bull fighters, Costillares, a very famous one.

'You are pardoned,' Goya tells her, 'You may return to Madrid.'

The Duchess laughs gaily. Once again she has become the great lady, worldly, frivolous. 'Really,' she says to Goya, 'How good of Maria Louisa. You must come.'

In the presence of these people, Goya suddenly feels dismally alone. Somehow he is made to feel a peasant who is graciously welcomed in good society. Is this the Duchess of Alba who embraced him so fervently at their last meeting?

At the bull fight Costillares puts on a grand show. Goya observes that the Duchess is completely enthralled, and when she throws a flower to the hero a slight groan escapes from Goya's lips. Now Costillares executes the veronica, which he has invented, and the Duchess appears overcome with admiration. Goya can stand no more. Very quietly he rises and leaves.

Costillares in the ring is magnificent. Cheering and wild applause rewards his virtuosity with the cape, and after each veronica he looks up to receive a warm smile from the Duchess. At last he kills the bull. Looking up again, the triumphant expression on his face is frozen. The Duchess is no longer smiling, she is not even looking at him. She has just discovered that Goya has disappeared.

It is a gay group that returns to the palace of Alba for a celebration. There is drinking and bright chatter in the sumptuous dining room as the servants bring in the platters of food. But the gaiety of Alba seems strained. She has just learned from her servants that Goya has departed for Madrid.

'You seem preoccupied,' says Costillares, placing his hand on her arm in a friendly manner. He is surprised when she impatiently brushes his hand away. Then she is contrite. 'Forgive me,' she says. 'I am terribly annoyed.'

Alba stands by the window, her eyes glued to the road that leads to Madrid. In her ears there is dinned the sounds of laughter and merry quips of her guests. Suddenly a look of weariness and disgust pinches her lovely features, and she turns abruptly on her guests. Her voice breaking with irritation, she tells them that she is feeling very ill, that they will have to leave at once. And not many minutes elapse before we find the unhappy Alba standing alone in the centre of the room, while in the background her servants stare dismally at the unconsumed repast on the table.

Goya, disillusioned, has become a recluse. Except for solitary walks at night, he has shut himself off from the world, and even his closest friends cannot get to him.

We see two of them knocking in vain at the door of his atelier.

'I know he's inside,' says one. 'I saw his light from across the street.'

'Something terrible has happened to his soul,' says the other sadly. 'Poor Goya. He just stays here, painting those blasphemous Caprichos, poking fun at the crown and the church. They will put him in prison.'

'Worse than that, if the Inquisition gets to him. Already they are scheming to get him in their clutches. Then it will mean torture – death . . .'

'Oh, well, the king will go on protecting him.'

'Yes, but for how long? That dreadful Inquisition!'

Goya, inside, is painting one of his Caprichos. Partly deaf, he doesn't hear at first the rapping at his door. But the rapping becomes louder, insistent. At last he turns around, walks to the door, and mutters that he doesn't wish to see anybody. As he turns away the rapping continues. With a gesture of extreme annoyance, Goya pulls open the door and beholds the Duchess of Alba!

Boiling with emotion, he refuses to let her in. 'Your place is with your aristocratic friends,' he says fiercely as he closes the door. 'I no longer wish to aspire to your level.'

Returning to his easel he sits in gloom, his shoulders hunched in misery.

That night he takes his wonted walk. From the darkness three masked men spring upon him. The powerful artist battles valiantly until one of his assailants, a tall man with a short pointed beard, fells him with a cruel blow to the side of the head. Blindfolded and trussed, Goya is led away.

He is taken to the palace of Alba. It is her hands that undo the blindfold as he stands, still trussed, tied upright to a pillar.

'You!' Goya exclaims, and he heaps upon her a tirade of fury. Alba is equally furious. 'You resort to such methods!' Goya blurts out. 'Your stubborn nature requires such methods,' she retorts. Then they belabour each other with a storm of imprecations, while Goya, helpless, struggles in his bonds.

Then Alba explains to him that he was wrong to have been jealous. A lady of her station couldn't fly into his arms and betray great emotion. Of course she was grateful, Alba says, and she loved him too. Then why be jealous of the others who were only friends? Goya, still bitter, is not impressed. 'You think I don't love you!' cries the Duchess. Goya is silent. A look of exasperation comes over her face. She slaps him several times. Then, beholding him mute and helpless in his bonds, the rage in her collapses. Now, overwhelmed with tenderness, she embraces him passionately, cries, 'I love you.' Their lips meet in a kiss.

Some time later they sit close together, her hands in his. 'Let me prove my love,' says Alba passionately. 'Here, in Madrid, our different stations make it so difficult. Let us flee Madrid where our love won't be poisoned by the rigid walls of caste.'

Goya tells her that her sacrifice would be too great, and he cannot abandon his career as a painter. Now he is convinced of her love. They will remain in Madrid.

As he leaves the castle, Goya recognizes one of the servants by his short pointed beard, the tall man who had brutally knocked him down. With one blow of his fist, Goya sends the man sprawling. Then, lifting him up bodily, he suspends him by his pants to the bough of a tree.

We next see Goya in his studio, finishing a portrait of Alba. She dips a brush into the oil and paints two rings on the hand of her portrait – the symbol of betrothal. On these rings she inscribes the names Alba and Goya.

Godoy's chamber. The Duchess comes to him. She is accompanied by her pet, a mischievous little Negro girl of four.

The Duchess asks Godoy to secure pardon for one of her servants who has been guilty of a petty misdemeanour. While they speak, the little Negro girl idles about the room, picks up a sheet of paper that has been lying on the desk. This the child twists into a doll's hat.

Back in the carriage, the child proudly shows it to her mistress. The Duchess, amused at first, observes writing on the paper hat. As she reads, her eyes widen. This is an incriminating letter, written by Maria Louise to Godoy, mentioning their love child. A sly look comes over Alba's face. Folding the letter carefully, she placed it in her bodice.

Godoy, missing the letter, goes to the queen in alarm. They quarrel violently when Maria Louise accuses him of negligence. 'Anyway,' the queen says furiously, 'this time the Duchess has gone too far. She will never annoy me again.'

Several days later, Goya is working in his studio when the Duchess bursts in on him. She is breathless, thoroughly alarmed.

'We must leave Madrid,' she says, 'And we must not delay.'

'But I cannot leave my work,' says Goya, 'I thought we had agreed . . .'

Alba tells him that her life is in imminent danger. 'I have just learned,' she says, 'that Maria Louise means to have me killed.'

Goya's manner changes instantly. 'Then we will leave, of course,' he says.

They agree to depart on the following day. Alba returns to her palace after her lover agrees to call for her next morning.

That night a terrible storm breaks out. Rain and a howling wind rage outside while Goya lies in his bed, unable to sleep. As if visited by a foreboding of evil, his face is contorted with fear and doubt. Once he cries out, 'Who is there?' and springs from his bed only to discover that he is quite alone. Just as he crawls back into bed a fierce gust of wind knocks down a portrait of Alba. Goya hastens to set the portrait upright. As he stumbles about the room in his agitation, he hears a furious knocking at his door. He opens it.

One of Alba's servants comes in, drenched to the skin, his teeth chattering with cold and fright. 'Come at once,' he says, 'the Duchess is dying.'

Goya rushes to the bedside of his love.

Still stunned by the news, he gazes in bewilderment at the assembly of servants, the weeping little Negro girl, the physicians, and the notary who listens carefully as Alba dictates terms of her will.

Goya violently seizes one of the servants. 'Tell me quickly,' he demands. 'What has happened?'

'The physician thinks it is poison,' the servant tells him.

The Duchess, raising her eyes, sees Goya, calls to him. As he plunges forward her arms rise feebly as if to embrace him. 'Francho!' she cries as he falls to her side and presses her hand to his face.

The physician tries to make Goya leave, but the Duchess restrains him, says she wishes to be alone with the painter. In a few moments the others clear the room.

Alba's eyes flutter open as she smiles faintly. 'Still the same Francho,' she says, 'always around when I'm in trouble.'

Goya groans. 'I'll be around with you for ever, from now on,' he whispers, as his hand moves significantly to his sword. The dying woman places a restraining hand on his arm. 'No, no,' she gasps. 'You must not die.' She makes him promise that he will go on living for the sake of his immortal art. Even though he goes on living, she tells him they will still be united in love, for his portraits of her had blended them in a marriage of the spirit and for all posterity. Fighting back his tears, Goya slips a ring from his finger, places it on the finger of Alba, next to the one she is wearing.

We see those two rings on her limp hand . . .

Then that hand becomes the hand of the portrait of the Duchess of Alba . . .

We draw away from the portrait, our attention receding in space and time, we behold a very old Goya, aged 80, reverently contemplating the same hand.

The aged genius at last draws his eyes away. He is nearly stone deaf, employs the use of a trumpet when his servants address him. He wears two pairs of thick spectacles and his body is quite feeble, but he hasn't lost all of his old fire. He is still brusque and impatient with his servants, but there is an element of mellowness and humour in his old eyes.

One of his servants straightens the blanket over his legs and announces that his physician is coming. Goya exclaims with some heat, 'What, that old fool again!'

The physician understands Goya's temperament. He both chides and humours him while performing the routine of looking at his tongue, examining his pulse, etc. The physician says, 'You persist in disobeying me, you old rogue. Your servant tells me you demanded mutton yesterday.' 'I have no prejudice against mutton,' says Goya calmly. 'But I have,' the physician tells him, 'for your table. Good broth is what you need.' 'Broth,' scoffs the old man, 'I wouldn't wash my paint brushes in it.'

The physician has just tested his patient's reflexes. Then he takes Goya's hand in his own. 'Now squeeze,' he orders, 'as hard as you can.' The painter squeezes and there comes over the face of the physician a look of intense pain. He is glad when Goya releases him. 'Bah!' he exclaims, 'still strong as a mule. I guess you'll live for ever.'

A subtle change comes over Goya's face. 'I may not,' he says, 'I don't know.' His eyes travel back to the portrait of the Duchess. As he gazes at the picture his face becomes exalted. '. . . but she will. I know that.'

THE END

Ilegible, son of Flauta

Synopsis. Fragment of an original, unrealized scenario by Juan Larrea and Luis Buñuel, based on a lost book by Juan Larrea. Deposited in the Museum of Modern Art, New York, and first published in *Cine Nuevo* (Mexico), November 1961.

Ilegible is a film of two dimensions, external and interior. One which, by the force of the images and the surprising concatenation, acts in a direct way on the spectator's consciousness; the other which addresses the subconscious in its own language. It is a dream of poetic character which develops beyond social consciousness, to excite the depths of the psyche.

This film is a conglomeration of symbols, not literary nor artificial, but the ordinary and natural symbols of our culture. Nothing in the human spirit is conceived without symbols. The language which we use to communicate with one another is a fabric of symbols articulated according to the logical needs of our intellect. Magic, religion organize a harmonious framework of symbols determined by a creative reason.

Nevertheless it would be an error to present these symbols naked. As the flesh covers and conceals the skeleton, so in this film the apparent covers the symbol which the spectator must feel more than discover. Otherwise the aesthetic effect of the work would be defeated, converting it more into a philosophic work than an artistic one, that is to say, that it would be directed more to the intelligence than to the imagination.

This film, like all dynamic reality, has a point of departure and a terminal point of arrival. Uprooted from a determined place in space, time, psyche, 'situated in the old world' (where the spectator himself is already situated) to arrive at possession of another place in space, time and psyche proper to the 'new world'. Hence it is that the protagonist and the city to which he belongs are one. They have the same name, Villalobos, whose fundamental reality is the deception. Hence the woman deceives him. But when the historic moment of dénouement arrives, the deception is visible and the policeman suicides, that is to say that that which constitutes, on the psychic plane, the repression or censorship, which our consciousness imposes, disappears.

In other words, that which impedes the development of the creative imagination retreats, opening up all cinematographic possibilities.

From this point the film is launched into unlimited imaginary worlds. The sequence of time is transformed. The person who seems intended as the wife of the protagonist becomes his mother. This mother is the future liberty which brings with it the promise of a new day, a new light, a new conscience, the rupture of the particular ego which provides the shackles which imprison us.

FRAGMENTS

She walks with her eyes fixed on infinity, lit by the setting sun, like a sleepwalker, and stops before him. He has risen abruptly.

Scattered dismembered limbs appear. Blood.

Under the influence of cold blood and the tone of Carrillo's voice, they start to walk. He tells them he has a small vessel with a crew of four waiting for him at Finisterre, ready to sail the moment he is on board.

He explains that there exist several fundamental problems in man's social existence which cannot be solved in the over-populated regions of the contemporary world. Therefore he has conceived the idea of setting out in search of an island about which men have spoken since time immemorial, that island so elusive to navigators, endowed with its own life, which travels hither and thither upon the oceans, and which perhaps submerges from time to time like a whale. There in that floating, mobile dimension, in that virgin land, the realities that preoccupy him can be conceived.

Ilegible has become aware that there is no correct relation between the movement of his watch and that of the sun.

Above all, the doubt: Are they alive? Are they dead? Are they in another dimension of time, or perhaps in eternity?

A street in a quiet quarter, almost without shops. A few passers-by. A uniformed policeman appears, evidently agitated. It is easy to perceive that he is going through one of those critical moments in which radical solutions are taken. He wipes his eyes with the back of his hand. Arriving on a corner, he takes out his pistol and shoots himself in the mouth. He falls. Curious passers-by, between shock and consternation, start to form a circle around him. One of them, a man of some thirty-five years old, is passionately attracted to the pistol which the policeman still holds in his right hand. He looks at it, and the weapon is seen in close-up. The man pushes decisively through the crowd:

'Let me through, I am a doctor,' he says.

He approaches the policeman. He takes the weapon from his hand, and keeps it in his own

left hand while he takes from the policeman a photograph of a wrinkled woman. Taking advantage of the curiosity aroused by this picture, he puts the pistol in his pocket. He says:
'There is nothing we can do. He is dead. I will phone the Red Cross.'
It is a pretext. He goes swiftly through various streets and reaches a door. He climbs the stairs and stops in front of the door of an apartment. He puts the key into the lock and tries, fruitlessly, to open it. The door is barred from within. Thinking that he may have mistaken the door, he raises his gaze to a card on which he reads his name: 'Leandro Villalobos.' Then he tried the bell and knocks insistently with his knuckles. A woman's voice asks from within:
'Who is it?'
'It's me.'
At the word 'me' there is a loud noise like a huge lustre breaking. He jumps and looks all round as if seeking the cause.
At this moment the door is at last opened by a woman, surprised and ill-kempt.
'Is it you, Leandro? ... How have you come back so quickly?'
'And you – why have you shut yourself in?'
'You know how nervous I am . . .'
He enters, and the room is seen: a very old writing table, with a monkish chair. A huge cupboard with two doors which might hide one or two persons. Shelves of books. On one of the walls is displayed a huge print representing a human brain, in which are stuck little flags, as on a military map. There is also a mirror on the wall.
In one of the corners of the room is a large statue of Rodin's 'Thinker', with the helmet of a hair-drier on its head.
The man looks rapidly at the brain in the print, which looks like a mountainous landscape. He reflects a moment in front of it, and changes the position of some flags, as if carrying out a strategic operation, while his wife talks to him and he replies . . .
He pushes her without roughness to the door, which he locks behind her.
Then he goes to Rodin's 'Thinker'. He unplugs the hair-drier and carefully removes it. He puts a tiny key in a lock which the statue has in its left ear and after giving it a turn, takes a cloth to lift the lid of the brain so as not to burn himself. He takes from it a roast pigeon, whose form resembles that of a brain. He cuts off a wing and a little breast and eats them. At the same time he goes to the cupboard, takes out a bottle of water and a glass. He pours a little liquid into this and then a couple of tablets which he takes from a tube of Veronal. He shakes them and swallows them. A telephone bell rings. He goes to the mirror and takes down a little receiver whose cord comes out of the looking glass so that when he looks into it it appears that the wire is coming from between his own brows. Although two voices are heard, his own and another more nasal and metallic, it is as if he was talking to himself. The dialogue will express, with the fewest possible words, that finally he has arrived at the moment of finding the solution of the problem which has so much preoccupied him. This idea, this truth which he has sensed for a long time passing through his brain without being able to capture it, will now offer itself up. The pistol which has killed a policeman holds, fast, a special power. It is rather as if it were an irresistible magic instrument. Nevertheless he, in his consciousness, is unaware of the use which he can make of it. Something has to be done but he does not know what. It is not a matter of suicide or of shooting anyone. He has arrived at the conclusion that he must give way to what the subconscious manifests.
Practically, he has decided to sleep holding the pistol in his hand so that what must happen will happen. With this objective he takes the rest of the Veronal tablets.
The conversation ended, he replaces the receiver and sits before the writing desk. He takes a writing pad. With red ink he crosses out his name written on the letterhead: Leandro Villalobos, Disillusion, 27; and writes instead: Ilegible, Son of Flauta.

Filmography

1929   *Un Chien andalou*
France.
Production: Luis Buñuel.
Director: Luis Buñuel.
Script: Luis Buñuel, Salvador Dalí.
Photography: Albert Duverger.
Design: Pierre Schilzneck.
Editor: Luis Buñuel.
Music: At its first performance the film was accompanied by gramophone records, including Wagner's *Tristan and Isolde* and some Argentine tangos. In 1960 Buñuel advised on the compilation of a score for a synchronized version, based on the 1929 musical selections.
Leading Players: Pierre Batcheff (The Young Man); Simone Mareuil (The Girl); Jaime Miratvilles; Salvador Dalí (Marist Priest); Luis Buñuel (Man with razor).
430 metres. 17 minutes. Black and white.
Filmed in March 1928 in Paris, Le Havre.
First performance: April 1929, Studio Ursulines, Paris.

1930   *L'Age d'or*
France.
Production: Le Vicomte de Noailles.
Director: Luis Buñuel.
Script: Luis Buñuel, Salvador Dalí.

288

Photography: Albert Duverger.

Design: Pierre Schilzneck.

Editor: Luis Buñuel.

Music: Luis Buñuel; montage of extracts from Mozart, Beethoven, Mendelssohn, Debussy, Wagner; the final pasodoble by Georges van Parys.

Assistant directors: Jacques B. Brunius, Claude Heyman.

Leading Players: Lya Lys (The Woman); Gaston Modot (The Man); Caridad de Labaerdesque; Lionel Salem; Max Ernst (The Bandit Chief); Madame Noizet; Liorens Artigas; Duchange; Ibanez; Pierre Prévert (Péman, a bandit); Pancho Cossio; Valentine Hugo; Marie Berthe Ernst; Jacques B. Brunius; Simone Cottance; Paul Eluard; Manuel Angeles Ortiz; Juan Esplandio; Pedro Flores; Juan Castañe; Joaquin Roa; Pruna; Xaume de Maravilles.

60 minutes. Black and white.

Filmed at the Studios Billancourt-Epinay.

First performance: 28 November 1930, Studio 28, Paris.

1932   *Las Hurdes – Tierra sin pan*
Spain.

Production: Ramón Acín.

Director: Luis Buñuel.

Script: Luis Buñuel, inspired by a book by Maurice Legendre.

Commentary: Luis Buñuel and Pierre Unik; *read by* Abel Jacquin.

Photography: Eli Lotar.

Editor: Luis Buñuel.

Music: Brahms' 4th Symphony. The sound-track was added in 1937 when the film was put into distribution by Pierre Braunberger, Films du Panthéon.

Assistant directors: Rafael Sanchez Ventura and Pierre Unik.

27 minutes. Black and white.

Filmed in Las Hurdes region of Spain, April–May 1932.

First performance: 1933 in a private screening in the Palace of the Press, Madrid. Released in Paris, by Pierre Braunberger in 1937.

1933–34   Dubbing director for Paramount, Paris, at the Joinville Studios.

1935   Dubbing director for Warner Brothers, Madrid.

1935   *Don Quintín el amargao*
Spain.

Production: Filmófono, Ricardo Urgoiti, Spain.

Executive producer and supervisor: Luis Buñuel.

Directors: Luis Marquin, Luis Buñuel (uncredited).

Dialogue Director: Eduardo Ugarte.

Script: Eduardo Ugarte and Luis Buñuel, based on the comedy by Carlos Arniches and José Estremera.

Photography: José Maria Beltrán.

Editors: Luis Buñuel/Eduardo G. Maroto.

Art Direction: Mariano Espinosa.

Music: Jacinto Guerrero.

Settings: José Maria Torres.

Sound: León Lucas de Lapeña.
Assistant directors: José Martin, Francisco Lejuela.
Leading Players: Alfonso Muñoz (Don Quintín); Ana Maria Custodio (Teresa); Luisita Esteso (Felisa); Fernando Granada (Paco); Isabel Noguera (Margot); Porfiria Sanchíz (María); Luis de Heredia (Angelito); Consuelo Nieva; José Alfayate (Sefini); Manuel Arbó; Erna Rosal; José Marco Davó; María Amaya; Jacinto Higueras; Isabelita Urcola; Manuel Vico.
85 minutes. Black and white.
Filmed at CEA Studios, Madrid.

1935   *La hija de Juan Simón*
Spain.
Production: Filmófono, Ricardo Urgoiti, Spain.
Executive producer and supervisor: Luis Buñuel.
Directors: Nemesio M. Sobrevila, José Luis Sáenz de Heredia, Eduardo Ugarte, Luis Buñuel (uncredited).
Script: Nemesio M. Sobrevila, Eduardo Ugarte, Luis Buñuel, based on the play by Sobrevila.
Photography: José Maria Beltrán.
Editor: Eduardo G. Maroto.
Art Direction: Nemesio M. Sobrevila, Mariano Espinosa.
Music: Daniel Montorio, Fernando Remacha. Lyrics: Mauricio Torres.
Sound: Antonio Fernando Roces.
Assistant director: Honorio Martinez.
Leading Players: Angelillo (Angel); Pilar Muñoz (Carmen); Carmen Amaya (Soledad); Manuel Arbó (Juan Simón); Ena Sedeño (Angustias); Porfirio Sanchez ('La Roja'); Cándida Losada (Trini); Emilio Portes (Don Severo); Julián Pérez de Avila (Carlos); Fernando Freire de Andrade (Don Paco); Pablo Hidalgo (Curro); Angelito Sampedro; Baby Deny. (There is also a brief appearance by Buñuel, who is seen and heard singing in the prison.)
95 minutes. Black and white.
Filmed at Roptence Studios, Madrid.

1936   *Quién me quiere a mi?*
Spain.
Production: Filmófono, Ricardo Urgoiti, Spain.
Executive producer and supervisor: Luis Buñuel.
Director: José Luis Sáenz de Heredia.
Script: Eduardo Ugarte, Luis Buñuel.
Story: Enrique Horta.
Dialogue director: Eduardo Ugarte.
Photography: José Maria Beltrán.
Editor: Luis Buñuel.
Art Director: Mariano Espinosa.
Music: Fernando Remacha, Juan Tellería.
Sound: León Lucas de Lapeña.
Assistants: Domingo Pruna, Honorio Martinez, Edgundo Ter.
Leading Players: Lina Yegros (Marta Vélez); Mari-Tere; José Baviera (Alfredo Flores); José María Linares Rivas (Eduardo); Fernando Freire de Andrade ('El

Aguila'); Luis de Heredia ('El Lentes'); Carlos del Pozo (Don Ramón); Manuel Arbó (Cintohio Reyes); Emilio Portes (Editor); Raúl Cancio (The drug addict); Pablo Hidalgo; Juan de las Heras; Luis Ardenillo; Francisco René. 80 minutes. Black and white.
Filmed at Ballestros Studios, Madrid.

1936 *Centinela alerta!*
Spain.
Production: Filmófono, Ricardo Urgoiti, Spain.
Executive producer and supervisor: Luis Buñuel.
Directors: Jean Grémillon (uncredited), Luis Buñuel (uncredited).
Dialogue director: Eduardo Ugarte.
Script: Eduardo Ugarte and Luis Buñuel, based on the comedy *La alegría del batallón*, by Carlos Arniches.
Photography: José Maria Beltrán.
Editor: Jean Grémillon.
Music: Fernando Remacha and Daniel Montero (song lyrics).
Sound: León Lucas de Lapeña.
Leading Players: Angelillo; Ana María Custodio; Luis Heredia; Mari-Tere; José María Linares Rivas; Raúl Cancio; Mary Cortés; Pablo Hidalgo; Emilio Portes; Pablo Alvarez Rubio; Mario Padreco.
Luis Buñuel and Eduardo Ugarte dub the voices of two peasants.
90 minutes. Black and white.
Filmed at the Roptence Studios, Madrid.

1937 *Espagne 1937/España leal en armas!*
France/Spain.
Production: Ciné-Liberté, Paris.
Supervision and assembly of material: Luis Buñuel.
Commentary: Pierre Unik and Luis Buñuel, read by Gaston Modot.
Photography: Roman Karmen, Manuel Villegas Lopez and an unnamed Spanish cameraman.
Editor: Jean Paul Dreyfus (Jean-Paul le Chanois).
Music: Beethoven's 7th and 8th Symphonies, selected by Luis Buñuel.
40 minutes. Black and white.

1938 *Cargo of Innocence.* The first of two films on the war in Spain which Buñuel was to have supervised. *Cargo of Innocence* was initiated, but the whole project was abandoned on account of the turn of events in Spain.

1938 *La Duquesa de Alba y Goya* (Project)

1939 *Triumph of the Will*
U.S.A.
Production: Museum of Modern Art, New York.
Producer: Kenneth MacGowan.
Direction, montage and commentary: Luis Buñuel.
A nine-reel montage made up from material from Leni Riefenstahl's 12-reel

The Triumph of the Will (1936) and Hans Bertram's 12-reel *Baptism of Fire* (1939).

1939–43   Supervisor of dubbing, translation and adaptation for Spanish–American versions of documentaries at the Museum of Modern Art. Among versions known to have been supervised by Buñuel are:
Los Pasaros No Conocen Fronteras (*High Over the Border*)
Producer: John Grierson.
Director/photography: John Fernhout.
El Vaticano de Pio XII (*The History of the Vatican*)
U.S.A.
Production: Louis de Rochemont, *The March of Time.*
Editor: Lothar Wolff.

1942   Commentator for U.S. Army Intelligence films.

1944   *The Sewer of Los Angeles* (Project for a Surrealist film)
Scenario: Man Ray, Luis Buñuel.

1944–45   Dubbing director for Warner Brothers, Hollywood.

1945   *The Beast With Five Fingers*
U.S.A.
Production: Warner Brothers.
Director: Robert Florey.
One sequence planned by Luis Buñuel.

1946   *Ilegible, hijo de Flauta* (Project)
This was to be a medium-length Surrealist sound film, based on a novel by Juan Larrea.
Scenario: Juan Larrea, Luis Buñuel.

1946   *La Casa de Bernarda Alba* (Project)
Based on a play by García Lorca.

1946   *Gran Casino* (*Tampico*)
Mexico.
Production: Ultramar Films. Anahuac. Oscar Dancigers.
Director: Luis Buñuel.
Script: Mauricio Magdaleno, Edmundo Baez, based on a story by Michel Weber.
Dialogue: Javier Mateos.
Photography: Jack Draper.
Editor: Gloria Schoemann.
Art Director: Javier Torres Torija.
Music: Manuel Esperón. Songs: 'Dueño de mi amor' by Manuel Esperón; 'Adiós, Pampa mia' by Francisco Canaro and Mariano Mores; 'El Choclo' by A. G. Villoldo; 'El reflector del amor' by Francisco Alonso; 'La Norteña' by F. Vigil.

Sound: Javier Mateos, José de Pérez.
Assistant director: Moisés Delgado.
Leading Players: Libertad Lamarque (Mercedes Irigoyen); Jorge Negrete (Gerardo Ramírez); Mercedes Barba (Camelia); Agustín Isunza (Heriberto); Francisco Jambrina (José Enrique); Charles Rooner (Van Eckerman); Julio Villareal (Demetrio García); Alfonso Bedoya (El Rayado); Fernanda Albany (Nanette); Berta Lenar (Raquel); el Trio Calaveras; José Baviera (Fabio); Ignacio Peón; Julio Ahuet; Juan García.
85 minutes. Black and white.
Filmed at Clasa Studios.

1949   *El gran calavera*
Mexico.
Production: Ultramar Films. Fernando Soler and Oscar Dancigers.
Director: Luis Buñuel.
Script: Luis Alcoriza and Raquel Rojas, based on the novel by Adolfo Torrado.
Photography: Ezequiel Carrasco.
Editor: Carlos Savage.
Art directors: Luis Moya, Dario Cabañas.
Music: Manuel Esperón.
Sound: Rafael Ruiz Esparza.
Assistant director: Moisés Delgado.
Leading Players: Fernando Soler (Don Ramiro); Rosario Granados (Virginia); Rubén Rojo (Pablo); Gustavo Rojo (Eduardo); Maruja Grifell (Milagros); Andrés Soler (Ladislao); Francisco Jambrina (Gregorio); Luis Alcoriza (Alfredo); Antonio Bravo (Alfonso); Antonio Monsell (Juan, the butler); Nicolás Rodríguez (Carmelito); María Luisa Serrano; Juan Pulido; Pepe Martínez; José Chávez; Gerardo Pérez Martínez.
90 minutes. Black and white.
Filmed at Tepeyec Studios.

1950   *Los Olvidados*
Mexico.
Production: Ultramar Films, Oscar Dancigers.
Director: Luis Buñuel.
Script: Luis Buñuel, Luis Alcoriza.
Photography: Gabriel Figueroa.
Editor: Carlos Savage.
Art Directors: Edward Fitzgerald, W. W. Claridge.
Music: Rodolfo Halffter; themes by Gustavo Pittaluga.
Sound: José B. Carles (RCA).
Assistant Director: Ignacio Villarreal.
Leading Players: Alfonso Mejía (Pedro); Estella India (Pedro's mother); Miguel Inclán (Blind man); Roberto Cobo (Jaibo); Alma Delia Fuentes (Meche); Francisco Jambrina (Reform School Director); Angel Merino (Director's assistant); Efrain Arauz (Pockface); Javier Amézcua (Julián);

293

Mario Ramírez (Ojitos); Héctor López Portillo (Judge); Salvador Quiroz (Blacksmith); Victor Manuel Mendoza; Jesús Navarro (Julian's father); Diana Ochoa (Cacarizo's mother); Charles Rooner (Pederast); Sergio Villareal; Jorge Pérez; Juan Villegas (Cacarizo's grandfather); Daniel Corona (Boy); Roberto Navarrete (Boy); Antonio Martínez (Chamaquito); Ramón Martínez (Nacho, Pedro's brother); Antulio Jiminez Pons (Chicharronero); Humberto Mosti (Corrigendo); Juan Domínguez (Corrigendo); José Moreno Fuentes (Policeman). Filmed at Tepeyec Studios.

Cannes, 1951: Official Jury prize for best direction; FIPRESCI award in recognition of Buñuel's total work. Mexican 'Arieles' award for script, adaptation and direction.

1950   *Susana (Demonio y Carne)*
Mexico.
Production: Sergio Kogan. Internacional Cinematográfica, S.A. Manuel Reachi, Mexico.
Director: Luis Buñuel.
Script: Luis Buñuel, Jaime Salvador. Based on a story by Manuel Reachi.
Dialogue: Rodolfo Usigli.
Photography: José Ortiz Ramos.
Editor: Jorge Bustos.
Art Director: Gunther Gerzso.
Music: Raúl Lavista.
Sound: Nicolás de la Rosa (RCA).
Assistant director: Ignacio Villarreal.
Leading Players: Rosita Quintana (Susana); Victor Manuel Mendoza (Jésus); Fernando Soler (Don Guadelupe); María Gentil Arcos (Felíza); Luis López Somoza (Alberto); Matilde Paláu (Doña Carmen).
82 minutes. Black and white.
Filmed at Churubusco Studios.

1951   *La hija del engaño (Don Quintín el amargao)*
Mexico.
Production: Oscar Dancigers. Ultramar Films.
Director: Luis Buñuel.
Script: Raquel Rojas de Alcoriza, Luis Alcoriza. Based on the comedy by Carlos Arniches and José Estremera.
A remake of the 1935 film *Don Quintín el amargao*
Photography: José Ortiz Ramos.
Editor: Carlos Savage.
Art Director: Edward Fitzgerald.
Music: Manuel Esperón. Songs: 'Amorcito Corazón'; 'Jugando, mamá, Jugando'.
Sound: Eduardo Arjona.
Assistant director: Mario Llorca.
Leading Players: Fernando Soler (Don Quintín); Rubén Rojo (Paco); Alicia Caro (Marta); Nacho Contla (Jonrón); Fernando Soto (Mantequilla); Lili Aclemar (Jovita); Amparo Garrido (Maria); Alvaro Matute (Julio); Roberto Meyer (Lencho Garcia); Conchita Gentil Arcos (Toña).

80 minutes. Black and white.
Filmed at Tepeyec Studios.

1951   *Cuando los hijos nos juzgan (Una mujer sin amor)*
Mexico.
Production: Sergio Kogan and Oscar Dancigers. Internacional Cinematográfica.
Director: Luis Buñuel.
Script: Jaime Salvador. Based on the novel *Pierre et Jean* by Guy de Maupassant.
Photography: Raúl Martinez Solares.
Editor: Jorge Bustos.
Art Director: Gunther Gerzso.
Music: Raúl Lavista.
Sound: Rodolfo Benítez.
Assistant director: Mario Llorca.
Leading Players: Julio Villareal (Don Carlos Montero); Rosario Granados (Rosario); Tito Junco (Julio Mistral); Xavier Loyá (Miguel); Joaquín Cordero (Carlos); Jaime Colpe Jr. (Carlitos); Elda Peralta (Luisa); Miguel Manzano; Eva Calvo.
Black and white.
Filmed at Churubusco Studios.

1951   *Subida al cielo*
Mexico.
Production: Isla Films. Manuel Altolaguirre and María L. Gómez Mena.
Director: Luis Buñuel.
Script: Luis Buñuel, from a story by Manuel Altolaguirre and Juan de la Cabada.
Dialogue: Juan de la Cabada.
Photography: Alex Phillips.
Editor: Rafael Portillo.
Art Directors: Edward Fitzgerald and José Rodriguez Granada.
Music: Gustavo Pittaluga. Song: 'La Sanmarqueña' by Agustín Jiménez.
Sound: Eduardo Arjona.
Assistant Director: Jorge López Portillo.
Leading Players: Lidia Prado (Raquel); Esteban Márquez (Oliverio); Carmen González (Albina); Leonor Gómez (Mama); Luis Acevez Castañeda (Silvestre); Pitouto (Peg Leg); Manuel Dondé (Don Eladio); Roberto Cobo (Juan); Roberto Meyer (Don Nemesio Alvarez y Villalbazo); Beatriz Ramos (Expectant mother); Pedro Ibarra (Don Remigio); Manuel Noriega; P. V. de Orellana; Paula Rendón (Silvestre's mother); Chel López; Silvia Castro; Víctor Pérez (Felipe); Gilberto González (Sánchez Coello); Paz Villegas (Doña Ester); Pedro Elviro (El Cojo); Francisco Reiguera (Miguel Suárez); Leonor Gómez (Doña Linda).
85 minutes. Black and white.
Filmed at Tepeyac Studios.
Prize for best *avant-garde* film, Paris, 1952.
FIPRESCI Prize, Cannes Film Festival 1952.
Mexican 'Ariel' Prize for Direction.

1952	*El Cadillac* (Project)
	Production: George Pepper.
	Script: Luis Buñuel, Hugo Butler.

1952   *El Bruto*
Mexico.
Production: Oscar Dancigers. Internacional Cinematográfica.
Director: Luis Buñuel.
Script: Luis Buñuel and Luis Alcoriza.
Photography: Agustín Jiménez.
Editor: Jorge Bustos.
Art Director: Gunther Gerzso.
Music: Raúl Lavista.
Sound: Javier Mateos.
Assistant Director: Ignacio Villarreal.
Leading Players: Katy Jurado (Paloma); Pedro Armendariz (Pedro); Andrés Soler (Cabrera); Rosita Arenas (Meche); Roberto Meyer; Beatriz Ramos; Paco Martínez; Gloria Mestre.
83 minutes. Black and white.
Filmed at Churubusco Studios.

1952   *Las aventuras de Robinson Crusoe* (*Adventures of Robinson Crusoe*)
Mexico/U.S.A.
Production: Oscar Dancigers, Henry F. Ehrlich. Ultramar Films OLMEC/- United Artists.
Director: Luis Buñuel.
Script: Luis Buñuel and Mozo (pseudonym for Hugo Butler), after Daniel Defoe.
Photography: Alex Phillips.
Colour: Pathécolor.
Editors: Carlos Savage, Alberto Valenzuela.
Art Director: Edward Fitzgerald.
Music: Anthony Collins, Luis Hernández Breton.
Sound: Javier Mateos, Jesus Gonzalez Gonzalez.
Assistant Director: Ignacio Villarreal.
Leading Players: Dan O'Herlihy (Robinson Crusoe); Jaime Fernández (Man Friday); Felipe Alba (Captain Oberzo); José Chávez (Mutineer); Emilio Garibay (Mutineer); Chel López (Bosun).
89 minutes. Colour.
Filmed at Tepeyac Studios and at Manzanillo and Chapultepec.
Mexican 'Ariel' for Direction, 1955.
Special mention at Punta del Este Festival.
Prize of *Parents* magazine, New York.

1952   *El*
Mexico.
Production: Oscar Dancigers. Nacional Films.
Director: Luis Buñuel.
Script: Luis Buñuel and Luis Alcoriza, based on the novel by Mercedes Pinto.

Photography: Gabriel Figueroa.
Editors: Carlos Savage, Alberto Valenzuela.
Art Directors: Edward Fitzgerald, Pedro Galvan.
Music: Luis Hernández Bretón.
Sound: Jose D. Pérez, Jesus Gonzalez Gonzalez.
Assistant Director: Ignacio Villarreal.
Leading Players: Arturo de Córdova (Francisco); Delia Garcés (Gloria); Luis Beristáin (Raúl); José Pidal; Aurora Walker (Doña Esperanza); Carlos Martinez Baena (Father Velasco); Manuel Donde (Pablo); Fernando Casanova (Beltrán); Rafael Banquells (Ricardo); Roberto Meyer.
100 minutes. Black and white.
Filmed at Tepeyac Studios.
FIAF Prize, Basilea.

1953   *Abismos de pasión (Cumbres borrascoses)*
Mexico.
Production: Oscar Dancigers, Abelardo Rodríguez.
Director: Luis Buñuel.
Script: Luis Buñuel, Pierre Unik, after *Wuthering Heights* by Emily Brontë.
Adaptation: Luis Buñuel, Julio Alejandro, Arduino Mauvri.
Photography: Agustín Jiménez, Sergio Vejar.
Editor: Carlos Savage.
Art Directors: Edward Fitzgerald, Raymundo Ortiz.
Costumes: Armando Valdes Peza.
Music: Raúl Lavista, adapted from Wagner's *Tristan and Isolde*.
Sound: Eduardo Arjona, Galindo Samperio.
Assistant Director: Ignacio Villarreal.
Leading Players: Jorge Mistral (Alejandro); Irasema Dilian (Catarina); Lilia Prado (Isabel); Ernesto Alonso (Eduardo); Luis Aceves Castañeda (Ricardo); Francisco Regueira; Hortensia Santoveña; Jaime Gonzalez.
90 minutes. Black and white.
Filmed at Tepeyac Studios.

1953   *La ilusión viaja en tranvía*
Mexico.
Production: Armando Orive Alba. Clasa Films Mundiales.
Director: Luis Buñuel.
Script: Luis Buñuel, Luis Alcoriza, José Revueltas, Mauricio de la Serna, based on a story by Mauricio de la Serna.
Photography: Raúl Martínez Solares.
Editor: Jorge Bustos.
Art Director: Edward Fitzgerald.
Music: Luis Hernández Bretón.
Sound: José D. Pérez.
Assistant director: Ignacio Villarreal.
Leading Players: Lilia Prado (Lupa); Carlos Navarro (Caireles); Agustín Isunza (Papa Pinillos); Miguel Manzano; Javier de la Parra; Guillermo Bravo Sosa; Felipe Montoyo; Fernando Soto; Domingo Soler (Tarrajas); José

Fidas; Pal Villegas; Conchita Gentil; Diana Ochea; Victor Alcover.
90 minutes. Black and white.
Filmed at Clasa Studios.

1954   *El rio y la muerte*
Mexico.
Production: Armando Orive Alba. Clasa Films Mundiales.
Director: Luis Buñuel.
Script: Luis Buñuel, Luis Alcoriza, based on *Muro blanco sobre roca negra* by
Lic. Miguel Alcarez Acosta.
Photography: Raúl Martínez Solares.
Editor: Jorge Bustos.
Art Directors: Gunther Gerzso, Edward Fitzgerald.
Music: Raúl Lavista.
Sound: Jose D. Pérez.
Assistant director: Ignacio Villarreal.
Leading Players: Columba Domínguez (Mercedes); Miguel Torruco (Felipe
Anguiano); Joaquín Cordero (Gerardo Anguiano); Jaime Fernández (Rómulo
Menchaca); Victor Alcover (Polo); Silvia Derbez (Elsa); Huberto Almazón
(Crescencio); Carlos Martínez Baena; Alfredo Varela Jr. (Chinelas); Fernando
Soto; Mantequilla; Jose Elías Moreno; Miguel Manzona; Manuel Donde;
Jorge Arriaga; Roberto Meyer; Chel López; José Muñoz.
90 minutes. Black and white.
Filmed at Clasa Studios.

1955   *Ensayo de un crimen* (*La Vida Criminal de Archibaldo de La Cruz*)
Mexico.
Production: Alfonso Patiño Gómez, Alianza Cinematografica ACSA.
Director: Luis Buñuel.
Script: Luis Buñuel, Eduardo Ugarte Pagés, from the novel by Rodolfo
Usigli.
Photography: Agustín Jiménez.
Editor: Jorge Bustos, Pablo Gómez.
Art Director: Jesús Brácho.
Music: Jorge Pérez Herrera.
Sound: Rodolfo Benítez.
Assistant Director: Luis Abbadie.
Leading Players: Miroslava Stern (Lavinia); Ernesto Alonso (Archibaldo);
Ariadna Welter (Carlota Cervantes); Rita Macedo (Patricia); José María
Linares Rivas (Willy Corduran); Andréa Palma (Señora Cervantes); Rodolfo
Landa (Alejandro Rivas); Leonor Llausás (Archibaldo's governess); Eva Calvo
(Archibaldo's mother); Enrique Indiano; Carlos Riquelme (Chief of Police);
Chabela Durán; Carlos Martínez Buena (Priest); Manuel Donde (An Officer);
Armando Velasco; Roberto Meyer; Rafael Banquells; Rodolfo Acosta;
Antonio Bravo Sanchez (Antique shop man).
91 minutes. Black and white.
Filmed at Clasa Studios.

1955 *Cela s'appelle l'Aurore*
France/Italy.
Production: Film Marceau (France), Laetitia Films and Insignia Films (Italy).
Director: Luis Buñuel.
Script: Luis Buñuel, Jean Ferry, based on the novel by Emmanuel Robles.
Photography: Robert Le Febvre.
Operator: Roger Delpuech; assistants: G. Sarthre, G. Muller.
Editor: Marguerite Renoir.
Art Director: Max Douy; assistants: J. Doiy, Jacques André.
Music: Joseph Kosma.
Sound: Antoine Petitjean.
Director of Production: André Cultet.
Assistant directors: Marcel Camus, Jacques Deray.
Leading Players: Georges Marchal (Dr Valerio); Lucia Bosè (Clara); Nelly Borgeaud (Angela); Gianni Esposito (Sandro); Julien Bertheau (Commissioner); Jean-Jacques Delbo (Gorzone); Henri Nassiet (Angela's father); Gaston Modot (Corsican peasant); Brigitte Elloy (Magda); Robert Levfort (Pietro); Simone Paris (Mme Gorzone); Pascal Mazotti (Azzopardi); Marcel Peres.
102 minutes. Black and white.
Filmed at Photosonor Studios, Neuilly, 13 August to 14 October 1955.

1956 *La Mort en ce jardin (La muerte en este jardin)*
France/Mexico.
Production: Oscar Dancigers, Producciones Tepeyac (Mexico), David Mage, Dismage (Paris).
Director: Luis Buñuel.
Script: Luis Buñuel, Luis Alcoriza, Raymond Queneau, based on the novel by José-André Lacour.
Dialogue: Gabriel Arout, Raymond Queneau.
Photography: Jorge Stahl Jr.
Colour: Eastman Colour.
Editor: Marguerite Renoir; assistants: Denise Charveain, Alberto E. Valenzuela.
Art Director: Edward Fitzgerald.
Music: Paul Misraki.
Sound: José D. Pérez.
Assistant directors: Dossia Mage, Ignacio Villarreal.
Leading Players: Georges Marchal (Chark); Simone Signoret (Gin); Charles Vanel (Castin); Michèle Girardon (Maria); Michel Piccoli (Father Lizzardi); Tito Junco (Chenko); Raúl Ramírez (Alvaro); Luis Aceves Casteñeda (Alberto); Jorge Martinez de Hoyos (Capt. Ferrero); Alberto Pedret (Lieutenant); Stefani; Marc Lambert (1st worker); Alia del Lago (2nd worker).
97 minutes. Colour.

1957 *La Femme et le pantin* (Project)
Based on the novel by Pierre Louys.
The film was eventually made by Julien Duvivier (1959).

1957   *Thérèse Etienne* (Project)
Based on the novel by Joseph Knittel.

1957   *Lord of the Flies* (Project)
Based on the novel by William Golding.
The subject was filmed in 1963 by Peter Brook.

1957   *Los Náufragos de la calle Providencia* (Project)
From a Surrealist script originally written in 1952–54, and eventually filmed in 1962 as *El ángel exterminador.*

1958   *Nazarín*
Mexico.
Production: Manuel Barbachano Ponce. Producciones Barbachano Ponce.
Director: Luis Buñuel.
Script: Luis Buñuel, Julio Alejandro, from the novel by Benito Pérez Galdós.
Dialogue: Emilio Carballido.
Photography: Gabriel Figueroa.
Operator: Ignacio Rovero; assistant: Pablo Rioj.
Editor: Carlos Savage.
Art Director: Edward Fitzgerald.
Costumes: Georgette Somopano.
Sound: José Pérez; engineer: James L. Field.
Assistant Directors: Ignacio Villarreal, Juan Luis Buñuel.
Executive producer: Federico Amerigao.
Production Adviser: Carlos Velo.
Leading Players: Francisco Rabal (Nazarín); Marga López (Beatriz); Rita Macedo (Andara); Ignacio López Tarso (Church thief); Ofelia Guilmain (Chanfa); Luis Aceves Castañeda (Parricide); Noé Murayama (El Pinto); Rosenda Monteros (La Prieta); Jesús Fernández (Ujo, the dwarf); Aurora Molina; Pilar Pellicer; Antonio Bravo; Edmundo Barbero; Raúl Dantés; Ada Callasio; David Reinoso.
94 minutes. Black and white.
Filmed at the Churubusco Studios.
Palme d'or, Cannes Film Festival 1959
André Bazin Prize, Acapulco Festival 1959 and numerous other awards.

1959   *Los Seres Queridos* (*The Loved One*) (Project)
Mexico/U.S.A.
Production: OLMEC.
Director: Luis Buñuel.
Script: Luis Buñuel and Hugo Butler, from the novel by Evelyn Waugh.
The cast was planned to include Alec Guinness.

1959   *La Fièvre monte à El Pao* (*Los Ambiciosos*)
France/Mexico.
Production: Raymond Borderie. Groupe des Quatre. Cinematografica Filmex.
Director: Luis Buñuel.

Script: Luis Buñuel, Luis Alcoriza, Charles Dorat, Louis Sapin, Henri Castillou, based on the novel by Henri Castillou.
Dialogue: Louis Sapin, José L. González de Léon.
Photography: Gabriel Figueroa, Ignacio Romero.
Editors: James Cuenet, Rafael López Ceballos.
Art Directors: Jorge Fernández, Pablo Galván.
Music: Paul Misraki.
Sound: William Robert Sivel, Enrique Rodríguez, Roberto Camecho.
Assistant Director: Ignacio Villarreal.
Director of Production: Charles Borderie.
Leading Players: Gérard Philipe (Ramón Vásquez); Maria Félix (Inés Vargas); Jean Servais (Alejandro Gual); Miguel Angel Ferriz (Vargas); Raúl Dantés (García); Domingo Soler (Prof. Gardenas); Tito Junco (Inclarte); Roberto Cañedo (Olivares); Andrés Soler; Luis Aceves Castañeda (López); Augusto Benedito; Miguel Arenas; David Reynoso; Antonio Bravo; Armando Acosta; Enrique Lucero; Alberto Pedret; José Chavez; Francisco Jambrina; José Muñoz.
97 minutes. Black and white.

1959   *Beau Clown* (Project)
Script: from the novel by Bert Grimault.

1960   *The Young One* (*La Joven: La Jeune Fille*)
Mexico/U.S.A.
Production: OLMEC (Mexico). George P. Werker (U.S.A.).
Director: Luis Buñuel.
Script: Luis Buñuel and H. B. Addis (Hugo Butler) from the novel 'Travellin' Man' by Peter Matthieson.
Photography: Gabriel Figueroa.
Editor: Carlos Savage.
Art Director: Jesús Bracho.
Music: Jésus Zarzosa. Song: 'Sinner Man' sung by Léon Bibb.
Sound: José B. Carlos, James L. Field, Galdino Samperio.
Assistant directors: Ignacio Villarreal, Juan Luis Buñuel.
Production director: Antonio de Salazar.
Leading Players: Zachary Scott (Miller); Bernie Hamilton (Travers); Kay Meersman (Evvie); Crahan Denton (Jackson); Claudio Brook (Minister).
95 minutes.

1961   *Viridiana*
Spain.
Production: Gustavo Alatriste for UNINCI S.A. and Films 59.
Executive Producer: R. Muñoz Suay.
Director: Luis Buñuel.
Script: Luis Buñuel and Julio Alejandro.
Story: Luis Buñuel.
Photography: José F. Aguayo.
Editor: Pedro del Rey.

Art Director: Francisco Canet.
Music: selected by Gustavo Pittaluga.
Chief of Production: Gustavo Quintana.
Assistant Director: Juan Luis Buñuel.
Leading Players: Francisco Rabal (Jorge); Silvia Pinal (Viridiana); Fernando Rey (Don Jaime); Margarita Lozano (Ramona); Victoria Zinny (Lucia); Teresa Rabal (Rita); José Calvo; Joaquin Roa; Luis Heredia; José Manuel Martin; Lola Gaos; Juan García Tienda; Maruja Isbert; Joaquin Mayol; Palmira Guerra; Sergio Mendizábal; Milagros Tomás; Alicia Jorge Barriga (Beggars).
90 minutes.
Filmed at C.E.A. Studios, Madrid.

1962   *El ángel exterminador*
Mexico/Spain.
Production: Gustavo Alatriste for UNINCI S.A. and Films 59 (Madrid).
Director: Luis Buñuel.
Script: Luis Buñuel and Luis Alcoriza.
Story: Luis Buñuel, based on his play, *Los náufragos de la calle Providencia*.
Photography: Gabriel Figueroa.
Editor: Carlos Savage Jr.
Art Director: Jesús Bracho.
Costumes: Georgette.
Music: Raúl Lavista; Scarlatti, Paradisi.
Sound: José B. Carles.
Assistant director: Ignacio Villareal.
Leading Players: Silvia Pinal (The Valkyrie); José Baviera (Leandro); Augusto Benedico (Doctor); Luis Beristain (Cristian); Antonio Bravo (Russell); Claudio Brook (Majordomo); Cesar del Campo (Colonel); Rosa Elena Durgel (Silvia); Lucy Gallardo (Lucia); Enrique García Alvarez (Señor Roc); Ofelia Guilmain (Juana Avila); Nadia Haro Oliva (Ana Maynar); Tito Junco (Raúl); Xavier Loya (Francisco Avila); Xavier Masse (Eduardo); Angel Merino (Servant); Ofelia Montesco (Beatriz); Patricia Moran (Rita); Patricia de Morelos (Blanca); Bertha Moss (Leonora); Enrique Rambal (Nobile).
95 minutes.
Filmed at the Churubusco Studios.

1963   *Le Journal d'une femme de chambre*
France/Italy.
Production: Serge Silberman and Michel Safra, for Speva Films, Cine-Alliance, Filmsonor (Paris), Dear Film Produzione (Rome).
Executive Producer: Henri Baum.
Director: Luis Buñuel.
Script: Luis Buñuel, Jean-Claude Carrière, from the novel by Octave Mirbeau.
Photography: Roger Fellous (Franscope).
Camera: Adolph Chailet; assistants: Rene Schneider, Agathe Beaumont.
Editor: Louisette Hautecoeur.

Art director: Georges Wakhevitch; assistant: Arlette Lalande.
Music: none.
Sound: Antoine Petitjean, Robert Kambourakis.
Assistant director: Juan Luis Buñuel.
Leading Players: Jeanne Moreau (Celestine); Michel Piccoli (M. Monteil); Georges Géret (Joseph); Françoise Lugagne (Mme Monteil); Daniel Ivernel (Captain Mauger); Jean Ozenne (M. Rabour); Gilberte Géniat (Rose); Bernard Musson (Sacristan); Jean-Claude Carrière (Curé); Muni (Marianne); Claude Jaeger (Judge); Dominique Sauvage (Claire); Madeleine Damien; Geymond Vital; Jean Franval; Marcel Rouzé; Jeanne Pérez; Andrée Tainsy; Françoise Bertin; Pierre Collet; Aline Bertrand; Joelle Bernard; Dominique Zardi; Michelle Daquin; Marcel Le Floch; Marc Eyraud; Gabriel Gobin.
98 minutes.
Filmed at France Studio. Shooting commenced 21 October 1963.

1963   *Llanto por un bandido*
Spain/Italy/France.
Production: Agata Films (Madrid); Atlantica Cinematografica (Rome); Méditerranée Cinéma (Paris).
Director: Carlos Saura.
Script and story: Carlos Saura, Mario Camus.
Photography: Jean Julio Baena.
Art Director: Enrique Alarcón.
Music: Carlo Rustichelli.
Leading Players: Francisco Rabal; Lea Massari; Philippe Leroy; Lino Ventura; Manuel Zarzo; Silvia Soler; Antonio Prieto; and Luis Buñuel in the role of the executioner in the opening sequence.

1964   *Calanda* (Project)
Project for a three-reel film on the Semana Santa in Calanda, a mixture of documentary and childhood memories. No script; two cameramen were to have been employed. The film was eventually made in 1965 by Jean Luis Buñuel as a French production.

1964   *Cuatro Misterios* (Project)
Production: Gustavo Alatriste. Spanish/Mexican co-production.
Script: Luis Buñuel, based on the stories *Aura* by Carlos Fuentes; *Las Ménades* by Julio Cortazar; *La Gradiva* by Jensen; and *Secuestro* by Luis Buñuel.
Director: Luis Buñuel.

1965   *Simón del desierto*
Mexico.
Production: Gustavo Alatriste.
Director: Luis Buñuel.
Script and story: Luis Buñuel and Julio Alejandro, based on a theme from Federico García Lorca.
Photography: Gabriel Figueroa; assistant: Sigfrido García
Editor: Carlos Savage Jr.

Music: Raúl Lavista (Pilgrim's Hymn) and the Semana Santa drums of Calanda.

Sound: James L. Fields.

Assistant director: Ignacio Villarreal.

Leading Players: Claudio Brook (Simón); Silvia Pinal (Temptress); Hortensia Santovana (Mother of Simón); Jesús Fernández (Rabadan the dwarf); Enrique del Castillo (Cripple); Enrique Alvarez Félix (Brother Mathias); Luis Aceves Castañeda (Priest); Francisco Regueira (Priest); Antonio Bravo (Priest); Eduardo MacGregor; Enrique García Alvarez.

Awarded Silver Lion of St Mark and FIPRESCI prize, Venice, 1965.

1965	*Le Moine* (Project)

France.

Director: Luis Buñuel.

Script: Luis Buñuel and Jean-Claude Carrière, based on the novel *The Monk* by Matthew Gregory Lewis.

Intended players: Jeanne Moreau; and in an earlier project of the same subject, Gérard Philipe.

Buñuel's scenario was eventually realized in 1972 by Ado Kyrou, with Franco Nero.

1966	*Belle de Jour*

France.

Production: Paris Film Production, Robert and Raymond Hakim.

Director of Production: Henri Baum.

Director: Luis Buñuel.

Script: Luis Buñuel and Jean-Claude Carrière from the novel by Joseph Kessel.

Photography: Sacha Vierny. Eastman Colour.

Editor: Louisette Taverna.

Art Director: Robert Clavel.

Music: none.

Sound: René Longuet.

Assistant directors: Pierre Lary, Jacques Fraenkel.

Leading Players: Catherine Deneuve (Séverine); Jean Sorel (Pierre); Michel Piccoli (Husson); Geneviève Page (Anaïs); Francisco Rabal (Hyppolite); Pierre Clementi (Marcel); Georges Marchal (The Duke); Françoise Fabian (Charlotte); Maria Latour (Matilde); Francis Blanche (M. Adolphe); François Maistre (The Professor); Bernard Fresson (The pock-marked man); Macha Méril (Renée); Muni (Pallas); Dominique Dandrieux (Catherine); Brigitte Parmentier (Séverine as a child); Michel Charrel (Footman); D. de Roseville (Coachman); Iska Khan (The Asiatic client); Marcel Eharvey (Professor Henri); Pierre Marcay (Doctor); Adelaide Blasquez (Maid); Marc Eyraud (Bartender); Bernard Musson (Butler); Claude Cerval.

100 minutes.

Shooting commenced 10 October 1966.

Golden Lion of St Mark and UNICRIT prize, Venice Festival 1967.

1967   *Luis Buñuel*
France.
Production: Radio-Télévision Française.
Director: André S. Labarthe.
With Luis Buñuel interviewed by Georges Sadoul.
Film of reportage and homage to the film-maker.

1969   *La Voie Lactée (La Via Lattea)*
France.
Production: Serge Silberman, Greenwich Films Production (Paris)/Fraia Film (Rome).
Director: Luis Buñuel.
Script: Luis Buñuel and Jean-Claude Carrière.
Photography: Christian Matras. Eastman Colour.
Editor: Louisette Hautecoeur.
Art Director: Pierre Guffroy; assistant: Pierre Cadiou.
Costumes: Jacqueline Goyot.
Music: selected by Luis Buñuel.
Sound: Jacques Gallois; montage: Dominique Amy.
Assistant director: Pierre Lary.
Leading Players: Paul Frankeur (Pierre); Laurent Terzieff (Jean); Alain Cuny (Man in cape); Edith Scob (Virgin Mary); Bernard Verley (Jesus); François Maistre (French priest); Claude Cerval (Brigadier); Muni (Mother Superior); Julien Bertheau (M. Richard); Ellen Bahl (Mme Garnier); Michel Piccoli (The Marquis); Michel Etcheverry (Inquisitor); Agnès Capri (Teacher); Pierre Clémenti (Devil); Georges Marchal (The Jesuit); Jean Piat (The Jansenist); Denis Manuel (Rodolphe); Daniel Pilon (François); Claudio Brook (The Bishop); Julien Guiolar (Spanish priest); Marcel Pérès (The Posadero): Delphine Seyrig (Prostitute); Jean-Claude Carrière (Priscillian); Augusta Carrière (French nun); Jean-Daniel Ehrmann (Condemned man); Pierre Lary (Young monk); Bernard Musson (Innkeeper); Michel Dacquin (M. Garnier); Gabriel Gobin (Father); Pierre Maguelon (Civil Guard Corporal); Marius Laurey (Second blind man); Jean Clarieux (Apostle Peter); Christian Van Cau (Apostle Andrew); Claudine Berg (Mother); Christine Simon (Thérèse).
102 minutes (English release version, 98 minutes).
Shooting commenced 10 October 1966. Verona Studios S.A. Madrid.

1970   *Tristana*
Spain/France/Italy.
Production: Epoca Films, S.A. and Taliá S.A. (Madrid)/Films Corona (Paris)/ Selenia Cinematografica (Rome).
Director: Luis Buñuel.
Script: Luis Buñuel and Julio Alejandro, from the novel by Benito Pérez Galdós.
Photography: José F. Aguayo. Eastman Colour.
Editor: Pedro del Rey.
Art Director: Enrique Alarcón.
Music: none.

Sound: José Nogueira.
Assistant directors: José Puyol, Pierre Lary.
Leading Players: Catherine Deneuve (Tristana); Fernando Rey (Don Lope);
Franco Nero (Horacio); Jesús Fernández (Saturno); Lola Gaos (Saturna);
Vicente Solder (Don Ambrosio); Antonio Casas (Don Cosme); José Calvo
(Bellringer); Fernando Cabrian (Dr Miquis); Cándida Losada (Bourgeois lady);
Maria Paz Pondal (Girl); Juan José Menéndez (Don Cándido); Sergio
Mendizábal (Professor); Antonio Ferrándis; José Maria Caffarel; Joaquim
Pamplona.
105 minutes (English release version 98 minutes).
Shooting commenced October 1969.

1972   *Le Charme discret de la bourgeoisie*
France.
Production: Greenwich Productions.
Director: Luis Buñuel.
Script: Luis Buñuel, Jean-Claude Carrière.
Photography: Edmond Richard. Eastman Colour.
Editor: Hélène Plemiannikov.
Art Director: Pierre Guffroy.
Music: none.
Leading Players: Fernando Rey (Ambassador); Delphine Seyrig (Simone
Thévenot); Stéphane Audran (Alice Sénéchal); Jean-Pierre Cassel (Sénéchal);
Paul Frankeur (Thévenot); Claude Piéplu (Colonel); Bulle Ogier (Florence);
Julien Bertheau (Bishop); Michel Piccoli (Minister); Muni (Peasant); Milena
Vukotic.
105 minutes.
Shooting commenced 23 May 1972.

1973   *La Chute d'un Corps*
Production: Georges Casati, Albina Production.
France – long film.
Director: Michel Polac.
Actors: Fernando Rey, etc. – and Luis Buñuel as extra.

1974   *Le Fantôme de la Liberté* (*Fantasm of Liberty*)
Co-producers: Serge Silberman (France). 20th Century Fox (U.S.A.).
Story and Director: Luis Buñuel
Script: Luis Buñuel and J. L. Carrière

Bibliography

This selection of books and articles is based, with additions, upon the Bibliography compiled by the Information Department and Book Library of the British Film Institute.

Books

Aranda, J. Francisco *Luis Buñuel: Biografia Critica*. Madrid, Editorial Lumen, 1969. 424 pp. plates. bibliog. filmog.

Bazin, André: Los olvidados. In *Qu'est ce que le cinéma? vol. 3*. Paris, Editions du Cerf, 1961 (pp. 22–28).

Bellone, Julius (ed.): The devil and the nun: Viridiana, by Andrew Sarris. In *Renaissance of the film*. New York, Macmillan Co.: London, Collier-Macmillan, 1970 (pp. 330–339). Reprinted from *Movie* no. 1.

Brunius, Jacques: Quatrième période. In *En marge du cinéma français*. Paris, Arcanes, 1954 (pp. 134–143).

Buache, Freddy *Luis Buñuel*. Lyon, Serdoc, 1964. 126 pp. plates. bibliog. filmog. (Premier Plan no. 33).

Buache, Freddy *Luis Buñuel*. Lausanne, La Cité, 1970. 209 pp. plates. bibliog. filmog.

Buache, Freddy *The Cinema of Luis Buñuel*. trs. Peter Graham. London/N.Y. Tantivy/Barnes. 208 pp. plates. filmog.

Durgnat, Raymond *Luis Buñuel.* Studio Vista, 2nd edn. 1968. 152 pp. photos. bibliog. filmog. (Movie Paperbacks).

Esteve, Michel (ed.) *Luis Buñuel.* Paris, Lettres Modernes, 1962–63. 2 vols. plates. bibliog. filmog. (Etudes Cinématographiques nos. 20/21, 22/23).

Esteve, Michel: 'Nazarin et Le journal d'un curé de campagne: la Passion refusée et acceptée.' In *La Passion du Christ comme thème cinématographique.* Paris, Lettres Modernes, 1961 (pp. 217–234).

Farber, Manny: Luis Buñuel. In *Negative space: Manny Farber of the movies.* London, Studio Vista, 1971 (pp. 275–281).

Goetz, Alice, and Banz, Helmut W. *Luis Buñuel: eine dokumentation.* Verband der Deutschen Filmclubs e.V. 1965. 142, 127, 27 pp. bibliog. filmog.

Grange, Frèdèric, and Rebolledo, Charles *Luis Buñuel.* Paris, Editions Universitaires, 1964. 189 pp. bibliog. filmog.

Gregor, Ulrich: Luis Buñuel (interview). In *Wie sie filmen.* Gütersloh, Sigbert Mohn Verlag, 1966 (pp. 88–101).

Haredurt, Peter: 'Luis Buñuel: Spaniard and Surrealist' in *Six European Directors.* London, Penguin, 1974 (pp. 102–134).

Kyrou, Ado *Luis Buñuel.* Paris, Edition Seghers, 1962. 221 pp. plates. bibliog. filmog. (Cinéma d'Aujourd'hui no. 4).

Kyrou, Ado *Luis Buñuel: an Introduction.* New York, Simon and Schuster, 1963.

—— *English translation of Kyrou's* Luis Buñuel.

Kyrou, Ado: Luis Buñuel. In *Le surréalisme au cinéma.* Paris, Le Terrain Vague, 2nd edn. 1963 (pp. 207–268).

Lennig, Arthur (ed.): Los olvidados, by R. C. Dale [and] Viridiana, by Frederick J. Hoffman. In *Classics of the film.* Madison, Wisconsin Film Society, 1965 (pp. 188–199).

Lizalde, Eduardo *Luis Buñuel: odisea del demoledor.* Mexico, Universidad Autónoma de Mexico, 1962. 50 pp. plates. filmog. (Cuadernos de cine no. 2).

Lovell, Alan: Luis Buñuel. In *Anarchist cinema.* London. Peace News, 1964 (pp. 18–28).

Mainds, Roger (ed.): Viridiana, by Ian McD. Rowe. In *Screen education yearbook, 1968.* London, Society for Education in Film and Television, 1967. pp. 139–143.

Matthews, J. H. *Surrealism and Film.* University of Michigan Press, 1971, passim.

Mauriac, Claude: Luis Buñuel. In *L'amour du cinéma.* Paris, Editions Albin Michel, 1954 (pp. 58–65).

—— Luis Buñuel. In *Petite littérature du cinéma.* Paris, Editions du Cerf, 1957 (pp. 75–85).

Moullet, Luc *Luis Buñuel.* Brussels, Club Livre de Cinéma, 1957. 16 pp. (Les grands créateurs du cinéma no. 5).

Sarris, Andrew (ed.): Luis Buñuel. In *Interviews with film directors.* New York, Bobbs-Merrill, 1967 (pp. 45–50). Material reprinted from *Movie* no. 1 and *Film Culture* no. 24.

Taylor, John Russell: Luis Buñuel. In *Cinema eye, cinema ear*. Methuen, 1964 (pp. 82–114. bibliog. filmog.).

Whannel, Paddy, and Harcourt, Peter (ed.): Los olvidados, by Albert Hunt. In *Film teaching*. BFI Education Department, 1964 (pp. 64–71).

Periodical Articles

Anarchy, no. 6, Aug. 1961, pp. 183–189.
Rufus Seger – Luis Buñuel: reality & illusion.
Tristam Shandy – Another look at Buñuel: the tragic eye.
Cahiers du Cinema, no. 7, Dec. 1951, pp. 6–23, 52–54.
Pierre Kast – Une fonction de constat: notes sur l'oeuvre de Buñuel.
Pierre Kast – A la recherche de Luis Buñuel.
Jacques Doniol-Valcroze – Par dela la victime (*Los Olvidados*).
—— no. 36, June 1954, pp. 2–14.
Jacques Doniol-Valcroze and André Bazin – Entretien avec Luis Buñuel.
—— no. 37, July 1954, pp. 44–48.
Michel Dorsday – Du révolutionnaire au moraliste (*El*).
Jacques Doniol-Valcroze – Post-scriptum sur *El*.
—— no. 56, Feb. 1956, pp. 18–23.
Emmanuel Robles – A Mexico avec Luis Buñuel.
—— no. 63, Oct. 1956, pp. 13–17.
Gabriel Arout – En travaillant avec Luis Buñuel.
—— no. 76, Nov. 1957, pp. 53–55.
Philippe Demonsablon – Verdoux réconcilé (*Ensayo de un crimen*).
—— no. 93, March 1959, pp. 27–32.
J-F. Aranda – La passion selon Buñuel (*Nazarín*).
—— no. 115, Jan. 1961, pp. 46–49.
André S. Labarthe – Un désespoir actif (*Nazarín*).
—— no. 120, June 1961, pp. 41–42.
Jean Douchet – *Viridiana*.
—— no. 127, Jan. 1962, pp. 48–51.
Michel Mardore – L'envers des Fiorettis (*Viridiana*).
—— no. 176, March 1966, pp. 33–40.
Jean-André Fieschi – L'ange et la bête: croquis mexicains de Luis Buñuel. Translation in *Cahiers du Cinema in English*, no. 4.
—— no. 191, June 1967, pp. 13–24, 70–71.
J. Cobos and G. S. de Erice – Entretien avec Luis Buñuel.
Jean-André Fieschi – La fin ouverte (*Belle de Jour*).
Jean-Louis Comolli – Un catéchisme travesti (*Belle de Jour*).
—— no. 223, Aug/Sept. 1970, pp. 5–28.
Series of articles on *Tristana*.
Luis Buñuel – Textes 1927–28.
Buñuel's critical writing included in Aranda – Luis Buñuel, and translated from *Griffith* no. 1.

Cahiers du Cinema in English, no. 4, 1966, pp. 19–25.
Jean-André Fieschi – The angel and the beast: Luis Buñuel's Mexican Sketches.
From *Cahiers du Cinéma*, no. 176, March 1966.
Cinema 3, no. 2, June 1970, pp. 47–56; no. 3, Sept. 1970, pp. 21–30; no. 4.
Hamid Benani – L'ambiguité dans l'oeuvre de Buñuel.
Cinema 56, no. 13, Dec. 1956, pp. 8–12.
J. Trebouta – Une scandaleuse tendresse.
Cinema 57, no. 22, Nov. 1957, pp. 107–109.
Jacques Trebouta – *La vie criminelle d'Archibaldo de la Cruz.*
Cinema 57, no. 23, Christmas 1957, pp. 15–31.
J-F. Aranda – Buñuel espagnol. Translated from *Cinéma Universitario.*
Cinema 59, no. 37, June 1959, pp. 70–74.
Luis Buñuel – Poésie et cinéma.
Cinema 61, no. 52, Jan. 1961, pp. 21–30.
Manuel Michel – L'homme sans chaines.
Luis Buñuel – Sur *Nazarín.*
Cinema 62, no. 65, April 1962, pp. 98–100.
Marcel Martin – *Viridiana.*
Cinema 65, no. 94, March 1965, pp. 39–44; no. 95, April 1965, pp. 67–72.
Luis Buñuel: voix off (Interview by Manuel Michel).
Cinema 66, no. 105, April 1966, pp. 25–29.
Buñuel contre son mythe (Interview by Manuel Michel).
Cinema 66, no. 107, June 1966, pp. 96–100.
Guy Braucourt – Cinq inédits de Buñuel.
Cinema 68, no. 123, Feb. 1968, pp. 48–53.
Augusto M. Torres – Luis Buñuel/Glauber Rocha: échos d'une conversation.
Cinemages, no. 1, 1955.
Special Buñuel issue.
Cinemages, v. 2, 1956, Compilation 1955 issue, pp. 6–15.
Gideon Bachmann – Films of Luis Buñuel.
Cinema Universitario, no. 4, Dec. 1956, pp. 7–19.
J-F. Aranda – Buñuel español. Translated in *Cinéma 57*, no. 23.
Film Comment (New York) July–August 1974.
Raymond Durgnat – *La Voie Lactée.*
Film Culture, no. 21, Summer 1960, pp. 41–62.
Luis Buñuel – A Statement.
Emilio Garcia Riera – The Eternal Rebellion of Luis Buñuel.
—— no. 24, Spring 1962, pp. 74–76, 81–82.
Luis Buñuel – On *Viridiana.*
Kenji Kanesaka – Interview with Luis Buñuel.
Emilio Garcia Riera – *Viridiana.*
Translated from *Revista de la Universidad de México.*
—— no. 41, Summer 1966, pp. 60–65.
Kenji Kanesaka – A visit to Luis Buñuel.

Film Heritage, vol. 1 no. 1, Autumn 1965, pp. 25–34.

Robert M. Hammond – Luis Alcoriza and the films of Luis Buñuel.

Film Quarterly, vol. 12 no. 2, Winter 1958, pp. 7–9.

Daniel Aubry and Jean Michel Lacor – Luis Buñuel [interview].

—— vol. 13 no. 3, Spring 1960, pp. 30–31.

Gavin Lambert – *Nazarín*.

—— vol. 15 no. 2, Winter 1961/62, pp. 55–56.

David Stewart Hull – *Viridiana*.

—— vol. 20 no. 3, Spring 1967, pp. 2–19.

Peter Harcourt – Luis Buñuel: Spaniard and surrealist.

—— no. 45, April 1960, p. 11.

Jean Baroncelli – Breve encuentro con Luis Buñuel.

Films and Filming, vol. 8 no. 1, Oct. 1961, pp. 17–18, 39; no. 2, Nov. 1961, pp. 29–30, 45.

Francesco Aranda – Surrealist and Spanish giant.

Francesco Aranda – Back from the wilderness.

—— vol. 8 no. 9, June 1962, p. 32.

Paul Rotha – *Viridiana*.

—— vol. 10 no. 1, Oct. 1963, p. 23.

Gordon Gow – *Nazarín*.

Guardian, 7 Jan. 1964.

Fetishiana: Luis Buñuel talks to Peter Lennon.

—— 27 Oct. 1966.

Peter Lennon – La fin morale.

Image et Son, no. 152, June 1962, pp. 34–35.

Raymond Lefèvre – *Viridiana*, ou les infortunes de la charité.

—— no. 153/154, Summer 1962, pp. 50–53.

M. Cegretin – *Los Olvidados*.

—— no. 157, Dec. 1962, pp. 3–29.

Issue devoted to Buñuel, including a fiche on *Nazarín*.

—— no. 187, Oct. 1965, pp. 53–62.

Raymond Lefèvre – *El* (fiche).

—— no. 193, April 1966, pp. 100–103.

Raymond Lefèvre – Film inédits de Buñuel.

—— no. 214, 1968, pp. 197–199.

Raymond Lefèvre – *La vie criminelle d'Archibaldo de la Cruz* (fiche).

—— no. 250, May 1971, pp. 18–76.

Buñuel par lui-même: dossier établi par André Cornand.

Jacqueline Lajeunesse and Hubert Arnault – Entretien avec Julien Guiomar.

Hubert Arnault – Entretien avec Serge Silberman.

Table ronde sur Buñuel.

René Gardier – L'ouvert et le clos.

Pierre Guenoun – Quotidien et tradition ibériques chez Buñuel.

Jeune Cinema, no. 12, Feb. 1966, pp. 3–7.

Jean Delmas – Buñuel le mexicain.

Jeune Cinema, no. 38, April 1969, pp. 1–20.
Series of articles and interviews with particular reference to *La Voie Lactée*.
Listener, no. 1965, 24 Nov. 1966, pp. 765–766.
Owen Holloway – The wilderness of this world.
London Magazine, Nov. 1962, pp. 66–72.
David Robinson – The old surrealist.
La Methode, no. 7, Jan. 1962, pp. 1–23.
Issue devoted to Buñuel.
Monogram, No. 5.
David Morse – *Tristana*.
Monthly Film Bulletin, vol. 19, June 1952, p. 76.
L. G. A.(nderson) – *Los Olvidados*.
—— vol. 27, Dec. 1960, p. 164.
Robert Vas – *Ensayo de un crimen*.
—— vol. 29, May 1962, p. 65.
Robert Vas – *Viridiana*.
—— vol. 30, Oct. 1963, p. 141.
Tom Milne – *Nazarín*.
—— vol. 35, Feb. 1968, pp. 19–20.
Tom Milne – *El*.
Movie, no. 1, 1962, pp. 14–16.
Andrew Sarris – Luis Buñuel: the devil and the nun – *Viridiana*.
New York Film Bulletin, no. 28, 13 Feb. 1961, pp. 4–6.
Luis Buñuel – The Cinema: an instrument of poetry. Reprinted from *McCarter Theatre Bulletin*, Autumn 1960.
Objectif, no. 21, July 1963, pp. 15–20.
Nestor Almendros – Luis Buñuel: cinéaste hispanique.
Positif, no. 1, May 1952, pp. 11–22.
Bernard Chardère – *Los Olvidados*.
—— no. 10, 1954, pp. 39–56.
Ado Kyrou – La grande tendresse de Luis Buñuel.
Jacques Demeure – Luis Buñuel: poète de la cruaute.
Un chef d'oeuvre – *El*.
—— no. 27, Feb. 1958, pp. 41–42.
Louis Seguin – *La vie criminelle d'Archibaldo de la Cruz*.
—— no. 31, Nov. 1959, pp. 44–46.
Robert Benayoun – *Nazarín*, ou les points sur les i.
—— no. 33, April 1960, pp. 21–31.
P-L. Thirard, Louis Seguin, Marcel Martin and Ado Kyrou on *Nazarín*.
—— no. 38, March 1961, pp. 61–64.
Jean-Paul Thorok – La passion de *Nazarín*.
— no. 42, Nov. 1961, pp. 2–62.
Special issue on Buñuel.
—— no. 44, March 1962, pp. 70–72.
Robert Benayoun – *Viridiana*.

Positif, no. 47, July 1962, pp. 75–80.
Louis Seguin – *Viridiana* et les critiques.
—— no. 50/52, March 1963, pp. 12–22.
Jean Larrea and Luis Buñuel – Illisible, fils de flûte: synopsis d'un scénario non réalisé.
Ado Kyrou – Buñuel et *L'ange exterminateur*.
—— no. 74, March 1966, pp. 52–66.
Charles Chabouel – Buñuel et le nouveau cinéma mexicain (interview with Buñuel and others).
—— no. 103, March 1969, pp. 1–25.
La Voie Lactée: deux extraits du scénario.
Bernard Cohn – Les overtures théologiques de Don Luis de Calanda.
Bernard Cohn – Jean-Claude Carrière: scénariste de Luis Buñuel (entretien).
Pierre Guffroy – Pourquoi les décorateurs? (by the designer of *La Voie Lactée*).
—— no. 108, Sept. 1969, pp. 1–11.
Jacques Goimard – Quelques refléxions sur Buñuel et le Christianisme (à propos de *Simon du Désert*).
Quarterly of Film, Radio and Television, vol. VII no. 4, Summer 1953, pp. 392–401.
J. Rubia Barcia – Luis Buñuel's *Los Olvidados*.
Screen Education, no. 43, March/April 1968, pp. 64–71.
Daniel Millar – Luis Buñuel: naturalist and supernaturalist.
Sequence, no. 14, New Year 1952, pp. 30–32.
Gavin Lambert – Buñuel and *Los Olvidados*.
Sight and Sound, vol. 20 no. 1, May 1951, p. 4.
Kenneth Tynan – Movie crazy (*Los Olvidados*).
—— vol. 21 no. 4, April/June 1952, pp. 167–168.
John Maddison – *Los Olvidados*.
—— vol. 23 no. 3, Jan./March 1954, pp. 125–130.
Tony Richardson – The films of Luis Buñuel.
—— vol. 24 no. 4, Spring 1955, pp. 181–185.
Jacques Doniol-Valcroze and André Bazin – Conversation with Buñuel. Abridged from *Cahiers du Cinéma*, no. 36, June 1954.
—— vol. 25 no. 2, Autumn 1955, pp. 87–88.
Basil Wright – *The criminal life of Archibaldo de la Cruz*.
—— vol. 29 no. 3, Summer 1960, pp. 118–119.
Derek Prouse – Interviewing Buñuel.
—— vol. 31 no. 3, Summer 1962.
David Robinson – 'Thank God – I am still an atheist' (on *Viridiana*).
—— vol. 32 no. 4, Autumn 1963, pp. 194–195.
Geoffrey Nowell-Smith – *Nazarín*.
—— vol. 35 no. 1, Winter 1965/66, pp. 37–39.
Tom Milne – The Mexican Buñuel.
—— vol. 36 no. 4, Autumn 1967, pp. 173–175.
Elliott Stein – Buñuel's Golden Bowl (*Belle de Jour*).

Sight and Sound, vol. 41 no. 1, Winter 1972–73.
Jonathan Rosenbaum – 'Interruption as Style' (on *Le Charme discret de la bourgeoisie*).
Telegine, no. 96, May 1961, Fiche no. 381, 16 pp.
Jean-Claude Philippe and Gilbert Salachas – *Nazarín.*
—— no. 106, Aug./Sept. 1962, Fiche no. 407, 15 pp.
José Pena and Gilbert Salachas – *Viridiana.*
Tiempo de Cine, no. 14/15, 1963, pp. 7–12.
Emir Rodriguez Monegal – El mito Buñuel.
Yale French Studies, no. 17, 1965, pp. 54–66.
Luis Garcia-Abrines – Rebirth of Buñuel.

Scripts

Collections

Buñuel, Luis *Three screenplays: Viridiana, The exterminating angel, Simon of the desert.* New York, Orion Press, 1969. 245 pp. illus.
Buñuel, Luis *The Exterminating Angel/Nazarín/Los Olvidados.* London, Lorrimer Scripts no. 35, 1972.
L'Avant-Scene du Cinema no. 27/28, July 1963, pp. 1–80. *Un Chien andalou, L'Age d'or, L'ange exterminateur.*

L'Age d'or and Un Chien andalou

Buñuel, Luis *L'age d'or and Un chien andalou*; translated from the French by Marianne Alexander. Lorrimer Publishing, 1968. 120 pp. plates. filmog.
Dali, Salvador *Un Chien andalou*: scenario (and) *L'Age d'or*: scenario. (In *The secret life of Salvador Dali*. London, Vision Press, 1948. pp. 401–409).

L'ange exterminateur

Buñuel, Luis *El ángel exterminador*, con un prólogo de Manuel Villegas López; translated from the French by Juan Luis Marfany. Barcelona, Aymá S.A. Editora, 1964. 135 pp. plates. filmog.

Belle de Jour

Buñuel, Luis: Belle de Jour; English translation and description of action by Robert Adkinson. Lorrimer Publishing, 1971. 168 pp. plates.

Un Chien andalou

In La Revue du Cinema, no. 5, Paris, 15 November 1929. *The first Buñuel script to be published.*

Las hurdes

L'Avant-Scene du Cinema, no. 36, April 1964, pp. 58–62. *Las hurdes.*

Le Journal d'une femme de chambre

L'Avant-Scene du Cinema, no. 36, April 1964, pp. 1–62. *Le Journal d'une femme de chambre.*

Nazarín
L'Avant-Scene du Cinema, no. 89, Feb. 1969, pp. 3–94. *Nazarín.*

Simón del desierto
Kovacs, Yves, Simon de desert: extraits inédits du scénario. (In *Surréalisme et cinéma vol. 2.* Paris, Lettres Modernes, 1965. pp. 275–281.)
L'Avant-Scene du Cinema, no. 94/95, July/Sept. 1969, pp. 71–91. *Simon du désert.*

Tristana
Buñuel, Luis *Tristana;* translated by Nicholas Fry. Lorrimer Publishing, 1971. 144 pp. plates.
L'Avant-Scene du Cinema, no. 110, Jan. 1971, pp. 1–62. *Tristana.*

Viridiana
Buñuel, Luis *Viridiana,* prologo de Georges Sadoul. Mexico, Ediciones Era, 1963. 159 pp. plates.
Buñuel, Luis *Viridiana.* Paris, Inter Spectacles, 1962. 156 pp. plates.

La Voie Lactée
L'Avant-Scene du Cinema, no. 94/95, July/Sept. 1969, pp. 1–70. *La Voie Lactée.*
Cinestudio, no. 76, pp. 18–35; no. 78, pp. 11–24. *La Via Lattea.*

Index of Names and Film Titles

317